Ecclesiastical, Medieval, and Neo-Latin Sentences

RICHARD UPSHER SMITH, JR.

Bolchazy-Carducci Publishers, Inc.

Mundelein, Illinois USA

Editor: Bridget Dean
Contributing Editor: Laurel Draper
Design & Layout: Adam Phillip Velez
Cover Image: A section of the arcade mosaic "Christ and the Procession of Martyrs" in the Basilica of Sant' Apollinare Nuovo, Ravenna, Italy, 6th century CE.

Ecclesiastical, Medieval, and Neo-Latin Sentences

Richard Upsher Smith, Jr.

Bolchazy-Carducci Publishers, Inc.
1570 Baskin Road
Mundelein, Illinois 60060
www.bolchazy.com

Printed in the United States of America
2018
by Kingery Printing Company

ISBN 978-0-86516-798-8

Library of Congress Cataloging-in-Publication Data

Smith, Richard Upsher, author.
  Ecclesiastical, medieval, and neo-Latin sentences / Richard Upsher Smith, Jr.
    pages cm
  Includes bibliographical references.
  ISBN 978-0-86516-798-8 (pbk. : alk. paper) 1. Latin language--Sentences. 2. Latin language, Medieval and modern--Sentences. I. Title.
  PA2293.S55 2013
  475--dc23
                                                                                    2013036721

In memory of my great-great-grandfather
Charles Moreau Davis (1824–1900), AM, of Bloomfield, NJ,
classical scholar and teacher, whose Greek New Testament
has descended to me.

Parvīs imbūtus temptābis grandia tūtus.
If you have been trained in small things, you will
attempt great things safely.

– Marbod of Rennes (c. 1035–1123),
as quoted by Hugh of Saint Victor,
Didascalicon 6.3

Table of Contents

---

[1]   N.B. In the chapter titles, syntax introduced in this book is in **boldface** type.

List of Images

Preface

Latin is one language. Although we may speak of Classical or Medieval or Neo-Latin, nevertheless the Latin of these different historical periods constitutes one language. Moreover, Classical Latin provided the model of Latinity for all subsequent periods. To be sure, ecclesiastical and medieval authors adapted old words, coined new words, and adopted constructions from Hebrew and Greek, as well as from their own vernaculars, to suit their new circumstances. Moreover, modern authors continue to make up terms to meet the needs of modern society, such as *autocinētum locīs inīquīs aptum*, "jeep." Nevertheless, the ancient authors, particularly Terence and Cicero, have remained throughout western history the models to which writers of Latin have returned. Therefore, it is crucial that the new student of Latin learn the classical language in the introductory and intermediate years.

However, the field of Medieval Studies has grown significantly in the last decades, and many students now have a legitimate and laudable interest in the Latin of the Church, of the Middle Ages, and of Modernity. Many students wish to read liturgical and theological texts in the original language, as well as texts in the many other genres employed after the fall of Rome and into the Renaissance, and even beyond. Therefore, while it is vitally important that Latin students learn the classical language, it also seems quite important that they be introduced as early as possible to some of the neologisms and new syntax of Ecclesiastical, Medieval, and Neo-Latin. This manual is intended to provide such an introduction, and has been designed for use with *Wheelock's Latin.*[2] In addition, one who already knows Classical Latin could use this book for a quick introduction to ecclesiastical Latin and the Latin of the Middle Ages and Renaissance. Indeed, it could also be used as a reader.

The *Sententiae ē Fontibus nōn Antīquīs Haustae* are the most important feature of this handbook. They are meant to supplement the original readings from the classical authors in each chapter of *Wheelock* with readings

---

[2]   Frederic M. Wheelock, *Wheelock's Latin*, rev. Richard A. LaFleur, 7th ed. (New York, 2011).

from the writers and writings of the Church and other post-classical sources. Sentences from Scripture have been placed first in each chapter, next, sentences from the liturgy, finally, sentences from ecclesiastical and other post-classical sources. When a sentence is taken from a liturgical book, but is a direct quotation of Holy Scripture or of another source, it is placed not with sentences from the Liturgy, but with the scriptural sentences or with the sentences from other sources.

Most frequently, the *Sententiae ē Fontibus nōn Antīquīs Haustae* will illustrate the same morphology and grammar as Professor Wheelock's *Sententiae Antīquae*. However, sometimes they will also illustrate either new constructions employed by the later authors or more advanced classical syntax. When this is the case, a brief introduction to the new construction will be given under the heading *Syntaxis Supplēmentum*, with references to appropriate grammar books, or reference will be made to the appropriate place in Professor Wheelock's *Supplementary Syntax*. In the *Syntaxis Supplēmentum*, I have endeavored to introduce all the grammar covered in the chapters of Floyd L. Moreland and Rita M. Fleischer's *Latin: An Intensive Course* (Berkeley: University of California Press, 1977) that is not introduced in *Wheelock*.

In addition, a few vocabulary items will be assigned for memorization in each chapter.[3] These will be found under the heading *Verba Memoriā Comprehendenda*. These words have also been gathered in a glossary at the end of the book.

A set of unadapted readings of greater length has also been provided for use when the text has been completed. It is entitled *Locī Immūtātī*, as in *Wheelock*. Several different kinds of writing have deliberately been represented: poetry and prose; the Bible, biblical commentary, and homiletic material; philosophy and theology; a charter and historical narrative; mathematics and pedagogical reflection.

Two appendices are provided: one, a short manual of some of the developments of Ecclesiastical and Medieval Latin; the other, a collection of brief biographies of the authors quoted in the *Sententiae* and the *Locī*.

Finally, indices of quotations from Holy Scripture, from ecclesiastical and magisterial documents, and from ecclesiastical and other post-classical authors have been added.

The orthographical and typographical conventions of *Wheelock's Latin* are followed in this manual. However, accent marks have been eschewed.

---

[3]   Sometimes a CL word will be assigned, too.

I would like to thank my colleagues Dr. Joseph A. Almeida, Dr. Sarah K. Wear, and Dr. Steven M. Hildebrand for using drafts of this supplement in their classes at Franciscan University of Steubenville since 2007. In addition, Dr. Almeida checked my transliterations from the Hebrew. I would also like to thank Catherine S. Ryland for making the indices, and my very patient editor, Bridget Dean, to whom I presented an unusually difficult manuscript. Needless to say, any mistakes that remain are my responsibility.

Suggestions for Using This Book

This book is designed to accompany *Wheelock's Latin* by supplementing the *Sententiae Antīquae* with sentences drawn from ecclesiastical and other non-classical sources. The sentences have been chosen with an eye to the grammar and vocabulary of the chapters which they accompany, and they are presented in the same format as the sentences in *Wheelock*. Only accent marks have been eschewed. A student will, of course, need either a copy of *Wheelock* or a dictionary for the vocabulary not contained in this book.

The annotations to each sentence gloss any word that has not appeared to that point in the chapter vocabularies in *Wheelock*. A word will be glossed only once in a chapter. Moreover, only those principal parts of a verb necessary to understand the form of the verb in the sentence being read will be given in the annotations.

I have used *Wheelock* since I began teaching Latin in the late '90s. In fact, I received my own introduction to Latin in *Wheelock's* pages in the late '70s. I have used *Wheelock's Latin* happily, except for the two following reservations, which have occurred to me in using Moreland and Fleischer in teaching intensive summer Latin courses. First, I have come to believe that Moreland and Fleischer are correct in presenting more syntax in their book than *Wheelock* does. Second, I think that Moreland and Fleischer are right to set more difficult sentences for student reading than *Wheelock* does. Both aspects of Moreland and Fleischer's pedagogy prepare the student better, I believe, for the transition to the reading of unadapted, extended Latin prose.

Therefore, I have sought both to cover all the grammar in Moreland and Fleischer that *Wheelock* does not cover, and to set many rather difficult sentences for student reading. This means that the teacher must pick and choose the sentences for use in class based on an assessment of the capabilities of the students. The most difficult sentences, if not assigned for homework, could be done at sight in class under the direction of the instructor. They could also be omitted. I expect that, given the constraints of time, some sentences will have to be omitted anyway. A teacher could also decide which additional elements of syntax should be introduced, based on the difficulty of the reading to be attempted upon *Wheelock's* completion. If *Wheelock's Latin Reader*[4] is to be studied next, then I think that the additional grammar in this book will be found pertinent.

Those Latinists who, desiring a quick introduction to ecclesiastical and medieval Latin, use this book will find the more difficult sentences a great benefit, I believe. The book could also be used as a reader.

To assist the teacher or reader in determining the level of difficulty of a sentence, I have added one of the following symbols at the end of each sentence in the book.

I	Introductory Level
I/M	Introductory to Middling Level
M	Middling Level
M/A	Middling to Advanced Level
A	Advanced Level

My assessment of these levels rests on my experience of teaching college students of varied abilities. One constant for students of all levels of ability is the difficulty of word order. Even the best students, once they have mastered the SOV concept, will set up that concept as a fixed mark by which to orient their reading of Latin. Thus, variations from that order will throw them off. I have, therefore, marked some sentences at a higher level of difficulty than their syntax may warrant, simply because of their word order.

At the risk of some repetition, an outline of a good many of the grammatical changes in Ecclesiastical and Medieval Latin has been provided in the appendix. The outline does not pretend to completeness.

Throughout this book, as in Professor Wheelock's *Vocābula*, a regular first conjugation verb will be identified with a parenthetical numeral one, e.g. **amō** (1).

---

[4] Frederic M. Wheelock, *Wheelock's Latin Reader, Selections from Latin Literture,* 2nd ed., rev. Richard A. LaFleur, New York: HarperResource, 2001.

Abbreviations

In addition to abbreviations employed in *Wheelock's Latin*, the following abbreviations are used in this handbook.

Blaise — Blaise, Albert, *Manuel du latin chrétien* (Strasbourg: Le Latin Chrétien, 1955); Eng. tr., *A Handbook of Christian Latin: Style, Morphology, and Syntax*, tr. Grant C. Roti (Washington, DC: The Catholic University of America Press, 1994)

BH — Pascale Bourgain, with Marie-Clotilde Hubert, *Le latin médiéval*, L'Atelier du Médiéviste 10 (Turnhout, Belgium: Brepols, 2005)

BR — *Breviarium Romanum ex Decreto SS. Concilii Trident. Restitutum ... cum Textu Psalmorum e Versione Pii Papae XII Auctoritate Edita*, two vols. (Tournai: Desclée & Socii, 1961)

CDD — Sacrosanctum Œcumenicum Concilium Vaticanum II, *Constitutiones, Decreta, Declarationes* (Vatican City: Secretaria Generalis Concilii Œcumenici Vaticani II, 1974; orig. pub. 1966)

Collins — Collins, John F., *A Primer of Ecclesiastical Latin* (Washington, DC: The Catholic University of America Press, 1985; corr., 1988)

Connelly — Connelly, Joseph, *Hymns of the Roman Liturgy* (Westminster, MD: The Newman Press, 1957)

Deferrari — Deferrari, Roy J., *A Latin-English Dictionary of St. Thomas Aquinas, Based on* The Summa Theologica *and Selected Passages of His Other Writings* (Boston: St. Paul Editions, 1960)

Fauroux   *Recueil des Actes des Ducs de Normandie (911–1066)*, ed. Marie
           Fauroux, Mémoires de la Société des Antiquaires de Normandie
           36 (Caen: Société des Antiquaires de Normandie, 1961)

GL   Gildersleeve, Basil L., and Gonzalez Lodge, *Gildersleeve's Latin
           Grammar*, 3rd ed., repr. with foreword and comprehensive
           bibliography (Wauconda, IL: Bolchazy-Carducci Publishers,
           2003; orig. pub. 1895)

KJV   [King James Version.] *The Holy Bible, Containing the Old
           and New Testaments: Translated out of the Original Tongues;
           and with the Former Translations Diligently Compared and
           Revised, By His Majesty's Special Command* (London: Eyre
           and Spottiswoode, 1898; orig. pub. 1611)

LAM   *More: Utopia, Latin Text and English Translation*, ed. George M.
           Logan, Robert M. Adams, and Clarence H. Miller (Cambridge:
           Cambridge University Press, 1995)

Lampe   Lampe, G. W. H., *A Patristic Greek Lexicon* (Oxford: Clarendon
           Press, 1961)

Latham   Latham, R. E., ed., *Revised Medieval Latin Word-List from
           British and Irish Sources* (London: The British Academy, 1965)

LH   *Officium Divinum ex Decreto Sacrosancti Œcumenici Concilii
           Vaticani II Instauratum, Auctoritate Pauli PP. VI Promulgatum,
           Liturgia Horarum iuxta Ritum Romanum.* Editio Typica, four
           vols. (Vatican City: Libreria Editrice Vaticana, 1977; orig.
           pub. 1971)

LLMA   *Lexicon Latinitatis Medii Aevi Praesertim ad Res Ecclesiasticas
           Investigandas Pertinens*, ed. Albert Blaise, Corpus Christianorum
           Continuatio Mediaevalis (Turnhout, Belgium: Brepols, 1975)

LS   Lewis, Charlton T., and Charles Short, *A Latin Dictionary*
           (Oxford: Clarendon Press, 1975; orig. pub. 1879)

LSJ   Liddell, Henry George and Robert Scott, *A Greek–English
           Lexicon*, 9th ed. Revised and augmented by Sir Henry Stuart
           Jones and Roderick McKenzie. Oxford: Clarendon Press, 1996
           (orig. pub. 1843)

LXX   *Septuaginta, Id Est Vetus Testamentum Graece iuxta LXX
           Interpres*, ed. Alfred Rahlfs, 2 vols. in one (Stuttgart: Deutsche
           Bibelgesellschaft, 1979; orig. pub. 1935)

Moynihan   Lewis, C. S., and Don Giovanni Calabria, *The Latin Letters of C. S. Lewis*, ed. Martin Moynihan (South Bend, IN: St. Augustine's Press, 1998)

MR   *Missale Romanum, Ex Decreto SS. Concilii Tridentini Restitutum Summorum Pontificum Cura Recognitum*, Editio Typica 1962, ed. Manlio Sodi and Alessandro Toniolo (Vatican City: Libreria Editrice Vaticana, 2007)

MRi   Mantello, F. A. C., and A. G. Rigg, *Medieval Latin, An Introduction and Bibliographic Guide* (Washington, DC: The Catholic University of America Press, 1996)

Nunn   Nunn, H. P. V., *An Introduction to Ecclesiastical Latin*, 2nd ed. (Cambridge: Cambridge University Press, 1927)

NV   *Nova Vulgata Bibliorum Sacrorum Editio Sacrosancti Œcumenici Concilii Vaticani II Ratione Habita Iussu Pauli PP. VI Recognita Auctoritate Ioannis Pauli PP. II Promulgata*, editio typica altera (Vatican City: Libreria Editrice Vaticana, 1986; orig. pub. 1979)

OED   Weiner, E.S.C. and J.A. Simpson, eds. *The Compact Edition of the Oxford English Dictionary*, 2 vols. Oxford: Oxford University Press, 1971 (orig. pub. as *The New English Dictionary*, 10 vols., 1884–1928).

OLD   *The Oxford Latin Dictionary*, ed. P. G. W. Glare, reprinted with corrections (Oxford: Clarendon Press, 1996; orig. pub. 1968–1982)

PIB   the version of the Psalter prepared by the Pontificium Institutum Biblicum and promulgated for liturgical use by Pope Pius XII March 24, 1945 (found in BR and V)

PW   Plater, W. E., and H. J. White, *A Grammar of the Vulgate, Being an Introduction to the Latinity of the Vulgate Bible* (Oxford: Clarendon Press, 1926; repr. 1997)

Smith   Smith, Richard Upsher, Jr., *A Glossary of Terms in Grammar, Rhetoric, and Prosody for Readers of Greek and Latin, A Vade Mecum* (Mundelein, IL: Bolchazy-Carducci Publishers, repr. with corrections, 2012; orig. pub. 2011)

Souter   Souter, Alexander, *A Glossary of Later Latin to 600 A.D.* (Oxford: Clarendon Press, 1949; repr. 1996)

Strecker   Strecker, Karl, *Introduction to Medieval Latin,* tr. and rev. Robert B. Palmer (Berlin Charlottenburg: Weidmannsche Verlagsbuchhandlung, 1957)

Symphonia   Hildegard of Bingen, *Symphonia, A Critical Edition of the* Symphonia armonie celestium revelationum *with Introduction, Translations, and Commentary,* 2d ed., ed. and tr. Barbara Newman, Ithaca, NY: Cornell University Press, 1998

V   *Biblia Sacra iuxta Vulgatam Clementinam, Nova Editio,* ed. A. Colunga, O. P., and L. Turrado, O. P., 5th ed. (Madrid: Biblioteca de Autores Cristianos, 1977)

Woodcock   Woodcock, E. C., *A New Latin Syntax,* Bristol Classical Press Advanced Language Series (London: Gerald Duckworth and Co. 2002; orig. pub. 1959)

CL   Classical Latin

EL   Ecclesiastical Latin

Gr.   Greek

Heb.   Hebrew

PIE   Proto-Indo-European

I   Introductory Level

I/M   Introductory to Middling Level

M   Middling Level

M/A   Middling to Advanced Level

A   Advanced Level

N.B. Abbreviations of books of the Bible cited in the *Sententiae* and *Locī* can be found in Index I.

Notes on Pronunciation

EL is pronounced the same way as CL, except for the following differences.

ae   like CL ē, and frequently spelled *e* in incunabula and manuscripts

oe   like CL ē, and frequently spelled *e* in incunabula and manuscripts

c   like **ch** in *cheese* before *e, i, ae, oe*

g   like **j** in *juice* before *e, i, y*

gn   like **ny** in *banyan*

ti   **tsi** before a vowel, unless the **ti** is preceded by *s, t, x*

One finds such spellings as *charitas* (*caritas*) and *michi* (*mihi*) in the manuscripts, which suggest that some speakers in the Middle Ages treated the letter *h* as a guttural in certain positions. Church musicians pronounce the *ch* in such words as *k*, e.g., *miki* for *mihi*. Church musicians also tend to allow to each vowel only its long sound. I see no reason why this practice should be followed in speaking EL or in reciting it in the liturgy. After all, word stress, even in EL, depends on the length or weight of the penultimate syllable (see Smith, 37–38, s.v. "Syllable"), so that speakers must know the quantities of syllables, if they are to pronounce EL correctly.

See further Appendix I, § I.

(handwritten top-left margin: Hw)

CAPVT I

Verbs; First and Second Conjugations; Adverbs

Verba Memoriā Comprehendenda

Dāvīd, indecl. Heb. name, or **Dāvīd, -vīdis,** m., *David,* second king of Israel

Ābraham, indecl. Heb. name, or **Ābraham, -hae,** m., the patriarch *Abraham*

Sententiae ē Fontibus nōn Antīquīs Haustae[5]

1. Torrentēs Belial terrent mē.
   [II Sam. 22:5 V.—**torrentēs,** *torrents,* = subject.—**Belial,** *of Belial,* a Canaanite god.] I

2. Quid vidēs in Sulamiten?
   [Song 7:1 V.—**in,** prep. + abl., *in.*—**Sulamitis, -tis,** f., *Shulamite,* = object of prep. *in.*] I

3. Errat et cōgitat stulta.
   [Ecclus. 16:23 V.—**stulta,** *foolish things,* = dir. obj.] I

4. Simon, amās mē? *Simon, do you love me?*
   [Jn. 21:17 V.—**Sīmon, -ōnis,** m., *Simon,* = voc.] I

5. Saulus videt nihil. *Saul was blind.*
   [Acts 9:8 V.—**Saulus, -ī,** m., *Saul,* i.e., Paul, = subject.] I

---

[5] In keeping with Professor Wheelock's policy with the *Sententiae Antiquae,* the author or source of each sentence will be identified. If the quotation is verbatim, an asterisk will be placed before the name of the author or source. If there is no asterisk, the sentence has been altered. Cf. *Wheelock's Latin,* 18–19.

1

6.   Tē Deum laudāmus. *We praise you, God*

         [*Tē Deum,[6] ad Mātūtīnum, BR 1.(5).—**tē,** *you,* = dir. obj.—**Deum,**
         God, = pred. acc. (see Smith, 71, s.v. "Objective Complement.").]
         I/M

7.   Dā mihi intellēctum. *Give to me understanding*

         [*Respōnsōrium, ad Laudēs Mātūtīnās, Fēria II, Hebdomada I,
         LH 3.570.—**mihi,** *to me,* = ind. obj.—**intellēctum,** *understanding,*
         = dir. obj.] I

8.   Iūbilāte Deō. *Sing for joy to God.*

         [*Antiphona 3, Fēria IV, ad Laudēs Mātūtīnās, Hebdomada I,
         LH 3.609.—**iūbilō** (1), *raise a shout of joy.*—**Deō,** m. dat. sg., *to/
         for God.*] I

9.   Sēmitās tuās dēmōnstrā mihi. *Show me Your narrow ways.*

         [Respōnsōrium, ad Tertiam, Fēria IV, Hebdomada I, LH 3.613.—
         sēmitās, f. acc. pl., = dir. obj., *narrow ways.*—**tuās,** modifies
         sēmitās, = *thy, your.*—**dēmōnstrō** (1), *point out, show.*—**mihi,**
         see Sentence 7.] I/M

10.   Salvē, diēs.

         [*Hymnus II, Dominica, ad Officium Lēctiōnis, Hebdomada II,
         LH 3.672.—**diēs,** f. voc. sg., = *(o) day.*] I

11.   Ūnitātem tenēre firmiter dēbēmus. *We should Hold to unity firmly.*

         [St. Cyprian of Carthage, *Dē ecclēsiae catholicae ūnitāte* 5.—
         ūnitātem, *unity,* = dir. obj.—**teneō, -ēre,** *hold.*—**firmiter,** adv.,
         firmly.] I/M

12.   Adenulfus abbātem asportat.

         [Leo Marsicanus, *Chronica Monastēriī Casīnensis* 2.1.—**Adenulfus,**
         Adenulf, a count of Aquino in the early tenth century, = subject.—
         abbātem, *abbot,* = dir. obj.—**asportō** (1), *carry away,* i.e., kidnap.] I

13.   Laudāte eum, caelum et terra. *Praise God, heaven & earth.*

         [*St. Francis of Assisi, *Exhortātiō ad Laudem Deī.*—**eum,** *him,*
         i.e., God, = dir. obj.—**caelum,** *heaven,* which is being directly
         addressed.—**terra,** *earth,* also being directly addressed.] I

---

6   St. Niceta of Remesiana has been suggested as the author. This identification has not
       been widely accepted. See *Oxford Dictionary of the Christian Church,* 3rd ed. corr.,
       ed. F. L. Cross and E. A. Livingstone (Oxford: Oxford University Press, 1998), s.v.
       "Niceta, St."

14.   Vīsitat Franciscus Clāram.
      [Thomas of Celano, *Legenda Sānctae Clārae Virginis* 5.—**vīsitō**
      (1), *go to visit.*—**Franciscus**, *Francis*, = subject.—**Clāram**, *Clare*,
      = dir. obj.] I/M

15.   Deus ōrdinātē gubernat.
      [St. Bonaventure, *Breviloquium* 1.5.—**Deus**, *God*, = subject.—
      ōrdinātē, adv., *in an orderly manner; providentially.*—**gubernō**
      (1), *govern.*] I

The Bayeux Tapestry is a series of several embroidered linen panels. Over fifty scenes were
worked in the cloth to narrate the events that led up to the Battle of Hastings in 1066. The
battle itself is vividly depicted. The tapestry, which was embroidered in England, is over
230 feet long. It was probably commissioned in the 1070s by William the Conqueror's
brother Odo, bishop of Bayeux, Normandy, and earl of Kent, England. The scene repro-
duced here shows the death of Harold, Earl of Wessex and King of England, at the Battle
of Hastings. The caption says, "Hārold rēx interfectus est." This image is included here
to illustrate the arms of the eleventh-century soldier, as well as the conditions of battle.
Count Adenulf of Aquino (see Capvt I, Sentence 12) would have been armed similarly, as
also would the Normans who conquered Southern Italy and Sicily in the eleventh century
(Locī XII). (© Wikimedia Commons)

CAPVT II

First Declension Nouns and Adjectives; Prepositions, Conjunctions, Interjections; **Predicate Accusative**[7]

Syntaxis Supplēmentum

Predicate Accusative. Although not introduced by *Wheelock* until Capvt XVI, this construction occurred already in Capvt I, and will occur again several times before Capvt XVI; therefore, I introduce it here. A predicate accusative, as it is called in Latin grammar, completes the meaning of a verb by showing what effect the action of the verb had on its direct object. An example can be found in Capvt I, Sentence 6, as well as below in Sentence 9. In the former example, the expletive *as* must be added in English, i.e., *We praise you as God*. In English grammar, the predicate accusative is called the objective complement. See Smith, 71.

Verba Memoriā Comprehendenda

anima, -ae, f. (dat. and abl. pl. sometimes **animābus**), *breath; vital principle; life; soul; mind*

enim, postpositive conj., *truly; for; in fact*

super, prep. + abl., *over, above, concerning, about, besides, beyond;* + acc. *over, above, upon, beyond, besides.*

---

[7] N.B. In the chapter titles, syntax introduced in this book is in **boldface** type.

4

SENTENTIAE Ē FONTIBUS NŌN ANTĪQUĪS HAUSTAE

1. Amat enim puellam valdē.
   [Gen. 34:19 V, said of Shechem's passion for Dinah.—**valdē,** adv., *intensely.*] I

2. Plāga leprae est in domō.
   [Lev. 14:35 V.—**plāga, -ae,** f., a *blow; plague*—**lepra, -ae,** f., *leprosy.*—**domō,** *house,* = obj. of prep. *in.*] I/M

3. Nōn enim est bona fāma.
   [*I Sam. 2:24 V, the priest Eli to his sons.—**bonus, -a, -um,** *good.*] I/M

4. Quālis est fōrma eius?
   [*I Sam. 28:14 V, Saul to the witch of Endor.—**quālis, -e,** *of what sort?*—**eius,** *his,* i.e., Samuel's.] I/M

5. Dant autem pecūniās.
   [Ezra 3:7 V, said of the Jews' donations for rebuilding the temple.—**autem,** postpositive conj., *however.*] I

6. Laudā, anima mea, Dominum.
   [*Ps. 145:2 V.—**anima mea,** voc. case.—**Dominum,** *the Lord,* = dir. obj.] I

7. Et nōn est īra super īram mulieris.
   [*Ecclus. 25:23 V—**mulieris,** *of a woman.*] I/M

8. Ō mulier, magna est fidēs tua.
   [*Mt. 15:28 V.—**mulier,** *woman,* = voc. case.—**fidēs, -eī,** f., *faith,* third decl. nom. sg., = subject.] I

9. Dāvīd vocat eum Dominum.
   [*Mt. 22:45 V.—**eum,** *him,* = dir. obj.—**Dominum,** *Lord,* = pred. acc.] I/M

10. In ipsō vīta est.
    [Jn. 1:4 V.—**in,** prep. + abl., *in.*—**ipsō,** *him,* = obj. of prep. *in.*] I

11. In viā tuā vīvificā mē. *In your way, vivify/revive me.*
    [*Respōnsōrium, ad Hōram Mediam, Dominica, Hebdomada I, LH 3.561.—**in,** prep. + abl., *in, on.*—**via, -ae,** f., *road, way.*—**vīvificō** (1), *make alive, vivify.*] I/M

12.   Innocentiae proxima est misericordia. *Mercy is next to innocence*
         [*Lactantius, *Epitomē Īnstitūtiōnum Dīvīnārum* 65.—**innocentia,**
         -ae, f., *innocence, integrity.*—**proximus, -a, -um,** *nearest, next* (+
         dat.).—**misericordia, -ae,** f., *mercy, pity*] I/M

13.   Amant filiōs et ferae. *Even the beasts love their children*
         [*St. Augustine of Hippo, *Sermō* 149.2.2.—**fīliōs,** *sons, children,*
         = dir. obj.—**fera, -ae,** f., *a wild animal.*] I/M

14.   Deus amīcitia est.
         [*St. Aelred of Rievaulx, *Dē Spīrituālī Amīcitiā* 1.69.—**Deus,** *God,*
         = subject.—**amīcitia,** *friendship,* = pred. nom.] I

15.   Propria animae vīta est. *Life is characteristic of the soul.*
         [*Marsilio Ficino, *Theologia Platōnica* 5.12.7.—**proprius, -a, -um,**
         peculiar, proper, characteristic (+ gen.).] I/M

CAPVT III
Second Declension Masculine Nouns and Adjectives; Apposition; Vocative Case

Syntaxis Supplēmentum

Vocative Case. EL sometimes uses the nominative case for the vocative with second declension masculine nouns. Even in CL, the nominative and the vocative forms of *deus, -ī*, m., *god,* were the same.

Verba Memoriā Comprehendenda

Dominus, -ī, m., *master, owner, lord; the Lord*
ecce, interj., *behold*
sānctus, -a, -um, *holy; Saint*

Sententiae ē Fontibus nōn Antīquīs Haustae

1. Nōē, vir agricola, plantat vīneam. *Noah, a farmer (man) planted a vineyard.*
   [Gen. 9:20 V.—**Nōē,** indecl. Heb. name, m., *Noě, Noah.*—**plantō** (1), *plant.*—**vīnea, -ae,** f., *vineyard.*] I/M

2. Quis es tū, fīlī mī?
   [*Gen. 27:18 V, Isaac to Jacob.—**quis,** *who?*—**es,** *art, are,* second pers. sg.—**tū,** *thou, you,* nom. sg.] I

3. Quis est vir ut est Iōb? *Who is a man as/like Job?*
   [*Job 34:7 V.—**ut,** *as.*—**Iōb, -is,** m., *Job.*] I/M

4. Quid est autem sapientia?
   [*Wis. 6:24 V.—**autem,** postpositive conj., *moreover.*] I

5. Sapientia laudat animam suam. *Wisdom praises its own -self*
   [Ecclus. 24:1 V.—**suus, -a, -um,** *his/her/its own.*] I *(nephesh) ~~spirit~~ soul*

7

6.   Vocā virum tuum.
   [*Jn. 4:16 V, Christ Jesus to the Samaritan woman.] I

(7.)   Vōs amīcī meī estis.   *Your friends are mine.*
   [*Jn. 15:14 V.—**vōs**, *you*, nom. pl.—**estis**, *are*, second pers. pl.] I

8.   Habēs fōrmam scientiae.
   [Rom. 2:20 V, said of the Jews and the Law.—**scientia, -ae,** f.,
   knowledge.] I

(9.)   Nōn est masculus, neque fēmina.   *It's masculine or feminine*
   [*Gal. 3:28 V.—**masculus, -ī,** m., *male.*—**neque**, conj., *and not.*—
   fēmina, *female,* its basic meaning.] I

10.   Tua est, Domine, magnificentia et potentia et glōria atque victōria,
   allēlūia.
   [*Antiphona 3 (Tempore Paschālī), Fēria III, ad Vesperās,
   Hebdomada IV, LH 2.1168.—**magnificentia, -ae,** f.,
   magnificence.—**potentia, -ae,** f., *power.*—**glōria, -ae,** f., *glory.*—
   atque, conj., *and also.*—**victōria, -ae,** f., *victory.*] I/M

(11.)   Adōrāte Dominum in aulā sānctā eius.   *Worship the Lord in his holy temple.*
   [*Antiphona 3, Fēria II, ad Laudēs Mātūtīnās, Hebdomada I, LH
   3.573.—**adōrō** (1), *entreat; worship.*—**aula, -ae,** f., *a palace; court;
   temple.*—**eius,** = *his.*] I

12.   Domine, magnus es tū.
   [*Antiphona 2, Fēria IV, ad Laudēs Mātūtīnās, Hebdomada I,
   LH 3.608.] I

(13.)   Vītam dominī meī Karolī narrō.   *I tell of the life of my Lord King Charlemagne.*
   [Einhard, *Vīta Karolī Magnī Imperātōris*, Prologus.—**Karolus, -ī,**
   Charles, i.e., Charlemagne.—**narrō** (1), *tell, relate.*] I

14.   Caecī sunt, quia vērum lūmen nōn vident.
   [St. Francis of Assisi, *Epistola ad Fidēlēs* (Recensiō Prior) 2.—
   caecus, -a, -um, *blind.*—**sunt,** *they are.*—**quia**, conj., *because.*—
   vērus, -a, -um, *true.*—**lūmen,** third decl. n. acc. sg., *light,* = dir.
   obj.] I/M

(15.)   Fīlī, nunc docēbō tē viam pācis.   *Son, now I will teach you the way of peace.*
   [*Thomas à Kempis, *Dē Imitatiōne Chrīstī* 3.23.1.—**nunc**, adv.,
   now.—**docēbō,** = *I shall teach* (with a double acc.; Smith, 56).—**tē,**
   thee, you, = dir. obj.—**via, -ae,** f., *way.*—**pācis,** = *of peace.*] I/M

CAPVT IV

Second Declension Neuters; Adjectives; Present of *Sum*; Predicate Nominatives; Substantives

VERBA MEMORIĀ COMPREHENDENDA

chrīstus, -ī, m., the anointed; Chrīstus, -ī, m., *the Anointed, the Messiah, (the) Christ*, a Greek borrowing

peccātum, -ī, n., *error; sin*

SENTENTIAE Ē FONTIBUS NŌN ANTĪQUĪS HAUSTAE

1. Et animam suam dat perīculīs. *And he gives his mind to*
   [Judg. 9:17 V, Abimelech speaking about his father Jerubbaal to *dangers,* the Shechemites.—**suus, -a, -um**, possessive adj., *his own*.] I/M

2. Saūl chrīstus Dominī est.
   [I Sam. 24:7 V, David about Saul.—**Saūl**, indecl. Heb. name, or **Saūl, -ūlis**, m., *Saul*, first king of Israel.] I

3. Iactā super Dominum cūram tuam. *Cast your care upon the Lord.*
   [*Ps. 54:23 V.—**iactō** (1), *throw*.] I

4. Laudāte Dominum, quia bonus est Dominus.
   [Ps. 134:3 V.—**quia**, conj., *because*.] I

5. Chrīstī estis. *You are the of Christ,*
   [*Mk. 9:40 V.—**Chrīstī**, a gen. of "appurtenance," a borrowing from Greek. See Blaise, § 84.5, and Appendix I, § 7 N 2.] I/M

6. Servus est peccātī.
   [*Jn. 8:34 V, said of everyone who does sin.—**servus, -ī**, m., *slave*.] I/M

7. Vōs vocātis mē "Magister et Domine." *[handwritten: you call me Master and Lord.]*
   [*Jn. 13:13 V.—**vōs**, *you*, nom. pl.] I

8. Iūstae et vērae sunt viae tuae.
   [*Apoc. 15:3 V, LH 3.776.—**iūstus, -a, -um**, *just.*—**via, -ae**, f., *way.*] I/M

9. Sine Deō nihil est validum. *[handwritten: Without God, nothing is Valid (strong).]*
   [Ōrātiō XVII Dominicālis et Cotidiāna, LH 3.31.—**Deus, -ī**, m., *God.*—**validus, -a, -um**, *strong, powerful.*] I

10. Inclīnā cor meum, Deus, in testimonia tua.
    [*Respōnsōrium, ad Hōram Mediam, Dominica, Hebdomada I, LH 3.561.—**inclīnō** (1), *bend, incline.*—**cor**, n. acc. sg., *heart; mind.*—**deus**, here = voc. See Capvt III Syntaxis.—**in**, prep. + acc., *towards.*—**testimōnium, -iī**, n., *testimony.*] I

11. Ēloquia Dominī ēloquia casta. *[handwritten: The words of the Lord are chaste (pure) words.]*
    [*Antiphona 3, Fēria III, ad Officium Lēctiōnis, Hebdomada I, LH 3.587.—**ēloquium, -iī**, n., *eloquence; word, speech.*—**castus, -a, -um**, *clean, pure.* —Note that *sunt* must be supplied.] I/M

12. Magnum est poenitentiae auxilium, magnum sōlācium.
    [*Lactantius, *Epitomē Īnstitūtiōnum Dīvīnārum* 67.—**poenitentia, -ae**, f., *penitence, repentance.*—**auxilium, -iī**, n., *help, aid.*—**sōlācium, -iī**, n., *consolation, comfort, relief.*] I/M

13. Dēcollant sanctum Albānum pāgānī. *[handwritten: The pagan beheaded the holy Alban.]*
    [St. Bede the Venerable, *Historia Ecclēsiastica Gentis Anglōrum* 1.7.—**dēcollō** (1), *behead.*—**Albānus, -ī**, m., *Alban*, the first British martyr.—**pāgānus, -ī**, m., *a pagan.*] I/M

14. Chaldaea et Syra lingua Hebraeae vīcīna est.
    [*Hugh of St. Victor, *De Grammatica* 1.—**Chaldaeus, -a, -um**, *Chaldaean.*—**Syrus, -a, -um**, *Syrian.*—**Hebraeus, -a, -um**, *Hebrew.*—**lingua, -ae**, f., *tongue; language.*—**vīcīnus, -a, -um**, *near, neighboring.*—N.B. Chaldean and Syriac, both branches of Aramaic, and Hebrew all belong to the North-West Semitic group of languages.] M

15. Gustāmus, dēlībāmus, odōrāmur, et [Deus] prope est.
    [*Arnold of Bonneval, *Liber dē Cardinālibus Chrīstī Operibus*, Prologus 4.—**gustō** (1), *taste.*—**dēlībō** (1), *sip.*—**odōror, -ārī**, first pers. pl. pres. ind. depon., i.e., a pass. form with an act. meaning, = *we smell* (at or out).—**prope**, adv., *near.*] I/M
    [handwritten: We taste, we drink, we smell, and God is near.]

CAPVT V

First and Second Conjugations: Future and Imperfect; Adjectives in -er

Verba Memoriā Comprehendenda

Israël or **Israhel,** m., indecl. Heb. name, or **Israël/Israhel, -ēlis,** *Israel*

ergō, adv., *therefore* *Cogito ergo sum.*

gar

Sententiae ē Fontibus nōn Antīquīs Haustae

1. Oculī enim Israël cālīgābant. *For Israel's eyes were became dark*
   [*Gen. 48:10 V, on the aged Jacob.—**cālīgō** (1), *be dark*.] I/M

2. Et Saūl pugnābat per circuitum et superābat.
   [I Sam. 14:47 V.— **Saūl,** indecl. Heb. name, or **Saūl, -ūlis,** m., *Saul.*—**pugnō** (1), *fight.*—**per circuitum,** *round about* (the borders of his kingdom).] I

3. Dā mihi in animō cōnstantiam. *Give me steadfastness of spirit*
   [*Jud. 9:14 V.—**mihi,** dat. pron., *(to) me.*—**cōnstantia, -ae,** f., *steadfastness, resolution*.] I

4. Caelī ēnārrant glōriam Deī.
   [*Ps. 18:2 V.—**ēnārrō** (1), *explain, tell in detail.*—**Deus, -ī,** m., *God*.] I

5. Tuī sunt caelī, et tua est terra. *Yours are the heavens, & yours is the earth.*
   [*Ps. 88:12 V.—**terra, -ae,** f., *earth*.] I/M

6. Crās dabō tibi.
   [*Prov. 3:28, what one should *not* say to a needy neighbor when one has the wherewithal to give.—**tibi,** dat. pron., *to you*.] I

11

7. Ecce tū pulchra es, amīca mea!

     [*Song 1:14 V.—**tū,** *thou, you,* nom. sg.] I/M

8. Mathathias habēbat filiōs quīnque.

     [1 Mac. 2:1–2 V.—**Mathathias,** Heb. name, nom. sg., *Mattathias,* the father of the Maccabees.—**quīnque,** indecl. numeral, *five.*] I

9. Et cēnābō cum illō.

     [*Apoc. 3:20 V, Christ of the person who opens the door to him.— **cum,** prep. + abl., *with.*—**illō,** abl. sg, *that man/him.*] I

10. Glōria in excelsīs Deō.

     [*Gloria, MR, p. 218 *(302).*—**excelsus, -a, -um,** *lofty, high, elevated.*] I/M

11. Manē nōbīscum, Domine.

     [*Respōnsōrium, Fēria IV, ad Nōnam, Hebdomada IV Temporis Paschālis, LH 2.614.—**nōbīscum,** = with us.]

12. Docēbit [Dominus] mītēs viās suās.

     [*Respōnsōrium, Fēria III, ad Officium Lēctiōnis, Hebdomada I, LH 3.588.—**doceō, -ēre,** *teach* (+ double acc. See Smith, 56.)— **mītēs,** third decl. adj. m. acc. pl., = *the meek.*—**via, -ae,** f., *road, way.*—**suus, -a, -um,** reflex. possessive adj., *his/her/its own.*] I/M

13. Nōn dabit in ūsūrā pecūniam. Hoc est enim dē aliēnīs malīs lucra captāre.

     [*Lactantius, *Epitomē Īnstitūtiōnum Dīvīnārum* 64, speaking of the follower of God.—**dabit,** here = *will lend.*—**ūsūra, -ae,** f., *interest paid for money borrowed, usury.*—**hoc,** = *this.*—**aliēnus, -a, -um,** *belonging to another.*—**lucrum, -ī,** n., *gain, profit.*—**captō** (1), *grab, seek to get.*] M

14. Fīliam imperātor Chuonrādus Mahthildam, pulchram puellam, Heinrīcō rēgī Francōrum dēspondēbat.

     [Wipo, *Gesta Chuonrādī Imperātōris* 32.—**imperātor,** *emperor,* nom., in apposition to *Chuonrādus.*—**Chuonrādus, -ī,** m., *Conrad.*— **Mahthilda, -ae,** f., *Mathilda.*—**Heinrīcus, -ī,** m., *Henry.*—**rēgī,** *king* = dat., in apposition to *Heinrīcō.*—**Francus, -ī,** m., *a Frank, a Frenchman.*—**dēspondeō, -ēre,** *promise in marriage.*] M/A

15. Internus mōtus vīta est.

     [*Marsilius Ficino, *Theologia Platōnica* 5.1.2.—**internus, -a, -um,** *internal, inward.*—**mōtus,** fourth decl. m. nom., sg., *motion, movement.*] I

CAPVT VI

Sum and *Possum*; Complementary Infinitive; **Objective Infinitive**

Syntaxis Supplēmentum

Objective Infinitive. See *Wheelock's Latin*, "Supplementary Syntax," 494. Note that both the complementary and the objective infinitive are neuter verbal nouns in the accusative case.

Verba Memoriā Comprehendenda

inimīcus, -ī, m., *(personal) enemy*

salvus, -a, -um, to the definitions in *Wheelock* add, *saved* (from sin by Christ)

Sententiae ē Fontibus nōn Antīquīs Haustae

1. Lōt timēbat manēre in Segor. *Lot was afraid to remain in Zoar*
   [Gen. 19:30 V.—**Lōt,** indecl. Heb. name, m., *Lot,* the nephew of Abraham.—**timeō, -ēre,** *be afraid (of).*—**Segor,** indecl. Heb. place name taken as abl., *Zoar.*] I

2. Nōn poterō immūtāre verbum Dominī Deī meī.
   [*Num. 22:18 V, Balaam to Balak.—**immūtō** (1), *change, alter.*] I

3. Quārē prōvocās malum? *Why call forth bad thing*
   [*II Kings 14:10 V, King Jehoash to King Amaziah.—**prōvocō** (1), *call forth.*] I

4. Et ab inimīcīs meīs salvus erō.
   [*Ps. 17:4 V.—**ab,** prep. + abl., *from.*] I

odds

5. Sī potes, respondē mihi.
   [*Job 33:5 V, Elihu to Job.—**respondeō, -ēre,** *answer.*—**mihi,**
   dat. pron., *(to) me.*] I

6. Multae enim sunt īnsidiae dolōsī.
   [*Ecclus. 11:31 V.—**multus,** can mean *large, considerable.*—
   dolōsus, -a, -um, *crafty, deceitful.*] I/M

7. Quis ergō poterit salvus esse?
   [*Mt. 19:25 V, who can, if the rich man can't?—**quis,** interrog.
   pron., *who?*] I

8. Nōn potest meus esse discipulus.
   [*Lk. 14:27 V, said of him who does not take up his cross and
   follow.] I

9. Graecīs et barbarīs dēbitor sum.
   [Rom. 1:14 V.—**barbarus, -a, -um,** *Greekless, barbarian.*—
   dēbitor, -tōris, m., *debtor.*] I

10. Diem vidēre nōn poterant, lūcernam forte poterant tolerāre.
    [*St. Augustine of Hippo, *Sermō* 342.2, speaking of those who
    came to see John the Baptist.—**diem,** *the day,* = dir. obj.—
    lūcerna, -ae, f., *a lamp.*—**forte,** adv., *as it happened.*] M

11. Sī enim bona est vīta creāta, quam bona est vīta creātrīx?
    [*St. Anselm of Canterbury, *Proslogion* 24.—**creātus, -a, -um,**
    created.—**quam,** adv., *how.*—**creātrīx, -trīcis,** in EL used as a
    third decl. adj., here f. nom. sg., modifying *vīta, creative, creating.*]
    I/M

12. Deus sōlus, quī exordium nōn habet, vērae essentiae nōmen tenet.
    [*Peter Lombard, *Sententiae* 1.8.1.—**sōlus, -a, -um,** *alone,
    only.*—**quī,** m. nom. sg. rel. pron., *who* (subject of the rel.
    clause).—**exordium, -iī,** n., *a beginning.*—**essentia, -ae,** f.,
    essence, being.—**nōmen,** third decl. n. acc. sg., *name* (= dir.
    obj.).—**teneō, -ēre,** *hold, possess.*] I/M

13. Esse subsistēns nōn potest esse nisi ūnum. *Subsisting being is*
    [*St. Thomas Aquinas, *Summa Theologiae* 1, q.44, a.1 *resp.*—**esse,** *notable*
    n. nom. verbal noun, *being.*—**subsistēns,** third decl. n. nom. *to be*
    adj., modifying *esse, subsisting, existing* "for itself not in another" *unless*
    (Deferrari, s.v.).—**nisi,** conj., *if . . . not, unless, except.*—**ūnus, -a,** *as one.*
    -um, *one.*] M

14.   Unde nōn potest esse nisi ūna ecclēsia, quia nōn est nisi ūnus Petrus.
       [*Nicholas of Cusa, *Sermō* 160.3.—**unde,** adv., *wherefore.*—**ūnus,**
       -a, -um, *one.*—**ecclēsia, -ae,** f., *church.*—**Petrus, -ī,** m., *Peter,* the
       first pope.] M

15.   Nōn potest esse fōrma prīma, sī nōn est vēra.
       [*Marsilius Ficino, *Theologia Platōnica* 1.3.2.—**prīmus, -a, -um,**
       first.] I

CAPVT VII
Third Declension Nouns; Ellipsis

Syntaxis Supplēmentum

Ellipsis. Ellipsis is the omission of a word that is important to the sense of the clause. The reader must supply the word, frequently from a parallel clause, e.g., *nōstī quod Esau frāter meus homō pilōsus sit et ego [sit] lenis,* "you know that my brother Esau is a hairy man and I [am] a smooth man" [Gen. 27:11]. More difficult for English speakers is the fact that ellipsis is very common in Latin with present forms of the verb *esse.* The present infinitive of the same verb is also often omitted. There are examples of this phenomenon in the *Sententiae* in this chapter.

Verba Memoriā Comprehendenda

Iēsūs, -ū, -ū, -ūm, -ū, -ū, m. irreg., *Joshua; Jesus* (Collins' quantities are followed)

Ierūsalem or **Hierūsalem,** indecl. Heb. name, or **Hierosolyma, -ae,** f., or **Hierosolyma, -ōrum,** n., *Jerusalem*

scrīptūra, -ae, f., *a writing; (Holy) Scripture*

Sententiae ē Fontibus nōn Antīquīs Haustae

1. Erunt enim in hominibus et iūmentīs ulcera.
   [*Ex. 9:9 V, the sixth plague of the Egyptians.—**iūmentum, -ī,** n., *a draught-animal.*—**ulcus, -eris,** n., *an ulcer.*] I

2. Tempus bellī, et tempus pācis.
   [*Eccles. 3:8 V.] I/M

3. Liber generātiōnis Iēsū Chrīstī fīliī Dāvīd, fīliī Ābraham.
   [*Mt. 1:1 V.— **generātiō, -ōnis,** f., *a begetting, generation.*] I/M

4. Ecce virgō in uterō habēbit.
    [*Mt. 1:23 V.—**uterus, -ī,** m., *womb; belly.*—**in uterō habēre** =
    be pregnant.] I

5. Et homō adhaerēbit ad uxōrem suam.
    [Mk. 10:7 V.—**adhaereō, -ēre,** *stick, cling to.*—**ad,** prep. + acc.,
    to. —**suus, -a, -um,** *his/her/its own.*] I

6. Et nēmō iam audēbat eum interrogāre.
    [*Mk. 12:34 V.—**nēmō,** nom. pron., *no one.*—**iam,** adv., *now.*—
    eum, acc. pron., *him.*—**interrogō** (1), *ask.*] I

7. Labor vester nōn est inānis in Dominō.
    [*I Cor. 15:58 V.—**inānis,** m. nom. sg. third decl. adj., *futile.*] I

8. Glōrificāte et portāte Deum in corpore vestrō.
    [*I Cor. 6:20 V, an exhortation to continence.—**glōrificō** (1),
    glorify.—**portō** (1), *bear* or *carry along.*] I

9. Animās vestrās castificāte in oboedientiā caritātis in fraternitātis
    amōre simplicī.
    [I Pet. 1:22 V.—**castificō** (1), *purify.*—**oboedientia, -ae,** f.,
    obedience. Take as an instrumental abl. See *Wheelock,* 13.—**cāritās,
    -tātis,** f., *affection, love.*—**frāternitas, -tātis,** f., *brotherhood,
    fraternity.*—**in fraternitātis amōre simplicī,** < εἰς φιλαδελφίαν
    ἀνυπόκριτον, = *for an unfeigned love of the brethren* (KJV). NV has
    ad . . . amōrem nōn fictum. PW, § 117.B, s.v. *In* (7), notice that *in* +
    abl. is often used mistakenly for εἰς + acc. (Cf. Appendix I, § 6 N
    3).—**simplicī,** third decl. m. abl. sg. adj., *simple, unfeigned.*] M

10. Et scrībam super eum nōmen Deī meī, et nōmen cīvitātis Deī meī,
    novae Ierūsalem. [*Apoc. 3:12 V, said of the Christian who shall conquer.—
    scrībam, *I shall write.*—**eum,** acc. pron., *him.*] I

11. Crucem tuam adōrāmus, Domine, et sānctam resurrēctiōnem tuam
    laudāmus et glōrificāmus. Ecce enim propter lignum vēnit gaudium
    in ūniversō mundō.
    [*Improperia III, Fēria VI In Passiōne et Morte Dominī, MR,
    p. 178 (262).—**crux, crucis,** f., *a cross.*—**adōrō** (1), *worship,
    honor, adore.*—**resurrēctiō, -ōnis,** f., *resurrection.*—**glōrificō**
    (1), *glorify.*—**lignum, -ī,** n., *wood; tree.*—**gaudium, -iī,** n., *joy,
    gladness, delight.* —**vēnit,** = *has come.*—**ūniversus, -a, -um,** *whole,
    entire.*—**mundus, -ī,** m., *the world, universe.*] I

12. Maiestātem tuam laudant Angelī, adōrant Dominātiōnēs, tremunt
     Potestātēs. Caelī caelōrumque Virtūtēs ac beāta Seraphim sociā
     exsultātiōne concelebrant.
     [*Praefātiō dē Beātā Marīā Virgine, MR, p. 247 (331).—**maiestās,
     -tātis,** f., *greatness, dignity, majesty.*—**angelus, -ī,** m., *an angel.*—
     dominātiō, -ōnis, f., *a ruler; a spiritual ruler, a Domination* (a
     member of one of the hierarchies of angels).—**tremō, -ere,** *tremble
     (at).*—**potestās, -tātis,** f., *power; a Power* (a member of another
     of the hierarchies of angels).—**beātus, -a, -um,** *happy, fortunate,
     blessed.*—**Seraphim,** indecl. Heb. pl. noun, n., *the Seraphim,*
     the highest choir of angels.—**socius, -a, -um,** *joint, common.*—
     exsultātiō, -ōnis, f., *a leaping; a rejoicing.*—**concelebrō** (1),
     celebrate a solemnity in great numbers, celebrate, solemnize.] M/A

13. Ignōrātiō scrīptūrārum ignōrātiō Chrīstī est.
     [*St. Jerome, *Commentāriōrum in Ēsāiam*, Prologus.—**ignōrātiō,
     -ōnis,** f., *ignorance.*] I/M

14. Cantāte vōcibus, cantāte cordibus, cantāte ōribus, cantāte mōribus:
     "cantāte Dominō canticum novum."
     [*St. Augustine of Hippo, *Sermō* 34.6, in LH 2.559. **vōx, vōcis,** f.,
     voice; word.—**cor, cordis,** n., *heart; mind.*—**ōs, ōris,** n., *mouth;
     face.*—**canticum, -ī,** n., *a song.*] I

15. Grammatica ā litterīs nōmen accēpit. "Grammata" enim Graecī
     litterās vocant.
     [Hugh of St. Victor, *Dē Grammaticā, in initiō.*—**grammatica,
     -ae,** f., *grammar, philology.* **ā,** prep. + abl., *from.*—**accēpit,** *has
     received.*] I/M

CAPVT VIII
Third Conjugation: Present System; Dum, Dōnec

SYNTAXIS SUPPLĒMENTUM

Dum, dōnec. In this chapter, *Wheelock* says that **dum** means *while, as long as, at the same time that* with the indicative, *until* with the subjunctive. **Dōnec**, included here but not in *Wheelock*, means the same things with the same moods. However, both words can mean *until* with certain tenses of the indicative, if "Suspense and Design" are not involved. See GL, § 569. Frequently, however, EL ignores the distinction between the meaning with the indicative and the meaning with the subjunctive. In fact, the Vulgate employs the subjunctive with *dōnec* most of the time. *Dum* does not appear in the Vulgate, except in combination as *dummodo*. See PW, §§ 142–143; Nunn, § 154; Blaise, §§ 310–312. For the encroachment of *dum* on the conjunction **cum**, *when, since, although*, see Capvt XXXI.

VERBA MEMORIĀ COMPREHENDENDA

dōnec, conj., *while, as long as, at the same time that, until* + indicative; *until* + subjunctive

valeō, in EL *valeō* often = *possum*

SENTENTIAE Ē FONTIBUS NŌN ANTĪQUĪS HAUSTAE

1. Vōx sanguinis frātris tuī clāmat ad mē dē terrā.
    [*Gen. 4:10 V, God to Cain.—**vōx, vōcis,** f., *voice.*—**sanguis, -guinis,** m., *blood.*—**clāmō** (1), *shout.*] I

2. Quid agis, Agar?
    [*Gen. 21:17 V, the angel to Hagar.—**quid agis?** = *how are you?*—**Agar,** indecl. Heb. name, f., *Hagar.*] I

19

3. Et dōnec putābam vōs aliquid dīcere, cōnsīderābam.
    [*Job 32:12 V, Elihu to Job's interlocutors.—**putō** (1), *think;
    suppose.*—**vōs,** acc. pl. m. pron., *you.*—**aliquid,** acc. sg. n. pron.,
    something.—**dīcō, -ere,** *say.*—**vōs aliquid dīcere** = *that you were
    saying something.*—**cōnsīderō** (1), *consider, contemplate.*] A

4. Quis ēnārrābit caelōrum ratiōnem?
    [*Job 38:37 V.—**quis,** nom. interrog. pron., *who?*—**ēnārrō** (1),
    explain, relate in detail.] I

5. Poenitentiam agite.
    [*Mt. 3:2 V.—**poenitentia** (or **paen-**), **-ae,** f., *repentance, penitence,
    penance.*—**agere** is used with "a *verbal subst.*, as a favorite
    circumlocution for the action indicated by the *subst.*" [LS, s.v.
    "agō" II.D.4.] Thus, this phrase = **poenitēte,** *be sorry, repent.*] I

6. Dūc in altum, et laxāte rētia vestra in captūram.
    [*Lk. 5:4 V, Jesus to Simon Peter.—**in,** prep. + acc., *into.*—**altum,
    -ī,** n., *the deep.*—**Dūc in altum** = *draw into the deep.*—**laxō** (1),
    expand, open up.—**rētia,** n. acc. pl., *nets.*—**in,** prep. + acc., *for.*—
    captūra, -ae, f., *a catch* (of animals or fish).] M

7. Fodere nōn valeō.
    [Lk. 16:3 V, the unjust steward ponders his future.—**fodiō,
    fodere,** *dig.*] I

8. Deus, grātiās agō tibi, quia nōn sum sīcut cēterī hominum.
    [*Lk. 18:11 V, the Pharisee at prayer.—**tibi,** dat. pron., *(to) you.*—
    quia, conj., *that.*—**sīcut,** adv., *as, just as.*—**cēterī, -ae, -a,** *the
    rest.*] I/M

9. Trahēbant Iāsonem et quōsdam frātrēs ad prīncipēs cīvitātis.
    [*Acts 17:6 V.—**Iāson, -onis,** m., *Jason,* an early convert at
    Thessalonica.—**quōsdam,** acc. pl. indef. adj., *certain.*—**prīnceps,
    -cipis,** m., *a chief (man).*] I

10. Salūtant tē fīliī sorōris tuae ēlēctae.
    [*II Jn. 13 V, St. John conveys greetings from one church to
    another.—**salūtō** (1), *wish well, greet.*—**ēlēctus, -a, -um,** *chosen.*]
    I/M

11. Hanc vītam dōnec apprehendimus, peregrināmur ā Dominō.
    [St. Augustine of Hippo, *Sermō* 346.2.—**hanc,** fem. acc. sg.
    demonstrative adj., = *this.*—**apprehendō, -ere,** *lay hold upon,*

seize. Note that Augustine actually wrote the subjunctive here, although he did mean *as long as.*—**peregrināmur,** first pers. pl. pres. ind. depon., i.e., a pass. form with an act. meaning, = *we are absent from, strangers to* (*ā* + abl.).] M

12. Astronomia est astrōrum lēx.
    [*St. Isidore of Seville, *Etymologiae* 3.24.—**astronomia, -ae,** f., *astronomy.*—**astrum, -ī,** n., *a star.*—**lēx, lēgis,** f., *law, a law.*] I

13. Sānitās est integritās corporis et temperantia nātūrae ex calidō et hūmidō.
    [*St. Isidore of Seville, *Etymologiae* 4.5.—**sānitās, -tātis,** f., *health.*—**integritās, -tātis,** f., *wholeness, soundness.*—**temperantia, -ae,** f., here = *a proportionate mixture.* See LLMA, s.v.—**nātūra, -ae,** f., *nature.*—**calidus, -a, -um,** *warm, hot.*—**hūmidus, -a, -um,** *wet, moist.*] I

14. Rēx autem Ludovīcus, ut erat vir mīlitiae aptus, ulcīscī in Theobaldum comitem frequentābat et cum multīs aliīs barōnibus terram eius expōnēbat.
    [Suger of St. Denis, *Vīta Ludovīcī Grossī Rēgis* 19.—**Ludovīcus, -ī,** m., *Lewis* VI the Fat, king of France (reigned 1108–1137).—**mīlitia, -ae,** f., *military service, warfare.*—**aptus, -a, -um,** *ready* (+ dat.).—**ulcīscī,** third decl. depon. pres. inf., = *to take revenge on* (*in* + acc.).—**Theobaldus, -ī,** m., *Theobald* II, count of Blois-Champagne (ruled 1102–1152).—**comes, -itis,** m., *a companion; a count.*—**frequentō** (1), here = *try* (see LLMA, s.v. 5).—**cum,** prep. + abl., *with.*—**alius, alia, aliud,** *other.*—**bārō, -ōnis,** m., *a dunce; a baron.*—**expōnō, -ere,** here = *despoil, ravage.*] M/A

15. Nātūra ad artis facilitātem nōn pervenit. Artium tamen omnium parēns est.
    [John of Salisbury, *Metalogicon* 1.11.—**ars, artis,** f., *art, skill.*—**facilitās, -tātis,** f., *ease, facility; capability.*—**pervenit,** fourth conjugation pres., ind. act. third pers. sg., = *arrive at, reach* (*ad* + acc.).—**omnium,** third decl. adj. f. gen. pl., *of all.*—**parēns,** f. nom. sg., *a parent.*] I/M

CAPVT IX

Demonstratives *Hic, Ille, Iste;*
Special *-īus* Adjectives;
More on *Iste* and *Alius*

SYNTAXIS SUPPLĒMENTUM

Iste, ista, istud. In CL, *hic, iste,* and *ille* act as first, second, and third person demonstratives. *Hic* refers to someone or something near or with the speaker, *iste* refers to someone or something near or with the person addressed, and *ille* refers to someone or something neither near nor with the persons involved in the conversation. In EL, *iste, ista, istud* can replace any demonstrative (Blaise, §§ 164–166), and frequently means no more than *is, ea, id,* to be introduced in Capvt XI. Note too that *hic, iste,* and *ille* sometimes approach the meaning of the definite article, especially the latter, from which developed the definite articles in the Romance languages (PW, §§ 99, 107). See also Nunn, § 64.

Alius, alia, aliud. This adjective can be used distributively. If the adjective is used twice in the same clause, but in different forms, what is said of the one must also be said of the other, e.g., *Aliī aliud faciunt,* Some men do one thing, other men do another. See Capvt XXVI, Sentence 12.

VERBA MEMORIĀ COMPREHENDENDA

mulier, -eris, f., *a woman; wife*
cāritās, -tātis, f., *costliness, high price; affection, love; charity*
cor, cordis, n., *the heart; mind*
dīvīnus, -a, -um, divine

Sententiae ē Fontibus nōn Antīquīs Haustae

1. Dēlēbimus enim locum istum, Sodomam.
    [Gen. 19:13 V.—**dēleō, -ēre,** *destroy.*—**Sodoma, -ae,** f., *Sodom.*] I

2. Duo virī erant in cīvitāte ūnā, ūnus dīvēs, alter pauper.
    [*II Sam. 12:1 V, the prophet Nathan to King David.—**duo, duae, duo,** *two.*—**dīves, -vitis,** third decl. adj., *rich.*—**pauper, -eris,** third decl. adj., *poor.*] I

3. Deus caelōrum, creātor aquārum, et Dominus tōtīus creātūrae, exaudī mē.
    [*Jud. 9:17 V.—**creātor, -ōris,** m., *creator.*—**aqua, -ae,** f., *water.*—**Dominus,** voc.—**creātūra, -ae,** f., *creation, creature.*—**exaudī,** fourth conj. second pers. sg. pres. imperative, *hear.*] I

4. Virī pulchritūdinis studium habēbant.
    [Ecclus. 44:6 V, said of those rich in virtue.—**pulchritūdō, -dinis,** f., *beauty.*] M

5. Excaecā cor populī huius.
    [*Is. 6:10 V.—**excaecō** (1), *blind.*] I

6. Quid molestī estis huic mulierī?
    [*Mt. 26:10 V, Jesus to his disciples about the woman who anointed his feet.—**quid,** *why?*—**molestus, -a, -um,** *disagreeable* (+ dat.).] I

7. Cūram illīus habē.
    [*Lk. 10:35 V, the Good Samaritan to the innkeeper.—**cūram habēre** = *take care (of).*] I/M

8. Hī hominēs conturbant cīvitātem nostram.
    [*Acts 16:20 V, the charge against Paul and Silas at Philippi.—**conturbō** (1), *upset, throw into confusion.*] I

9. Nūllus est Deus nisi ūnus.
    [*I Cor. 8:4 V.—**nisi,** conj., *if not, unless, except.*] I/M

10. Mundā cor meum ac labia mea, omnipotēns Deus.
    [*Munda Cor Meum, MR, p. 219 (303).—**mundō** (1), *make clean, cleanse.*—**labium, -iī,** n., *a lip.*—**omnipotēns,** third decl. adj. modifying *Deus, omnipotent, all-powerful.*] I

11.   Deō Patrī sit glōria, eiusque sōlī Fīliō, cum Spīritū Paraclitō.
[*Hymnus, Fēria Quīnta ad Laudēs II, BR 2.522.—**pater, -tris,**
m., *father.*—**sit,** third pers. sg. pres. subjunctive of **esse,** *be.*—**eius,**
gen. third pers. sg. pron., *his.*—**cum,** prep. + abl., *with.*— **Spīritū,**
fourth decl. m. abl. sg. noun, *Spirit.*—**Paraclitus, -ī,** m., *Paraclete.*]
I/M

12.   Hunc habet poētica licentia modum.
[*Lactantius, *Epitomē Īnstitūtiōnum Dīvīnārum* 11.—**poēticus,**
-a, -um, *poetic.*—**licentia, -ae,** f., *freedom, liberty.* **modus, -ī,** m.,
manner, method, way.] M

13.   Illud etiam maximum argūmentum immortālitātis, quod Deum
sōlus homō agnōscit.
[*Lactantius, *Epitomē Īnstitūtiōnum Dīvīnārum* 70.—**maximus, -a,**
-um, *greatest.*—**argūmentum, -ī,** n., *proof, evidence, argument.*—
immortālitās, -tātis, f., *immortality.*—**quod,** explanatory *that.*—
agnōscō, -ere, *know again from previous acquaintance; know by*
inference or *report, understand; acknowledge.*] M

14.   Cāritās alia est dīvīna, alia hūmāna; alia est hūmāna licita, alia illicita.
[*St. Augustine of Hippo, *Sermō* 349.1.1.—**alius . . . alius,** =
(the) one . . . (the) other.—**hūmānus, -a, -um,** *human.*—**licitus,**
-a, -um, *allowed, permitted.*—**illicitus, -a, -um,** *not allowed,*
impermissible.] M

15.   Neutrum dictum [est genus], quia nec hoc est nec illud, id est nec
masculīnum nec fēminīnum.
[*St. Isidore of Seville, *Etymologiae* 1.7.28, speaking of the gender
of nouns.—**genus, generis,** n., *kind;* (grammmatical) *gender.*—
dictum est, here = *is called.*—**quia,** conj., *because.*—**nec . . .**
nec, *neither . . . nor.*—**id est,** *that is, i.e.*—**masculīnus, -a, -um,**
masculine.—**fēminīnus, -a, -um,** *feminine.*] M

CAPVT X
Fourth Conjugation and -*iō* Verbs of the Third Conjugation

VERBA MEMORIĀ COMPREHENDENDA

amīcitia, to the definitions in *Wheelock* add *compact, treaty*
clāmō (1), *shout*

SENTENTIAE Ē FONTIBUS NŌN ANTĪQUĪS HAUSTAE

1. Sī facitis misericordiam et vēritātem cum dominō meō Ābraham, indicāte mihi.
    [Gen. 24:49 V, Eliezer bargains with Laban for Rebecca.—
    misericordia, -ae, f., *compassion, pity, mercy*; **misericordiam facere** = *show mercy.*—**indicō** (1), *point out; set a price.*—**mihi,** dat. pron., *to/for me.*] I

2. Fac mēcum amīcitiās, et erit manus mea tēcum.
    [*II Sam. 3:12 V, Abner to David.—**cum** follows a personal pron. as an enclitic.—**manus,** fourth decl. f. nom. sg., *a hand.*] I

3. Et per multās hōrās in ecclēsiā clāmābant ad Deum.
    [Jud. 7:18 V, the reaction of the people of Bethulia to an Assyrian siege.—**per,** prep. + acc., *through; for.*—**ecclēsia, -ae,** f., *assembly; church.*] I

4. Immortālitās est in cōgnātiōne sapientiae, et in amīcitiā illīus dēlectātiō bona.
    [*Wis. 8:17–18 V.—**immortālitās, -tātis,** f., *immortality.*—**cōgnātiō, -ōnis,** f., *relationship by birth; affinity.*—**dēlectātiō, -ōnis,** f., *delight, pleasure.*] I/M

5. Mulieris bonae vir beātus.
    [*Ecclus. 26:1 V.] M

6. Nōn omnēs capiunt verbum istud.
    [Mt. 19:11 V, the "word" is the exhortation to celibacy.—**omnēs,**
    m./f. nom. pl. adj., *all.*] I/M

7. Ego sum via, et vēritās, et vīta. Nēmō venit ad Patrem nisi per mē.
    [*Jn. 14:6 V.—**ego,** nom. sg. pron., *I.*—**nēmō,** nom. sg. pron., *no
    one.*—**pater, -tris,** m., *father.*—**nisi,** conj., *except, unless.*] I

8. Nec ipsa nātūra docet vōs?
    [I Cor. 11:14 V, on men's and women's hair lengths.—**nec,** conj.,
    and . . . not.—**ipse, ipsa, ipsum,** *himself, herself, itself.*—**vōs,** acc.
    pl. pron., *you.*] I

9. Rādīx enim omnium malōrum est cupiditās.
    [*I Tim. 6:10 V.—**rādīx, -īcis,** f., *root.*—**omnium,** third decl. n.
    gen. pl. adj., *of all.*] I

10. Prīmum autem iūstitiae officium est Deum agnōscere ut praesentem,
    eumque metuere ut dominum, dīligere ut patrem.
    [*Lactantius, *Epitomē Īnstitūtiōnum Dīvīnārum* 59.—**prīmus,**
    -a, -um, *first.*—**autem,** postpositive conj., *moreover; however.*—
    iūstitia, -ae, f., *justice, righteousness.*—**agnōscō, -ere,** *recognize;
    acknowledge.*—**ut,** conj., *as.*—**praesentem,** third decl. m. acc.
    sg. adj., *present, at hand.*—**eum,** = *him* (dir. obj.).—**metuō, -ere,**
    fear.—**dīligō, -ere,** *esteem, love.*] M

11. Et quī nescit scrīptūrās, nescit Deī virtūtem eiusque sapientiam.
    [*St. Jerome, *Commentāria in Ēsāiam,* Prologus.—**quī,** nom. m. sg.
    rel. pron. = *he who.*—**nesciō, -īre,** *not to know, be ignorant of.*] I/M

12. Fugit homō, et sēcum trahit bellum suum, quōcumque it.
    [*St. Augustine of Hippo, *Sermō* 25.4.4.—**sēcum,** = *with
    him(self).*—**suus, -a, -um,** *his/her/its own.*—**quōcumque,** adv.,
    whithersoever, wherever.—**it,** irreg., = *he goes.*] I/M

13. Pendēbat ergō [Chrīstus] in cruce dēfōrmis, sed dēfōrmitās illīus
    pulchritūdō nostra erat.
    [*St. Augustine of Hippo, *Sermō* 27.6.6.—**pendō, -ere,** *hang, be
    suspended.*—**crux, crucis,** f., *a cross.*—**dēfōrmis,** third decl. m.
    nom. sg. adj., *misshapen, ugly, disgraceful, base.*—**dēfōrmitās,**
    -tātis, f., *ugliness, baseness.*—**pulchritūdō, -inis,** f., *beauty.*] I/M

14. Peccāta vērō remittere sōlus Deus potest.
    [*St. Thomas Aquinas, *Compendium Theologiae* 146.—**vērō,** adv.,
    indeed.—**remittō, -ere,** *send back; relax; forgive.*] I

15.   Creatūra enim sine Creatōre ēvānescit.

[*Gaudium et Spēs, no. 36.—**creatūra, -ae,** f., *a creature; the creation.*—**creātor, -tōris,** m., a *creator; the Creator.*—**ēvānescō, -ere,** *vanish, disappear, pass away.*] I

A pupil of El Greco, Luis Tristán de Escamilla (c. 1585–1624), painted this evocative head of St. Monica (c. 331–387), the mother of St. Augustine of Hippo (354–430). The picture originally formed part of the altarpiece of the church in Yepes, a small town near Toledo, Spain, but now hangs in the Prado Museum in Madrid. St. Monica, a Christian, was the wife of Patricius, a pagan and a member of the Roman gentry of North Africa. She had three children with him, the eldest of whom was Augustine. Monica devoted her life to the conversion of her husband and children, and her heart was broken many times by Augustine in particular (see Capvt XXXVII, Sentence 9). When Augustine moved to Italy to further his oratorical career in 384, Monica soon followed, and was rewarded by witnessing Augustine's conversion in 387. In his early dialogues, written just after his conversion, Augustine describes his mother with great respect as a philosopher. They resolved to return to Africa that year, and were waiting for a ship at the Roman port of Ostia, when the famous mutual ecstasy of mother and son occurred (*Cōnfessiōnēs* 9.10.23–26; Capvt XXXIX, Sentence 8). Monica died shortly afterwards in Ostia. Her relics are now in Rome. (© Wikimedia Commons)

CAPVT XI
Personal Pronouns *Ego*, *Tū*, and *Is*;
Demonstratives *Is* and *Īdem*

VERBA MEMORIĀ COMPREHENDENDA

angelus, -ī, m., *a messenger; angel*

Marīa, -ae, f., *Mary*

sacer, -cra, -crum, *sacred, holy*

SENTENTIAE Ē FONTIBUS NŌN ANTĪQUĪS HAUSTAE

1. Dominus mittet angelum suum tēcum, et dīriget viam tuam.
    [Gen. 24:40 V, Eliezer quoting Abraham to Laban.—**dīrigō,
    -ere**, *direct, guide*.] I

2. Quid est hoc quod agis?
    [*Num. 23:11 V, Balak to Balaam.—**quod**, n. acc. rel. pron., *which,
    that*.] I

3a. In tempore istō, et in hāc eādem hōrā, sī vīta comes erit, habēbis in
    uterō fīlium.
    [II Kings 4:16 V.—**comes, -itis**, m., *a companion, partner*.[8]—
    uterus, -ī, m., *womb; belly*.] A

---

[8] The strange phrase *sī vīta comes erit* (*fuerit* in the original) has an interesting history,
as far as I can reconstruct it. I include it here as an indication of the difficulties one
encounters in the Vulgate. The LXX, which was the basis of the Vulgate translation,
reads, Εἰς τὸν καιρὸν τοῦτον ὡς ἡ ὥρα ζῶσα σὺ περιειληφυῖα υἱόν. It is clear from the
use of the phrase ὡς ἡ ὥρα ζῶσα in the next verse that ζῶσα modifies ὥρα and not σύ.
Therefore, the translation of 4:16 from the Greek should be, "At the right time when the
season is living, thou shalt have embraced a son." The phrase ὡς ἡ ὥρα ζῶσα is a translation of the Hebrew *kā'ēt ḥayyâh*, "at the living/reviving time," i.e., "in the spring." Thus,
the Greek can be made to fit the meaning of the Hebrew; but the Vulgate translation
of the LXX is incorrect, for the translator seems to have thought that ζῶσα modified
σύ, giving the sense, "if life will be your comrade," meaning perhaps, "if you are alive."
Sentence 3b above gives the NV rendering of this verse for comparison.

3b.   In tempore istō, in annō alterō, amplexāberis fīlium.
        [II Kings 4:16 NV.—**annus, -ī,** m., *year.*—**amplexāberis,** second
        pers. sg. fut. depon., = *you will embrace.*] M

4.   Tunc intellegēs timōrem Dominī, et scientiam Deī inveniēs.
        [*Prov. 2:5 V, the result of seeking wisdom.—**tunc,** adv., *then, at
        that time.*—**scientia, -ae,** f., *knowledge, science, skill.*] I

5.   Dīc sapientiae, "Soror mea es," et prūdentiam vocā amīcam tuam.
        [*Prov. 7:4 V.—**prūdentia, -ae,** f., *foresight, wisdom, discretion.*—
        amīcam tuam, = pred. acc.] M

6.   Lūcius cōnsul Rōmānōrum Ptolemaeō rēgī salūtem.
        [*I Mac. 15:16 V, a formulaic classical epistolary greeting. Note
        the ellipsis of *dīcit,* as was customary.—**Lūcius,** = *Lucius* Caecilius
        Metellus Calvus (consul 142 BCE).—**Ptolemaeus, -ī,** m., *Ptolemy
        VIII Euergetes II* (c. 182/1–116 BCE).—**salūs, -ūtis,** f., *health,
        safety; greeting.*—**salūtem dīcere,** = *greet, salute.*] I

7.   Ecce ego mittō angelum meum ante faciem tuam, quī praeparābit
        viam tuam ante tē.
        [*Mk. 1:2 V.—**ante,** prep. + acc., *before, in front of.*—**faciem,**
        fourth decl. f. acc. sg., *face.*—**quī,** m. nom. sg. rel. pron., *who.*—
        praeparō (1), *prepare.*] I

8.   Et nōmen virginis Marīa.
        [*Lk. 1:27 V.] I

9.   Vir caput est mulieris, sīcut Christus caput est Ecclēsiae.
        [*Eph. 5:23 V.—**sīcut,** adv., *as.*] I

10.   Hoc enim sentīte in vōbīs, quod et in Christō Iēsū.
        [*Phil. 2:5 V.—**quod,** n. nom. rel. pron., *which.*] I/M

11.   Capiunt ergōne tē[, Deus,] caelum et terra, quoniam tū implēs ea?
        [*St. Augustine of Hippo, *Cōnfessiōnēs* 1.3.3.—**impleō, -ēre,** *fill
        up, fill full.*] M

12.   Vēritās enim dīcit mihi, "Nōn est Deus tuus terra et caelum neque
        omne corpus." Hoc dīcit eōrum nātūra.
        [*St. Augustine of Hippo, *Cōnfessiōnēs* 10.6.10.—**omne,** third
        decl. n. nom. sg. adj., *every.*] I/M

13.   Rollō dīcēbat, "Dānī sumus. Tū vērō quis es, quī tam facētē nōbīs dīcis?"

      [William Calculus, *Historia Northmannōrum* 2.10.—**Rollō, -ōnis,** m., *Hrolfr, Rollo,* the Viking war leader who began the conquest of Normandy.—**Dānī, -ōrum,** m., *Danes.*—**quis,** m. nom. sg. interrog. pron., = *who?*—**quī,** m. nom. sg. rel. pron., = *who.*—**tam,** adv., *so.*—**facētē,** adv., *pleasantly, wittily,* used ironically.] I/M

14.   Amīcōs autem illōs sōlōs dīcimus, quibus cor nostrum et quidquid in illō est committere nōn formīdāmus.

      [*St. Aelred of Rievaulx, *Dē Spīrituālī Amīcitiā* 1.32.—**quibus,** m. dat. pl. rel. pron., = *to whom.*—**quisquis, quidquid,** indef. pron., *whoever, whatever.*—**committō, -ere,** *entrust, commit.*—**formīdō** (1), *be terrified, tremble.*] M

15.   Tū docē mē viam rēctam. Prōpōne breve aliquod exercitium Sacrae Commūniōnī congruum.

      [*Thomas á Kempis, *Dē Imitātiōne Chrīstī* 4.6.2.—**rēctus, -a, -um,** *straight, right.*—**prōpōnō, -ere,** *set forth; propose.*—**aliquī, aliquae, aliquod,** indef. adj., *some.*—**exercitium, -iī,** n., *exercise, practice.*—**commūniō, -ōnis,** f., *a sharing, communion.*—**congruus, -a, -um,** *fit, suitable* (+ dat.).] I/M

CAPVT XII
Perfect Active System; Syncope

SYNTAXIS SUPPLĒMENTUM

Syncope, Syncopation. Latin speakers regularly dropped the syllables -*ve*- and -*vi*- from perfect forms of the verb, e.g, *amāstī* for *amāvistī*, and *amārunt* for *amāvērunt*. See also Smith, 38.

VERBA MEMORIĀ COMPREHENDENDA

cūnctī, -ae, -a, *all together, all* (the sg. number exists, but is used less often than the pl.)

Petrus, -ī, m., *Peter*

SENTENTIAE Ē FONTIBUS NŌN ANTĪQUĪS HAUSTAE

1. Et creāvit Deus hominem ad imāginem suam: ad imāginem Deī creāvit illum, masculum et fēminam creāvit eōs.
    [*Gen. 1:27 V.—**ad,** = *in comparison with, according to.*—**imāgō, -inis,** f., *image.*—**suus, -a, -um,** reflex. possessive adj., *his/her/its own.*—**masculus, -a, -um,** *male.*—**fēmina, -ae,** f., *a female*, its basic meaning.] I

2. Servus autem cūncta quae gesserat narrāvit Isaac.
    [*Gen. 24:66 V, Eliezer reports to Isaac about his negotiations for Rebecca.—**servus, -ī,** m., *slave.*—**quae,** n. acc. pl. rel. pron., *which, that.*—**narrō** (1), *tell.*—**Isaac,** indecl. Heb. name, m., *Isaac,* = dat.] I

3. Rachel dūxit uxōrem Iacob.
    [Gen. 29:28.—**Rachel,** indecl. Heb. name, f., *Rachel,* = dir. obj.— **dūxit uxōrem,** an idiom, = *marry* (in the case of a man). *Uxōrem* serves as a pred. acc. in this construction.] I/M

31

4. Iōsēph vīdit Beniamin frātrem suum uterīnum, et āit, "Iste est frāter vester parvulus, dē quō dīxerātis mihi?"
    [Gen. 43:29 V, Joseph sees Benjamin for the first time after years in Egypt.—**Iōsēph,** indecl. Heb. name, m., *Joseph.*—**Beniamin,** indecl. Heb. name, m., *Benjamin.*—**uterīnus, -a, -um,** *uterine, of the same mother.*—**āit,** = *said.*—**parvulus, -a, -um,** *young.*—**quō,** m. sg. abl. rel. pron., = *whom.*] I

5. Et posteā intellēxerit peccātum suum, offeret prō peccātō suō vitulum.
    [*Lev. 4:14 V, part of the law on a sin offering.—**posteā,** adv., *after.*—**offeret,** = *he shall offer.*—**vitulus, -ī,** m., *a bull calf.*] I/M

6. Verbum mīsit Dominus in Iacob, et cecidit in Israël.
    [*Is. 9:8 V, the beginning of a prophecy.—**verbum** should be understood both as the dir. obj. of *mīsit* and as the subject of *cedidit.*—**Iacob,** indecl. Heb. name, m., *Jacob.*] I

7. In prīncipiō erat Verbum, et Verbum erat apud Deum, et Deus erat Verbum. Hoc erat in prīncipiō apud Deum.
    [*Jn. 1:1–2 V.—**apud,** prep. + acc., *at, by, near, with.*] I

8. Iēsūs autem dīxit, "Pater, grātiās agō tibi quōniam audīstī mē."
    [Jn. 11:41 V, Jesus speaks at the raising of Lazarus.—**audīstī,** for *audīvistī* by syncope.] I

9. Deinde post annōs trēs vēnī Hierosolymam vidēre Petrum, et mansī apud eum diēbus quīndecim.
    [*Gal. 1:18 V, Paul is speaking.—**deinde,** adv., *then, next.*—**post,** prep. + acc., *after.*—**trēs,** m. acc. pl. adj., *three.*—**Hierosolymam,** acc. of motion towards, = *ad H.*—**vidēre,** = inf. expressing purp. See Appendix I, § 50.—**diēbus quīndecim,** abl. of time during which, = *for fifteen days.* See Appendix I, § 24.] I/M

10. Benedictus Dominus Deus Israël, quia vīsitāvit et fēcit redēmptiōnem plēbis suae.
    [*Benedictus,* Ōrdinārium, Ad Laudēs mātūtīnās, LH 3.529.—**benedictus, -a, -um,** *blessed.*—**quia,** conj., *because.*—**vīsitō (1),** *visit.*—**redēmptiō, -ōnis,** f., *a ransoming, redemption.*—**plēbs, -bis,** f., (common) *people.*] I

11. Fēcit Deus mundum propter hominem.
    [*Lactantius, *Epitomē Īnstitūtiōnum Dīvīnārum* 69.—**mundus, -ī,** m., *the world, universe.*] I

12. Tū in viā ambulā; veniēs ad patriam, sī nōn dēserās viam. Tenēte
     ergō Chrīstum, tenēte fidem, tenēte viam.
       [St. Augustine of Hippo, *Sermō* 362.25.27.—**ambulō** (1), *walk*.—
       dēserō, -ere, *desert, abandon,* here in the second sg. pres. act.
       subjunctive, = *should* [not] *desert*.—**teneō, -ēre,** *hold, keep*.—
       fidem, *faith,* = dir. obj.] M

13. Et ideō dē nihilō fēcistī "caelum et terram," magnum quiddam et
     parvum quiddam . . . magnum caelum et parvam terram. Tū erās et
     aliud nihil, unde fēcistī "caelum et terram."
       [*St. Augustine of Hippo, *Cōnfessiōnēs* 12.8.7, praying to God.—
       ideō, adv., *for that reason*.—**nihilum, -ī,** n., *nothing*.—**quīdam,**
       quaedam, quiddam, indef. pron., *someone, something*.—**parvus,**
       -a, -um, *small, little*.—**unde,** adv., *whence; from which*.] M

14. Nūptiae autem sīve mātrimōnium est virī et mulieris coniūnctiō,
     indīviduam cōnsuetūdinem vītae cōntinēns.
       [*Tribonian, Theophilus, and Dorotheus, *Imperātōris Iūstiniānī*
       Īnstitūtiōnēs 1.9.1.—**nūptiae, -ārum,** f., *marriage*.—**sīve,**
       conj., *or*.—**mātrimōnium, -iī,** n., *matrimony*.—**coniūnctiō,**
       -ōnis, f., *a union, association*.—**indīviduus, -a, -um,** *indivisible,*
       inseparable.—**cōnsuetūdō, -inis,** f., *companionship*.—**continēns,**
       f. nom. sg. pres. act. partic., modifying *coniunctiō,* = *containing*.] M

15. Mīsit [Deus] enim Fīlium suum, aeternum scīlicet Verbum.
       [*Deī Verbum* 1.4, CDD, p. 425.—**suus, -a, -um,** *his/her/its own*.—
       aeternus, -a, -um, *eternal*.—**scīlicet,** adv., *namely*.] I

CAPVT XIII

Reflexive Pronouns and Possessives; Intensive Pronoun; **Reflexive Possessives in EL**

Syntaxis Supplēmentum

Reflexive Possessives. Note that EL is not always as careful as CL to distinguish between *suus, -a, -um*, and *eius* or *eōrum*, as in the fifth sentence below. In fact, generally speaking, the classical rules governing the use of reflexives "tombent en désuétude," "are falling into abeyance," according to Blaise (§ 172). See also PW, §§ 96–98; Blaise, §§ 172–180; Nunn, § 61.

Verba Memoriā Comprehendenda

cibus, -ī, m., *food*

salvum, -am, -um facere, to the meanings of **faciō** in *Wheelock* add this biblical idiom, = *save* (someone or something, also in the acc.)

voluntās, -tātis, f., *will, wish, inclination*

Sententiae ē Fontibus nōn Antīquīs Haustae

1. Ipse vērō Ābraham stābat iuxtā eōs sub arbore.
   [Gen. 18:8 V, Abraham serves the angels at Mamre.—**vērō,** adv., *in truth.*—**iuxtā,** prep. + acc., *near (to).*—**arbor, -oris,** f., *tree.*] I

2. Sēparāvit vōs Deus Israël ab omnī populō, et iūnxit sibi.
   [*Num. 16:9 V, Moses addresses Korah.—**sēparō** (1), *separate.*—**ab,** prep. + abl., *from.*—**omnī,** third decl. m. abl. sg. adj., *every.*] I

34

3. Populus Philisthīnōrum laudābat deum suum.
   [Judg. 16:24 V, just before Samson brought the temple down.—
   Philistīnus, -ī, m., *a Philistine.*] I

4. Percussit autem cor Dāvīd eum, et dīxit ad Dominum, "Peccāvī valdē
   in hōc factō."
   [II Sam. 24:10 V, David repents after the census.—**percutiō, -ere,**
   -cussī, *strike hard.*—**valdē,** adv., *exceedingly.*—**in** + abl., here = *in*
   the case of, in reference to.] I

5. Manum suam illa mīsit ad fortia, et digitī eius apprehendērunt fūsum.
   [Prov. 31:19 V, from the description of a good wife.—**manum,**
   fourth decl. f. acc. sg., *hand.*—**fortia,** third decl. n. acc. pl. adj., =
   respectable things. Cf. Plautus, *Trinummus* 5.2.9, cited at LS, s.v.,
   II.A.—**digitus, -ī,** m., *finger.*—**apprehendō, -ere, -hendī,** *lay hold*
   of.—**fūsus, -ī,** m., *spindle.*] I

6. Alit enim animam suam cibīs aliēnīs.
   [Ecclus. 40:30 V, from some advice against indigency.—**aliēnus,**
   -a, -um, *belonging to another.*—**cibīs aliēnīs,** abl. of means, supply
   with.] I

7. Hoc fēcit initium signōrum Iēsūs in Canā Galilaeae; et manifestāvit
   glōriam suam, et crēdidērunt in eum discipulī eius.
   [*Jn. 2:11 V.—**initium, -iī,** n., *beginning.*—**Cana, -ae,** f., *Cana.*—
   Galilaea, -ae, f., *Galilee.* This is a topographical genitive. See
   Blaise, § 91.12, and Appendix I, § 9.—**manifestō** (1), *make*
   public.—**crēdō, -ere, -didī,** *believe.* The construction of **crēdere**
   with **in** + acc. of the person belongs to EL. CL uses the dat. of the
   person. See Appendix I, § 6 N 3. Of course, the dat. of the person
   is found in EL, too, but not with the present nuance.] I/M

8. Dīligēs proximum tuum sīcut tē ipsum.
   [*Gal. 5:14 V.—**dīligēs,** fut. jussive = *you shall . . . .* See Appendix
   I, § 44.—**proximus, -ī,** m., *neighbor.*—**sīcut,** adv., *as.*] I

9. Ecce stō ad ōstium, et pulsō: sī quis audierit vōcem meam, et aperuerit
   mihi iānuam, intrābō ad illum, et cēnābō cum illō, et ipse mēcum.
   [*Apoc. 3:20 V, Jesus addresses the Laodiceans.—**ōstium, -iī,** n.,
   a door.—**pulsō** (1), *beat, strike.*—**quis,** indef. pron. m. nom. sg.,
   anyone.—**vōx, vōcis,** f., *voice.*—**aperiō, -īre, -ruī,** *open.*—**iānua,**
   -ae, f., *door.*—**intrō** (1), *walk in, enter.*] M

10.   Domine, salvum fac rēgem.
       [*Ōrdinārium, ad Vesperās dē Precibus, BR 2.(13).] I

11.   Interrogāvī mundī mōlem dē Deō meō, et respondit mihi, "Nōn ego
       sum, sed ipse mē fēcit."
       [*St. Augustine of Hippo, *Cōnfessiōnēs* 10.6.9.—**interrogō** (1),
       ask.—**mundus, -ī,** m., *the world, universe.*—**mōles, -is,** f., *a massive
       construction.*—**respondeō, -ēre, -spondī,** *answer, reply.*] M

12.   Iūstitia est cōnstāns et perpetua voluntās iūs suum cuīque tribuēns.
       [*Tribonian, Theophilus, and Dorotheus, *Imperātōris Iūstiniānī
       Īnstitūtiōnēs* 1.1.1.—**iūstitia, -ae,** f., *justice; righteousness.*—
       cōnstāns, -antis, *steady, firm, unchanging.*—**iūs, iūris,** n., *right,
       justice, law.*—**tribuō, -ere,** *grant, give; yield, concede.*] M/A

13.   Iūris praecepta sunt haec: honestē vīvere, alterum nōn laedere, suum
       cuique tribuere.
       [*Tribonian, Theophilus, and Dorotheus, *Imperātōris Iūstiniānī
       Īnstitūtiōnēs* 1.1.3.—**praeceptum, -ī,** n., *a precept.*—**honestē,**
       adv., *decently, properly, virtuously.*—**laedō, -ere,** *hurt, injure,
       damage.*] M/A

14.   Dā tē ad cordis compūnctiōnem, et inveniēs dēvōtiōnem.
       [*Thomas à Kempis, *Dē Imitātiōne Chrīstī* 1.21.1.—**compūnctiō,
       -ōnis,** f., *the prick of conscience; penitential sorrow.*—**devotiō,
       -ōnis,** f., *piety, devotion.*] I/M

15.   Dum tempus habēs, congregā tibi dīvitiās immortālēs.
       [*Thomas à Kempis, *Dē Imitātiōne Chrīstī* 1.23.8.—**congregō** (1),
       gather together.—**immortālis, -e,** *not subject to death.*] I

CAPVT XIV

I-Stem Nouns of the Third Declension; Ablatives of Means, Accompaniment, and Manner; *In* with the Ablative of Instrument/Means

Syntaxis Supplēmentum

In with the Instrumental Ablative. EL sometimes employs the preposition *in* with the instrumental ablative. This is a Hebraism (PW, § 22[b]). Examples will be found below. See also Appendix I, § 21.

Verba Memoriā Comprehendenda

gaudium, -iī, n., *joy, delight*

psallō, -ere, psallī, *play upon a stringed instrument; sing the Psalms of David* (EL)

Sententiae ē Fontibus nōn Antīquīs Haustae

1.   Deus, auribus nostrīs audīvimus.
      [*Ps. 43:2 V.] I

2.   Hoc mare magnum: illīc reptilia quōrum nōn est numerus, animālia pusilla cum magnīs.
      [Ps. 103:25 V.—**illīc,** adv., *there.*—**reptile, -is,** n., *a creeping thing, reptile.*—**quōrum,** n. gen. pl. rel. pron., *of which.*—**pusillus, -a, -um,** *very little, "wee little"* (as Maritime Canadians say).] I

37

3.   Et mīsit rēx prīncipem tribūtōrum in cīvitātēs Iūda, et vēnit Ierūsalem
     cum turbā magnā.
     [I Mac. 1:30 V, Antiochus IV Epiphanes (c. 215–154 BCE)
     sets in motion the train of events that leads to the Maccabean
     rebellion.—**prīnceps, -cipis,** m., *a chief, head.*—**tribūtum, -ī,** n.,
     tribute, tax.—**Iūda,** indecl. Heb. name, or **Iūdas, -ae,** m., *Judah.*—
     Ierūsalem, names of cities do not require a prep. (see *Wheelock,*
     313–314); supply *ad.*] I/M

4.   Stīpendia enim peccātī mors. Grātia autem Deī vīta aeterna in Chrīstō
     Iēsū Dominō nostrō.
     [*Rom. 6:23 V.—**stīpendium, -iī,** n., *tax; wage, pay.*—**aeternus,
     -a, -um,** *eternal, imperishable.*] I/M

5.   Audīvī vōcem quārtī animalis dīcentis, "Venī," et vīdī, et ecce equus
     pallidus.
     [*Apoc. 6:7b-8a V.—**vōx, vōcis,** f., *voice.*—**quārtus, -a, -um,**
     fourth.—**dīcentis,** pres. act. partic., n. gen. sg., modifying *animalis,*
     = *saying.*—**equus, -a, -um,** *a horse.*—**pallidus, -a, -um,** *pale.*] I/M

6.   Ēsurientēs implēvit bonīs.
     [*Canticum Ēvangelicum, ad Vesperās, Ōrdinārium, LH 3.538,
     speaking of God's care for his people.—**ēsurientēs,** m./f. acc.
     pl. partic., *those who are hungry, the hungry.*—**impleō, -ēre, -ēvī,**
     fill (up).] I

7.   Omnia in sapientiā fēcistī.
     [*Respōnsōrium Breve, ad I Vesperās, Dominica, Hebdomada
     I, LH 3.548.—**in sapientiā,** instrumental, but cf. Capvt XVI,
     Sentence 11.] I

8.   Magnō cum gaudiō coetuī dominicālī dā nōbīs interesse.
     [*Precēs, ad Laudēs mātūtīnās, Dominica, Hebdomada I, LH
     3.558.—**coetuī,** fourth decl. m. dat. sg. noun, *assembly.*—
     dominicālī, third decl. m. dat. sg. adj., modifying *coetuī,*
     dominical.—**dā nōbīs** = *grant (to) us.*—**intersum, -esse,** + dat.,
     take part in.] M

9.   Iūdicābit Dominus in iūstitiā pauperēs.
     [*Antiphona 1, Fēria III, ad Officium Lēctiōnis, Hebdomada I,
     LH 3.586.—**iūdicō** (1), *judge.*—**iūstitia, -ae,** f., *justice.*—**pauper,
     -eris,** m., *a poor man.*] I

10. Psallite spīritū, psallite et mente, hoc est: glōrificāte Deum et animā
     et corpore vestrō.
     [*Hesychius, in capite psalmī secundī, ad Laudēs Mātūtīnās,
     Dominica, Hebdomada IV, LH 3.926.—spīritū, fourth decl. m.
     abl. sg. noun, *spirit.*—mēns, mentis, f., *mind.*—hoc est, = *i.e.*—
     glōrificō (1), *glorify.*] I/M

11. Laudāmus Dominum in vītā nostrā, id est in mōribus nostrīs.
     [*Arnobius, in capite psalmī secundī, ad Laudēs mātūtīnās, Fēria
     IV, Hebdomada IV, LH 3.976.—id est = *i.e.*, or is it the other way
     around?] I

12. Mare est aquārum generālis collēctiō.
     [*St. Isidore of Seville, *Etymologiae* 13.14.1.—generālis, third
     decl. f. nom. sg. adj., = *universal, general.*—collēctiō, -ōnis, f., *a
     collecting together.*] I

13. Terra est in mediā mundī regiōne posita, omnibus partibus caelī in
     modum centrī aequālī intervallō cōnsistēns.
     [*St. Isidore of Seville, *Etymologiae* 14.1.1.—medius, -a, -um,
     middle.—mundus, -ī, m., *the universe, cosmos.*—in modum, *in the
     manner.*—centrum, -ī, n., *the center* (of a circle).—regiō, -ōnis, f.,
     a region.—positus, -a, -um, *placed.*—omnibus, third decl. f. abl.
     pl. adj., modifying *partibus*, take as an abl. of separation, = *from
     all.*—aequālī, third decl. n. abl. sg. adj., modifying *intervallō*, take
     as an abl. of respect, = *at an equal.*—intervallum, -ī, n., *an interval,
     distance.*—cōnsistēns, third decl. f. nom. sg. partic., modifying
     terra, = *standing.*] A

14. *Vestis virum facit.*
     [*Desiderius Erasmus, *Adagia* 3.1.60, quoting a proverb already
     hoary in his day.—vestis, -is, f., *clothing, clothes.*] I

15. Homō etenim ex intimā suā nātūrā ēns sociālis est, atque sine
     relatiōnibus cum aliīs nec vivere nec suās dōtēs expandere potest.
     [*Gaudium et Spēs*, no. 12.—etenim, conj., *for indeed.*—intimus,
     -a, -um, *inmost; deepest; most secret.*—ēns, entis, n., *a being.*—
     sociālis, -e, *companionable, sociable, social.*—relātiō, -ōnis, f.,
     relation.—dōs, dōtis, f., *a dowery; an endowment, a quality.*—
     expandō, -ere, *stretch out, expand, spread out.*] M

CAPVT XV

Numerals; Genitive of the Whole; Ablative with Numerals and Ablative of Time; **Ablative of Time in EL; Genitive of the Whole with Cardinal Numbers in EL**

SYNTAXIS SUPPLĒMENTUM

Ablative of Time. EL sometimes uses the preposition *in* with the ablative of time, e.g., *in hāc diē et in hōc tempore*, on this day and at this time (I Kings 14:14 V). EL also sometimes uses the ablative to convey the sense of duration of time, e.g., *multō tempore*, for a long time (Deut. 4:40).[9] CL prefers the accusative in this construction, but note, e.g., Livy 21.4.10, *trienniō*, for three years.

Genitive of the Whole (Partitive Genitive) with Cardinal Numbers. EL sometimes employs the genitive of the whole with other cardinal numbers than *mīlia*, e.g., *super ūnum mōntium*, on one of the mountains (Gen. 22:2 V).

Dative of Advantage or Disadvantage. The dative is used not only to indicate the indirect object of a verb, i.e., the person indirectly affected by an action, but also persons with a more remote interest in the action of a verb. One category of this more general use of the dative is the Dative of Advantage or Disadvantage, which shows who gains or loses some advantage—glory, wealth, or pleasure—by an action. See Sentence 2 below.

---

[9]   Both of these examples are taken from PW, § 115.

VERBA MEMORIĀ COMPREHENDENDA

carō, carnis, f., *flesh*

prex, precis, f., *a prayer*

psalmus, -ī, m., *a psalm*

SENTENTIAE Ē FONTIBUS NŌN ANTĪQUĪS HAUSTAE

1. Et vīdit puteum in agrō, et trēs gregēs ovium accubābant iuxtā eum.
    [Gen. 29:2 V, Jacob at the well in the land of the east.—**puteus, -ī,**
    m., *a well.*—**grex, gregis,** m., *a flock.*—**ovis, ovis,** f., *a sheep.* The
    gen. is a gen. of material. See *Wheelock's Latin,* "Supplementary
    Syntax," 491–492.—**accubō, -āre,** *lie near.*—**iuxtā,** prep. + acc.,
    by.] I/M

2. Et Salomon mactāvit Dominō hostiās pācificās, boum vīgintī duō
    mīlia, et ovium centum vīgintī mīlia. 120k
    [I Kings 8:63 V, Solomon's sacrifice at the dedication of the temple.—
    Salomon, -ōnis, m., *Solomon.*—**mactō** (1), *slaughter.*—**Dominō,** =
    dat. of advantage. —**hostia, -ae,** f., *a sacrificial animal.*—**pācificus,**
    -a, -um, *peace-making.*—**boum,** contr. from **bovum,** from **bōs**
    (bovis), bovis, m., *ox.*—**vīgintī,** indecl. adj., *twenty.*] I/M

3. Diēs annōrum nostrōrum sunt septuāgintā annī, et maior pars eōrum
    labor et dolor.
    [Ps. 89:10 NV, LH 3.940.—**diēs,** fifth decl. m. nom. pl., *days.*—
    septuāgintā, indecl. adj., *seventy.*—**maior,** f. nom. sg. adj.,
    greater.—**dolor, -ōris,** m., *pain, grief.*] I/M

4. Et tū dās illīs ēscam in tempore opportūnō.
    [*Ps. 144:15 NV, LH 3.1019.—**ēsca, -ae,** f., *food.*—**opportūnus,**
    -a, -um, *fit, suitable.*] I

5. Et psalmōs nostrōs cantābimus cūnctīs diēbus vītae nostrae.
    [*Is. 38:20 V, LH 3.713.—**diēbus,** fifth decl. m. abl. pl., *days.*] I/M

    3rd conq. present

6. Mittit duōs ex discipulīs suīs in castellum.
    He sends
    [Mk. 11:1 V.—**mittit,** an historical present. See Capvt XVI
    Syntaxis.—**castellum, -ī,** n., *a fortified settlement.*] I

7. Nihil nunc damnātiōnis est iīs quī in Christō Iēsū sunt.
    [*Rom. 8:1, ad Vesperās, Fēria VI, Hebdomada IV, LH 3.1020.—
    damnātiō, -ōnis, f., *condemnation.*—**quī,** m. nom. pl. rel. pron.,
    who.] I/M

8. Adestō, Domine, precibus nostrīs, et diē noctūque nōs protege.
    [*Ōrātiō ad Vesperās, Fēria IV, Hebdomada I, LH 3.618.—adestō,
    second or fut. imperative second pers. sg. of adsum, -esse, be
    present; aid (+ dat.).—diē, fifth decl. m. abl. sg., day.—noctū,
    collateral form of nocte, from nox, noctis, f., night.—prōtegō,
    -ere, protect.] I/M

9. Deus omnipotēns, hoc laudis suscipe.
    [Ōrātiō ad Vesperās, Fēria II, Hebdomada II, LH 3.705.—
    omnipotēns, third decl. m. voc. sg. adj., omnipotent.—suscipiō,
    -ere, undertake; accept.] I

10. Manē nōbīscum, Domine, tōtō diē.
    [*Precēs, ad Laudēs mātūtīnās, Fēria IV, Hebdomada II, LH
    3.733.—diē, fifth decl. m. abl. sg., day.] I/M

11. Vīvit ergō [Fīlius] per Patrem; et quō modo per Patrem vīvit, eōdem
    modo nōs per carnem eius vīvimus.
    [*St. Hilary of Poitiers, Dē Trīnitāte 8.16, in LH 2.612.—quō
    modo (sometimes quōmodo), relative adv., as.—modus, -ī, m.,
    manner, way.] I/M

12. Disciplīnae līberālium artium septem sunt.
    [*St. Isidore of Seville, Etymologiae 1.2.1.—disciplīna, -ae, f.,
    instruction; a science.—līberālium, third decl. f. gen. pl. adj., =
    of the liberal.] I

13. Sīcut autem quattuor sunt elementa, sīc et quattuor hūmōrēs, et
    ūnusquisque hūmor suum elementum imitātur: sanguis āerem,
    cholera ignem, melancholia terram, phlegma aquam. Et sunt
    quattuor hūmōrēs, sīcut quattuor elementa, quae cōnservant
    corpora nostra.
    [*St. Isidore of Seville, Etymologiae 4.5.3.—sīcut . . . sīc, advs.,
    as . . . so.—elementum, -ī, n., an element, first principle.—
    hūmor, -ōris, m., moisture, fluid.—ūnusquisque, ūnaquaeque,
    ūnumquodque, indef. adj., every.—imitātur, third pers. sg.
    pres. ind. depon., a pass. form with an act. meaning, imitate,
    copy.—sanguis, -inis, m., blood.—āēr, āeris, m., the lower air,
    the earth's atmosphere.—cholera, -ae, f., yellow bile.—ignis,
    ignis, m., fire.—melancholia, -ae, f., black bile.—phlegma,
    -atis, n., phlegm.—quae, n. nom. pl. rel pron., subject of rel.
    clause, which.] M

14. Omnium dīmensiōnum tria genera sunt: longitūdō, lātitūdō, altitūdō.
     [*Hugh of St. Victor, *Practica Geōmetriae*, Praenotanda.—
     omnium, third decl. f. gen. pl. adj., = *of all.*—**dīmensiō, -ōnis,**
     f., *a measuring; dimension.*—**genus, generis,** n., *sort, kind,*
     class.—**longitūdō, -inis,** f., *length.*—**lātitūdō, -inis,** f., *breadth.*—
     altitūdō, -inis, f., *height; depth.*] I

15. Trēs sunt mūsicae [artēs]: mundāna, hūmāna, īnstrūmentālis.
     [*Hugh of St. Victor, *Didascalicon* 2.13.—**mūsicus, -a, -um,**
     belonging to music, musical.—**mundānus, -a, -um,** *pertaining to*
     the world or *cosmos, cosmic.*—**īnstrūmentālis,** third decl. f. nom.
     sg. adj., *pertaining to an intrument, instrumental.*] I

CAPVT XVI

Third Declension Adjectives; Jussive Future; Historical Present

SYNTAXIS SUPPLĒMENTUM

Jussive Future. EL employs the future indicative in the second person as an equivalent of the future or second imperative (see Capvt XXVIII below). An example of the jussive future is found in Sentence 9 below.

Historical Present. In historical narrative, the present indicative is often used instead of a past tense to lend vividness to the account. English speakers use this device frequently in conversation, but infrequently in good prose. Examples can be found in Capvt XV, Sentence 6, and below in Sentence 9. The historical present is usually translated by a past tense in English.

VERBA MEMORIĀ COMPREHENDENDA

aeternus, -a, -um, *eternal*

stultus, -a, -um, *foolish, simple, silly*

SENTENTIAE Ē FONTIBUS NŌN ANTĪQUĪS HAUSTAE

1. Et id fēcērunt cum ingentī gaudiō.
   [II Chron. 30:23 V, at the passover as reformed by King Hezekiah.] I

2. Brevēs diēs hominis sunt; numerus mēnsium eius apud tē est.
   [*Job 14:5 V.—**diēs,** fifth decl. m. nom. pl. *days.*—**mēnsis, -sis,** m., *month.*—**apud,** prep. + acc., *at, by, near, with.*] I/M

3. Sūmite psalmum, et date tympanum, psaltērium iūcundum, cum
citharā.
   [*Ps. 80:3 V.—**sūmō, -ere,** *take up.*—**date,** here = *beat.*—
   tympanum, -ī, n., *a drum.*—**psaltērium, -iī,** n., *a mandolin.*—
   cithara, -ae, f., *a guitar.*]

4. Corōna senum filiī filiōrum, et glōria filiōrum patrēs eōrum.
   [*Prov. 17:6 V.—**corōna, -ae,** f., *a crown.*] I

5. Anima saturāta calcābit favum, et anima ēsuriēns etiam amārum prō
dulcī sūmet.
   [*Prov. 27:7 V.—**saturātus, -a, -um,** *filled to satiety.*—**calcō** (1),
   tread under foot.—**favus, -ī,** m., *a honeycomb.*—**ēsuriēns,** third
   decl. f. nom. sg., adj., *hungry.*—**amārus, -a, -um,** *bitter.*] I/M

6. Tria sunt difficilia mihi, et quārtum penitus ignōrō.
   [*Prov. 30:18 V, a reference to the ways of the eagle, snake, ship, and
   young man!—**penitus,** adv., *utterly.*—**ignōrō** (1), *be ignorant of.*] I

7. Facile est enim in oculīs Deī subitō honestāre pauperem.
   [*Ecclus. 11:23 V.—**subitō,** adv., *suddenly.*—**honestō** (1), *honor;
   grace.*—**pauperem,** 3rd decl. adj. m. acc. sg., *poor.*] I

8. Et arrogantiam fortium humiliābō.
   [*Is. 13:11 V.—**arrogantia, -ae,** f., *conceitedness, haughtiness.*—
   humiliō (1), *abase, humble.*] I

9. Āit illī Iēsūs, "Dīligēs Dominum Deum tuum ex tōtō corde tuō, et
in tōtā animā tuā, et in tōtā mente tuā.
   [Mt. 22:37 V.—**āit,** third pers. sg. pres. ind., from the defective
   verb **āiō,** *say, affirm;* treat as hist. pres.—**ex,** note that the Gr. has
   intrumental ἐν here, which is equivalent to EL instrumental *in.*] I

10. Grātiās agō Deō meō in omnī memoriā vestrī.
    [Phil. 1:3 V.—**vestrī,** see *Wheelock's Latin,* 492, "Objective
    Genitive."] I

11. "Omnia in sapientiā fēcistī." Simul enim Pater et sapientiam suam
genuit et in ipsā omnia fēcit.
    [John Scotus Eriugena, *Dē Divisiōne Nātūrae* 2.20, quoting and
    explaining Ps. 103:24 V.—**in sapientiā,** instrumental, but John
    clearly takes it locally, thinking that the the primordial causes
    are in Wisdom, i.e., the Second Person of the Blessed Trinity.—
    simul, adv., *at once, at the same time, together.*—**gignō, -ere, genuī,**
    beget, bring forth.] M

12.   Annō Dominī MXXXVI Heinrīcus rēx, fīlius imperātōris, Chnutōnis rēgis Anglōrum fīliam, nomine Chunelindem, prō rēgīnā cōnsecrātam rēgālibus nūptiīs in coniugium dūxit.

       [*Wipo, *Gesta Chuonrādī II Imperātōris* 35.—**Heinrīcus, -ī,** m., *Henry III, king of East Francia from 1028, son of the Holy Roman Emperor Conrad II (d. 1039).*—**imperātor, -ōris,** m., *emperor.*—**Chnutō, -ōnis,** m., *Canute the Great, king of England and Denmark (1016/1019–1035).*—**Anglī, -ōrum,** m., *the English.*—**Chunelindis, -is,** f., *Gunnhilde.*—**cōnsecrātus, -a, -um,** *consecrated.*—**rēgālis, -e,** *royal.*—**nūptiae, -ārum,** f., *a wedding.*—**coniugium, -iī,** n., *marriage, wedlock.*] A

13.   Praetereā, quemadmodum sē habet tuus oculus ad corpus tuum, sīc tua mēns ad animam tuam. Est enim mēns tua animae oculus.

       [*Marsilio Ficino, *Theologica Platōnica* 1.6.4.—**praetereā,** adv., *further.*—**quemadmodum,** adv., *as.*—**sē habēre,** = *be.*—**sīc,** adv., *so.*] I/M

14.   Nātūra hominis nōn potest nōn esse fallāx.

       [*René Descartes, *Meditātiōnēs dē Prīmā Philosophiae* 6.—**fallāx, -ācis,** adj., *deceitful, treacherous, false.*] I/M

15.   Homō enim tōtīus vītae oeconomicae-sociālis auctor, centrum, et fīnis est.

       [*Gaudium et Spēs* 63, CDD, 783.—**oeconomicus-sociālis, -a-is, -um-e,** *economic and social.*—**auctor, -ōris,** m., *originator, author.*—**centrum, -ī,** n., *center.*—**fīnis, -is,** m., *goal, end.*] I

CAPVT XVII

The Relative Pronoun; Connecting Relative

SYNTAXIS SUPPLĒMENTUM

Connecting Relative. Both CL and EL often begin a sentence with a relative pronoun that has no genuine relative function. The sentence is an independent clause, and the relative pronoun can be resolved into a conjunction and the appropriate form of *is, ea, id*. Here is an example from the life of St. John Eudes: *Tot labōribus frāctus, mortī proximus, diē decimā augustī . . . exspīrāvit.* ***Quem** Pius Papa decimus mīrāculīs clārum, inter Beātōs . . . retulit,* Broken by so many labors [and] near death, he died on the nineteenth day of August. **Whom,** famous for his miracles, Pope Pius X recorded among the Blesseds. (Lēctiō III, ad Mātūtīnum, Diē 19 augustī, BR 2.831.] In the second sentence, *quem* is equivalent to *et eum*, the sentence to which it belongs being an independent clause. Sometimes, too, a neuter connecting relative summarizes the points of a preceding argument, e.g., ***Quod** nē ipsum quidem mihi accidit,* Not even which thing itself happened to me, i.e., but not even this thing actually happened to me. (St. Ambrose, *Dē Officiīs Ministrōrum* 1.1.4.) The connecting relative here (= *et id*) summarizes a process which Ambrose has just described.

VERBA MEMORIĀ COMPREHENDENDA

iūstus, -a, -um, *just, righteous*

proprius, -a, -um, *peculiar to, characteristic of* (+ gen.). See Appendix I, § 29.

Sententiae ē Fontibus nōn Antīquīs Haustae

1. Plantāverat autem Dominus Deus paradīsum voluptātis ā prīncipiō, in quō pōsuit hominem quem fōrmāverat.
   [*Gen. 2:8 V.—**plantō** (1), *plant.*—**paradīsus, -ī,** m., *a* (royal) *park.*—**pōnō, -ere, pōsuī,** *put, place.*] I

2. Quae flēre coepērunt, et dīcere, "Tēcum pergēmus ad populum tuum."
   [Ruth 1:9–10 V, Naomi's daughters-in-law refuse to leave her.— **fleō, -ēre,** *weep.*—**pergō, -ere,** *go on.*] I/M

3. Beātus vir cui nōn imputāvit Dominus peccātum.
   [*Ps. 31:2 V.—**imputō** (1), *impute, ascribe.*] I

4. Beāta gēns cuius est Dominus Deus eius.
   [*Ps. 32:12 V.—**gēns, gentis,** f., *a clan; race; nation.*—**eius,** a "redundant demonstrative" in imitation of the Heb. use of a demonstrative pron. with the rel. pron., which does not decline. See Appendix I, § 30.] I/M

5. Beātus homō quem tū ērudieris, Domine, et dē lēge tuā docueris eum.
   [*Ps. 93:12 V.—**ērudiō, -īre, -iī,** *instruct.* Translate *ērudieris* here, and *docueris* next, as English pres. indic., though they are, in fact, perf. subj. The LXX has a pres. general indef. rel. clause here.—**lēx, lēgis,** f., *law.*—**eum,** another redundant demonstrative.] A

6. Beātus vir quī timet Dominum.
   [*Ps. 111:1 V.] I

7. Beātī omnēs quī timent Dominum, quī ambulant in viīs eius.
   [*Ps. 127:1 V. **ambulō** (1), *walk.*] I

8. Multī prophētae et iūstī cupiērunt vidēre quae vidētis, et nōn vidērunt, et audīre quae audītis, et nōn audiērunt.
   [*Mt. 13:17 V.—**prophēta, -ae,** m., *prophet.*—**cupiērunt,** for *cupīvērunt* by syncope.—**audiērunt,** for *audīvērunt* by syncope.] I

9. Et beāta quae crēdidistī.
   [*Lk. 1:45 V, Elizabeth to Mary.—**crēdō, -ere, crēdidī,** *trust, believe.*] I

10. Omnis sapientia ā Dominō Deō est, et cum illō fuit semper, et est ante aevum.
    [*Antiphona ad Magnificat, ad Vesperās, Dominica III augustī, BR 2.190.—**aevum, -ī,** n., *never-ending time; a life, an age.*] I

11. Bona etiam misericordia, quae et ipsa perfectōs facit.

[*St. Ambrose, *Dē Officiīs Ministrōrum* 1.11.38.—**misericordia, -ae,** f., *pity, mercy.*—**perfectus, -a, -um,** *perfect, complete.*] I/M

12. Sīcutī ūnīus hominis caput et corpus, ipse ūnus homō, sīc Fīlius ille Virginis et ēlēcta eius membra, ipse ūnus homō et ūnus hominis Fīlius. "Tōtus," inquit Scrīptūra, "et integer Chrīstus caput et corpus"; sīquidem omnia simul membra ūnum corpus, quod cum suō capite ūnus hominis Fīlius, quī cum Deī Fīliō ūnus Deī Fīlius, quī et ipse cum Deō ūnus Deus.

[*Blessed Isaac of Stella, *Sermō* 42, in LH 2.670.—**sīcutī,** adv., *as, just as.*—**ēlēctus, -a, -um,** *chosen, elect.*—**membrum, -ī,** n., *a limb, member of the body.*—**inquit,** third pers. sg. defective verb, = *says.*—**inquit Scrīptūra,** I cannot locate this passage in a concordance. Perhaps Isaac had in mind Eph. 4:15–16.—**integer, -gra, -grum,** *complete, whole.*—**sīquidem,** adv., *if indeed; since.*—**simul,** adv., *at the same time, at once, together.*] A

13. Ergō et tōtum corpus cum capite hominis Fīlius et Deī Fīlius, et Deus. . . . Itaque et omnia cum Deō ūnus Deus; sed Fīlius Deī cum Deō nātūrāliter, et cum ipsō Fīlius hominis persōnāliter, cum quō suum corpus sacrāmentāliter.

[*Blessed Isaac of Stella, *Sermō* 42, in LH 2.670–671, continuing the previous entry.—**omnia,** third decl. n. nom. pl. adj., = *all.*—**nātūrāliter,** adv., *naturally, by nature, according to nature.*—**persōnāliter,** adv., *personally, by a person.*—**sacrāmentāliter,** adv., *sacramentally, by a sacrament.*] A

14. Fidēlia igitur et ratiōnabilia Chrīstī membra dīcere sē vērāciter possunt hoc, quod est ipse, etiam Deī Fīlium, ac Deum. Sed quod ipse nātūrā, hoc ipsa cōnsortiō; quod ipse plēnitūdine, hoc ipsa participātiōne; dēnique quod Deī Fīlius generātiōne, hoc eius membra adoptiōne.

[*Blessed Isaac of Stella, *Sermō* 42, in LH 2.671, continuing the previous entry.—**fidēlis, -e,** *faithful.*—**ratiōnālis, -e,** *reasonable, rational.*—**vērāciter,** adv., *truthfully.*—**cōnsortium, -iī,** n., *fellowship, society.*—**plēnitūdō, -inis,** f., *fullness; completeness.*—**participātiō, -ōnis,** f., *a sharing, partaking, participation.*—**dēnique,** adv., *finally.*—**generātiō, -ōnis,** f., *a begetting, generating.*—**adoptiō, -ōnis,** f., *the adoption of a child.*] A

15.   Quamobrem ipsa ūnitās, vēritās, bonitās, quam invēnimus super
        angelum, ex mente Platōnis omnium est prīncipium, deus ūnus
        vērusque et bonus.
        [*Marsilio Ficino, *Theologia Platōnica* 2.1.4.—**quamobrem,** adv.,
        for which reason.—**ūnitās, -tātis,** f., *unity.*—**bonitās, -tātis,** f.,
        goodness.—**ēx,** here = *according to.*—**Platō, -ōnis,** m., *Plato.*] I/M

Marsilio Ficino (1433–1499), a Florentine, spent his scholarly and philosophical career
under the patronage of Cosimo de' Medici (1398–1464). Cosimo acted as patron to a group
of scholars and philosophers who knew Greek and who were enthusiastic about the texts
of Plato, the Neo-Platonic philosophers, especially Plotinus, the Corpus Hermeticum,
and the Jewish Kabbalah. Ficino, who was the head of this group, which was called the
Platonic Academy, translated Plato and Plotinus and other Greeks into Latin. He was or-
dained priest in 1473. Several sentences from Ficino's great work, the *Theologia Platōnica
dē Immortālitate Animōrum*, are included in this volume. He is depicted here in a marble
bust of 1889 in the Villa Borghese at Rome by Carlo Panati (1850–1935). (© Wikimedia
Commons, PaulineM)

CAPVT XVIII

First and Second Conjugations: Present System Passive; Ablative of Agent

Verba Memoriā Comprehendenda

cantō (1), *make melody* (with instrument or voice); *sound* (of an instrument); *play* (of an instrument); *sing* (of a voice); *sing* (a song); *use enchantments*

nātūrālis, -e, *natural*

Sententiae ē Fontibus nōn Antīquīs Haustae

1. In Isaac vocābitur tibi sēmen.
    [*Gen. 21:12 V.—**Isaac,** indecl. Heb. name, m., *Isaac.*—**sēmen, -minis,** n., *seed.*] I

2. Haec quoque inter pollūta reputābuntur dē hīs quae moventur in terrā: mustēla et mūs et crocodīlus.
    [*Lev. 11:29 V.—**pollūtus, -a, -um,** *defiled, polluted.*—**reputō** (1), *reckon, calculate.*—**moventur,** to be taken as reflexive, *move oneself* (LS, s.v. II).—**mustēla, -ae,** f., *a weasel.*—**mūs, mūris,** m./f. gender, *a mouse.*—**crocodīlus, -ī,** m., *a crocodile.*] I

3. Frūstrā serētis sēmentem, quae ab hostibus dēvorābitur.
    [*Lev. 26:16 V.—**frūstrā,** adv., *in vain.*—**serō, -ere,** *sow, broadcast* (seed).—**sēmentis, -tis,** f., *a sowing; a crop.*—**dēvorō** (1), *devour.*] I

4. Vēnimus in terram, ad quam mīsistī nōs, quae rēvērā fluit lacte et melle.
    [*Num. 13:28, their scouts report back to Moses and Aaron.—**rēvērā,** adv., *in reality.*—**lac, lactis,** n., *milk.*—**mel, mellis,** n., *honey.*] I

5. Est via quae vidētur hominī iūsta, novissima autem eius dēdūcunt ad mortem.

> [*Prov. 14:12 V.—**novissimus, -a, -um,** *last; most recent; utmost.*—**dēdūcō, -ere,** *lead down.*] I/M

6. Omnēs autem stultī miscentur contumēliīs.

> [*Prov. 20:3 V.—**misceō, -ēre,** *mix, mingle; associate, combine* (+ abl.).—**contumēlia, -ae,** f., *insult.*] I

7. Omnia flūmina intrant in mare, et mare nōn redundat.

> [*Eccles. 1:7 V.—**redundō** (1), *flow back; overflow.*] I

8. Omnis enim creātūra ad suum genus ab initiō refigūrābātur.

> [*Wis. 19:6 V. **creātūra, -ae,** f., *a creature.*—**initium, -iī,** n., *beginning.*—**refigūrō** (1), *form again, refashion,* with reference to the miracles wrought by God in the exodus of his people from Egypt.] I/M

9. Et Petrus quidem servābātur in carcere.

> [*Acts 12:5 V.—**carcer, -eris,** m., *jail, prison.*] I

10. Virī, quid haec facitis? Et nōs mortālēs sumus, similēs vōbīs hominēs.

> [*Acts 14:14 V, Barnabas and Paul try to prevent the Lycaonians from worshipping them.—**similis, -e,** *like* (+ dat.).] I/M

11. Scientia īnflat, caritās vērō aedificat.

> [*I Cor. 8:1 V.—**īnflō** (1), *blow into; puff out.*—**vērō,** adv., *in truth.*—**aedificō** (1), *build.*] I

12. Deus nōn continētur locō, nōn tenētur spatiō.

> [St. Augustine of Hippo, *Sermo* 4.4.5.—**contineō, -ēre,** *keep in, surround, contain.*—**spatium, -ī,** n., *space.*] I

13. Iūs nātūrāle est, quod nātūra omnia animalia docuit. Nam iūs istud nōn hūmānī generis proprium est, sed omnium animalium ... Hinc dēscendit maris atque fēminae coniugātiō, quam nōs mātrimōnium appellāmus, hinc līberōrum prōcreātiō et ēducātiō.

> [*Tribonian, Theophilus, and Dorotheus, *Imperātōris Iūstiniānī Īnstitūtiōnēs* 1.2.—**hinc,** adv., *hence.*—**dēscendō, -ere, -scendī,** *come down, descend.*—**mas, maris,** m., *the male.*—**fēmina, -ae,** f., *the female.*—**mātrimōnium, -iī,** n., *marriage.*—**coniugātiō, -ōnis,** f., *a mingling.*—**līberī, -ōrum,** (one's) *children.*—**prōcreātiō, -ōnis,** f., *begetting.*—**ēducātiō, -ōnis,** f., *rearing, bringing up.*] M

14. Wilelmus comes, filius Robertī ducis Normanōrum, dedit terram
dē Calvelvillā, per auctōritātem Hugōnis mīlitis, in cuius beneficiō
manet. Testēs sunt Wilelmus filius Osbertī, Wimunt Cusel, Hugō
dē la Ferte, Nigellus, Willelmus, Rodulphus, Ioannēs abbās.
[*Carta Wilelmī Normannōrum Comitis prō Villarensī
Monasteriō,[10] Fauroux, no. 166.—**Wilelmus, -ī,** m., *William* the
Bastard and Conqueror.—**comes, -itis,** m., *a count.* This was the
normal title in the eleventh century for those rulers whom we
call the dukes of Normandy.—**Robertus, -ī,** m., *Robert* I, count
of Normandy.—**dux, ducis,** m., *a duke.* This was a title adopted,
without royal authority, by Richard II in 1006, whose son Robert I
also used it at times, as did his other successors, until it became the
normal title.[11]—**Normanus, -ī,** m., *a Norman.*—**terra,** here prob.
= *estate.*—**dē,** note the locative sense, = *of.*—**Calvelvilla, -ae,** f.,
Cauville.—**Hugō, -ōnis,** m., *Hugh.*—**mīles, -itis,** m., *a knight.*—
beneficium, -iī, n., *a fief.*—**testis, -is,** m., *a witness.*—**Osbertus,
-ī,** m., *Osbert.*—**Wimunt,** = *Witmundus, Guimundus,* both second
decl. m.—**la Ferte,** prob. = *La Ferté-en-Bray,* now La Ferté-St-
Samson.[12]—**Nigellus, -ī,** m., *Nigel, Niall.*—**Rodulphus, -ī,** m.,
Ralph.—**Iōannes, -is,** m., *John.*—**abbās, -ātis,** m., *an abbot.*] I/M

15. Sīcut igitur generātiō hominis est ex nōn ente quod est nōn homō,
ita creātiō, quae est ēmānātiō tōtīus esse, est ex nōn ente quod est
nihil.
[*St. Thomas Aquinas, *Summa Theologiae* 1, q.45, a.1 *resp.*—**sīcut,**
adv., *as, just as,* correlative with *ita.*—**generātiō, -ōnis,** f., *birth.*—
ēns, entis, n., *a being, being.*—**ita,** adv., *so.*—**creātiō, -ōnis,** f.,
creation.—**ēmānātiō, -ōnis,** f., *a flowing out, emanation.*—**esse,**
= *being.*] M/A

---

[10] The monastery was the Abbey of Montivilliers, a foundation of Benedictine nuns. See
David Bates, *Normandy before 1066* (London: Longman, 1982), 196.

[11] On the use of the titles "count" and "duke" by the rulers of Normandy, see Bates, op.
cit., 148–151.

[12] See Daniel Power, *The Norman Frontier in the Twelfth and Early Thirteenth Centuries*
(Cambridge: Cambridge University Press, 2004), 190, 504–505.

CAPVT XIX

Perfect Passive System; Interrogative Pronouns and Adjectives; **Perfect Passive System in EL**

Syntaxis Supplēmentum

Perfect Passive System in EL. In CL, forms from the perfect stem of *esse*, i.e., *fu-*, were sometimes used to construct the perfect passive system, instead of forms from the present system of *esse*. This was done, especially with *fuī* and the other persons of the perfect, when the participle was thought of purely as an adjective. It was also done, with all tenses of the perfect system, to indicate that the action no longer persisted in its effects. GL, § 250, give this example: "**amātus fuī,** *I have been loved* (but I am loved no longer)." In EL, however, perfect passives are often contructed with the forms made from the stem *fu-* with no real difference in meaning from the perfect passives constructed with present forms of *esse*. Thus, *fuī* frequently corresponds to *sum, fueram* to *eram,* and *fuerō* to *erō* in the perfect passive system.

Verba Memoriā Comprehendenda

benedīcō, -ere, -dīxī, -dictum, *speak well of* (+ dat.); *bless* (+ dat. or acc.)
sanguis, -guinis, n., *blood; blood relationship*

Sententiae ē Fontibus nōn Antīquīs Haustae

1. Erat autem Iudith relicta eius vidua annīs tribus et mēnsibus sex.
    [*Jud. 8:4 V.—**Iudith,** indecl. Heb. name, f., *Judith*.—**relinquō, -ere, -līquī, -lictum,** *leave (behind), abandon.*—**vidua, -ae,** f., *a widow.*—**mēnsis, -sis,** m., *month.*] M

2. Per quam viam spargitur lūx?
    [*Job 38:24 V.—**spargō, -ere,** *scatter, spread.*—**lūx, lūcis,** f., *light.*] I

3. Et [Dominus] firmāvit orbem terrārum, quī nōn commovēbitur.
    [*Ps. 92:2 PIB, Dominica ad Laudēs, Psaltērium, BR 2.377.—
    firmō (1), *make firm* or *fast.*—**orbis, -is,** m., *circle;* **orbis
    terrārrum,** *the world.*—**commoveō, -ēre,** *disturb.*] I

4. In viā testimōniōrum tuōrum dēlectātus sum, sīcut in omnibus
    dīvitiīs.
    [*Ps. 118:14 V.—**testimōnium, -iī,** n., *testimony; proof.*—**sīcut,**
    adv., *just as.*] I/M

5. Quod factum est, ipsum permanet.
    [*Eccles. 3:15 V.—**permaneō, -ēre,** *stay to the end, persist.*] I/M

6. Parāta sunt dērīsōribus iūdicia.
    [*Prov. 19:29 V.—**dērīsor, -ōris,** m., *scoffer.*] I/M

7. Nūptiae quidem parātae sunt, sed quī invītātī erant, nōn fuērunt dignī.
    [*Mt. 22:8 V.—**nūptiae, -ārum,** f., *a wedding, marriage.*—**quidem,**
    postpositive conj., *indeed.*—**invītō** (1), *invite, summon.*—**dignus,
    -a, -um,** *worthy.*] I/M

8. Et hic bibet dē vīnō īrae Deī, quod mistum est merō in calice īrae ipsīus.
    [*Apoc. 14:10 V said of the worshipper of the beast.—**bibō, -ere,**
    drink.—**vīnum, -ī,** n., *wine.*—**mistum = mixtum.**—**merum, -ī,**
    n., *pure wine.* In ancient times, it was the custom to mix wine with
    water.—**calix, -icis,** m., *cup; chalice.*] I/M

9. V. Diffūsa est grātia in labiīs tuīs. R. Proptereā benedīxit tē Deus in
    aeternum.
    [Versūs, ad Laudēs, Diē 23 augustī, BR 2.838.—**V. = versiculus,
    -ī,** m., *little verse.*—**diffundō, -ere, -fūsī, -fūsum,** *pour forth,
    diffuse.*—**labium, -iī,** n., *lip.*—**R. = respōnsum, -ī,** n., *response.*—
    proptereā, adv., *therefore.*] I/M

10. Quis nōn timēbit tē, Domine, et magnificābit nōmen tuum?
    [*Canticum (Apoc. 15:4 V), ad Vesperās, Fēria VI, Hebdomada
    IV, LH 3.1020.—**magnificō** (1), *exalt, magnify.*] I

11. Ecce in quō prīncipiō fēcit Deus caelum et terram. Caelum ergō et
    terram fēcit Deus in Fīliō, per quem facta sunt omnia, et sine quō
    factum est nihil.
    [*St. Augustine of Hippo, *Sermō* 1.2.2.] I/M

12.   Vidētur mihi dīvīsiō nātūrae per quattuor differentiās quattuor
       speciēs recipere: quārum prīma est in eam quae creat et nōn creātur;
       secunda in eam quae creātur et creat; tertia in eam quae creātur et
       nōn creat; quārta, quae nec creat nec creātur.

       [*John Scotus Eriugena, *Dē Dīvīsiōne Nātūrae* 1.1, speaking of God,
       the primordial causes, man, and sin.—**dīvīsiō, -ōnis,** f., *division;
       distribution,* take as the subject of *vidētur.*—**differentia, -ae,** f.,
       difference, distinction.—**speciēs,** fifth decl. f. acc. pl. noun, *kinds,
       species.*—**recipiō, -ere,** *admit, receive.*—**prīmus, -a, -um,** *first.*] M

13.   Eōdem annō hībernō tempore, collēctō exercitū, imperātor
       trānscendens Padum ad Parmam cīvitātem vēnit; ibi nātālem Dominī
       celebrāvit. . . . In ipsā diē nātīvitātis Dominī inter Teutonicōs et
       cīvēs Parmensēs magna sēditiō orta est, et quīdam bene valēns vir
       Chuonrādus, infertor cibōrum imperātōris, cum aliīs interfectus est.

       [*Wipo, *Gesta Chuonrādī Imperātōris* 37.—**hībernus, -a, -um,**
       of winter, winter.—**collēctō exercitū,** an abl. abs., = *when he had
       gathered the army together.*—**imperātor, -ōris,** m., *emperor.*—
       trānscendens, pres. act. partic. m. nom. sg., modifying *imperātor,
       passing over.*—**Padus, -ī,** m., *the Po* (River).—**Parma, -ae,** f.,
       Parma. Note that *Parmam* is in apposition to *cīvitatem,* where
       English would prefer a "defining genitive." This is a classical
       usage.—**nātālis, -is,** m., *birthday.*—**celebrō** (1), *celebrate.*—**diē,**
       fifth decl. f. abl. sg., *day.*—**nātīvitās, -tātis,** f., *birth, nativity.*—
       Teutonicus, -a, -um, *German.*—**Parmensis, -e,** *pertaining to
       Parma, Parman.*—**sēditiō, -ōnis,** f., *a riot.*—**orior, -īrī, ortus
       sum,** a depon. verb, having pass. forms with act. meanings, *arise,
       begin.*—**quīdam, quaedam, quoddam,** indef. adj., *a certain.*—
       bene valēns, = *very strong.*—**Chuonrādus, -ī,** m., *Conrad* (not the
       emperor).—**infertor, -ōris,** m., *a waiter, steward.*—**cibus, -ī,** m.,
       food.—**interficiō, -ere, -fēcī, -fectum,** *kill, murder.*] M

14.   Quod creātum est dē nihilō factum est. Nam quod dē aliquō factum
       est, factum quidem est, sed creātum nōn est, quia dē nihilō factum
       nōn est. Fēcit ergō Deus caelum et terram, nec sōlum fēcit, sed
       creāvit, hoc est dē nihilō fēcit.

       [*Hugh of St. Victor, *Dē Sacramentīs* 1.1.1.—**nihilum, -ī,** n.,
       nothing.—**aliquō,** n. abl. sg. indef. pron., *something.*—**quia,** conj.,
       because.] M

15.   Quid Ecclēsia dē homine sentit? . . . Quid est autem homō?
       [*Gaudium et Spēs,* nos. 11 and 12.—**ecclēsia, -ae,** f., *church.*] I

CAPVT XX

Fourth Declension; Ablatives of Place from Which and Separation; Subjective Genitive; Objective Genitive

SYNTAXIS SUPPLĒMENTUM

Subjective Genitive. When a noun contains the idea of an action, it can be modified by another noun in the genitive to show the agent of the action, e.g., *Quis ergō nōs sēparābit ā cāritāte Chrīstī?* "Who then shall separate us from the love of Christ?" i.e., the love that Christ feels for us (Rom. 8:35). See also Sentence 10 below.

Objective Genitive. See *Wheelock*, 492. See also Sentence 6 below.

VERBA MEMORIĀ COMPREHENDENDA

cornū, cornūs, n., to the meaning in *Wheelock* add *power, might* (by analogy with the horn of a bull), both from CL and as a Hebraism (LS s.v. II)

pius, -a, -um, *dutiful; pious*

impius, -a, -um, *undutiful; impious*

SENTENTIAE Ē FONTIBUS NŌN ANTĪQUĪS HAUSTAE

1. Anima sī peccāverit per ignōrantiam, fēceritque ūnum ex hīs quae Dominī lēge prohibentur, offeret arietem immaculātum dē gregibus sacerdōtī.

   [Lev. 5:17 V.—**peccō** (1), *sin*. Note that both *peccāverit* and *fēcerit* may be translated as pres. ind., as this is a Future More Vivid conditional sentence.—**ignōrantia, -ae,** f., *ignorance*.—**lēx, lēgis,** f., *law*.—**offeret,** third pers. sg. fut. ind. act. of **offerō, -ferre,** *offer*: = *will offer*.—**ariēs, -etis,** m., *a ram*.—**immaculātus, -a, -um,** *unblemished, immaculate*.—**grex, gregis,** m., *a flock*.—**sacerdōs, -dōtis,** m., *a priest*.] M

2. Remānserant autem in castrīs duo virī, super quōs requiēvit Spīritus. Nam et ipsī dēscrīptī fuerant.

   [Num. 11:26 V, Eldad and Medad, two of the seventy chosen to help Moses.—**castra, -ōrum,** n., (military) *camp*.—**requiēscō, -ere, -quiēvī,** *rest*.—**dēscrībō, -ere, -psī, -ptum,** *copy; enroll*.] I/M

3. Dominus interrogat iūstum et impium. Quī autem dīligit inīquitātem, ōdit animam suam.

   [*Ps. 10:6 V.—**interrogō** (1), *question, examine*.—**inīquitās, -tātis,** f., *unfairness, iniquity*.] I

4. Et omnia cornua peccātōrum cōnfringam, et exaltābuntur cornua iūstī.

   [*Ps. 74:11 V.—**peccātor, -ōris,** m., *a sinner*.—**confringō, -ere,** *break in pieces*.—**exaltō** (1), *raise, exalt*.] I

5. Iūstus dē angustiā līberātus est, et trādētur impius prō eō.

   [*Prov. 11:8 V.—**angustia, -ae,** f., *narrow place; difficulty*.—**trādētur,** third decl. third pers. sg. fut. ind. pass., = *will be handed over*.] I

6. Et ecce ūniversa vānitās et afflictiō spīritūs.

   [*Eccles. 1:14 V.—**ūniversus, -a, -um,** *all together* or *collectively*.—**vānitās, -tātis,** f., *emptiness; futility*.—**afflictiō, -ōnis,** f., *pain, torment*.] I/M

7. Cum autem vēnerit ille Spīritus vēritātis, docēbit vōs omnem vēritātem.

   [*Jn. 16:13 V.—**vēnerit,** this may be translated as a pres. ind., as this is on the model of a Future More Vivid conditional sentence.] I

8. Īnfēlīx ego homō; quis mē līberabit dē corpore mortis huius? Grātia
    Deī per Iēsūm Chrīstum Dominum nostrum.
    [*Rom. 7:24–25 V.—**īnfēlīx, -īcis,** third decl. nom. m./f./n. sg.
    adj., *unlucky, unhappy.*] I/M

9. Nam sī ōrem linguā, spīritus meus ōrat, mēns autem mea sine frūctū
    est. Quid ergō est? Ōrābō spīritū, ōrābō et mente: psallam spīritū,
    psallam et mente.
    [*I Cor. 14:14–15 V.—**ōrem,** first. pers. sg. pres. act. subjunctive
    of *ōrō* (1), *beg; pray,* = *should pray.*—**lingua, -ae,** f., *tongue.*] M

10. Grātia Dominī nostrī Iēsū Chrīstī, et cāritās Deī, et commūnicātiō
    Sānctī Spīritūs sit cum omnibus vōbīs.
    [*II Cor 13:13 V.—**commūnicātiō, -ōnis,** f., *an imparting,
    communicating.*—**sit,** third pers. sg. pres. subjunctive of *esse,*
    = *be.*] I

11. Prae cēterīs, frātrēs, ā lītibus et discordiīs iēiūnāte.
    [*St. Augustine of Hippo, *Sermo* 205.3.— **prae cēterīs,** = *for the
    rest.*—**līs, lītis,** f., *a legal controversy; contention, strife.*—**discordia,
    -ae,** f., *dissension, disagreement.*—**iēiūnō** (1), *fast, abstain.*] I

12. Iūris duae sunt positiōnēs: pūblicum et prīvātum. Pūblicum iūs est,
    quod ad statum reī Rōmānae spectat; prīvātum, quod ad singulōrum
    ūtilitātem pertinet. Iūs igitur prīvātum est tripertītum: collēctum est
    enim ex nātūrālibus praeceptīs aut gentium aut cīvīlibus.
    [Tribonian, Theophilus, and Dorotheus, *Imperātōris Iūstiniānī
    Īnstitūtiōnēs* 1.1.4.—**positiō, -ōnis,** f., here perh. = *branches of
    study.*—**pūblicus, -a, -um,** *of* or *belonging to the people, public.*—
    prīvātus, -a, -um, *of* or *belonging to an individual, private.*—
    status, -ūs, m., *condition, state.*—**rēs Rōmāna, reī Rōmānae,**
    the Roman state, the Republic.—**spectō** (1), *consider, observe, have
    a regard for.*—**singulī, -ae, -a,** *single, separate.*—**ūtilitās, -tātis,**
    f., *advantage, profit.*—**pertineō, -ēre,** *pertain to, belong to* (ad +
    acc.).—**tripertītus, -a, -um,** *divided into three parts.*—**colligō,
    -ere, -lēgī, -lēctum,** *gather together.*—**praeceptum, -ī,** n., *a
    precept.*—**gēns, gentis,** f., *a people, nation.*—**cīvīlis, -e,** *pertaining
    to the* cīvitās, *civic, civil.*] I/M

13. Nōn est strepitus oris, sed iūbilus cordis; nōn sōnus labiōrum, sed mōtus gaudiōrum; voluntātum, nōn vocum cōnsōnantia. . . . Est quippe nūptiāle carmen.

[*St. Bernard of Clairvaux, *Sermō I super Cantica* 6.11, discussing the nature of the songs which the Song contains.—**strepitus, -ūs,** m., *a loud noise; a crashing, rumbling.*—**iūbilus, -ī,** m., *a joyful melody.*—**sonus, -ī,** m., a *noise, sound, din.*—**labium, -ī,** n., *lip.*—**mōtus, -ūs,** m., *a motion, movement.*—**vōx, vōcis,** f., *voice, word.*—**cōnsonantia, -ae,** f., *an agreement, harmony, consonance.*—**quippe,** adv., *certainly, indeed.*—**nūptiālis, -e,** *of marriage, nuptial.*] M

14. Omnia participant aliquāliter lēgem aeternam, inquantum scīlicet ex impressiōne eius habent inclīnātiōnēs in propriōs āctūs et finēs. Inter cētera autem ratiōnālis creātūra excellentiōrī quōdam modō dīvīnae prōvidentiae subiācet, inquantum et ipsa fit prōvidentiae particeps, sibi ipsī et aliīs prōvidēns.

[*St. Thomas Aquinas, *Summa Theologiae* 1–2, q.91, a.2 *resp.*—**participō** (1), *cause to participate in, impart; partake of, participate in.*—**aliquāliter,** adv., *in some measure.*—**lēx, lēgis,** f., *law.*—**inquantum,** *according as, insofar as.*—**scīlicet,** adv., *of course; namely.*—**impressiō, -ōnis,** f., *an impression.*—**inclīnātiō, -ōnis,** f., *a tendency, inclination.*—**āctus, -ūs,** m., *an action, activity, act.*—**fīnis, -is,** m., *an end; a purpose.*—**cēterī, -ae, -a,** *the rest, the others.*—**ratiōnālis, -e,** *rational.*—**creātūra, -ae,** f., *a creature; creation.*—**excellentior, -ōris,** comparative adj., *more excellent, loftier, more eminent.*—**quīdam, quaedam, quoddam,** *a certain.*—**modus, -ī,** m., *mode, manner, way.*—**prōvidentia, -ae,** f., *foresight, foreknowledge, providence.*—**subiaceō, -ēre,** *be subject to* (+ dat.).—**fit,** third sg. pres. irreg. verb, *becomes, is made.*—**particeps, -cipis,** *a partaker of, participant in* (+ gen.).—**prōvidēns,** f. nom. sg. partic., modifying *ipsa,* = *forseeing, providing.*] M

15. Unde et in ipsā [i.e., rātiōnālī creātūrā] participātur ratiō aeterna, per quam habet nātūrālem inclinātiōnem ad dēbitum āctum et fīnem. Et tālis participātiō lēgis aeternae in rātiōnālī creātūrā lēx nātūrālis dīcitur.

[*St. Thomas Aquinas, *Summa Theologiae* 1–2, q.91, a.2 *resp,* continuing the previous sentence.—**unde,** adv., *whence; therefore.*—**dēbitus, -a, -um,** *morally binding.*—**tālis, -e,** *such, of such a sort.*—**participātiō, -ōnis,** f., *a sharing, participation.*—**dīcitur,** *is called.*] M

CAPVT XXI
Third and Fourth Conjugations: Present System Passive

Verba Memoriā Comprehendenda

fōns, fontis, m., *a spring; fountain*

potentia, -ae, f., *power*

sermō, -ōnis, m., *conversation, talk, discourse; a sermon*

Sententiae ē Fontibus nōn Antīquīs Haustae

1. Reliqua autem gestōrum Manasse, et obsecrātiō eius ad Deum suum, verba quoque videntium ad eum in nōmine Dominī Deī Israël, continentur in sermōnibus rēgum Israël.
    [II Chron. 33:18 V.—**reliquus, -a, -um,** *remaining.*—**gesta, -ōrum,** n., *deeds.*—**Manasse,** indecl. Heb. name, m., *Manasseh, king of Israel,* take as gen.—**obsecrātiō, -ōnis,** f., *public act of prayer.*—**vidēns, -entis,** m., *a seer.*] I

2. Et relinquent gentēs īdōla sua, et venient in Ierūsalem, et inhabitābunt in eā, et gaudēbunt in eā omnēs rēgēs terrae.
    [*Tob. 14:8–9a, V.—**īdōlum, -ī,** n., *an idol.*—**inhabitō** (1), *dwell.*—**gaudeō, -ēre,** *rejoice.*] I

3. Contrā folium, quod ventō rapitur, ostendis potentiam tuam.
    [*Job 13:25 V, Job rebukes his friends.—**folium, -iī,** n., *a leaf.*—**ventus, -ī,** m., *wind.*—**ostendō, -ere,** *display.*] I

4.   Et dīxī, "Ūsquequō, Domine?" Et dīxit, "Dōnec dēsōlābuntur
      cīvitātēs absque habitātōre, et domūs sine homine, et terra relinquētur
      dēserta."
      [Is. 6:11 V.—**ūsquequō?**, adv., *how long?*—**dōnec** + fut. ind., =
      until, with no implied sense of suspense. See Capvt VIII Syntaxis.
      The LXX has ἕως ἄν + subjunctive, which is indefinite.—**dēsōlō**
      (1), *abandon.*—**absque**, prep. + abl., *without.*—**habitātor, -tōris**,
      m., *inhabitant.*—**domūs,** fourth decl. f. nom. pl., *houses.*—
      dēsertus, -a, -um, *desert, waste.*] M

5.   Sciētur prophēta quem mīsit Dominus in vēritāte.
      [*Jer. 28:9 V, Jeremiah rebukes a false prophet.—**prophēta, -ae**,
      m., *a prophet.*] I

6.   Vēnit autem Numenius, et quī cum eō fuerant ab urbe Rōmā, habentēs
      epistolās rēgibus et regiōnibus scrīptās, in quibus continēbāntur haec.
      [*I Mac. 15:15 V.—**Numenius, -iī,** m., *Numenius,* a Jewish
      ambassador.—**habentēs,** m. nom. pl. partic. modifying both
      Numenius and *quī,* the compound subject, *having (= with).*—
      epistola, -ae, f., *a letter.*—**regiō, -ōnis,** f., *a district.* —**scrīptās,** f.
      acc. pl. partic. modifying *epistolās, written.*—**haec,** = *the following
      things.* See GL, § 305.6.] I/M

7.   Dīcēbat enim intrā sē, "Sī tetigerō tantum vestīmentum eius, salva
      erō."
      [*Mt. 9:21, the woman with the flow of blood encourages
      herself.—**tetigerō,** translate as pres. in a Future More Vivid
      conditional sentence.—**intrā,** prep. + acc., *within.*—**tantum,**
      adv., *only.*—**vestīmentum, -ī,** n., *clothing.*] I/M

8.   Petrus autem dīxit, "Domine, sī tū es, iubē mē ad tē venīre super
      aquās."
      [Mt. 14:28 V.] I

9.   Quem ergō frūctum habuistis tunc in illīs, in quibus nunc ērubēscitis?
      Nam fīnis illōrum mors est.
      [*Rom. 6:21 V.—**tunc,** adv., *then, at that time.*—**ērubēscō, -ere,**
      blush with shame, feel ashamed.—**in quibus,** a causal abl., = *because
      of which.* See GL, § 408 N 3.] M

10.   Benedīcite, fōntēs, Dominō; benedīcite, maria et flūmina, Dominō.
      [*Canticum Trium Puerōrum (Dan. 3:77a and 78a V), Dominica
      ad Laudēs, BR 2.379.] I

11. Deum et animam scīre cupiō.
   [*St. Augustine of Hippo, *Sōliloquia* 1.2.7.] I

12. Apparuit mēnse Augustō stēlla quae dīcitur comēta, et mātūtīnīs
   horīs oriēbātur.
   [St. Bede the Venerable, *Historia Ecclēsiastica* 4.12.—**appareō,
   -ēre, -uī,** *become visible, appear.*—**mēnsis, -sis,** m., *month.*—
   Augustus, -a, -um, *of* or *relating to Augustus.*—**stēlla, -ae,** f., *star,
   planet.*—**comētus** = **comātus, -a, -um,** *hairy.* A *stēlla comāta* was
   a comet.—**mātūtīnus, -a, -um,** *pertaining to the morning.*—**orior,
   orīrī,** a depon. with a pass. form, but an act. meaning, *arise.*] I/M

13. Petrus autem singulāriter dīcitur commissārius et vīcārius Chrīstī,
   quia commissārius comissāriōrum.
   [Nicholas of Cusa, *Sermō* 144.2, speaking of St. Peter, the first
   pope.—**Petrus, -ī,** m., *Peter.*—**singulāriter,** *singly; particularly,
   exceedingly.* —**quia,** conj., *because.*—**commissārius, -iī,** m., *a
   deputy, commissary.*—**vīcārius, -iī,** m., *a substitute, vicar.*] I/M

14. *Animus in pedēs dēcidit.* Quī vehementer consternāntur atque
   expavescunt, iīs "animus in pedēs dēcidere" dīcitur.
   [*Desiderius Erasmus, *Adagia* 1.8.70.—**pēs, pedis,** m., *a foot.*—
   dēcidō, -ere, *fall down.*—**vehementer,** adv., *powerfully.*—
   cōnsternō (1), *alarm, frighten.*—**expavescō, -ere,** *grow very
   frightened.*] M

15. Sacra Trāditiō ergō et Sacra Scrīptūra artē inter sē conectuntur atque
   commūnicant.
   [*Deī Verbum* no. 9, CDD, p. 430.—**trāditiō, -ōnis,** f., *a giving up,
   surrender; a giving over, instruction; traditon.*—**artē,** adv., *close,
   closely, firmly.*—**cōnectō, -ere,** *fasten, tie together, connect.*—
   commūnicō (1), *divide something with somebody, communicate,
   impart, share (inter sē).*] I/M

CAPVT XXII
Fifth Declension; Ablative of Place Where

Verba Memoriā Comprehendenda

sīcut, adv. and conj., *as, just as*

tenebrae, -ārum, f. pl., *darkness*

Sententiae ē Fontibus nōn Antīquīs Haustae

1. Appelāvitque lūcem Diem, et tenebrās Noctem: factum est vespere et māne, diēs ūnus.
   [*Gen. 1:5 V.—**lūx, lūcis,** f., *light.*—**nox, noctis,** f., *night.*—**vesper, -eris,** m., *evening.*—**māne,** n. indecl., *morning.*] I

2. Complēvitque Deus diē septimō opus suum quod fēcerat.
   [*Gen. 2:2 V.—**compleō, -ēre, -ēvī,** *complete.*—**septimus, -a, -um,** *seventh.*—**opus, operis,** n., *work.*] I

3. Sīcut dēsīderat cervus ad fontēs aquārum, ita dēsīderat anima mea ad tē, Deus.
   [Ps. 41:2 V.—**dēsīderō** (1), *desire, long for.*—**cervus, -ī,** m., *a hart, stag.*—**ita,** adv., *so.*] I

4. Statēra dolōsa abōminātiō est apud Deum, et pondus aequum voluntās est.
   [*Prov. 11:1 V.—**statēra, -ae,** f., *a balance, scale.*—**dolōsus, -a, -um,** *deceitful.*—**abōminātiō, -ōnis,** f., *abomination.*—**apud,** prep. + acc., *among, in the presence of.*—**pondus, -eris,** n., *weight.*] I/M

5. Cūnctae rēs difficilēs; nōn potest eās homō explicāre sermōne.
   [*Eccles. 1:8 V.—**explicō** (1), *unfold; disentangle.*] M

6.   Et respondit rēx Ptolemaeus, dīcēns, "Fēlīx diēs, in quā reversus es
     ad terram patrum tuōrum, et sēdistī in sēde rēgnī eōrum."
     [*I Mac. 10:55 V.—**respondeō, -ēre, -spondī,** *answer.*—
     Ptolemaeus, -ī, m., *Ptolemy* VI *Philometor,* king of Egypt
     180–145 BCE, addressing Alexander I Epiphanes, king of Syria
     150–ca. 145 BCE.—**dīcēns,** m. nom. sg. partic., modifying
     Ptolemaeus, saying.—**diēs,** here feminine, a common usage
     when a special day, as a birthday, is the subject.—**revertor,
     -ī, -versus sum,** a depon., pass. in form, act. in meaning, = *you
     have returned.*—**sedeō, -ēre, sēdī,** *sit.*—**sēdēs, -dis,** f., *seat.*—
     rēgnum, -ī, n., *kingdom.*] I/M

7.   Suprā modum autem māter mīrābilis et bonōrum memoriā digna,
     quae, pereuntēs septem fīliōs sub ūnīus diēī tempore cōnspiciēns,
     bonō animō ferēbat propter spem quam in Deum habēbat.
     [*II Mac. 7:20 V.—**suprā,** prep. + acc., *above.*—**mīrābilis, -e,**
     extraordinary.—**dignus, -a, -um,** *worthy of* (+ abl.).—**pereuntēs,**
     m. acc. pl. partic., modifying *fīliōs,* = *perishing.*—**cōnspiciēns,**
     f. nom. sg. partic., modifying *quae,* = *seeing.*—**ferēbat,** third sg.
     impf. act. ind., *was bearing/enduring, tried to bear/endure.*] M

8.   Omnis ergō arbor quae nōn facit frūctum bonum excidētur et in
     ignem mittētur.
     [*Mt. 3:10 V.—**arbor, -oris,** f., *a tree.*—**excīdō, -ere,** *cut off.*] I/M

9.   Petrus vērō ad illōs, "Paenitentiam," inquit, "agite, et baptizētur
     ūnusquisque vestrum in nōmine Iēsū Chrīstī in remissiōnem
     peccātōrum vestrōrum: et accipiētis dōnum Spīritūs Sānctī."
     [*Acts 2:38 V.—**vērō,** adv., *in truth;* conj., *but.*—**paenitentiam
     . . . agite,** for this idiom, see Capvt VIII, Sentence 5 above.—
     baptizētur, third sg. pres. subjunctive pass., *let . . . be baptized.*—
     ūnusquisque, ūnaquaeque, ūnumquodque, *everyone,
     everything.*—**remissiō, -ōnis,** f., *forgiveness.*—**accipiō, -ere,**
     receive.] I

10. Iūstitia enim Deī in eō [i.e., Ēvangeliō] revēlātur ex fidē in fidem;
     sīcut scrīptum est, "Iūstus autem ex fidē vīvit."
     [*Rom. 1:17 V.—**iūstitia, -ae,** f., *justice, righteousness.*—**revēlō**
     (1), *disclose, reveal.*] I/M

11. Surrēxit Chrīstus spēs mea.
     [*Victimae Paschālī,* Sequentia in Dominicam Resurrēctiōnis, MR,
     p. 330 (414).—**surgō, -ere, surrēxī,** *get up, arise.*] I

12. Rērum omnium conditōrem Deum sēnsus hominum iūdiciō nātūrālī mōtūque cognoscit.

    [*Marius Victorinus Afer, *Dē Physicīs* 1.—**conditōr, -ōris,** m., *a founder; an author.*—**mōtus, -ūs,** m., *a motion, movement.*— **cognōscō, -ere,** *become acquainted with, learn, recognize.*] I/M

13. Voluntās mōtus mentis est.

    [St. Hilary of Poitiers, *Dē Trīnitāte* 8.12.] I

14. Servō Deī nūlla rēs displicere dēbet praeter peccātum.

    [*St. Francis of Assisi, *Admonitiōnēs* 11.—**servus, -ī,** m., *a slave, servant.*—**displiceō, -ēre,** + dat., *be displeasing to, displease.*— **praeter,** prep. + acc., *besides, except.*] I/M

15. *Elephantum ex muscā facis,* id est, rēs exiguās verbīs attolis atque amplificās.

    [*Desiderius Erasmus, *Adagia* 1.9.69.—**elephantus, -ī,** m., *an elephant.*—**musca, -ae,** f., *a fly.*—**exiguus, -a, -um,** *small, little.*— **attolō, -ere,** *raise up, lift up.*—**amplificō** (1), *enlarge.*] I/M

16. Rē quidem vērā *erōs* et *agapē*—amor ascendēns atque amor dēscendēns—nōn sē sinunt umquam inter sē sēiungī.

    [*Pope Benedict XVI, *Deus Cāritās Est* 1.7.—**rē vērā,** adv., *in truth.*—**erōs,** Gr., = *love,* often of a sexual nature, which in Plato becomes the desire to be united with beauty that gradually leads the soul away from bodies to God.—**agapē,** Gr., *fondness,* which Christians adapted to mean *brotherly love, charity.*—**ascendēns, -dentis,** *ascending.*—**dēscendēns, -dentis,** *descending.*—**sinō, -ere,** *allow, permit.*—**umquam,** adv., *ever.*—**sēiungō, -ere,** *separate, disjoin.*] M

CAPVT XXIII

Participles; Greek Periphrastic Tenses

SYNTAXIS SUPPLĒMENTUM

Greek Periphrastic Tenses. In imitation of Gr., EL sometimes combines present participles with forms of *esse* to make progressive tenses. With the present tense of *esse* this construction is like the English present progressive. With the imperfect tense of *esse* it is equivalent to the CL imperfect in its past progressive sense. With the future tense of *esse* this construction is like the English future progressive. Examples: *Nōn enim vōs estis loquentēs, sed Spīritus sānctus,* You are not indeed speaking, but the Holy Spirit (Mk. 13:11). *Erat enim docēns eōs,* He was indeed teaching them (Mk. 1:22). *Hominēs eris capiēns,* You will be capturing men (Lk. 5:10). See Blaise, § 225, and Nunn, § 90.

VERBA MEMORIĀ COMPREHENDENDA

iūstitia, -ae, f., *justice; righteousness*

vōx, vōcis, f., *a voice; word*

SENTENTIAE Ē FONTIBUS NŌN ANTĪQUĪS HAUSTAE

1. Fūrtō sublatus sum dē terrā Hebraeōrum, et hīc innocēns in lacum mīssus sum.
    [*Gen. 40:15 V, Joseph to his cellmates.—**fūrtum, -ī,** n., *a trick, deception.*—**Hebraeus, -a, -um,** *Hebrew.*—**hīc,** adv., *here.*—**innocēns, -entis,** *innocent.*—**lacus, -ūs,** m., *vat; lake; pit; dungeon.*] I

2. Vēnēruntque Achior et Nabath cōnsōbrīnī Tobīae, gaudentēs ad
Tobīam et congrātulantēs eī dē omnibus bonīs quae circa illum
ostenderat Deus.
[*Tob. 11:20 V.—**Achior,** indecl. Heb. name, m., *Ahikar.*—
Nabath, indecl. Heb. name, m., *Nadab.*—**cōnsōbrīnus, -ī,** m.,
a cousin.—**Tobīas, -ae,** m., *Tobit.*—**congrātulor, -ārī,** depon.,
with a pres. act. partic., = *congratulating* (+ dat.).—**circā,** prep. +
acc., *around; concerning.*] I/M

3. Versa est in lūctum cithara mea, et organum meum in vōcem flentium.
[*Job 30:31 V.—**lūctus, -ūs,** m., *sorrow.*—**cithara, -ae,** f., *lyre.*—
organum, -ī, n., *pipe.*—**fleō, -ēre,** *weep.*] I

4. Corpus illīus [i.e., leviathan] quasi scūta fūsilia, compāctum squamīs
sē prementibus.
[*Job 41:6 V.—**leviathan,** indecl. Heb. noun, *leviathan; a
crocodile.*—**quasi,** adv., *as it were.*—**scūtum, -ī,** n., *shield.*—
fūsilis, -e, *molten; of molten metal, cast.*—**compingō, -ere, -pēgī,
-pāctus,** *join together into a whole.*—**squāma, -ae,** f., a *scale; small
metal plates used in making armor.*] M

5. Dominus regit mē, et nihil mihi dēerit: in locō pascuae ibi mē
collocāvit. Super aquam refectiōnis ēducāvit mē.
[*Ps. 22:1–2 V.—**dēsum, -esse,** + dat., *be wanting (to), be
lacking (to).*—**pascua, -ae,** f., *a pasture.*—**collocō** (1), *place,
set.*—**refectiō, -onis,** f., *refreshment.*—**ēducō** (1), *foster, educate;
nourish, support.*] M

6. Anima nostra sīcut passer ērepta est dē laqueō vēnantium.
[*Ps. 123:7 V.—**passer, -eris,** m., *a sparrow.*—**laqueus, -ī,** m., *a
snare.*—**vēnāns, -antis,** m., *one who hunts, a hunter.*] I

7. Nōn in fortitūdine equī voluntātem habēbit [Deus], nec in tībiīs virī
benēplacitum erit eī.
[*Ps. 146:10 V.—**fortitūdō, -inis,** f., *strength.*—**voluntātem
habēbit,** < LXX, θελήσει (+ ἔν τινι), *will delight in, love* (see LSJ,
s.v. ἐθέλω I.9).—**tībia, -ae,** f., *the shin.*—**benēplaceō, -ēre, -uī,
-ītum,** *please.* Take **benēplacitum erit** as an impersonal passive,
= *it will be pleasing.*] M

8. Haec dīcit Dominus, "Facite iūdicium et iūstitiam, et līberāte vī
oppressōs de manū calumniātōris."
[*Jer. 22:3 V.—**calumniātor, -ōris,** m., *false accuser.*] I/M

9. Et erant discipulī Iōannis et Pharisaeī iēiūnantēs.
    [Mk. 2:18 V.—**Iōannes, -nis,** m., *John.*—**Pharisaeus, -ī,** m., *a Pharisee.*—**iēiūnō** (1), *fast.*] I/M

10. Rēx āit puellae, "Pete ā mē quod vīs, et dabō tibi." Et iūrāvit illī, "Quia quidquid petieris, dabō tibi, līcet dīmidium rēgnī meī."
    [*Mk. 6:22–23 V, Herod to Salome.—**vīs,** second pers. sg. pres. ind. of *vōlō,* = *you wish.*—**Quia,** sometimes used in EL to signal a direct quotation. Do not translate. See Appendix I, § 70 N 2.—**petieris,** fut. pf. of *petō,* translate as pres. as if in a Future More Vivid conditional sentence.—**iūrō** (1), *swear.*—**līcet,** conj., *although.*—**dīmidium, -iī,** n., *half.*—**rēgnum, -ī,** n., *a kingdom.*] M

11. Omnī autem petentī tē tribue.
    [*Lk. 6:30 V.—**tribuō, -ere,** *grant.*] M

12. Ipsa creātūra aliquem fabricātōrem suī ēnuntiat.
    [*Marius Victorinus Afer, *Dē Physicīs* 2.—**creātūra, -ae,** f., *a creature; creation.*—**fabricātōr, -ōris,** m., *a maker, artificer.*—**ēnuntiō** (1), *tell, divulge, disclose.*] I/M

13. Deus factus est homō quia hominem accēpit; sīc dīcitur esse homō, quia hominem habet, vel quia est habēns hominem; et homō factus Deus, quia assumptus est ā Deō; et homō esse Deus, quia habēns hominem est Deus.
    [*Peter Lombard, *Sententiārum Librī Quattuor* 3.8.10.—**accipiō, -ere, -cēpī,** *take, receive, accept.*—**assūmō, -sūmere, -sumpsī, -sumptum,** *take to oneself.*] M/A

14. Annō Dominī MCCXXIV, tempore dominī Honōriī papae, scīlicet eōdem annō quō cōnfirmāta est ab eō rēgula beātī Franciscī, annō dominī rēgis Henrīcī, filiī Iōannis, octāvō, fēriā tertiā post fēstum nātīvitātis Beātae Virginis, quod illō annō fuit diē dominicā, applicuērunt prīmō Frātrēs Minōrēs in Angliam apud Dovoriam, quattuor scīlicet clēricī et quīnque laicī.
    [*Thomas of Eccleston, *Dē Adventū Minōrum in Angliam* 1.— MCCXXIV, = *millēsimō duocentēsimō vīcēsimō quārtō* (see *Wheelock's Latin,* 500).—**Honōrius, -iī,** m., *Honorius* III (d. 1227).—**papa, -ae,** m., *a pope.*—**scīlicet,** adv., *namely.*—**cōnfirmō** (1), *confirm.*—**rēgula, -ae,** f., *a rule.*—**Franciscus, -ī,** m., St. *Francis* of Assisi.—**Henrīcus, -ī,** m., *Henry* III, king of England, 1216–1272.—**Iōannes, -is,** "Bad" King *John,* ruled 1199–1216.—**octāvus, -a, -um,** *eighth.*—**fēria, -ae,** f.,

a weekday.—**tertius, -a, -um,** *third.*—**fēstum, -ī,** n., *a feast.*—
nātīvitās, -tātis, f., *birth* (a feast which falls on September
8th).—**dominicus, -a, -um,** *pertaining to a lord* or *to the Lord.*—
applicō, -āre, -cuī, here = *land* (from a boat or ship).—**prīmō,**
adv., *first.*—**Frātrēs Minōrēs, Frātrum Minōrum,** = *the Friars
Minor,* the Franciscans.—**Anglia, -ae,** f., *England.*—**Dovoria,
-ae,** f., (presumably) *Dover,* called *Dubrae, -ārum,* f., in EL.—
clēricus, -ī, m., *a clergyman.*—**lāicus, -ī,** m., *a layman.*] M/A

15.   Sacra Trāditiō et Sacra Scrīptūra ūnum verbī Deī sacrum dēpositum
       cōnstituunt Ecclēsiae commissum.
       [*Deī Verbum* no. 10, CDD, p. 431.—**trāditiō, -ōnis,** f., *a giving
       up, surrender; a giving over, instruction; traditon.*—**dēpositum, -ī,**
       n., *a deposit.*—**cōnstituō, -uere,** *set up, establish, arrange.*] I/M

This fresco depicts the Blessed Mother and the Infant Jesus being adored by St. Francis
(1181/2–1226) and St. Clare (1194–1253), the two great saints of Assisi. The fresco is
located in the Cappellina della Vergine sulla Piazetta (The Little Chapel of the Virgin on
the Little Court) at the Church of San Damiano just outside Assisi. St. Francis' conversion
began at the old chapel on this spot, which he rebuilt, and St. Clare founded her order of
nuns here. Francis wrote his *Canticle of the Sun* in Clare's convent. Several sentences from
Francis's works are included in this book. The painter of this medieval fresco is unknown.
(© Wikimedia Commons)

CAPVT XXIV

Ablative Absolute; Passive Periphrastic; Dative of Agent; Active Periphrastic; Ablative Absolute in EL

Syntaxis Supplēmentum

Active Periphrastic. The future active participle can be combined with any form of *esse*, in order to make a vivid future. (Cf. *Wheelock*, p. 247.) The forms made with the perfect stem, however, are less common. Examples:

> *rīsūrus (-a, -um) sum*, I am about to / am likely to / intend to laugh

> *rīsūrus (-a, -um) eram*, I was about to / was likely to / intended to laugh

> *rīsūrus (-a, -um) erō*, I shall be about to / be likely to / intend to laugh

> *rīsūrus (-a, -um) fuī*, I was (have been) about to / was (have been) likely to / intended (have been intending) to laugh

> *rīsūrus (-a, -um) fueram*, I had been about to / been likely to / intended to laugh

> *rīsūrus (-a, -um) fuerō*, I shall have been about to / have been likely to / have intended to laugh

This construction also occurs in all the tenses of the subjunctive, and in the present and perfect infinitive.

Ablative Absolute. EL did not always strictly observe the classical rules for the use of the ablative absolute. See Sentence 3 below and Capvt XXVI, Sentence 1.

71

Verba Memoriā Comprehendenda

ratiōnālis, -e, *rational, reasonable*

sacrāmentum, -ī, n., *a sum deposited in a suit by the two parties involved; a civil suit; an army recruit's initial promise of service; the military oath of allegiance; a solemn obligation;* (in EL) *a secret; a mystery; a sacrament*

Sententiae ē Fontibus nōn Antīquīs Haustae

1. Lōt locūtus est ad generōs suōs quī acceptūrī erant fīliās eius et dīxit, "Surgite, ēgrediminī dē locō istō, quia dēlēbit Dominus cīvitātem hanc."

    [*Gen. 19:14, V, Lot's warning on the destruction of Sodom.—**Lōt,** indecl. Heb. name, m., *Lot.*—**locūtus est,** depon. third pers. sg. pf. ind., a pass. form with an act. meaning, = *(he) spoke.*—**gener, -ī,** m., *a son-in-law.*—**surgō, -ere,** *get up, arise.*—**ēgrediminī,** depon. second pers. pl. imperative, a pass. form with an act. meaning, = *get out.*] M

2. Tū rēx rēgum es, et Deus caelī rēgnum et fortitūdinem et imperium et glōriam dedit tibi.

    [*Dan. 2:37 V, Daniel to King Nebuchadnezzar.—**rēgnum, -ī,** n., *a kingdom.*—**fortitūdō, -dinis,** f., *strength.*] I/M

3. Apertīs thēsaurīs suīs, obtulērunt eī mūnera: aurum, tūs et myrrham.

    [*Mt. 2:11 V, LH 3.757.—**aperiō, -īre, -ruī, -rtum,** *open.*—**thēsaurus, -ī,** m., *a treasure.*—**offerō, -ferre, obtulī,** an irreg. verb, but conjugated regularly in the perf., *offer.*—**mūnus, -eris,** n., *a duty; gift.*—**tūs, tūris,** n., *frankincense.*—**myrrha, -ae,** f., *myrrh,* used in "perfumes, cosmetics, and medicines."[13]] M

4. Ego autem dīcō vōbīs, quia omnis quī dīmīserit uxōrem suam, exceptā fornicātiōnis causā, facit eam moechārī; et quī dīmissam dūxerit, adulterat.

    [*Mt. 5:32 V.—**quia,** introduces indirect statement, = *that.*—**dīmittō, -ere, -mīsī,** *send away, dismiss; divorce.*—**fornicātiō, -ōnis,** f., *fornication.*—**moechārī,** pres. depon. inf., a pass. form with an act. meaning, = *to commit adultery.*—**dūxerit,** here = *lead in marriage, marry* (said of a man).—**adulterō** (1), *to commit adultery (with).*] M

---

13 Daniel Thomas Potts, "myrrh," *The Oxford Classical Dictionary*, 3rd ed. rev., ed. Simon Hornblower and Antony Spawforth (Oxford: Oxford University Press, 2003), 1017.

5. Hī sōlī sunt adiūtōrēs meī in rēgnō Deī, quī mihi fuērunt sōlāciō.
   [*Col. 4:11 V, Paul refers to certain faithful mission helpers.—
   adiūtor, -ōris, m., *helper.*—**sōlāciō,** a dat. of purpose; with **mihi,**
   a dat. of reference, it makes a double dative, = *were a comfort to
   me.* See Capvt XXXVIII *Syntaxis.*] A

6. Grātiās agimus tibi, Domine Deus omnipotēns, quī es et quī erās et
   quī ventūrus es.
   [Apoc. 11:17 V, LH 3.881.—**omnipotēns, -entis,** *all-powerful.*] I/M

7. Gāvīsī sunt discipulī, Allēlūia, allēlūia, vīsō Dominō, Allēlūia, allēlūia.
   [*Respōnsōrium, ad Vesperās, Fēria II, Hebdomada II Temporis
   Paschālis, in LH 2.508.] I/M

8. Verbō inhabitante, aeternāliter exsultābunt quī eum intrā sē
   recēpērunt.
   [*In psalmō prīmō, ad Laudēs mātūtīnās, Fēria II, Hebdomada I,
   LH 3.575.—**inhabitō** (1), *dwell in.*—**aeternāliter,** adv., *forever.*—
   exsultō (1), *leap up; exult.*—**intrā,** prep. + acc., *within.*] I/M

9. Deus autem, in ipsīs rationālis animae sēcrētīs, quī homō interior
   vocātur, et quaerendus et dēprecandus est.
   [*St. Augustine of Hippo, *Dē magistrō* 1.2. **sēcrētus, -a, -um,**
   secret; hidden.—**interior, -oris,** *inner, more inward.*—**dēprecor,**
   -ārī, depon. verb, forming the fut. pass. partic. as any other verb,
   pray (for the averting of evil).] M/A

10. Hoc exemplīs plānum faciendum est.
    [*St. Augustine of Hippo, *Dē Trīnitāte* 5.7.8, Augustine begins
    an explanation.—**exemplum, -ī,** n., *example.*—**plānus, -a, -um,**
    plane; plain.] I/M

11. Pāce per tōtam Italiam cōnfirmātā, imperātor Chuonrādus prosperō
    reditū in Alamanniam vēnit et, in Augustā Vindelicā colloquium
    familiāre cum suīs fidēlibus tenēns, dē prōditōribus patriae tractāre
    coepit.
    [*Wipo, *Gesta Chuonrādī Imperātōris* 20.—**confirmō** (1), *make
    firm, confirm, strengthen.*—**Chuonrādus, -ī,** m., *Conrad.*—**prosper,**
    -a, -um, *according to one's hope: fortunate, prosperous.*—**reditus, -ūs,**
    m., *a return.*—**Alamannia, -ae,** f., *Germany.*—**Augusta Videlica,**
    -ae -ae, f., *Augsburg.*—**colloquium, -ī,** n., *a conference.*—**familiāris,**
    -e, *intimate, friendly.*—**prōditor, -tōris,** m., *a betrayer, traitor.*—
    tractō (1), *handle, treat, discuss.*] M/A

12.   Virō dēfūnctō, bona pauperibus distribuit.
> [*Initia Sānctae Elisabeth Lūsitāniae, LH 3.1257.—**dēfungor, -ī, dēfūnctus sum,** depon., the perf. part. of which has an active meaning, = *having died.*—**pauper, -eris,** *poor.*—**distribuō, -ere, -uī,** *divide, distribute.*] I/M

13.   In omnī congregātiōne, quamdiū dūrat amor, tamdiū ōrdō, sīve in familiīs, cīvitātibus, rēgnīs, monastēriīs, etc. Amor igitur causa est ōrdinis, quō cessante cessat ōrdō. Sīcut in corpore, dūrante amōre inter hūmōrēs, homō est temperātus, sed cessante concordiā et amōre distemperātus. Sānctus Petrus valdē ōrdinātus, ideō sibi ecclēsia fuit commissa.
> [*Nicholas of Cusa, *Sermō* 12.6.—**congregātiō, -ōnis,** f., *a gathering together, society.*—**quamdiū . . . tamdiū,** advs., *as long as . . . so long.*—**dūrō** (1), *harden; endure.*—**ōrdō, -inis,** m., *order.*—**sīve,** conj., *whether.*—**rēgnum, -ī,** n., *a kingdom.*—**monastērium, -iī,** n., *a monastery.*—**cessō** (1), *cease (from), stop.*—**hūmor, -ōris,** m., *any liquid; a humor* (i.e., blood, phlegm, yellow bile, black bile), the balance of the humors being thought necessary for good health.—**temperātus, -a, -um,** *correctly mixed, ordered; healthy.*—**concordia, -ae,** f., *harmony, agreement.*—**distemperātus, -a, -um,** *out of balance; unhealthy.*— **valdē,** adv., *very much, greatly.*—**ōrdinō** (1), *set in order.*—**ideō,** adv., *for that reason.*] A

14.   *Ūnus vir, nūllus vir.* Sēnsus est nihil ēgregium praestārī posse ab ūnō homine, omnī auxiliō dēstitūtō.
> [*Desiderius Erasmus, *Adagia* 1.5.40.—**ēgregius, -a, -um,** *admirable, excellent.*—**praestō, -āre,** *perform, execute; show, exhibit.*—**auxilium, -iī,** n., *help, aid.*—**dēstituō, -tuere, -stituī, -stitūtum,** *place apart; forsake.*] M/A

15.   Quī magistrātum ūllum ambīerit exspēs omnium redditur.
> [*St. Thomas More, *Ūtopia* 2, LAM, p. 194, reporting a salutary practice of the Utopians.—**magistrātus, -ī,** m., *a magistracy, public office.*—**ūllum,** instead of *aliquem* because of the negative judgment implicit in the sentence.—**ambiō, -īre, -īvī,** here = *go around canvassing for* (votes), *campaign for* (office).—**exspēs,** adj., only in nom. sg., *without hope, hopeless.*—**reddō, -ere,** here = *make, render, cause to be.*] M/A

CAPVT XXV

Infinitives; Indirect Statement; Direct Quotation; Indirect Statement in EL; Future Passive Infinitive; Predicate Genitive

SYNTAXIS SUPPLĒMENTUM

Direct Quotation. In imitation of a Greek construction, EL sometimes introduces a direct quotation with the word *quia* or *quoniam*. This introductory word is not translated. Capvt XXIII, Sentence 10, provides an example.

Indirect Statement. In addition to the CL construction with the accusative and infinitive, EL also uses a finite verb introduced by *quod*, *quia*, or *quoniam*, a construction modelled on the Greek. The verb can be either in the indicative or in the subjunctive. Blaise, §§ 261–263, observes that with *quod* the subjunctive is used frequently to give a subjective nuance, or when the main verb is negated or is interrogative. With *quia* and *quoniam* the indicative is used for the most part. Sentences 1, 2, and 3 below provide examples.

Future Passive Infinitive. The future passive infinitive is not in common use, although one can be found in Sentence 10 below. Instead, the future active infinitive of *esse*, i.e, *futūrum esse*, or its alternative *fore*, is used in combination with a consecutive clause. See Capvt XXX, *Syntaxis*.

Predicate Genitive (Genitive of Characteristic). Mentioned by *Wheelock* on p. 348, the predicate genitive is a noun in the possessive genitive or in the genitive of description (or quality, which also requires an adjective), used in the predicate of a sentence to indicate a characteristic or class appertaining to a person or a thing, e.g., *audītor istīus doctrīnae nōn est ūnīus generis*, The auditor of that doctrine (i.e., of Sacred Scripture) is not of one kind [*St. Bonaventure, *Breviloquim*, Prologus 4.3). Or, *Tōtum quod est hominis est in resurrēctiōne reparandum*, All that is characteristic of man must be renewed in the resurrection (St. Thomas Aquinas, *Compendium Theologiae* 2.6.563.)

VERBA MEMORIĀ COMPREHENDENDA

necessitās, -tātis, f., *necessity; poverty*

quia, conj., *because; that.* See also notes above.

sēcrētus, -a, -um, *secret, hidden*

SENTENTIAE Ē FONTIBUS NŌN ANTĪQUĪS HAUSTAE

1.   Et sciētis quia ego Dominus.
   [*Ezek. 37:13 V, LH 3.803.] I

2.   Nōtum sit vōbīs quoniam gentibus missum est hoc salūtāre Deī.
   [*Acts 28:28 V, LH 3.837.—**nōtus, -a, -um,** *known,* < γνωστόν.—
   sit, third pers. sg. pres. subjunctive of *esse,* = *let it be.*—**salūtāre,**
   -ris, n., *salvation.*] I/M

3.   Quisquis cōnfessus fuerit quoniam Iēsūs est fīlius Deī, Deus in eō
   manet et ipse in Deō.
   [*I Jn. 4:15 V, LH 3.838.—**cōnfiteor, -ērī, -fessus sum,** depon.,
   having pass. forms with act. meanings, = *will have confessed* or
   better *confesses.*] I

4.   Iūdex crēderis esse ventūrus.
   [*Tē Deum, ad Officium lēctiōnis, Ōrdinārium, LH 3.526.—
   crēdō, -ere, crēdidī, *believe.* Note that in this construction Latin
   prefers a personal subject, while English prefers an impersonal.]
   I/M

5.   Quī promīsistī tē aquam esse datūrum salientem in vītam aeternam,
   Spīritum tuum effunde super omnēs hominēs.
   [*Precēs, ad Laudēs mātūtīnās, Fēria VI, Hebdomada III, LH
   3.891.—**prōmittō, -ere, -mīsī,** *promise.*—**saliō, -īre,** *leap.*—
   effundō, -ere, *pour out.*] I/M

6.   Quis enim ambigit ōrdinem, quī in rērum nātūrā est, ab aliquō esse
   positum, nōn ā sē?
   [*Marius Victorinus Afer, *Dē Physicīs* 1.—**ambigō, -ere,** *doubt.*—
   ōrdō, -inis, m., *a series; order.*] I/M

7.   AUGUSTĪNUS. Cōnstat ergō inter nōs verba signa esse. ADEŌDATUS. Cōnstat.

      [*St. Augustine of Hippo, *Dē magistrō* 2.3.—**cōnstat,** impers. verb, *it is agreed.*] I

8.   Fatendum est Patrem et Fīlium prīncipium esse Spīritūs Sānctī, nōn duo prīncipia.

      [St. Augustine of Hippo, *Dē Trīnitāte* 5.15.16.—**fateor, -ērī,** depon., having a fut. pass. partic. like any other verb's, *confess, admit.*] I/M

9.   Sed sī per aeternitātem tuam fuistī et es et eris, et fuisse nōn est futūrum esse, et esse nōn est fuisse vel futūrum esse, quōmodo aeternitās tua tōta est semper?

      [*St. Anselm of Canterbury, *Proslogion* 19.—**aeternitās, -tātis,** f., *eternity.*—**quōmodo,** adv., *in what way?, how?*] M/A

10.   Nec sānē praesūmō mē ōsculātum īrī ab ōre ipsīus [id est, Deī]: est hoc assūmptī hominis ūnicae fēlīcitātis et praerogātīvae singulāris; sed humilius ab ōsculō ōris suī petō mē ōsculārī, quod commūne utique est multōrum, quī dīcere possunt, "Et nōs omnēs dē plēnitūdine eius accēpimus."

      [*St. Bernard of Clairvaux, *Sermō II in Cantica* 2.2.—**sānē,** adv., *rationally; admittedly, to be sure.*—**praesūmō, -ere,** *anticipate; suppose.*—**osculō** (1), *kiss.* Note the fut. pass. inf.—**assūmō, -ere, -sūmpsī, -sūmptum,** *take up, receive, adopt, accept, take.*—**ūnicus, -a, -um,** *one and no more, sole; alone of its kind, unique.*—**fēlīcitās, -tātis,** f., *happiness.*—**praerogātīva, -ae,** f., *privilege, prerogative.*—**singulāris, -e,** *single; singular; unique.*—N.B. Take *ūnicae fēlīcitātis et praerogātīvae singulāris* as pred. gen., = "characteristic of the unique happiness and of the singular privilege".—**ōsculum, -ī,** n., *a kiss.*—**utique,** adv., *certainly, at least.*—**plēnitūdō, -tūdinis,** f., *fullness.*—**Et nōs omnes,** etc., John 1:16.] A

11.   Igitur dēsertum Chrīstus ingreditur. Locus sēcrētus ēligitur, quia sōlīus Deī iūdiciō ieiūnia sunt agenda.

      [Arnold of Bonneval, *Liber dē cardinālibus Chrīstī operibus* 5.2, from a sermon on the temptations of Christ.—**dēsertus, -a, -um,** *desert, lonely, waste;* here supply *locum.*—**ingredior, -dī,** a third conjugation depon., having pass. forms with act. meanings, = *(he) enters.*—**ēligō, -ere,** *choose.*—**ieiūnium, -iī,** n., *a fast.*] M

12. Cito etiam cum grātiā et benedictiōne vestrā [archiepīscopum nostrum] remittendum esse et nōs ōrāmus et ipsa multiplex regiōnis necessitās implōrat.

[*Peter the Venerable, *Epistola* 21, from a letter to the pope, requesting him to send back the local archbishop.—**benedictiō, -ōnis,** f., *blessing.*—**archiepīscopus, -ī,** m., *an archbishop.*—**remittō, -ere,** *send back.*—**multiplex, -icis,** *manifold.*—**regiō, -ōnis,** f., *a region.*—**implōrō** (1), *ask, entreat.*] M/A

13. Dīcēbat Bernardus Carnōtensis nōs [i.e., modernōs] esse quasi nānōs gigantum umerīs īnsīdentēs.

[*John of Salisbury, *Metalogicon* 3.4.—**Bernardus Carnōtensis, -ī -sis,** m., *Bernard of Chartres.*—**modernus, -ī,** m., *a modern person.*—**quasi,** adv., *as, as if, as good as.*—**nānus, -ī,** m., *a dwarf.*—**gigās, -gantis,** m., *a giant.*—**umerus, -ī,** m., *a shoulder.*—**īnsīdō, -ere,** *sit in* or *on* (+ dat.).] I

14. Vīdērunt summī philosophī nūllum corpus esse Deum, et ideō cūncta corpora transcendērunt quaerentēs Deum. Vīdērunt etiam quidquid mūtābile est, nōn esse summum Deum omniumque prīncipium, et ideō omnem animam mūtābilēsque spīritūs transcendērunt. Deinde vīdērunt omne quod mūtābile est nōn posse esse nisi ab illō quī incommūtābiliter et simpliciter est. Intellēxērunt ergō eum et omnia ista fēcisse et ā nūllō modō fierī potuisse.

[*Peter Lombard, *Sententiae* 1.3.3.—**summus, -a, -um,** *highest.*—**philosophus, -ī,** m., *philosopher.*—**ideō,** adv., *for that reason.*—**transcendō, -ere, -scendī,** *step over, pass over.*—**mūtābilis, -e,** *changeable, mutable.*—**incommūtābiliter,** adv., *unchangeably, immutably.*—**simpliciter,** adv., *simply, uncompoundedly.*—**ā nūllō modō** (must = **nūllō modō;** see BH, p. 89), adv., *by no means.*—**fierī,** = *to be made.*] M/A

15. Respondeō dīcendum sacram doctrīnam ūnam scientiam esse.

[*St. Thomas Aquinas, *Summa Theologiae* 1, q.1, a.3 *resp.*—**respondeō, -ēre,** *answer.*—**dīcendum,** supply *esse,* and take impersonally.—**doctrīna, -ae,** f., *teaching, instruction, learning.*] M

CAPVT XXVI
Comparison of Adjectives; Ablative of Comparison; **Ablative of Degree; Ablative of Charge or Penalty**

Syntaxis Supplēmentum

Ablative of Degree of Difference. See *Wheelock*, Appendix, p. 493. An example of this construction can be found in Sentence 11 below.

Ablative of the Charge or Penalty. With judicial verbs of "condemning or acquitting," the ablative is used to express the charge or penalty, e.g., *damnāre capite*, to condemn to death (GL, § 378.3). See Sentence 5 below. Cf. the Genitive of the Charge in Capvt XXXIII.

Verba Memoriā Comprehendenda

ēligō, -ere, -lēgī, -lēctum, *choose*

trādō, -ere, -didī, -ditum, *hand over; hand down, transmit*

Sententiae ē Fontibus nōn Antīquīs Haustae

1. Et ērēctō ibi altārī, invocāvit super illud fortissimum Deum Israël.
   [*Gen. 33:20 V, said of Jacob.—**ērigō, -ere, -rēxī, -rēctum,** *erect, build.*—**altāre, -is,** n., *an altar.*—**invocō** (1), *call upon, invoke.*]
   I/M

2. Cūr tristior est hodiē solitō faciēs vestra?
   [*Gen. 40:7, Joseph to his cellmates.—**solitum, -ī,** n., *what is usual, the usual.*—**faciēs, -ēī,** f., *face.*] I/M

3. Ūna sapientior cēterīs uxōribus eius haec socruī respondit, "Forsitan nunc dīvidit spolia et pulcherrima fēminārum ēligitur eī. Vestēs dīversōrum colōrum Sisarae traduntur in praedam."

    [*Judg. 5:29–30 V, Deborah imagines the plight of murdered Sisera's wives.—**cēterī, -ae, -a,** *the rest (of).*—**socrus, -ūs,** f., *mother-in-law.*—**respondeō, -ēre, -spondī,** *respond, answer.*—**forsitan,** adv., *perhaps.*—**dīvidō, -ere,** *divide, distribute.*—**spolium, -ī,** n., *booty, spoil.*—**vestis, -is,** f., *a garment, clothing.*—**dīversus, -a, -um,** *different.*—**color, -ōris,** m., *color.*—**Sisara, -ae,** m., *Sisera, a Canaanite general.*—**in,** here = *for.*—**praeda, -ae,** f., *loot; prey.*] M/A

4. Mulierem fortem quis inveniet? Longē super gemmās pretium eius.

    [*Prov. 31:10 NV. —**inveniet,** translates the Heb. imperf., which here has the meaning of a Lat. pres. subjunct., = *can find.*—**longē,** adv., *far.*—**gemma, -ae,** f., *a jewel, gem.*—**pretium, -iī,** n., *price; reward.*] M

5. Morte turpīssimā condemnēmus eum.

    [*Wis. 2:20 V, the unjust plot against the just man.—**condemnēmus,** first pers. pl. pres. subjunctive act. of **condemnō** (1), = *let us condemn,* constructed with the acc. of the per. and abl. of the charge or penalty.] M

6. Tunc omnēs simul benedīxērunt misericordem Dominum et convaluērunt animīs, nōn sōlum hominēs, sed et bēstiās ferōcissimās et mūrōs ferreōs parātī penetrāre.

    [*II Mac. 11:9 V, the Maccabean troops brace themselves to attack the Macedonians.—**tunc,** adv., *at that time.*—**simul,** adv., *together.*—**misericors, -cordis,** *merciful.*—**convalescō, -ere, -luī,** *grow strong.*—**bēstia, -ae,** f., *a beast.*—**mūrus, -ī,** m., *a wall.*—**ferreus, -a, -um,** *(of) iron.*—**penetrō** (1), *pierce.*] M

7. Et dīxit quī sedēbat in thronō, "Ecce nova faciō omnia." Et dīxit mihi, "Scrībe, quia haec verba fidelissima sunt et vēra."

    [*Apoc. 21:5 V.—**sedeō, -ēre,** *sit (upon).*—**thronus, -ī,** m., *throne.*] I

8. Trādunt nōbilissimī disputātiōnum magistrī nōmine et verbō plēnam cōnstāre sententiam.

    [*St. Augustine of Hippo, *Dē magistrō* 5.16, making a basic point of notional grammar.—**trādō, -ere,** *hand down, teach.*—**nōbilis,**

-e, *famous; noble.*—**disputātiō, -ōnis,** f., *an argument, debate.*—**nōmen,** here = *a noun.*—**verbum,** here = *a verb.*—**cōnstō** (1), *consist in* or *of* (+ abl.).] M/A

9. Est autem animus vīta quaedam, unde omne quod animātum est vīvere, omne autem inanime quod animārī potest mortuum, id est vītā prīvātum, intellegitur. Nōn ergō potest animus morī. Nam sī carēre poterit vītā, nōn animus, sed animātum aliquid est.

   [*St. Augustine of Hippo, *Dē Immortālitāte Animae* 9.16.—**animō** (1), *animate, give life to.*—**inanimis, -e,** *lifeless, inanimate.*—**mortuus, -a, -um,** *dead.* Supply *esse.*—**prīvō** (1), *deprive.*—**morī,** pres. inf. of *morior,* depon., having pass. forms with act. meanings, = *to die.*—**poterit,** take as pres. ind., = *proves to be able.* See GL, § 596.1.] A

10. Et quid erat quod mē dēlectābat, nisi amāre et amārī?

   [*St. Augustine of Hippo, *Cōnfessiōnēs* 2.2, thinking of his student days.—**dēlectō** (1), *entice; delight.*] I/M

11. Sīc enim virtūtēs quae sunt in animō hūmānō nūllō modō sēparantur ab invicem. Quantō ergō magis in illā incommūtābilī aeternāque substantiā, incomparābiliter simpliciōre quam est animus hūmānus, haec ita sē habent?

   [St. Augustine of Hippo, *Dē Trīnitāte* 6.4.6.—**sīc,** adv., *so, thus.*—**hūmānus, -a, -um,** *human.*—**sēparō** (1), *separate.*—**invicem,** adv. used here as obj. of the prep. *ab, each other.*—**quantus, -a, -um,** *how much.*—**magis,** adv., *more.*—**incommūtābilis, -e,** *unchangeable.*—**substantia, -ae,** f., *being, essence, substance.*—**incomparābiliter,** adv., *incomparably.*—**simplex, -plicis,** *simple.*—**ita,** adv., *so, thus.*—**sē habēre,** *be constituted, be.*] M/A

12. Omnēs autem lēgēs aut dīvīnae sunt aut hūmānae. Dīvīnae nātūrā, hūmānae mōribus cōnstant, ideōque haec discrepant, quoniam aliae aliīs gentibus placent. Fās lēx dīvīna est, iūs lēx hūmāna. Transīre per aliēnum fās est, iūs nōn est.

   [*St. Isidore of Seville, *Etymologiae* 5.2.1–2.—**cōnstō, -āre,** *rest upon* (+ abl.).—**ideō,** adv., *for that reason.*—**discrepō** (1), *differ, be unlike.*—**placeō, -ēre,** *be pleasing to, please* (+ dat.).—**fās,** indecl., n., *right, sacred duty.*—**transīre,** pres. act. inf. used as a gerund = *to cross, crossing.*—**aliēnum, -ī,** n., *the property of a stranger.*] M/A

13.   Magis tamen [sacra doctrīna] est speculatīva quam practica, quia
      prīncipālius agit dē rēbus dīvīnīs quam dē āctibus hūmānīs.
      [*St. Thomas Aquinas, *Summa Theologiae* 1, q.1, a.4 *resp.*—**magis,**
      adv., *more.*—**doctrīna, -ae,** f., *teaching, instruction, learning.*—
      speculātīvus, -a, -um, *concerned with seeing, contemplative,*
      speculative.—**practicus, -a, -um,** *concerned with doing, active,*
      acting.—**prīncipālius,** comp. adv., *more chiefly.*—**āctus, -ūs,** m.,
      action, act.] M

14.   Deum cognōscimus ex perfectiōnibus prōcēdentibus in creātūrās ab
      ipsō. Quae quidem perfectiōnēs in Deō sunt secundum ēminentiōrem
      modum quam in creātūrīs.
      [*St. Thomas Aquinas, *Summa Thelogiae* 1, q.13, a.3 *resp.*—
      cognōscō, -ere, *become acquainted with, recognize.*—**perfectiō,**
      -ōnis, f., *an accomplishment, perfection.*—**prōcēdō, -ere,** *go forth,*
      proceed.—**creātūra, -ae,** f., *a creature.*—**secundum,** prep. + acc.,
      according to.—**ēminēns, -entis,** *outstanding, distinguished.*] M

15.   Quālitās fōrma quaedam est.
      [*Marsilio Ficino, *Theologica Platōnica* 1.3.1.—**quālitās, -tātis,**
      f., *a quality.*] I

CAPVT XXVII

Irregular Comparison of Adjectives; Historical Infinitive

Syntaxis Supplēmentum

Historical Infinitive. In historical narrative, Latin speakers sometimes used present infinitives with nominative subjects instead of finite forms of the verb. This device focuses attention upon the action, and lends a rapid and intense feeling to the account, e.g., *Fēles trāns viam currere, canēs persequī*, The cat ran across the street, the dogs chased. *Woodcock*, § 20, traces this use (though not the form) of the infinitive to a very primitive stage of language development, when only verbal nouns were in use to express action and states of being. Examples can be found in Capvt XXX, Sentence 8.

Verba Memoriā Comprehendenda

cēterī, -ae, -a, or **caeterī, -ae, -a,** *the others, the rest*

rēgnum, -ī, n., *royal rule; kingdom*

Sententiae ē Fontibus nōn Antīquīs Haustae

1a. Mulier dīligēns corōna est virō suō, et putrēdō in ossibus eius quae cōnfūsiōne rēs dignās gerit.
     [*Prov. 12:4 V.—**corōna, -ae,** f., *a crown.*—**putrēdō, -inis,** f., *rottenness; festering.* Supply *ea est.*—**os, ossis,** n., *a bone.*—**cōnfūsiō, -ōnis,** f., *disorder.*—**dignus, -a, -um,** *worthy, worthy of* (+ abl.).] M/A

1b. Mulier dīligēns corōna est virō suō, et quasi putrēdō in ossibus eius quae est inhonesta.
     [*Prov. 12:4 NV.—**quasi,** adv., *as if, as it were.*—**inhonestus, -a, -um,** *disgraceful.*] I/M

2. Audīvimus superbiam Mōab, superbus est valdē. Superbia eius et arrogantia eius et indignātiō eius plūs quam fortitūdō eius.

    [*Is. 16:6 V, in Lēctiōne II, Fēria quārta, Ad Mātūtīnum, Infrā hedomadam II Adventūs, BR 1.25.—**superbia, -ae,** f., *pride.*—**Mōab,** indecl. Heb. name, m., *Moab.*—**valdē,** adv., *exceedingly.*—**arrogantia, -ae,** f., *arrogance.*—**indignātiō, -ōnis,** f., *indignation.*—**fortitūdō, -dinis,** f., *strength.*] I

3. Et redūcam captīvitātem Aegyptī, et collocābō eōs in terrā nātīvitātis suae, et erunt ibi in rēgnum humile. Inter cētera rēgna erit humillima, et nōn ēlevābitur ultrā super nātiōnēs.

    [Ezek. 29:14, 15 V, prophesying the restoration of Egypt as a humble kingdom.—**redūcō, -ere,** *lead* or *bring back.*—**captīvitās, -tātis,** f., *captivity.*—**Aegyptus, -ī,** f., *Egypt.*—**collocō** (1), *gather together* (in a place).—**nātīvitās, -tātis,** f., *birth.*—**in,** here = *for, as.*—**ēlevō** (1), *raise up.*—**ultrā,** adv., *anymore.*—**nātiō, -ōnis,** f., *nation.*] I

4. Simile est rēgnum caelōrum fermentō, quod acceptum mulier abscondit in farīnae satis tribus, dōnec fermentātum est tōtum.

    [*Mt. 13:33 V.—**fermentum, -ī,** n., *yeast.*—**abscondō, -ere, -dī,** *conceal, hide.*—**farīna, -ae,** f., *flour.*—**satum, -ī,** n., *a Hebrew measure.*—**fermentō** (1), (act.) *to cause to rise* or *ferment*; (pass.) *to rise, ferment.*] I/M

5. Respondit Iēsūs et dīxit eī, "Quia dīxī tibi, 'Vīdī tē sub fīcū,' crēdis. Maius hīs vidēbis."

    [*Jn. 1:50 V, Christ Jesus to Nathanael.—**respondeō, -ēre, -dī,** *answer.*—**fīcus, -ūs,** f., *a fig tree.*—**crēdō, -ere,** *believe.*] I

6. Et signum magnum appāruit in caelō: mulier amicta sōle et lūna sub pedibus eius, et in capite eius corōna stēllārum duodecim.

    [*Apoc. 12:1 V.—**appāreō, -ēre, -ruī,** *appear.*—**amiciō, -īre, -cuī, -ctum,** *wrap in, clothe.*—**lūna, -ae,** f., *moon.*—**pēs, pedis,** m., *foot.*—**stēlla, -ae,** f., *star; planet.*—**duodecim,** indecl. adj., *twelve.*] I

7. Servitūs autem est cōnstitūtiō iūris gentium, quā quis dominiō aliēnō contrā nātūram subicitur.

    [*Tribonian, Theophilus, and Dorotheus, *Imperātōris Iūstiniānī Īnstitūtiōnēs* 1.3.2.—**cōnstitūtiō, -ōnis,** f., *an arrangement.*—**quis,** m. nom. sg. indef. pron., used regularly in a rel. clause instead of *aliquis* (GL, § 315), = *someone*.—**dominium, -iī,** n., *rule, ownership.*—**aliēnus, -a, -um,** *belonging to another person.*—**subiciō, -ere,** *make subject, subject.*] I

8.   Dē beātō pāpā Gregoriō nōs convenit, quia nostram, id est, Anglōrum, gentem dē potestāte Satanae ad fidem Chrīstī suā industriā convertit, lātiōrem in nostrā *Historiā Ecclēsiasticā* facere sermōnem, quem rēctē nostrum appellāre possumus et dēbēmus apostolum.

    [St. Bede the Venerable, *Historia Ecclēsiastica* 2.1.—**pāpa, -ae,** m., *a pope.*—**Gregorius, -iī,** m., *Gregory* the Great.—**convenit,** impers. verb, = *it is fitting* (+ inf. with acc. subject).—**Anglī, -ōrum,** m., *the Angles; the English.*—**potestās, -tātis,** f., *power.*—**Satanas, -ae,** m., *Satan.*—**industria, -ae,** f., *activity, assiduity.*—**convertō, -ere, -vertī,** *cause to turn around, convert.*—**lātus, -a, -um,** *broad, wide, extensive.*—**historia, -ae,** f., *history.*—**rēctē,** adv., *rightly.*—**apostolus, -ī,** m., *apostle.*] M/A

9.   Dēlectābat Hēraldum vīta inimīcī Alverādī, gravior morte.

    [William of Poitiers, *Gesta Guillelmī* 1.3, Harold takes delight in the blinding of his rival.—**Hēraldus, -ī,** m., *Harold* I Harefoot, king of England, 1035–1040.—**inimīcus, -ī,** m., (personal) *enemy.*—**Alverādus, -ī,** m., *Alfred,* son of Harold's father's first wife's first marriage.—**morte,** take as an ablative of comparison.] A

10.   Convincitur ergō etiam insipiēns esse vel in intellēctū aliquid quō nihil maius cogitārī potest, quia hoc cum audit intellegit, et quidquid intellegitur in intellēctū est. Et certē id quō maius cogitārī nequit nōn potest esse in sōlō intellēctū. Sī enim vel in sōlō intellēctū est, potest cogitārī esse et in rē, quod maius est. Sī ergō id quō maius cogitārī nōn potest est in sōlō intellēctū, id ipsum quō maius cogitārī nōn potest est quō maius cogitārī potest. Sed certē hoc esse nōn potest. Exsistit ergō procul dubiō aliquid quō maius cogitārī nōn valet et in intellēctū et in rē.

    [*St. Anselm of Canterbury, *Proslogion* 2.—**convincō, -ere,** *convict; convince.*—**insipiēns, -entis,** *a foolish person.*—**vel,** adv., *assuredly; even.*—**intellēctus, -ūs,** m., *reason, intellect.*—**certē,** adv., *certainly.*—**nequeō, -īre,** *be unable.*—**exsistō, -ere,** *come forth, appear; exist.*—**procul dubiō,** *without a doubt.*] A

11. Trēs quippe sunt hominum ōrdinēs, vidēlicet ōrāntēs, agricultōrēs, dēfēnsōres. Hōs autem ōrdinēs sīc ad dīversa Deus officia in hōc mundō disposuit, quōmodo quīdam paterfamiliās ovēs et bovēs canēsque maximōs suā in domō distribuit.

    [*St. Anselm of Canterbury, *Dē hūmānīs mōribus* 127.—**quippe,** adv., *indeed.*—**ōrdō, -dinis,** m., *order, rank.*—**vidēlicet,** adv., *namely.*—**ōrō** (1), *pray.*—**agricultor, -ōris,** m., *a husbandman.*—**dēfēnsor, -ōris,** m., *a defender, guardian.*—**sīc,** adv., *so.*—**dīversus, -a, -um,** *different.*—**dispōnō, -ere, -posuī,** *distribute, set in order.*—**quōmodo,** adv., here = *even as,* correl. with *sīc.*—**paterfamiliās, patrisfamiliās,** m., *a father of a family, head of a house, proprietor of an estate. Familiās is an archaic first decl. gen. sg.*—**ovis, ovis,** f., *a sheep.*—**bōs, bovis,** m./f., *a bull, ox, cow.*—**canis, -is,** m./f., *a dog, bitch.*—**domus, -ī,** f., *a house.*—**distribuō, -ere,** *divide, distribute.*] M/A

12. Profectō diī plūrēs nōn sunt, quia nequeunt plūra prīncipia.

    [*Marsilio Ficino, *Theologia Platōnica* 2.2.1.—**profectō,** adv., *truly, indeed.*] M

13. Deus enim summus summa est ūnitās.

    [*Marsilio Ficino, *Theologia Platōnica* 4.1.9.—**ūnitās, -tātis,** f., *unity.*] I/M

14. Magis valet homō propter id quod est, quam propter id quod habet.

    [*Gaudium et Spēs,* no. 35, Officium Lēctiōnis, Hebdomada IV per annum, Lēctiō Altera, LH 4.124–125.—**magis,** adv., *more, rather.*—**valet,** here = *is worth* or *means/signifies.*] M

15. Oeconomia hodierna, nōn secus atque aliae vītae sociālis prōvinciae, crēscentī super nātūram hominis dominātiōne notātur, densiōribus impensiōribusque relātiōnibus atque mūtuā dēpendentiā, inter cīvēs, coetūs, et populōs, necnōn frequentiōrī polīticae potestātis interventiōne.

    [*Gaudium et Spēs,* no. 63, CDD, p. 783.—**oeconomia, -ae,** f., *the economy.*—**hodiernus, -a, -um,** *of today, today's.*—**secus atque,** *otherwise than, differently from.*—**aliae . . . prōvinciae,** take as nom. pl.—**sociālis, -is,** *social.*—**prōvincia, -ae,** f., *sphere of duty* or *activity.*—**crēscō, -ere,** *increase.*—**dominātiō, -ōnis,** f., *mastery, unrestricted power, absolute dominion.*—**notō** (1), *mark.*—**densus, -a, -um,** *thick, dense.*—**impensus, -a, -um,** *ample, considerable, great.*—**relātiō, -ōnis,** f., *a reference, relation,* *proportion.*—**mūtuus, -a, -um,** *reciprocal, mutual.*—**dēpendentia, -ae,** f., *dependence.*—**coetus, -ūs,** m., *an assemblage of persons, group.*—**necnōn,** adv., *nor not,* but as an example of litotes (Smith, 102-103), = *and also, and indeed.*—**frequēns, -entis,** *repeated, frequent, constant.*—**polīticus, -a, -um,** *political.*—**potestās, -tātis,** f., *power.*—**interventiō, -ōnis,** f., *intervention.*] A

This is a drawing of the seal of St. Anselm of Canterbury (c. 1033–1109). The inscription says, "Sigillum Anselmi grātiā Deī archiepīscopī." Note his pallium, the white woolen yoke with long pendant, worn over his chasuble, which symbolized his metropolitan authority, i.e., his participation in papal authority in his own ecclesiastical province. Even today, the Anglican archbishop of Canterbury is called the Primate of All England. Anselm was a Lombard, who became a monk at the Benedictine monastery of Bec in Normandy. He became prior and then abbot, but was nominated as archbishop of Canterbury in 1093 by King William II. Anselm was a great philosopher-theologian—there was as yet no formal distinction between the disciplines—and sentences from his works are included in this volume. (© Wikimedia Commons)

CAPVT XXVIII

Subjunctive Mood; Present Subjunctive; Jussive and Purpose Clauses; **Future Imperative; Hortatory Subjunctive; Infinitive of Purpose in EL**

Syntaxis Supplēmentum

Future Imperative. In addition to the present or first imperative, Latin also has a future or second imperative. The future imperative occurs in both second and third persons. The following chart shows the endings.

	ACTIVE	PASSIVE
SINGULAR		
2nd person	-tō	-tor
3rd person	-tō	-tor
PLURAL		
2nd person	-tote	—
3rd person	-ntō	-ntor

The future imperative "looks forward to contingent fulfilment . . . and is used chiefly in laws, legal documents, maxims, recipes, and the like; likewise in familiar language" (GL 268.2). It can be translated *you shall, he shall,* etc. Certain verbs have only the future imperative, e.g., *scītō,* know, from *scīre.*

Hortatory Subjunctive. The jussive subjunctive, when in the first person, is sometimes called the hortatory subjunctive. These two uses of the subjunctive belong to the optative subjunctive or subjunctive of wish (negative *nē*). See further Capvt XXIX Syntaxis.

Infinitive of Purpose. Although the Roman poets had sometimes used an infinitive to express purpose instead of *ut* plus the subjunctive or some other construction, EL extended the usage on the model of Greek, e.g., *vēnimus adōrāre eum*, we have come to worship him (Mt. 2:2). See PW, §§ 50(a) and 127(7).

VERBA MEMORIĀ COMPREHENDENDA

misericordia, -ae, f., *mercy, pity*

saeculum, -ī, n., *a race, breed; an ordinary lifetime, a generation; a maximum lifetime, a century; an indefinitely long time, an age*

SENTENTIAE Ē FONTIBUS NŌN ANTĪQUĪS HAUSTAE

1. Nōn auferētur scēptrum dē Iūda, et dux dē femore eius, dōnec veniat quī mittendus est, et ipse erit exspectātiō gentium.

    [*Gen. 49:10 V, Capitulum, Ad Vesperās, Ōrdinārium dīvīnī Officiī, Tempore Adventūs, BR 1.(23).—**auferētur,** third pers. pl. fut. ind. pass. of **auferō, -ferre,** = *will be taken away.*—**scēptrum, -ī,** n., *sceptre.*—**Iūda,** indecl. Heb. name, or **Iūdas, -ae,** m., *Judah.*— **femur, -moris,** n., *the upper part of the thigh; loins.* —**mittendus,** see Appendix I, § 60.—**exspectātiō, -ōnis,** f., *expectation.*] I/M

2. Dīxit Dominus Dominō meō, "Sedē ā dextrīs meīs, dōnec pōnam inimīcōs tuōs scabellum pedum tuōrum."

    [Ps. 109:1 PIB, Dominica ad Vesperās, BR 2.395.—**sedeō, -ēre,** *sit.*—**ā,** here = *at.*—**scabellum, -ī,** n., *a footstool.* See Capvt II Syntaxis.—**pēs, pedis,** m., *a foot.*] I/M

3. Cōnstāns est cor eius, nōn timēbit, dōnec cōnfūsōs videat adversāriōs suōs.

    [Ps. 111:8 PIB, Dominica ad Vesperās, BR 2.396.—**cōnstāns, -ntis,** *steadfast, firm.*—**cōnfundō, -ere, -fūdī, -fūsum,** *confuse, bewilder.*—**adversārius, -iī,** m., *an opponent, adversary.*] I

4. V. Domine, exaudī ōrātiōnem meam. R. Et clāmor meus ad tē veniat. V. Benedīcāmus Dominō. R. Deō grātiās. V. Fidēlium animae per misericordiam Deī requiēscant in pāce. R. Āmēn.

    [*Conclusiō Laudum, Ōrdinārium dīvīnī Officiī, BR (8).—**V.** = **versiculum, -ī,** n., *versicle.*—**exaudiō, -īre,** *hear, heed.*—**ōrātiō, -ōnis,** f., *prayer.*—**R.** = **respōnsum, -ī,** n., *response.*—**clāmor, -ōris,** m., *cry.*—**requiēscō, -ere,** *rest.*] I/M

5.   Excitā, quaesumus, Domine, potentiam tuam, et venī: et magnā nōbīs
      virtūte succurre; ut per auxilium grātiae tuae, quod nostra peccāta
      praepediunt, indulgentia tuae propitiātiōnis acceleret, quī vīvis et
      rēgnās cum Deō Patre in ūnitāte Spīritūs Sānctī, Deus, per omnia
      saecula saeculōrum.
         [*Ōrātiō, Dominica IV Adventūs, BR 1.50.—**excitō** (1), *rouse
      up; arouse.*—**quaesumus,** archaic first pers. pl. pres. ind. act.
      of **quaerō,** used, as here, in supplications.—**potentia, -ae,** f.,
      power.—**succurrō, -ere,** *run up under; help, succour.*—**auxilium,
      -iī,** n., *help, aid.*—**praepediō, -īre,** *entangle the feet; shackle;
      hinder.*—**indulgentia, -ae,** f., *kindness; gentleness.*—**propitiātiō,
      -ōnis,** f., *atonement; propitiation.*—**accelerō** (1), *hasten; make
      haste.*—**rēgnō** (1), *reign.*—**ūnitās, -tātis,** f., *unity.*] M/A

6.   Quod enim dē tuā glōriā, revēlante tē, crēdimus, hoc dē Fīliō tuō,
      hoc dē Spīritū Sānctō, sine differentiā discrētiōnis sentīmus, ut in
      cōnfessiōne vērae sempiternaeque Deitātis, et in persōnīs proprietās,
      et in essentiā ūnitas, et in māiestāte adōrētur aequālitās.
         [*Praefātiō dē Sānctissimā Trinitāte, MR, p. 245 (329).—**revēlō** (1),
      unveil, uncover, lay bare.—**differentia, -ae,** f., *difference, distinction.*—
      discrētio, -ōnis, f., *separation; difference, distinction; discernment,
      discrimination.*—**cōnfessiō, -ōnis,** f., *a confession, acknowledgement;
      praise.*—**sempiternus, -a, -um,** *continual, everlasting.*—**deitās,
      -tātis,** f., *the divine nature, deity.*—**persōna, -ae,** f., *a person.*—
      proprietās, -tātis, f., *a property, peculiarity, peculiar nature* or *quality
      of a thing.*—**essentia, -ae,** f., "the being or essence of a thing; trans.
      of the Gr. οὐσία" (LS).—**ūnitās, -tātis,** f., *unity.*—**māiestās, -tātis,**
      f., *greatness, dignity, majesty.*—**adōrō** (1), *entreat* (a deity); *honor,
      reverence, worship.*—**aequālitās, -tātis,** f., *equality.*] A

7.   Deus, ā quō bona cūncta prōcēdunt, tuīs largīre supplicibus, ut
      cōgitēmus, tē īnspīrante, quae rēcta sunt, et, tē gubernante, eadem
      faciāmus. Per Dominum nostrum.
         [*Ōrātiō 10 dominicālis et cotīdiāna, LH 3.30.—**prōcēdō, -ere,**
      go forth, proceed.—**largīre,** depon. second pers. sing. impera.,
      = *give* or *grant abundantly.*—**supplex, -icis,** m., *a suppliant.*—
      īnspīrō (1), *breathe upon* or *into; inspire.*—**gubernō** (1), *steer a
      ship; direct, govern.*] M/A

8.   Sed tē laudet anima mea, ut amet tē.
         [St. Augustine of Hippo, *Cōnfessiōnēs* 5.1.] M

9. Haec autem, ut crēdantur, vetus et nova īnfōrmat īnstructiō.
   [*Boethius, *Dē fidē catholicā* 29–30.—**haec,** = the generation
   of the Son and the procession of the Holy Spirit.—**crēdō,**
   -ere, *believe.*—**vetus, -teris,** *old.*—**īnfōrmō** (1), *give form to;*
   represent, sketch.—**īnstructiō, -ōnis,** f., *instruction* (here =
   Testament).] M

10. Cūnctum tempus vītae in eiusdem monastēriī habitātiōne
    peragēns, omnem meditandīs Scrīptūrīs operam dedī atque, inter
    observāntiam disciplīnae rēgulāris et cōtīdiānam cantandī in
    ecclēsiā cūram, semper aut discere aut docēre aut scrībere dulce
    habuī.
    [St. Bede the Venerable, *Historia Ecclēsiatica* 5.24, giving
    some autobiographical details.—**monastērium, -iī,** n., *a*
    monastery.—**habitātiō, -ōnis,** f., *a dwelling,* whether the act or
    the place.—**peragō, -ere,** *complete.*— **meditandīs Scrīptūrīs,**
    = *to meditating on the Scriptures.*—**operam dare** = *pay attention*
    to (+ dat.).—**observantia, -ae,** f., (obedient) *observance* (of
    duties).—**disciplīna, -ae,** f., *teaching, discipline.*—**rēgulāris,**
    -e, *of* or *pertaining to the* (Benedictine) *rule.*—**cōtīdiānus, -a,**
    -um, *daily.*—**cantandī,** gen. gerund, = *of singing.*—**discere . . .**
    docēre . . . scrībere, object infinitives.—**dulce,** = pred. acc. or
    complem.] A

11. Flecte cervīcem diīs et estō sorōribus exemplum correctiōnis et causa
    līberātiōnis.
    [*Hrosvitha of Gandersheim, *Dulcitius* 1.5, a pagan magistrate
    tries to persuade a Christian to lapse.—**flectō, -ere,** *bend, bow.*—
    cervīx, -īcis, f., *neck.*—**estō,** fut. imperative of *sum.*—**exemplum,**
    -ī, n., *example, model.*—**correctiō, -ōnis,** f., *amendment,*
    improvement.—**līberātiō, -ōnis,** f., *liberation, release.*] M

12. Retribuat vōbīs Deus misericordiam, quam fēcistis sānctō fīliō vestrō
    Goduinō.
    [St. Bernard of Clairvaux, *Epistola* 65.1, thanking another abbot
    for forgiving Godwin's desertion to the Cistercians.—**retribuō,**
    -ere, *repay:* = *may [God] repay* (optative subjunctive: see Capvt
    XXIX).—**vōbīs,** a polite plural, as with the other second pers.
    pl. forms in this sentence. See Appendix I, § 6 N 4.—**Goduinus,**
    -ī, m., *Godwin.*] M

13. Quia ergō fēmina mortem īnstruxit, clāra virgō illam interēmit, et
ideō est summa benedictiō in fēmineā fōrmā prae omnī creātūrā,
quia Deus factus est homō in dulcissimā et beātā virgine.

    [*St. Hildegard of Bingen, *Quia ergō fēmina*, in *Symphonia*, 116,
a non-metrical antiphon to the Blessed Mother.—**īnstruō, -ere,
-struxī,** *build; set in battle array; prepare, equip.*—**interimō,
-ere, -ēmī,** *take away; destroy, annihilate.*—**ideō,** adv., *for that
reason, therefore.*—**benedictiō, -ōnis,** f., *a praising; a blessing.*—
fēmineus, -a, -um, *relating to a woman, female.*—**creātūra, -ae,**
f., *a creature; creation.*] I

14. Vēritās nōn modo aliud est quam mēns, sed et superius aliquid. Eget
quippe mēns vēritāte, vēritās mente nōn indiget. Ac lātius sē fundit
vēritātis quam mentis imperium.

    [*Marsilio Ficino, *Theologia Platōnica* 1.6.6.—**quippe,** adv.,
certainly, indeed.—**indigeō, -ēre,** *stand in need of* (+ abl.).—**lātus,
-a, -um,** *broad, wide.*—**fundō, -ere,** *pour, pour out.*] M/A

15. Nūlla salūtiferō sē comparet herba Tabācō, / vīribus hoc omnēs
exsuperat relīquās.

    [*Iōannes Posthius, *Tabācum.*—**salūtifer, -fera, -ferum,** *health-
bringing.*—**comparō** (1), *compare.*—**herba, -ae,** f., *a green plant,*
esp. *grass; a weed.*—**tabācum, -ī,** n., *tobacco.*—**vīribus,** see
Wheelock, 492–493.—**exsuperō** (1), *mount up, appear above;
excel, surpass.*—**reliquiae, -ārum,** f., *remains, remainder.*] A

16. Deus auctor pācis et amātor, quem nōsse vīvere, cuī servīre rēgnāre
est, protege ab omnī oppugnātiōne supplicēs tuōs, ut, quī in tuā
prōtectiōne cōnfīdimus, nūllīus hostīlitātis arma timeāmus. Per
Chrīstum Dominum nostrum.

    [*Collecta pro Pāce, Mātūtīnae Precēs, Liber Precum Pūblicārum
in Ecclēsia Anglicānā (1560).—**amātor, -ōris,** m., *a friend,
lover.*—**nōscō, -ere, nōvī,** *learn;* (in perf.) *know.* Note that *nōsse*
= *nōvisse.*—**serviō, -īre,** *be a slave to, serve* (+ dat.).—**rēgnō** (1),
be a king, reign.—**prōtegō, -ere,** *cover, protect.*—**oppugnātiō,
-ōnis,** f., *an assault.*—**supplex, -icis,** m., *a suppliant.*—**prōtectiō,
-ōnis,** f., *protection.*—**cōnfīdō, -ere,** *have confidence in, believe
confidently.*—**hostīlitās, -tātis,** f., *enmity, hostility.*] A

CAPVT XXIX

Imperfect Subjunctive; Present and Imperfect Subjunctive of *Sum* and *Possum*; Result Clauses; **Potential Subjunctive; Optative Subjunctive; Deliberative Subjunctive; Note on the Subjunctive**

Syntaxis Supplēmentum

Potential Subjunctive (Negative *Nōn*). The potential subjunctive is used when the speaker acknowledges that his statement is a matter of possibility, not of fact. "The tone varies from vague surmise to moral certainty, from 'may' and 'might' to 'must.'" [GL, § 257.1]. The present and perfect subjunctive are used when the speaker's statement may prove valid. The imperfect subjunctive is used when reference is to the past. In CL the imperfect is chiefly used in the "ideal second person, an imaginary "you.'" [GL, § 258]. The potential subjunctive is said to be rare in the Vulgate [Nunn, § 103]. But note, *Nōn habitent in terrā tuā*, they must not dwell in your land [Ex. 23:33].

Optative Subjunctive (Negative *Nē*). The term "optative subjunctive" is used both to name a category of subjunctive uses, and a specific use. Specifically, the optative subjunctive is used to express a wish. The present subjunctive (rarely the perfect) is used when the wish is possible of fulfilment. The imperfect and pluperfect subjunctive are used when the wish is impossible of fulfilment. *Utinam* (= How, pray?, but translated "if only," "would that"), *utinam nē*, and even *utinam nōn* frequently introduce the optative subjunctive in CL [GL, §§ 260–261]. However, *utinam* is frequently omitted in EL [Blaise, § 240]. *Israël, utinam audiās mē*. Israel, if only you would hear me (Ps. 80:9 NV, LH 3.750). The term "optative subjunctive" is also used to denominate a general category of subjunctive usages that express the intention or wish of the speaker. To this category belong also the deliberative, jussive, and hortatory uses of the subjunctive.

Deliberative Subjunctive (Negative *Nōn*). While the deliberative subjunctive belongs to the optative subjunctive, the negative is *nōn*, since this use of the subjunctive does not express the intention of the speaker, but asks a question about the intention the speaker should form, and expects an imperative answer [*Woodcock*, § 109 N ii]. The deliberative is usually employed in the first person singular, or when the subjunctive would have been originally in the first person (see Sentence 2 below), and is in the form of a question that expects an imperative answer. [GL § 265; cf. § 428 N 1]. *Quid faciam populō huic?* What am I to do for this people? (Ex. 17:4 V). EL often employs the future indicative instead of the subjunctive in this construction, e.g., *Quid faciēmus et nōs?* What are we also to do? (Lk. 3:14; cited in Nunn, § 102). The deliberative subjunctive is also used to pose rhetorical questions.

Note on the Subjunctive. The CL subjunctive is misnamed. It is, according to historical linguistics, descended from the PIE optative mood, and has many of the same functions as the Greek optative. The PIE subjunctive was co-opted in Latin and the other Italic languages to serve as the simple future tense. See Sihler, §§ 501, 537, 543.

Verba Memoriā Comprehendenda

aliquī, aliquae/aliqua, aliquod, indef. pronominal adj., *some*

utinam, adv., *if only, how I wish that, would that* (archaic), used sometimes to introduce the optative subjunctive

Sententiae ē Fontibus nōn Antīquīs Haustae

1. Tibi serviat omnis creātūra tua.
    [*Jud. 16:17 V.—**serviō, -īre,** *serve* (as a slave) (+ dat.).—**creātūra, -ae,** f., *a creature; creation.*] I/M

2. Quandō fundāmenta ēvertuntur, iūstus quid faciat?
    [*Ps. 10:3 NV, LH 3.580.—**fundāmentum, -ī,** n., *foundation.*—**ēvertō, -ere,** *turn upside down.*] I/M

3. Utinam populus meus audīret mē, Israël ambulāret in viīs meīs!
    [*Ps. 80:14 PIB).—**ambulō** (1), *walk.*] I/M

4. Utinam hodiē vōcem eius audiātis.
    [*Ps. 94:7 NV, Ad Invītātōrium, Ōrdinārium, LH 3.524.] I/M

5. Hodiē sī vōcem eius audieritis.
    [*Ps. 94:8 V.—*sī* + fut. pf., according to PW, § 124, means, "if
    ye *shall* (not *will*) hear his voice," and does not represent a wish,
    but is part of a command. PW say that the fut. pf. is used most
    frequently in the Vulgate in the protasis of a Future More Vivid
    either with a fut. or an imperative in the apodosis, as it is in this
    verse, though here it is incomplete.] M/A

6. Percutiat mē iūstus in misericordiā et increpet mē.
    [*Ps. 140:5 NV, Ad I Vesperās, Dominica, Hebdomada I, LH
    3.546.—**percutiō, -ere,** *strike hard.*—**increpō, -āre,** *make a loud
    noise; make a loud protest* (against a person), *rebuke.*] I/M

7. Rēgnāvit Dominus Deus noster omnipotēns. Gaudeāmus et
    exsultēmus et dēmus glōriam eī.
    [*Apoc. 19:6b–7a V, LH 3.800.—**rēgnō** (1), *reign, hold sway.*—
    omnipotēns, -tentis, *all-powerful.*—**exsultō** (1), *jump around;
    exult.*] I/M

8. Nōtam fac mihi viam in quā ambulem.
    [*Respōnsōrium breve, Ad Laudēs mātūtīnās, Fēria VI,
    Hebdomada III, LH 3.891.—**nōtus, -a, -um,** *known.*—**in quā
    ambulem,** = *in order that I may walk in it,* a rel. clause of purpose:
    see Capvt XXXIV Syntaxis.] M

9. Dā nōbīs ita vīvere ut per societātem passiōnum ipsīus virtūtem
    resurrectiōnis consequī valeāmus.
    [Ōrātiō, Ad Vesperās, Fēria VI, Hebdomada III, LH 3.900.—
    societās, -tātis, f., *an association, fellowship.*—**passiō, -ōnis,** f.,
    suffering.—**resurrectiō, -ōnis,** f., *resurrection.*—**cōnsequor,
    -sequī,** depon., having pass. forms with act. meanings, here =
    to obtain.] M

10. Tū excitās [hominem], ut laudāre tē [eum] dēlectet, quia fēcistī nōs
    ad tē et inquiētum est cor nostrum, dōnec requiēscat in tē.
    [*St. Augustine of Hippo, *Cōnfessiōnēs* 1.1.—**excitō** (1), *rouse
    up; arouse.*—**inquiētus, -a, -um,** *unquiet, restless.*—**dōnec** +
    subjunctive, as in CL, must here imply purpose, intention, or
    futurity.—**requiēscō, -ere,** *rest.*] M

11.   Est ergō in nōbīs, ut ita dīcam, docta ignōrantia, sed docta Spīritū
       Deī quī adiuvat īnfīrmitātem nostram.
       [*St. Augustine of Hippo, *Epistola* 130.15.28 (ad Probam), on
       prayer.—**ignōrantia, -ae**, f., *want of knowledge, ignorance.*—**ut ita
       dīcam,** = *so to speak.*—**īnfīrmitās, -tātis,** f., *weakness, infirmity.*] I/M

12.   Admonitī sumus cantāre Dominō canticum novum. Homō novus
       canticum novum. Canticum rēs est hilaritātis, et, sī dīligentius
       cōnsiderēmus, rēs est amōris. Quī ergō nōvit novam vītam amāre,
       nōvit canticum novum cantāre.
       [*St. Augustine of Hippo, *Sermō* 34.1, in LH 2.558.—**admoneō,**
       = *moneō.*—**cantō** (1), *sing.*—**canticum, -ī,** n., *a song.*—**hilaritās,
       -tātis,** f., *cheerfulness, mirth.*—**dīligentius,** here = compar. adv.,
       which has the same form as the n. acc. sg. compar. adj.—**considerō**
       (1), *consider, reflect.* The subjunctive suggests *should reflect.*] I/M

13.   Sacrāmentum est in aliquā celebrātiōne, cum rēs gesta ita fit ut aliquid
       significāre intellegātur, quod sānctē accipiendum est.
       [*St. Isidore of Seville, *Etymologiae* 6.19.39.—**celebrātiō, -ōnis,**
       f., *a large gathering; festival; celebration.*—**cum,** conj., *when.*—**fit,**
       third pers. sg. pres. ind. of **fīō, fierī,** = *happens.*—**significō** (1),
       indicate, signify.—**sānctē,** adv., *solemnly, religiously.*] M

14.   Anima est fōrma ita simplex atque ita lībera, ut neque ex plūribus
       partibus compōnātur, neque ex matēriae visceribus ēruātur.
       [*Marsilio Ficino, *Theologica Platōnica* 5.13.2.—**simplex, -icis,**
       simple.—**compōnō, -ere,** *put together, compose.*—**matēria, -ae,**
       f., *matter.*—**viscus, -eris,** usu. pl., **viscera, -um,** n., *the internal
       organs; the inmost part.*—**ēruō, -ruere,** *tear out, dig up.*] M

15.   Āiunt enim sīlēnōs imāgunculās quāspiam fuisse sectilēs, et ita
       factās, ut dīdūcī et explicārī possent, et quae clausae rīdiculam ac
       mōnstrōsam tībīcinis speciem habēbant, apertae subitō nūmen
       ostendēbant, ut artem scalptōris grātiōrem iocōsus faceret errōr.
       [*Desiderius Erasmus, *Adagia* 3.3.1., explaining the origin of the
       adage *Sīlēnī Alcibiadis.*—**Sīlēnī, -ōrum,** m., *satyrs; also a type of
       ancient curio.*—**imāguncula, -ae,** f., *a little image.*—**quispiam,
       quaepiam, quodpiam,** *anyone, anything; someone, something,
       some.*—**sectilis, -e,** *cut, cleft, divided.*—**dīdūcō, -ere,** *draw apart,
       split, separate.*—**explicō** (1), *unfold, spread out.*—**claudō, -ere,
       clausī, clausum,** *close, shut.*—**rīdiculus, -a, -um,** *laughable.*—
       mōnstrōsus, -a, -um, *strange, monstrous.*—**tībīcen, -inis,** m., *a*

piper, oboist.—**speciēs, -ēī,** f., *outward appearance; shape, form, figure.*—**aperiō, -īre, aperuī, apertum,** *uncover; open.*—**subitō,** adv., *suddenly.*—**nūmen, -inis,** n., *a deity, god.*—**scalptōr, -ōris,** m., *a cutter, carver.*—**grātus, -a, -um,** *pleasing, agreeable.*—**iocōsus, -a, -um,** *humorous, droll.*—**errōr, -ōris,** m., *a mistake.*] A

Desiderius Erasmus of Rotterdam (1466/9–1536) was the great-est humanist of his generation, and perhaps of all time. His Latin style was elegant, yet vigorous, his reading complete both in Latin and Greek. His piety was genuine, but filtered through a scintillating wit. He worked for reform within the Church, yet strove mightily against the Protestant Martin Luther on the subject of good works. His editions of classical authors were widely used, as was his edition of the New Testament. His vast collection of proverbs, the *Adagia,* was a masterpiece of erudition and moral commentary. Some of the articles were really essays on the problems of his day. Several of the adages can be read in this volume. This portrait, painted in 1523, is by Hans Holbein the Younger (c. 1497–1543). Holbein also painted a portrait of Erasmus' friend St. Sir Thomas More. (© Wikimedia Commons)

CAPVT XXX

Perfect and Pluperfect Subjunctive; Indirect Questions; Sequence of Tenses; **Retained Indicative in Indirect Questions in EL; Subordinate Clauses in Indirect Statement;** *Futūrum Esse (Fore)* **Ut + Subjunctive;** *Quod***-Clause of Alleged Reason**

Syntaxis Supplēmentum

Retained Indicative in Indirect Questions. EL frequently employs the indicative instead of the subjunctive in indirect questions, e.g., *Discite quid est*, learn what it is (Mt. 9:13 V; cited at PW § 135).

Subordinate Clauses in Indirect Statement. In CL, the verb in a subordinate clause in indirect statement routinely appears in the subjunctive, even when it would have been in the indicative in direct statement. This is a usage of the potential subjunctive, and it indicates that the speaker is merely reporting an assertion, not vouching for it himself. See *Wheelock*, Appendix, 493–494; cf. *Woodcock*, § 272. This distinction is not always observed in EL.

Futūrum Esse (Fore) Ut **+ Subjunctive.** Latin speakers preferred a circumlocution to the future passive infinitive, which properly was expressed by the supine + *īrī*. This circumlocution was composed of the future active infinitive used impersonally, i.e., *futūrum esse* or its alternative *fore*, and a consecutive or result clause. See Capvt XXXV, Sentence 18, for an example.

Quod-Clause of Alleged Reason. The potential subjunctive can also be used in a causal clause to show that the reason given is not given on the speaker's authority, but is merely reported. This use is related to the usage in indirect statement mentioned above. See Sentence 8 below.

VERBA MEMORIĀ COMPREHENDENDA

Chrīstiānus, -a, -um, *Christian*

paenitentia, -ae, or poenitentia, -ae, f., *change of mind; repentance; penance.* For the idiom *paenitentiam agere*, see Capvt VIII, Sentence 5.

SENTENTIAE Ē FONTIBUS NŌN ANTĪQUĪS HAUSTAE

1. Invēnitque eum vir errantem in agrō, et interrogāvit quid quaereret.
   [*Gen. 37:15 V, a man finds Joseph looking for his brothers.—
   interrogō (1), *ask.*] I/M

2. Et āit rēx, "Interrogā tū, cuius fīlius sit iste puer."
   [*I Sam. 17:56 V, Saul asks about David.] I

3. Tobīas respondit, "Rogō tē, dē quā domō aut dē quā tribū es tū?"
   [Tob. 5:16 V, Tobit speaks with Raphael.—Tobīas, -ae, m.,
   Tobit.—rogō (1), *ask.*—domus, -ī, f., *a house.*—tribus, -ūs, f.,
   a tribe.] I

4. Et apprehēnsā manū caecī, ēdūxit eum extrā vīcum, et exspuēns in
   oculōs eius, impositīs manibus suīs, interrogāvit sī quid vidēret.
   [*Mk. 8:23 V.—apprehendō, -ere, -hendī, -hēnsum, *lay hold of,
   seize.*—ēdūcō, -ere, -dūxī, *lead out.*—extrā, prep. + acc., *outside.*—
   vīcus, -ī, m., *village.*—exspuō, -uere, *spit out.*—impōnō, -ere,
   -posuī, -positum, *put upon; impose.*—sī, here = *whether.*] M

5. Paenitentiam itaque age ab hāc nēquitiā tuā, et rogā Deum, sī forte
   remittātur tibi haec cōgitātiō cordis tuī.
   [*Acts 8:22 V.—ab, here = *for, because of.* See PW, § 117.A, *A,
   ab.*—nēquitia, -ae, f., *a bad moral quality of any sort; wickedness.*—
   forte, adv., *by chance.*—remittō, -ere, *send back; remit; forgive.*—
   cōgitātiō, -ōnis, f., *a thought; plan.*] M

6. Ūtile itaque est in immaculātā ūnitāte vōs esse, ut et semper
   participētis Deō.
   [*St. Ignatius of Antioch, *Epistola ad Ephesiōs* 5.2, Lēctiō
   Altera, Ad Officium Lēctiōnis, Dominica II per annum, LH

3.57.—**immaculātus, -a, -um,** *unstained.*—**ūnitās, -tātis,** f., *unity.*—**participō** (1), + abl. = *share in, partake of.*] M

7. Quod est in corpore anima, hoc sunt in mundō Chrīstiānī.
[*Epistola ad Diognētum* 6, in LH 2.659.] I

8. Flēre omnēs, ipsa sine flētū. Mīrārī plērīque quod tam facile vītae suae prōdiga, quam nōndum hauserat, iam quasi perfuncta dōnāret. Stupēre ūniversī quod iam Dīvīnitātis testis exsisteret, quae adhūc arbitra suī per aetātem esse nōn posset.
[*St. Ambrose of Milan, Dē Virginibus 1.2.8, speaking of the martyrdom of St. Agnes.—**fleō, -ēre,** weep. Note the historical infinitives here and below. See Capvt XXVII Syntaxis.—**flētus, -ūs,** m., weeping, tears.—**mīror, -ārī,** depon. verb, having pass. forms with act. meanings, wonder, marvel at.—**plērīque, -raeque, -raque,** the majority, most.—**prōdigus, -a, -um,** wasteful.— **nōndum,** adv., not yet.—**hauriō, -īre,** drink.—**quasi,** adv. or conj., as if.—**perfunctus, -a, -um,** performed, accomplished.—**dōnō, -āre,** give; sacrifice.—**stupeō, -ēre,** be astonished.—**ūniversus, -a, -um,** altogether.—**dīvīnitās, -tātis,** f., divinity.—**testis, -tis,** m./f., a witness.—**exsistō, -ere,** emerge, appear.—**adhūc,** adv., till now.—**arbitra, -ae,** f., a witness.] A*

9. ADEŌDATUS TO AUGUSTINE. "Quōmodo istud [argūmentum] sit, nōn intellegō."
[*St. Augustine of Hippo, Dē magistrō 5.12.—**Quōmodo,** adv., how? in what way?] I/M*

10. Deus hanc āvertat āmentiam!
[*St. Augustine of Hippo, Dē magistrō 9.28.—**āmentia, -ae,** f., madness; stupidity.] I*

11. Vērissima quippe ratiō est et vērissimē dīcitur, cum verba proferuntur, aut scīre nōs quid significent aut nescīre; sī scīmus, [nōs] commemorārī potius quam discere; sī autem nescīmus, nē commemorārī quidem, sed fortasse ad quaerendum admonērī.
[*St. Augustine of Hippo, Dē magistrō 11.36, Augustine speaks of the usefulness of words.—**quippe,** adv., indeed.—**ratiō,** here perh. = account, explanation.—**vērissimē,** superl. adv., very truly.— **prōferuntur,** = (they) are brought forth.—**significō** (1), mean.— **commemorō** (1), remind.—**potius,** adv., rather.—**fortasse,** adv., perhaps.—**ad quaerendum,** a gerund with ad expressing purpose, = to seek.—**admoneō** = moneō.] A*

12. Aeternitās igitur est interminābilis vītae tōta simul et perfecta possessiō.
     [*Boethius, *Cōnsōlātiō philosophiae* 5.6.—**aeternitās, -tātis,** f.,
     eternity.—**interminābilis, -e,** *endless.*—**simul et,** conj., *and also.*—
     perfectus, -a, -um, *complete.*—**possessiō, -ōnis,** f., *possession.*] M

13. Ovēs ergō eius pascua inveniunt, quia quisquis illum [i.e., Iēsūm]
     corde simplicī sequitur, aeternae viriditātis pābulō nūtrītur. Quae
     autem sunt istārum ovium pascua, nisi interna gaudia semper virentis
     paradīsī? Pascua namque ēlēctōrum sunt vultus praesēns Deī. Quī,
     dum sine dēfectū conspicitur, sine fīne mēns vītae cibō satiātur.
     [*Pope St. Gregory the Great, *Homilia* 14.3–6, in LH 2.592.—**ovis,**
     -is, f., *a sheep.*—**pascuus, -iī,** n., *a pasture.*—**simplex, -icis,** *simple,*
     unaffected.—**viriditās, -tātis,** f., *greenness; freshness.*—**pābulum,**
     -ī, n., *food; fodder.*—**nūtriō, -īre,** *nourish.*—**internus, -a, -um,**
     internal, inward.—**virēns, -entis,** *green; fresh.*—**paradīsus, -ī,**
     m., *a park; paradise.*—**ēlēctus, -a, -um,** *chosen.*— **vultus, -ūs,** m.,
     a face.—**praesēns, -entis,** *present.*—**dēfectus, -ūs,** m., *a failing,*
     ceasing.—**cōnspiciō, -ere,** *behold.*—**cibus, -ī,** m., *food.*] I/M

14. Duplex est autem homō: interior et exterior. Interior homō anima,
     et exterior homō corpus.
     [*St. Isidore of Seville, *Etymologiae* 11.1.6.—**duplex, -icis,** *double,*
     two-fold.—**interior, -ius,** *inner, interior.*—**exterior, -ius,** *outer,*
     exterior.] I

15. Tum Brettōnēs confitentur quidem intellexisse sē vēram esse viam
     iūstitiae quam praedicāret Augustīnus.
     [*St. Bede the Venerable, *Historia Ecclēsiastica* 2.2, the response of
     the British bishops to a miracle of St. Augustine of Canterbury's.—
     Brettō, -ōnis, m., *a Briton.*—**cōnfitentur,** depon., having pass.
     forms with act. meanings, = *(they) confess*; but here an historical
     pres., so = *(they) confessed.*—**praedicō** (1), *proclaim, preach.*] M/A

16. Ego Soror Adeleia dō terram dē Bellōmonte, quae mea probātur esse
     iūre hērēditāriō, favente virō Giraldō Boctoy, ecclēsiae Villarensis
     Monastēriī, ubi vōtum habeō convertī, et hoc per manum comitis
     Normannōrum Guillelmī, cuius est hoc signum + . Testibus hīs,
     Guillelmō fīliō Osbernī, Guillelmō Maleth.
     [*Carta Guillelmī Normannōrum Comitis, Fauroux, no. 173,
     p. 361.—**Adeleia, -ae,** f., *Adeleia.*—**terra,** here = *an estate,*
     property (see LLMA, s.v.).—**dē,** note the locative sense.—**Bellus**
     Mōns, Bellī Montis, m. = *Beaumont-le-Roger.*—**probō,** here =

prove.—**hērēditārius, -a, -um,** *hereditary.*—**faveō, -ēre,** *be favorable to, support.*—**Giraldus, -ī,** m., *Gerald.*—**Boctoy,** indecl. name.—**ecclēsia, ae,** f., here = *the monks or nuns* of a monastery taken as a group (see LLMA, s.v.).—**Villarense Monastērium, -sis, -iī,** n., *the Abbey of Montivilliers,* one of Count Robert I's foundations of Benedictine nuns.[14]—**vōveō, -ēre, vōvī, vōtum,** *vow* (+ inf., see Latham, s.v. "vot-").—**convertor, -ī,** *embrace the monastic life* (see LLMA, s.v. "converto").—**ubi vōtum habeō convertī,** = *where I have vowed to embrace the monastic life.* See Blaise, § 219, for the use of *habēre* with the acc. perf. pass. part. as a periphrastic perf. act., the origin of the French *passé composé.* See also Appendix I, § 48.—**comes, -itis,** m., *a count.*—**Normannus, -ī,** m., *a Norman.*—**Guillelmus, -ī,** m., *William* the Bastard and Conqueror.—**testis, -is,** m./f., *a witness.*—**Osbernus, -ī,** m., *Osbern* fitz Arfast, nephew of Gunnor, wife of Count Richard I of Normandy. He held the office of ducal *dapifer* or steward, held after him also by his son, William fitz Osbern, a witness of this document.[15]—**Maleth,** indecl. name, prob. = Malet, an aristocratic family of the Montivilliers vicinity.[16]] A

17.   Canis valdē calidus est, aliquod commūne et nātūrāle sibi in mōribus hominis habet, et ideō hominem sentit et intellegit, et eum amat, et libenter cum eō morātur, et fīdus est, et ideō diabolus canem ōdit et abhorret propter fidem quam ad hominem habet.

[*St. Hildegard of Bingen, *Physica* 7.20.—**canis, -is,** m./f., *a dog, bitch.*—**valdē,** adv., *intensely, very very.*—**calidus, -a, -um,** *warm, hot,* i.e., influenced by the sanguine humor.—**ideō,** adv., *therefore.*—**libenter,** adv., *gladly.*—**moror, -ārī,** depon., having pass. forms with act. meanings, *linger, tarry.*—**fīdus, -a, -um,** *true, trusty, faithful.*—**diabolus, -ī,** m., *a devil; the Devil.*—**abhorreō, -ēre,** *shrink back from, shudder at.*] I

18.   Ā Chrīstō igitur Chrīstiānī, ā Petrō fidēlēs dīcimur.

[*Nicholas of Cusa, *Sermō* 287.8.—**Petrus, -ī,** m., St. *Peter,* the first pope.] I

---

14   Bates, op. cit., 196.
15   Ibid., 117–118, 150.
16   Ibid., 102, 110.

19. *Bēstia bēstiam nōvit.*

[*Desiderius Erasmus, *Adagia* 4.7.57, citing a proverb.—**bēstia, -ae,** f., *an animal without reason, a beast.*] I

20. Eius reī pūblicae īnstitūtiō hunc ūnum scopum in prīmīs respicit: ut, quoad per pūblicās necessitātēs licet, quam plūrimum temporis ab servitiō corporis ad animī lībertātem cultumque cīvibus ūniversīs asserātur. In eō enim sitam vītae fēlīcitātem putant.

[*St. Thomas More, *Ūtopia* 2, LAM, p. 134, speaking of the Utopian constitution.—**īnstitūtiō, -ōnis,** f., *arrangement, disposition.*—**scopos, -ī,** m., *a target to shoot at.*—**in prīmīs,** = *especially.*—**respiciō, -ere,** *have a regard for, consider.*—**quoad,** adv., *as far as.*—**necessitās, -tātis,** f., *need;* (in pl.) *requirements.*—**licet,** = *it is permitted.*—**servitium, -ī,** n., *servitude, service.*—**lībertās, -tātis,** f., *freedom.*—**cultus, -ūs,** m., *culture, training, education.*—**ūniversī, -ae, -a,** *all together.*—**asserō, -ere,** *set free from, protect.*—**sinō, -ere, sīvī, situm,** *place, put down, situate.*—**fēlīcitās, -tātis,** f., *fertility; happiness.*] A

21. Nam etsī haud multī cuiusque urbis sunt quī cēterīs exonerātī labōribus sōlī disciplīnae dēputantur, . . . tamen omnēs puerī litterīs imbuuntur, et populī bona pars, virī fēminaeque, per tōtam vītam hōrās illās quās ab operibus līberās dīximus in litterīs collocant.

[*St. Thomas More, *Ūtopia* 2, LAM, p. 154.—**etsī,** conj., *even if, although.*—**haud,** adv., *not, not at all.*—**exonerō** (1), *disburden; free, release.*—**disciplīna, -ae,** f., *a being instructed; a branch of instruction; art, science.*—**dēputō** (1), *prune; appoint.*—**imbuō, -ere,** *steep, saturate; accustom, initiate.*—**opus, -eris,** n., *a work, task.*—**collocō** (1), *put, place.*] M

CAPVT XXXI

Cum Clauses, *Ferō*; ***Dum* for *Cum*; Genitive of Indefinite Value; Ablative of Price**

SYNTAXIS SUPPLĒMENTUM

***Dum* for *Cum*.** *Dum* encroaches upon *cum* in EL, and can be used to indicate time, circumstance, and cause as *cum* does. See Blaise, §§ 310–311, for examples.

Genitive of Indefinite Value. Mentioned by *Wheelock* on p. 260, the genitive of indefinite value, sometimes just called the genitive of value, is used with verbs of rating and buying, such as *aestimāre*, to value, and *emere*, to buy, in order to indicate the general value or price of a thing. See Sentences 15 and 20 below. A common ancient expression, also used in subsequent ages, employed *floccī*, of a flock of wool, as in *mē floccī facit*, he rates me (at the value) of a flock of wool, i.e., he doesn't give a darn about me. The genitive of *as, assis*, m., an as (a copper coin of small value), was employed the same way.

Ablative of Price. The ablative is used to indicate the definite price of an object. See Sentence 8 below. This usage is often extended to include other relations than those of the market.

VERBA MEMORIĀ COMPREHENDENDA

quamvīs, *although* (+ subjunctive)

tunc, adv., *then, at that time*

SENTENTIAE Ē FONTIBUS NŌN ANTĪQUĪS HAUSTAE

1. Terra autem erat inānis et vacua, et tenebrae erant super faciem abyssī, et Spīritus Deī ferebātur super aquās.
   [*Gen. 1:2 V.—**inānis, -e,** *empty, vain.*—**vacuus, -a, -um,** *empty, devoid (of), void.*—**faciēs, -ēī,** f., *face; beauty.*—**abyssus, -ī,** f., *a bottomless pit; the sea; hell.*] I

2. Vīdit igitur mulier quod bonum esset lignum ad vēscendum et pulchrum oculīs aspectūque dēlectābile, et tulit dē frūctū illīus et comēdit deditque virō suō, quī comēdit.
   [Gen. 3:6 V.—**lignum, -ī,** n., *wood; tree.*—**ad vēscendum,** a purp. construction with the gerund, = *to eat.*—**aspectus, -ūs,** m., *seeing;* here in the abl. of specification or respect, = *with respect to seeing.* See Capvt XL.—**dēlectābilis, -e,** *delightful, pleasing.*—**comedō, -ēsse, -mēdī,** irreg. verb, *eat up entirely, consume; waste.*] M/A

3. Ego fēcī et ego feram et ego portābō et ego salvābō.
   [*Is. 46:4 V, God speaks to Israel.—**portō** (1), *bear, carry.*—**salvō** (1), *save; heal.*] I

4. Prāvum est cor omnium et īnscrūtābile. Quis cognōscet illud?
   [*Jer. 17:9 V.—**prāvus, -a, -um,** *crooked, deformed; perverse; depraved.*—**īnscrūtābilis, -e,** *unsearchable, inscrutable.*] I

5. Cum enim īnfirmor, tunc potēns sum.
   [*II Cor. 12:10 V, LH 3.89.—**īnfirmō** (1), *weaken; diminish.*] I

6. Chrīstus Iēsūs, cum in formā Deī esset, nōn rapīnam arbitrātus est esse sē aequālem Deō, sed sēmetipsum exinānīvit.
   [*Phil. 2:6–7 V, LH 3.916.—**rapīna, -ae,** f., *robbery; the act of robbery; loot.*—**arbitror, -ārī, -ātus sum,** depon. verb, having pass. forms with act. meanings, = *(he) judged, thought.*—**aequālis, -e,** *even, equal.*—**sēmetipsum,** an even stronger form of *sēipsum.*—**exināniō, -īre, -īvī,** *empty, make empty.*] M

7. Quem [id est, Iēsūm Chrīstum] cum nōn vīderitis, dīligitis.
   [*I Pet. 1:8 V, LH 3.635. —**vīderitis,** why is the perf. subjunct. used here?] I

8. Bilībris trīticī dēnāriō et trēs bilībrēs hordeī denariō; et vīnum et oleum nē laeseris.
   [*Apoc. 6:6 V, in LH 2.543, an announcement at the opening of the Third Seal.—**bilībris, -is,** LS does not give the gender, but

perh. f., as it translates the Gr. *choinix*, also f., *a quantity of two pounds*, "the daily ration of grain for one man."[17]—**trīticum, -ī,** n., *wheat.*—**dēnārius, -ī,** m., *a Roman silver coin* "equivalent to one day's wages. The cost of wheat here is five to twelve times its normal price. Famine is indicated."[18]—**hordeum, -ī,** n., *barley.*—**oleum, -ī,** n., *olive oil.*—**laedō, -ere, laesī,** *hurt, injure, damage.* This is perh. a reference to the wine and olive oil used in temple sacrifices.[19]] A

9.   Ecce Dominus veniet cum splendōre dēscendēns, et virtūs eius cum eō, vīsitāre populum suum in pāce, et cōnstituere super eum vītam sempiternam.

[*Respōnsum, Lēctiō III, Ad mātūtīnum, Sabbatō, Īnfrā Hebdomadam II Adventūs, BR 1.30.—**splendor, -ōris,** m., *brilliance, magnificence.*—**dēscendō, -ere,** *go down.*—**vīsitō** (1), *go to see, visit.*—**cōnstituō, -ere,** *establish.*—**sempiternus, -a, -um,** *everlasting, sempiternal.*] I/M

10.   Exsultābunt labia mea, cum cantāverō tibi.

[*Respōnsōrium breve, ad Laudēs mātūtīnās, Sabbatō, Hebdomada II, LH 3.786.—**exsultō** (1), *jump for joy; rejoice.*—**labium, -iī,** n., *lip.*—**cantō** (1), *sing.*] I

11.   Quod accipis, corpus est illīus pānis caelestis, et sanguis est illīus sacrae vītis. Nam, cum pānem cōnsecrātum et vīnum discipulīs suīs porrigeret, sīc āit, "Hoc est corpus meum. Hic est sanguis meus." Crēdāmus, quaesō, cui crēdidimus. Nescit mendācium vēritās.

[*St. Gaudentius of Brescia, *Tractātus* 2, in LH 2.665–666, speaking of the Mass.—**pānis, -is,** m., *bread.*—**caelestis, -e,** *heavenly.*—**sanguis, -inis,** m., *blood.*—**vītis, -is,** f., *a vine.*—**cōnsecrō** (1), *consecrate, make holy.*—**porrigō, -ere,** *stretch out, extend; offer.*—**quaesō,** archaic form of *quaerō* used in supplications and prayers.—**mendācium, -iī,** n., *a lie.*] M

---

17   J. Massyngberde Ford, *Revelation*, Anchor Bible 38 (Garden City, NY: Doubleday and Co., 1975), 98.

18   Loc. cit.

19   Ibid., 98–99 and 107–108.

12. Agāmus ergō, dīlēctissimī, grātiās Deō Patrī, per Fīlium eius, in Spīritū Sānctō, quī propter multam misericordiam suam, quā dīlēxit nōs, misertus est nostrī; "et cum essēmus mortuī peccātīs, convīvificāvit nōs Chrīstō," ut essēmus in ipsō nova creātūra novumque figmentum. Dēpōnāmus ergō veterem hominem cum āctibus suīs; et adeptī participātiōnem generātiōnis Chrīstī, carnis renūntiēmus operibus.

> [*Pope St. Leo the Great, *Sermō I in Nātivitāte Dominī* 1–3, in LH 1.327.—**dīlēctus, -a, -um,** *beloved.*—**misereor, -ērī, misertus sum,** depon. verb, having pass. forms with act. meanings, = *(he) pitied* (+ gen.).—**morior, -ī, mortuus sum,** depon., = *we had died.*—**convīvificō** (1), *make alive together, restore to life with.* See Eph. 2:5.—**Chrīstō,** take as a dat. with a compound verb (Capvt XXXV) in imitation of the Greek, = *with Christ.*—**creātūra, -ae,** f., *a creature; creation.*—**figmentum, -ī,** n., *a production, creation.*—**dēpōnō, -ere,** *set down, lay aside.*—**vetus, -eris,** *old.*—**āctus, -ūs,** m., *motion, movement; performance, action.*—**adipiscor, -ī, adeptus sum,** depon., = *having obtained.*—**participātiō, -ōnis,** f., *a sharing, participation.*—**generātiō, -ōnis,** f., *a begetting, generating.*—**renūntiō** (1), *disclaim, renounce.*—**opus, operis,** n., *a work.*] M/A

13. Nam cum trēs sint partēs philosophiae speculātīvae,—nātūrālis, in mōtū inabstracta; mathēmatica, sine mōtū inabstracta, et theologica, sine mōtū abstracta,—in nātūrālibus igitur ratiōnābiliter, in mathēmaticīs disciplīnāliter, in dīvīnīs intellēctuāliter versārī oportēbit.

> [Boethius, *Dē Trinitāte* 2, describing the branches of philosophy and the methods by which they are studied.—**speculātīvus, -a, -um,** *speculative.*—**mōtus, -ūs,** m., *motion.*—**inabstractus, -a, -um,** *not separated,* i.e., from matter.—**mathēmaticus, -a, -um,** *mathematical.*—**theologicus, -a, -um,** *theological.*—**abstractus, -a, -um,** *separated,* i.e., from matter.—**ratiōnābiliter,** adv., *reasonably, rationally.*—**disciplīnāliter,** adv., *liberally,* i.e., by means of the liberal arts.—**intellēctuāliter,** adv., *intellectually.*—**versor, -sārī,** depon. verb, having pass. forms with act. meanings, = *to be engaged in, occupied with* (*in* + abl.).—**oportet, -ēre,** an impers. verb constructed with the infinitive, *it is necessary.* See Capvt XXXIX.] A

14. Mathēmatica Latīnē dīcitur doctrīnālis scientia, quae abstractam
    cōnsīderat quantitātem. Abstracta enim quantitās est, quam
    intellēctū ā māteriā sēparantēs vel ab aliīs accidentibus, ut est pār,
    impār, vel ab aliīs huiuscemodī in sōlā ratiōcinātiōne tractāmus.
    Cuius speciēs sunt quattuor, id est Arithmētica, Mūsica, Geōmetria,
    et Astronomia.
    [*St. Isidore of Seville, *Etymologiae* 3, *in initiō*.—**mathēmatica,
    -ae,** f., *mathematics.*—**Latīnē,** adv., *in Latin.*—**doctrīnālis, -e,**
    theoretical.—**quantitās, -tātis,** f., *quantity.*—**cōnsīderō** (1),
    consider, weigh, reflect on.—**intellēctus, -ūs,** m., *intellect.*—
    māteria, -ae, f., *matter.*—**sēparō** (1), *disjoin, separate.*—**accidēns,
    -entis,** n., *an accident* in the philosophical sense.—**pār, paris,**
    equal; even (of numbers).—**impār, -paris,** adj., *unequal; odd* (of
    numbers).—**huiuscemodī,** *of this kind, such.*—**ratiōcinātiō,
    -ōnis,** f., *reasoning.*—**tractō** (1), *treat, discuss.*—**speciēs, -ēī,** f.,
    kind, species.—**arithmētica, -ae,** f., *arithmetic.*—**mūsica, -ae,**
    f., *music.*—**geōmetria, -ae,** f., *geometry.*—**astronomia, -ae,** f.,
    astronomy.] M/A

15. Quantī tē fēcit [Deus], ex hīs quae prō tē factus est, agnōsce.
    [*St. Bernard of Clairvaux, *Sermō I in Epiphaniā Dominī* 2, *in*
    LH 1.361.—**quantī,** = *how much,* a common usage (genitive of
    indefinite value).—**fēcit,** = *value, esteem* (used as a verb of rating).
    Note that B. uses the indic. here in what is technically an ind.
    quest. Russell, 13, calls this type of construction "an archaic and
    also colloquial feature," and refers to GL, § 467.—**agnōscō, -ere,**
    recognize.] M

16. Cum sim servus omnium, omnibus servīre teneor et administrāre
    odōrifera verba Dominī meī.
    [*St. Francis of Assisi, *Epistola ad Fidēlēs* (Recensiō Posterior)
    2.—**serviō, -īre,** *be a slave to, serve* (+ dat.).—**administrō** (1),
    administer.—**odōrifer, -fera, -ferum,** *having a pleasant smell.*]
    I/M

17. Cum sacra Scrīptūra sit omni-sapiēns et vērissima, quia revēlāta
    et trādita ā Deō, quī est Vēritās et omnia sciēns, maximē sacrae
    Scrīptūrae est crēdendum.
    [*St. Thomas Aquinas, *Dē dīvīnīs nōminibus* 1.1.21.—**omni-
    sapiēns, -entis,** *all-wise.*—**revēlō** (1), *reveal.*—**crēdō, -ere,**
    believe, trust in (+ dat.).] M

18. Cum enim grātia nōn tollat nātūram, sed perficiat, oportet quod nātūrālis ratiō subserviat fideī.

   [*St. Thomas Aquinas, *Summa Theologiae* 1, q.1, a.8 ad 2.— **perficiō, -ere,** *accomplish; perfect.*—**oportet,** see Sentence 13 above. Here the verb is constructed with **quod,** as an ind. statement.—**subserviō, -īre,** *be subject to, subserve* + dat.] I

19. Ō salūtāris hostia, / quae caelī pandis ōstium, / bella premunt hostīlia: / dā rōbur, fer auxilium.

   [*St. Thomas Aquinas, *Verbum supernum prodiēns,* in LH 3.497.— **salūtāris, -e,** *healthful, beneficial.*—**hostia, -ae,** f., *an animal slain in sacrifice, a victim.*—**pandō, -ere,** *stretch out; throw open.*— **ōstium, -iī,** n., *entrance, door.*—**hostīlis, -e,** *unfriendly, hostile.*— **rōbur, -oris,** n., *hard wood; hardness, strength.*] I

20. Nōn magnī pendās, quis prō tē vel contrā tē sit, sed age et cūrā, ut Deus tēcum sit in omnī rē quam facis.

   [*Thomas à Kempis, *Dē Imitātiōne Chrīstī* 2.2.1, in LH 1.224.— **pendō, -ere,** *weigh; consider, judge.* Take either as a potentential subjunctive or as an EL prohibition.—**cūrō** (1), *take care* (+ purp. clause: GL, § 546N1.).] M

This is a fifteenth-century alabaster statue of St. Thomas Aquinas (c. 1225–1274) which was made in Spain. It now belongs to the Nelson-Atkins Museum of Art in Kansas City, Missouri. Thomas, who was of Lombard descent, was a son of the knight Landulf of Roccasecca, and was intended for a career as a Benedictine monk at the family abbey of Montecassino. To his family's consternation, however, he became a Dominican Friar. After his family failed to dissuade him by kidnapping and incarceration (Adenulf of Aquino was their ancestor; see Capvt I, Sentence 12), Thomas studied in Paris and Cologne under St. Albert the Great. Thomas wrote commentaries on books of Scripture, Aristotle, the Pseudo-Dionysius, Boethius, and the *Sententiae* of Peter Lombard. He wrote many other works, the greatest of which were the *Summa contrā Gentīlēs* and the *Summa Theologiae,* both of which are architectonic presentations of the entirety of Christian teaching. Thomas's writings are well represented in this book. (© Wikimedia Commons)

CAPVT XXXII

Formation and Comparison of Adverbs; *Volō, Mālō, Nōlō*; Proviso Clauses; **Greek Accusative;** *Nē* + **Second Person Present Subjunctive for** *Nōlī* + **Infinitive in EL;** *Priusquam, Antequam*

Syntaxis Supplēmentum

Greek Accusative. In Greek, the accusative can be used to indicate the respect in which the meaning of a passive or intransitive verb is true. This usage was imitated already by the CL poets, but received new impetus from the translation of Holy Scripture from Gr. into Latin, e.g., *amictī stolās albās*, clothed in white robes (Apoc. 7:9), and *ablūtī corpus aquā mundā*, washed with respect to the body with pure water (Hebrews 10:22). These examples, and others, can be found at PW, § 44(c).

Nē + **Subjunctive for** *Nōlī* + **Infinitive.** In CL, except in the comic poets, the second person present (optative) subjunctive was rarely employed as a negative imperative directed at an actual person. Instead, it was used of an "imaginary 'you'" [GL § 263.2]. It was rather like the American usage, "You never cross the street in the middle of the block." In EL, however, this subjunctive, generally in the singular, was used for *nōlī* + infinitive without distinction in meaning, e.g., *Nē perdās cum impiīs, Deus, animam meam*, Do not destroy my life with the impious, O God (Ps. 25:9). Both CL and EL did employ the perfect subjunctive in the second person, usually singular, for a negative command addressed to an actual person.

***Priusquam* and *Antequam*.** These two words mean *before* (= "earlier than"), and they introduce temporal clauses. In CL, when the the relationship of the verb in the temporal clause with the verb in the main clause is temporal and factual, the indicative is used. When some notion of "design, anticipation, or prevention" is present, the subjunctive is used. The use of these conjunctions can be subtle, and should be studied in a grammar. However, in EL the subjunctive tends to be used indiscriminately. *Istae generātiōnēs caelī et terra quandō creatae sunt, in diē quō fēcit Dominus Deus caelum et terram et omne virgultum agrī antequam orerētur in terrā omnemque herbam regiōnis priusquam germināret.* Those are the generations of heaven and earth when they were created, on the day God made heaven and earth and every shoot of the field before it sprang up, and every stalk before it shot forth (Gen. 2: 4–5a V). If this had been CL, a better translation for the subjunctive would have been *before it could spring up . . . before it could shoot up*. Notice, too, that the two elements of these words are sometimes split apart, *prius* and *ante* going in the main clause, *quam* in the subordinate clause. This is called *tmesis* (Smith, 38).

VERBA MEMORIĀ COMPREHENDENDA

antequam, conj., *before*

baptīzō (1), *baptize*

priusquam, conj., *before*

prophēta, -ae, m., *a prophet*

SENTENTIAE Ē FONTIBUS NŌN ANTĪQUĪS HAUSTAE

1. Habeō duās fīliās, quae necdum cognovērunt virum. Ēdūcam eās ad vōs et abūtiminī eīs sīcut vōbīs placuerit, dummodo virīs istīs nihil malī faciātis, quia ingressī sunt sub umbrā culminis meī.
    [*Gen. 19:8, V, Lot tries to prevent the abuse of the three angels.— **necdum,** conj., *(and) not yet.*—**ēdūcō, -ere,** *lead out.*—**abūtor, -tī,** depon., having pass. forms with act. meanings, here the imperative, = *use, abuse* (+ abl.).—**placeō -ēre, -uī,** *be pleasing to* (+ dat.), here used impersonally.—**ingredior, -dī, -gressus sum,** depon. verb, having pass. forms with act. meanings, here = *they have entered.*—**umbra, -ae,** f., *shade, shadow.*—**culmen, -inis,** n., *(roof-)top.*] I/M

2.   Nōlīte cōnfīdere in prīncipibus, in homine, per quem nōn est salūs.
      [Ps. 145:3 PIB, Fēria quārta ad Laudēs I, BR 2.480.—**cōnfīdō,
      -ere,** *have confidence in.*] I

3.   Cantāte Dominō, quoniam magnificē fēcit.
      [*Is. 12:5 V, LH 3.750.—**cantō** (1), *sing.*—**magnificus, -a, -um,**
      noble, magnificent.] I

4.   Et nē velītis dīcere intrā vōs, "Patrem habēmus Ābraham." Dīcō enim
      vōbīs quoniam potēns est Deus dē lapidibus istīs suscitāre fīliōs
      Ābrahae.
      [*Mt. 3:9 V.—**nē velītis dīcere,** = *do not expect to say,* in literal
      translation of the Grk.—**intrā,** prep. + acc., here = *inter.*—**potēns
      est . . . suscitāre,** < δύναται . . . ἐγεῖραι: *potēns est* should be taken
      as a periphrasis for *potest.*—**lapis, -idis,** m., *stone.*—**suscitō** (1),
      cause to rise.] I/M

5.   Omnia ergō quaecumque vultis ut faciant vōbīs hominēs et vōs facite
      illīs. Haec est enim lēx et prophētae.
      [*Mt. 7:12 V.—**quīcumque, quaecumque, quodcumque,** indef.
      pron., declined like the rel. pron., *whoever, whatever.*—**volō (ut)** +
      subjunctive, = a jussive noun clause. Cf. *Wheelock,* p. 304.] I/M

6.   Nōlī mē tangere, nōndum enim ascendī ad Patrem meum.
      [*Jn. 20:17 V.—**nōndum,** adv., *not yet.*—**ascendō, -ere, -ndī,**
      mount up, ascend.] I

7.   Nec faciō animam meam pretiōsiōrem quam mē, dummodo
      consummem cursum meum et ministerium verbī, quod accēpī ā
      Dominō Iēsū.
      [*Acts 20:24 V, Paul addresses the Ephesian elders for the last
      time.—**pretiōsus, -a, -um,** *valuable, precious.* This construction
      is difficult in the Greek, and may mean, "But I hold not my life
      of any account as dear unto myself."[20] This English translation
      is similar to the NV: "Sed nihilī faciō animam meam pretiōsam
      mihi." Note the gen. of indef. value. The Douay-Rheims Bible
      translates the Vulgate literally: "neither do I count my life more
      precious than myself."—**ministerium, -iī,** n., *service, ministry.*] A

[20]   J. Rawson Lumby, *The Acts of the Apostles with Maps, Notes and Introduction,* Cambridge
       Greek Testament for Schools and Colleges (Cambridge: Cambridge University Press,
       1887), 360.

8.   Sciō enim quia nōn habitat in mē—hoc est, in carne meā—bonum.
      Nam velle adiacet mihi; perficere autem bonum nōn inveniō. Nōn
      enim quod volō bonum, hoc faciō; sed quod nolō malum, hoc agō.
      [*Rom. 7:18–19 V.—**habitō** (1), *dwell.*—**adiaceō, -ēre,** *lie beside*
      or near to (+ dat.).—**perficiō, -ere,** *accomplish.*] M/A

9.   Nōlō enim vōs ignōrāre, frātrēs, quoniam patrēs nostrī omnēs
      sub nūbe fuērunt, et omnēs mare trānsiērunt, et omnēs in Mōÿse
      baptīzātī sunt in nūbe et in marī.
      [*I Cor. 10:1 V.—**nōlō** + acc. + inf.—**ignōrō** (1), *not know, not*
      recognize.—**trānseō, -īre, -iī,** irreg. verb with regular perf., *go*
      across, cross.—**Mōÿses, -is,** m., *Moses.* Note that *in Mōÿse* < εἰς
      τὸν Μωσῆν, into Moses, an example of a common mistranslation.
      See PW, § 117.B(7).] I

10.   Nē dīxeris, "Rediēns redī et crastinō diē dabō tibi." Nē quid inter
      prōpositum tuum et beneficium intercēdat.
      [*St. Gregory of Nazianzus, *Oratio* 14, *Dē pauperum amōre* 40, in
      LH 2.209.—**redeō, -īre,** *return.* Note that *rediēns* is an example of
      the pres. partic. of a verb being coupled with that verb to represent
      the Heb. infin. absolute, a construction which emphasized "the
      certainty of an action or fact." See PW, § 26(i), and Appendix
      I, § 58.—**crastinus, -a, -um,** *of tomorrow*; **crastinus diēs** =
      tomorrow.—**prōpositum, -ī,** n., *design, purpose, intention.*—
      intercēdō, -ere, *go between, come between.*] I/M

11.   Ratiō est aspectus animī, quō per sē ipsum, nōn per corpus, vērum
      intuētur, aut ipsa vērī contemplātiō nōn per corpus, aut ipsum vērum
      quod contemplātur.
      [*St. Augustine of Hippo, *Dē Immortālitāte Animae* 6.10.—**aspectus,**
      -ūs, m., *a seeing; the sense of sight.*—**intueor, -ērī,** depon. verb, having
      pass. forms with act. meanings, *look at attentively, contemplate.*—
      contemplātiō, -ōnis, f., *an attentive consideration, contemplation.*—
      contemplō (1), *consider attentively, contemplate.*] M/A

12.   Homō est animal ratiōnāle mortāle . . . Ūnō verbō ā bēstiīs, quod
      ratiōnāle, et aliō ā dīvīnīs [anima] sēparātur, quod mortāle dīcitur.
      Illud igitur nisi tenuerit, bēstia erit; hinc nisi sē āverterit, dīvīna
      nōn erit.
      [*St. Augustine of Hippo, *Dē ōrdine* 11.31.—**bēstia, -ae,** f.,
      beast.—**sēparō** (1), *separate, divide.*—**illud,** here = *the former.*—
      hinc, adv., here = *from the latter.*] M

13. "Obsecrō vōs per misericordiam Deī." Rogat Paulus, immō per
Paulum rogat Deus, quia plūs amārī vult quam timērī. Rogat Deus,
quia nōn tam Dominus esse vult quam pater.
> [*St. Peter Chrysologus, *Sermō* 108, in LH 2.604, commenting
> on Rom. 12:1 V, prob. from memory.—**obsecrō** (1), *beseech,
> entreat.*—**Paulus, -ī,** m., St. *Paul.*—**immō,** particle, *or rather.*]

14. Nōlīte timēre.
> [*St. Peter Chrysologus, *Sermō* 108, in LH 2.605, imagining what
> Christ might say to sinners.] I

15. Et quidem nātūrālī iūre commūnia sunt omnium haec: āēr et aqua
prōfluēns et mare et per hoc lītora maris. Nēmō igitur ad lītus maris
accēdere prohibētur, dum tamen vīllīs et monumentīs et aedificiīs
abstineat, quia nōn sunt iūris gentium.
> [*Tribonian, Theophilus, and Dorotheus, *Imperātōris Iūstiniānī
> Īnstitūtiōnēs* 2.1.1.—**āēr, āeris,** m., *the earth's atmosphere, air.*—
> **prōfluēns, -entis,** *flowing, running* (of water).—**accēdō, -ere,**
> *come near, approach.*—**dum,** = *dummodo.*—**vīlla, -ae,** f., *a country
> house; a farm.*—**monumentum, -ī,** n., *a monument.*—**aedificium,
> -iī,** n., *a building.*—**abstineō, -ēre,** *keep away from.*—**iūris,** a pred.
> gen., = *the business of the law.*] I/M

16. Nam id sōlum iūstum est quod vīs, [Deus,] et nōn iūstum quod
nōn vīs.
> [*St. Anselm of Canterbury, *Proslogion* 11.] I

17. Voluistī ergō[, Deus,] ut amārēmus tē, quī nec iūste poterāmus salvārī,
nisi amārēmus tē; nec amāre tē poterāmus, nisi prōcēderet ā tē. Ergō,
Domine, sīcut Apostolus amōris tuī dīcit, et nōs iam dīximus, prior
dīlēxistī nōs, et prior dīligis omnēs dīlēctōrēs tuōs.
> [*William of Saint-Thierry, *Dē contemplandō Deō* 9–11, in LH
> 1.219.—**salvō** (1), *save.*—**nisi amārēmus,** = *unless we were
> loving.*—**prōcēderet,** = *were proceeding.*—**apostolus, -ī,** m., *an
> apostle.*—**dīlēctor, -ōris,** m., *a lover.*] I/M

18. Ubi autem voluptātis rēgnum adsit, ibi difficile est virtūtem
cōnsistere.
> [*Battista Guarino, *Dē Ōrdine Docendī et Studendī* 3, speaking
> especially of adolescents.—**rēgnum, -ī,** n., *rule, authority,
> kingdom.*—**adsum, -esse,** *be near, be present.*—**cōnsistō, -ere,**
> *stand firmly, hold one's ground, keep one's footing.*] I/M

19.   Sī portārī vīs, portā et alium.
       [*Thomas à Kempis, *Dē Imitātiōne Chrīstī* 2.3.2.—**portō** (1),
       carry.] I

20.   Huiusmodī incrēmentum [i.e., facultātum hūmānārum], sī rēctē
       intellegātur, maiōris pretiī est quam externae quae colligī possunt
       dīvitiae.
       [*Gaudium et Spēs* 35, in LH 3.128.—**huiusmodī**, indecl., *of this
       sort, such.*—**incrēmentum, -ī,** n., *increase, growth.*—**facultās,
       -tātis,** f., *ability, skill, means, opportunity.* —**intellegātur,** = *should
       be understood.*—**pretium, -iī,** n., *price, value.*—**externus, -a, -um,**
       external.—**colligō, -ere,** *gather together, collect.*] M

CAPVT XXXIII

Conditions; Subjunctive and Indicative in Conditionals in EL; Genitive of the Charge

Syntaxis Supplēmentum

Subjunctive and Indicative in Conditionals in EL. EL often employs the subjunctive in the protasis of a conditional sentence, and the indicative in the apodosis. CL usually uses the same mood in both protasis and apodosis. Of course, CL does allow mixed conditionals, and, in some cases, the EL combinations of subjunctive and indicative clauses could be such mixed conditionals. Frequently, however, they appear to represent new developments. Thus, for example, one may find:

> sī + pres. subjunct., fut. ind. = Future More Vivid (as in Greek)

> sī + pres. subjunct., pres. ind. = Pres. General (as in Greek)

> sī + imperf. subjunct., imperf. ind. = Pres. Contrafactual (cf. GL, § 597R2)

> sī + plpf. subjunct., plpf. ind. = Past Contrafactual (cf. GL, § 597R2)

One should not, however, take this table as representing fixed forms of the conditional, but possibilities for interpretation. Nor should one view the table as being exhaustive of the possibilities for conditional forms.

An analysis of the constructions in this table, and of other constructions, with examples, can be found at Blaise, §§ 303–308. For the general principle, see PW, § 140.

Genitive of the Charge. Judicial verbs of "accusing, convicting, condemning, and acquitting" take the genitive of the charge, which expresses the charge or penalty, e.g., *damnāre capitis*, to condemn to death (GL, § 378). See Sentence 6 below. Cf. the Ablative of the Charge or Penalty in Capvt XXVI.

Verba Memoriā Comprehendenda

persōna, -ae, f., *an actor's mask; the character played by an actor; the function performed or part maintained by any person in the world; a personage; a grammatical person; one of the subsistent relations of the Holy Trinity*

superbia, -ae, f., *pride, arrogance*

Sententiae ē Fontibus nōn Antīquīs Haustae

1. Sī populus meus audīsset mē, Israël sī in viīs meīs ambulāsset, in brevī inimīcōs humiliāssem, et suprā tribulantēs eōs mīsissem manum meam.

    [Ps. 80:14–15 NV, LH 3.751.—**audīsset,** for *audīvisset* by syncope.—**ambulō** (1), *walk;* note the syncope.—**in brevī,** supply *tempore.*—**humiliō** (1), *abase, humble;* note the syncope.—**tribulō** (1), *oppress.*] M

2. Sī custōdierint fīliī tuī testāmentum meum, et testimōnia mea quae docēbō eōs, fīliī eōrum usque in saeculum sedēbunt super sēdem tuam.

    [Ps. 131:12 V.—**custōdiō, -īre, -iī,** *guard; preserve.*—**testāmentum, -ī,** n., *a testament, will.*—**testimōnium, -ī,** n., *witness, evidence.*—**sedeō, -ēre,** *sit.*—**sēdes, -is,** f., *seat.*] I

3. Initium superbiae hominis apostatāre ā Deō, quoniam ab eō, quī fēcit illum, recessit cor eius, quoniam initium omnis peccātī est superbia.

    [*Ecclus. 10:14–15 V, Lēctiō III Ad mātūtīnum, Fēria tertia, Īnfrā hebdomadam V augustī, BR 2.210.—**apostatō** (1), *forsake one's religion, apostatize.*—**recēdō, -ere, -cessī,** *go back, recede.*] I/M

4. Sī enim [principēs huius saeculī] cognōvissent, numquam Dominum glōriae crucifīxissent.

    [*I Cor. 2:8 V, LH 3.777.—**crucifīgō, -ere, -fīxī,** *fix to a cross, crucify.*] I

5.   Dīcō autem nōn nūptīs et viduīs. Bonum est illīs, sī sīc permaneant
     sīcut et ego.
     [I Cor. 7:8 V.—**nūpta, -ae,** f., *a married woman.*—**viduus, -a, -um,**
     bereft; widowed.—**permaneō,** strengthened form of *maneō.*] I

6.   ONE OF AUGUSTINE'S PUPILS INQUIRES OF ANOTHER. "Nam quaerō
     ex tē, quaesō," inquit, "iustusne sit Deus? . . . Sī enim Deum iūstum
     nōn esse respondēris, tū vīderis quid agās, quī mē dūdum impietātis
     arguēbās. Sī autem, ut nōbīs trāditur nōsque ipsīus ōrdinis necessitāte
     sentīmus, iūstus est Deus, sua cuīque distribuendō utīque iūstus
     est. Quae autem distribūtiō dīcī potest, ubi distīnctiō nūlla est?
     Aut quae distīnctiō, sī bona sunt omnia? Quidve praeter ōrdinem
     reperīrī potest, sī Deī iūstitiā bonōrum malōrumque meritīs sua
     cuīque redduntur? Iūstum autem Deum omnēs fatēmur. Tōtum
     igitur ōrdine includitur."
     [*St. Augustine of Hippo, *Dē ōrdine* 7.19, a pupil tries to
     demonstrate that even evil is within God's order.—**quaesō,**
     archaic form of *quaerō,* = *please.*—**respondēris . . . vīderis,** both
     perf. subjunctives, in a rare form of the FLV (see GL, § 596), = *if you
     (should have) answer(ed), you would (have) see(n).*—**dūdum,** adv., *a
     little while ago.*—**impietās, -tātis,** f., *impiety;* here = a genitive of the
     charge with *arguēbās.*—**arguō, -ere,** *accuse.* Note that his fellow
     pupil has just refuted such an argument.—**ōrdō, -inis,** m., *regular
     arrangement, order.* In this dialogue, the discussion about order
     is really a discussion about God's providence.—**distribuendō,**
     gerund, abl. of means, = *by dividing, distributing.*—**utīque,**
     adv., *certainly.*—**distribūtiō, -ōnis,** f., *division, distribution.*—
     distīnctiō, -ōnis, f., *distinction; difference.*—**praeter,** prep. + acc.,
     besides, except.—**reperiō, -īre,** *find, discover.*—**meritum, -ī,** n.,
     desert; merit. This is a dative of purpose. See *Wheelock,* Appendix,
     492.—**reddō, -ere,** *give back, return.*—**fateor, -ērī,** depon., having
     pass. forms with act. meanings, = *we confess.*—**inclūdō, -ere,**
     include, enclose.] A

7.   At sī ex tē quaererem quae sit pars ōrātiōnis "est," nōn (opīnor)
     nōmen, sed verbum esse dīcerēs.
     [*St. Augustine of Hippo, *Dē magistrō* 5.14, from the beginning
     of Augustine's argument on the usefulness of words.—**ōrātiō,**
     -ōnis, f., *speech.*—**opīnor,** = *I suppose.*—**nōmen,** here = *noun.*—
     verbum, here = *verb.*] M

8. Expergiscere, homō; prō tē Deus factus est homō. . . . In aeternum mortuus essēs, nisi in tempore nātus esset. Numquam līberārēris ā carne peccātī, nisi suscēpisset similitūdinem carnis peccātī. Perpetua tē possidēret miseria, nisi fieret haec misericordia. Nōn revīxissēs, nisi tuae mortī convēnisset. Dēfēcissēs, nisi subvēnisset. Perīssēs, nisi vēnisset.

[*St. Augustine of Hippo, *Sermō* 185.1.—**expergiscor, -ī,** depon. verb, having pass. forms with act. meanings; here the form is second pers. sg. pres. imperative, = *wake up!*—**factus est,** *was made* or *became.*—**morior, -ī, mortuus sum,** depon., = *would have died.*—**nāscor, -ī, nātus sum,** depon., = *had been born.*— **similitūdō, -inis,** f., *likeness.*—**possideō, -ēre,** *possess, have.*— **miseria, -ae,** f., *wretchedness, affliction, misery.*—**fieret,** *had happened* or *had been made.*—**revīvīscō, -ere, -vīxī,** *come to life again.*—**conveniō, -īre, -vēnī,** here = *be adapted to* (+ dat.).— **dēficiō, -ere, -fēcī,** *fail.*—**subveniō, -īre, -vēnī,** *come to help, relieve.*—**perissēs,** *would have perished.*] A

9. Deum, quem mundus nōn capit, angustus quōmodo capere poterat hūmānus aspectus? Quid erit, quid dēbeat, quid possit, nōn respicit iūs amōris. Amor ignōrat iūdicium, ratiōne caret, modum nescit. Amor nōn accipit dē impossibilitāte sōlācium, nōn recipit dē difficultāte remedium. Amor, nisi ad dēsīderāta pervāserit, necat amantem; et ideō vādit quō dūcitur, nōn quō dēbeat.

[St. Peter Chrysologus, *Sermō* 147, in LH 1.191.—**angustus, -a, -um,** *narrow, limited.*—**aspectus, -ūs,** m., *a seeing, looking, sight.*— **quid erit,** certainly an indirect question, as the two following indirect questions show. Perh. an example of anacoluthon (Smith, 93), or perhaps the deliberate use of the indicative for vividness. Cf. Blaise, § 270, the last example; cf. also Capvt XXXI, Sentence 15.—**respiciō, -ere,** *have regard for, consider.*—**ignōrō** (1), *be ignorant of, not to know.*—**impossibilitās, -tātis,** f., *impossibility.*— **difficultās, -tātis,** f., *difficulty.*—**pervādō, -ere, -vāsī,** *go through; attain, reach* (*ad* + acc.).—**vādō, -ere,** *go, hasten, rush.*—**quō,** adv., *whither, where.*] M

10. Amor parit dēsīderium, gliscit ardōre, ardōre ad inconcessa pertendit. Et quid plūra? Amor quod amat nōn potest nōn vidēre. Hinc est quod omnēs sānctī omnia quae meruerant parva dūxērunt, sī Dominum nōn vīdērunt. Hinc est quod amor quī cupit vidēre Deum, etsī nōn habet iūdicium, habet tamen studium pietātis.

[St. Peter Chrysologus, *Sermō* 147, in LH 1.192, continued from the last sentence.—**pariō, -ere,** *bring forth, bear, produce.*—**dēsīderium, -iī,** n., *a desire, longing.*—**gliscō, -ere,** *grow* or *swell up.*—**ardor, -ōris,** m., *heat; eagerness.*—**inconcessus, -a, -um,** *not allowed, impossible; forbidden.*—**pertendō, -ere,** *push on, proceed.*—**hinc,** adv., *hence.*—**mereō, -ēre, -uī,** *deserve, merit.*—**etsī,** conj., *even if, although.*—**pietās, -tātis,** f., *dutifulness towards God, piety.*] M

11.   Quōcircā sī persōna in sōlīs substantiīs est atque in hīs ratiōnābilibus substantiaque omnis nātūra est nec in ūniversālibus sed in indīviduīs cōnstat, reperta persōnae est dēfīnitiō: "nātūrae ratiōnābilis indīvidua substantia."

    [*Boethius, *Contrā Eutychēn* 3, Boethius' famous definition of a person.—**quōcircā,** conj., *for which reason.*—**substantia, -ae,** f., *that in which a thing consists, being, essence.*—**ūniversālis, -e,** *universal.*—**indīviduum, -ī,** n., *an atom; an individual.*—**cōnstō, -stāre,** *exist, abide.*—**reperiō, -īre, -pperī, -pertum,** *find, discover.*—**dēfīnitiō, -ōnis,** f., *a definition.*] A

12.   Et sī vetar Deum verbīs ōrāre, quōmodo possum veniam spērāre?
    [*Hrosvitha of Gandersheim, *Paphnutius* 7.14.—**vetō, -āre,** *forbid,* constructed with the infin.—**ōrō** (1), *pray.*—**quōmodo,** adv., *how?*—**venia, -ae,** f., *pardon.*] I

13.   Ego Rodbertus, Normannōrum dux, vīllam in Calcivō territōriō sitam, nomine Vuivellam, cum omnibus appendiciīs suīs Deō Sānctōque Petrō in Gemmeticō monastēriō trādō, et hanc dōnātiōnem hōc crucis signō cōnfirmō. +
    [*Carta Rodbertī Normannōrum Ducis, Fauroux, no. 75, p. 216.—**Rodbertus, -ī,** m., *Robert* I the Magnificent, duke of Normandy (ruled 1027–1035).—**Normannus, -ī,** m., *a Norman.*—**dux,** here = *duke.*—**villa, -ae,** f., *an estate.*—**Calcivum territōrium, -ī -iī,** n., *Le Pays de Caux.*—**Vuivella, -ae,** f., *Veauville.*—**situs, -a, -um,** *situated, lying.*—**appendix, -icis,** f., *a dependency* (cf. LLMA, s.v. *appendicium,* and related words).—**Gemmeticum monastērium, -ī -iī,** n., *the monastery of Jumièges.*—**dōnātiō, -ōnis,** f., *a gift, donation.*—**crux, crucis,** f., *a cross.*—**cōnfirmō** (1), *confirm.*] I

14.   Sī altrinsecus ad eandem basim alium cathetum ērēxerō, cum diagōnālēs mediō sē intersecāre coeperint, cathetōs parēs esse necesse est, et sunt duō triangula altrinsecus cōnstitūta paria ad eandem basim.

[Hugh of St. Victor, *Practica Geometria, Dē Altimetria* 1.9. Hugh
is discussing the erection of a second right triangle of equal size
on one of the sides (= the base) of another.—**altrinsecus,** adv.,
on the other side.—**basis, -is** or **-eos,** f., *base.* For the Gr. decl.,
see GL, § 65.—**cathetus, -ī,** f., *a perpendicular.*—**ērigō, -ere,
-rēxī,** *set up, erect.*—**diagōnālis, -e,** *diagonal.*—**intersecō** (1),
intersect.—**necesse,** indecl. adj. constructed with the acc. and
inf., *necessary.*—**triangulum, -ī,** n., *a triangle.*—**cōnstituō, -ere,
-stituī, -stitūtum,** *cause to stand, set up.*] A

15. Nihil enim habēmus et vidēmus corporaliter in hōc saeculō dē ipsō
     Altissimō, nisi corpus et sanguinem, nomina et verba, per quae factī
     sumus et redēmptī "dē morte ad vītam."
     [*St. Francis of Assisi, *Epistola ad Clēricōs.*—**corporālis, -e,** *relating
     to the body, corporeal.*—**sanguis, -inis,** m., *blood.*—**redimō, -ere,
     -ēmī, -ēmptum,** *redeem.*—**dē morte,** etc., I John 3:14.] I

16. Dīxit [Robertus Grosseteste] enim eī [Frātrī Petrō dē Theukesbury]
     aliquandō, quod nisi frātrēs fovērent studium et studiōsē vacārent
     lēgī dīvīnae, prō certō similiter contingeret dē nōbīs, sīcut dē aliīs
     religiōsīs, quōs vidēmus in tenebrīs ignōrantiae (proh dolor!)
     ambulāre.
     [*Thomas of Eccleston, *Dē Adventū Minōrum in Angliam* 14, relating
     an observation concerning the Friars Minor made by Robert
     Grosseteste, bishop of Lincoln (1235–1253), to the Franciscan Peter
     of Tewkesbury.—**aliquandō,** adv., *once.*—**foveō, -ēre,** *nurture,
     support.*—**studiōsus, -a, -um,** *eager.*—**vacō** (1), *be at leisure, have
     time.*—**prō certō,** = *for sure.*—**contingō, -ere,** *happen.*—Note that
     the condition *nisi…fovērent…vacārent…contingeret* is in indirect
     statement in secondary sequence, and is therefore equivalent to
     a Future Less Vivid.—**religiōsus, -ī,** m., *a religious (person), a
     member of a religious order.*—**ignōrantia, -ae,** f., *want of knowledge,
     ignorance.*—**proh dolor!,** *oh, sorrow!*—**ambulō** (1), *walk.*] M/A

17. Item [Robertus Grosseteste] iniūnxit cuīdam frātrī melancholicō, ut
     biberet calicem plēnum optimō vīnō pro paenitentiā, et cum ēbibisset
     licet invītissimē, dīxit eī, "Frāter cārissime, sī habērēs frequenter
     tālem paenitentiam, habērēs utique melius ōrdinātam cōnscientiam."
     [*Thomas of Eccleston, *Dē Adventū Minōrum in Angliam*
     14, relating a story told by Friar John of Dya about Robert
     Grosseteste.—**item,** adv., *also, likewise.*—**iniungō, -ere, -iūnxī,**

charge, enjoin (+ dat. of person).—**melancholicus, -a, -um,** *characterized by black bile, melancholy.*—**calix, -icis,** m., *a goblet, cup.*—**ēbibō, -ere, -bibī,** *drink up.*—**licet,** *although.*—**invītus, -a, -um,** *unwilling.*—**frequēns, -entis,** *repeated, frequent.*—**tālis, -e,** *such.*—**utique,** adv., *at any rate, certainly.*—**ōrdinō** (1), *set in order, order.*—**cōnscientia, -ae,** f., *conscience.*] M

18. *Amīcōrum commūnia sunt omnia.* . . . Quod quidem sī tam esset fīxum in hominum animīs, quam nūllī nōn est in ōre, profectō maximā malōrum parte vīta nostra levārētur.

   [*Desiderius Erasmus, *Adagia* 1.1.1, commenting on a famous proverb.—**fīgō, -ere, fīxī, fīxum,** *fix, fasten, make fast.*—**quam,** correlative to *tam, as.*—**nūllī nōn est,** note the use of litotes. See Smith, 102–103.—**profectō,** adv., *really, indeed.*—**levō** (1), *relieve, free.*] M

19. . . . Ex hōc prōverbiō Sōcratēs colligēbat omnia bonōrum esse virōrum nōn secus quam deōrum. Deōrum, inquit, sunt omnia. Bonī virī deōrum sunt amīcī et amīcōrum inter sē commūnia sunt omnia. Bonōrum igitur virōrum sunt omnia.

   [*Desiderius Erasmus, *Adagia* 1.1.1, continuing the thought in the sentence above.—**prōverbium, -ī,** n., *a proverb.*—**Sōcratēs, -is,** m., *Socrates.*—**colligō, -ere,** *gather together, collect; conclude, deduce.*—**nōn secus quam,** *not otherwise than.*] M/A

20. . . . Platō āit fēlīcem ac beātam fore cīvitātem in quā nōn audīrentur haec verba, "meum et nōn meum." Sed dictū mīrum [est] quam nōn placeat, immō quam lapidētur ā Chrīstiānīs illa commūnitās, cum nihil umquam ab ethnicō philosophō dictum sit magis ex Chrīstī sententiā.

   [*Desiderius Erasmus, *Adagia* 1.1.1, continuing the thought of the sentence above.—**Platō, -ōnis,** m., *Plato* (see *Republic* 462 C).—**fore,** = *futūrum esse.*—**mīrus, -a, -um,** *wonderful, surprising, extraordinary.*—**dictū,** a supine, = *to say.*—**quam,** *how.*—**placeō, -ēre,** *be pleasing to* (+ dat.).—**immō,** adv., *or rather.*—**lapidō** (1), *throw stones at, stone.*—**commūnitās, -tātis,** f., *a community, fellowship.*—**ethnicus, -a, -um,** *heathen.*—**magis,** adv., *more.*—**ex sententiā,** *according to (one's) wish, mind, liking.*] M/A

CAPVT XXXIV

Deponent Verbs; Ablative with Special Deponents; **Relative Clause of Purpose; Relative Clauses Introduced by Relative Adverbs**

Syntaxis Supplēmentum

Relative Clause of Purpose. Introduced only in passing on *Wheelock*, 328, the relative clause of purpose occurs frequently enough. According to *Woodcock*, § 134 (b), this construction arose from an original parataxis with the jussive subjunctive, e.g., *Fīlium mīsit. Frumentum meteret.* He sent his son. He was to harvest the grain. In hypotaxis, the construction became *Fīlium mīsit, quī frumentum meteret,* He sent his son to harvest the grain. See Sentence 3 below. If a comparative adjective or adverb is used in a purpose clause, the purpose clause is always introduced by *quō*, e.g., *Legit quō sapientior fīat.* He is reading to become wiser. See Sentence 11 below.

Relative Clauses Introduced by Relative Adverbs. Relative clauses can be introduced by the relative adverbs *quō*, whither, (to) where, *ubi*, where, and *unde*, whence, from where, e.g., *gaudē unde ille coāctus est flēre*, rejoice whence (from the same source that) that man has been compelled to weep (Pseudo-Cyprian, cited at Blaise, § 191). Such adverbs can also introduce relative clauses of purpose and of result (Capvt XXXVIII), e.g., *statim dīvīnae censūrae maiestāte percussus est, unde regrediēns impetū ac morsū leōnis necārētur*, he was struck immediately by the majesty of divine judgment, whence (in such a way that), in returning, he was killed by the attack and mauling of a lion (Cyprian, *Ep.* 59.6, cited also at Blaise, §191).

VERBA MEMORIĀ COMPREHENDENDA

ēvangelium, -ī, n., *good news; the Gospel*
faciēs, -ēī, f., *face; appearance*
habitō (1), *dwell*

Sententiae ē Fontibus nōn Antīquīs Haustae

1. Et fluvius ēgrediēbātur dē locō voluptātis ad irrigandum paradīsum,
    quī dīviditur in quattuor capita.
    [Gen. 2:10 V.—**ad irrigandum paradīsum,** a gerundival purp.
    construction, = *to water paradise.*—**dīvidō, -ere,** *divide.*—**caput,
    -itis,** n., *a head.*] I/M

2. Profectus inde Ābraham in terram austrālem, habitāvit inter Cādēs
    et Sūr, et peregrīnātus est in Gerārīs.
    [*Gen. 20:1 V.—**austrālis, -e,** *southern.*—**Cādēs,** indecl. Heb.
    name, *Kadesh.*—**Sūr,** indecl. Heb. name, *Shur.*—**peregrīnor, -nārī,
    -nātus sum,** *travel* or *reside abroad.*—**Gerāa, -ōrum,** n. pl., *Gerar.*
    LXX Gen. 26 supports the construing of this word as n. pl., here.]

3. Tulērunt autem tunicam eius et in sanguine haedī quem occīderant
    tinxērunt, mittentēs quī ferrent ad patrem et dīcerent, "Hanc
    invēnimus. Vidē utrum tunica fīliī tuī sit an nōn."
    [*Gen. 37:31–32 V, Joseph's brothers plot to deceive their father.—
    tunica, -ae, f., *tunic.*—**sanguis, -inis,** m., *blood.*—**haedus, -ī,** m., *a
    kid.*—**occīdō, -ere, -cīdī,** *kill.*—**tingō, -ere, -nxī,** *wet; dye.*—**quī,**
    an indef. antecedent must be supplied here for the rel. pron.] I/M

4. Postquam autem locūtī sunt, praecēpit Ragūel occīdī arietem et parārī
    convīvium. Cumque hortārētur eōs discumbere ad prandium, Tōbīas
    dīxit, "Hīc ego hodiē nōn mandūcābō neque bibam, nisi prius petītiōnem
    meam cōnfirmēs et prōmittās mihi dare Saram, filiam tuam."
    [*Tob. 7:9–10 V.—**postquam,** conj., *after.*—**praecipiō, -ere, -cēpī,**
    teach; order, constructed with the acc. + inf.—**Ragūel,** indecl.
    Heb. name, m., *Raguel.*—**ariēs, -etis,** m., *a ram.*—**convīvium,
    -iī,** n., *a banquet.*—**discumbō, -ere,** *lie down; recline at table.*—
    prandium, -iī, n., *dinner* (taken about noon).—**Tōbīas, -ae,** m.,
    Tobias, Tobit.—**mandūcō** (1), *chew; eat.*—**petītiō, -ōnis,** f., *a
    thrust; request.*—**cōnfirmō** (1), *confirm.*—**Sara, -ae,** f., *Sarah.*] I

5. Nē mōliāris amīcō tuō malum, cum ille in tē habeat fīdūciam.
    [*Prov. 3:29 V.—**fīdūcia, -ae,** f., *trust, confidence.*] I

6. Nōlī resistere contrā faciem potentis, nec cōnēris contrā ictūs fluviī.
    [*Ecclus. 4:32 V.—**resistō, -ere,** *resist, oppose.*—**conor,** here =
    endeavor, strive.—**ictus, -ūs,** m., *a blow.*—**fluvius, -iī,** m., *a river.*] I

7. Cum enim moriētur homō, hērēditābit serpentēs et bēstiās et vermēs.
    [*Ecclus. 10:13 V, Lēctiō III, Ad mātūtīnum, Fēria tertia, Īnfrā
    hebdomadam V augustī, BR 2.210.—**hērēditō** (1), *inherit.*—
    serpēns, -ntis, f., *a snake, serpent.*—**bēstia, -ae,** f., *a beast.*—
    vermis, -is, m., *a worm, maggot.*] I

8. Parvulus enim nātus est nōbīs, et fīlius datus est nōbīs.
    [*Is. 9:6 V.—**parvulus, -a, -um,** *little, small, tiny.*] I

9. Dīcō autem vōbīs, quia Ēlīās iam vēnit et nōn cognōvērunt eum, sed
    fēcērunt in eō quaecumque voluērunt. Sīc et Fīlius hominis passūrus
    est ab eīs.
    [*Mt. 17:12 V.—**Ēlīās, -ae,** m., *Elias, Elijah.*—**quīcumque,**
    quaecumque, quodcumque, indef. pron., declined like the rel.
    pron., *whoever, whatever.*] I

10. Venientēs autem et prīmī, arbitrātī sunt quod plūs essent acceptūrī.
    Accēpērunt autem et ipsī singulōs dēnāriōs.
    [*Mt. 20:10 V, from the parable of the Laborers in the Vineyard.—
    singulī, -ae, -a, *one each, single.*—**dēnārius, -iī,** m., *a denarius,*
    a silver coin.] M

11. Per passiōnem tuam tribue fidēlibus membra sua mortificāre, quō
    expedītiōrēs ad resurrēctiōnem tuam celebrandam occurrant.
    [*Precēs ad I Vesperās, Dominica in Palmīs, LH 2.319, a prayer
    addressed to Christ.—**passiō, -ōnis,** f., *a suffering, enduring.*—
    tribuō, -ere, *grant, give, allow, yield.* EL can use an infin. for an
    ind. command. See Appendix I, § 51.—**membrum, -ī,** n., *a limb*
    or *member* of the body.—**mortificō** (1), *kill, destroy; subject, reduce*
    to weakness.—**expedītus, -a, -um,** *unshackled, unimpeded; free,*
    ready.—**resurrēctiō, -ōnis,** f., *resurrection.*— **ad ... celebrandam,**
    a gerundival purp. construction, = *to celebrate your resurrection.*—
    occurrō, -ere, here prob. = hasten to *gather.*] M

12. Hinc gaudium numquam fīniendum, hinc in Deō persevērantia, hinc
    similitūdō cum Deō, et, quō nihil sublīmius expetī potest, hinc est
    ut deus fīās.
    [*St. Basil of Caesarea, *Dē Spīritū Sānctō* 9.23, in LH 2.768,
    speaking of the illumination of the Holy Spirit.—**hinc,** adv.,
    hence; from this.—**gaudium, -iī,** n., *joy, gladness, delight.*—**fīniō,**

-īre, *bound, limit; finish, end. Finiendum* is here a simple fut. pass. partic. See Appendix I, § 60.—**persevērantia, -ae,** f., *steadfastness, perseverance.*—**similitūdō, -inis,** f., *likeness, resemblance.*— **sublīmis, -e,** *lofty; noble.*—**expetō, -ere,** *require.*] M/A

13.   Dignior enim sequētur effectus, quem ferventior praecēdit affectus.
[*St. Augustine of Hippo, *Epistola* 130.9.18 (ad Probam), in LH 4.303, on prayer.—**effectus, -ūs,** m., *result, effect.*—**fervēns, -entis,** *glowing, hot, heated, fiery.*—**praecēdō, -ere,** *go before, precede.*—**affectus, -ūs,** m., *a feeling.*] I

14.   Duōbus igitur hōrum trium, memoriā et intellegentiā, multārum rērum nōtitia atque scientia continentur. Voluntās autem adest, per quam fruāmur eīs vel ūtāmur.
[*St. Augustine of Hippo, *Dē Trīnitāte* 10.10.13, Augustine is developing his famous analogy for the Holy Trinity.— **intellegentia, -ae,** f., *intellect, understanding.*—**nōtitia, -ae,** f., *conception, idea.*—**adest, -esse,** *be present.*—**fruor,** see *Wheelock,* 285.] M

15.   Sardonicīs quōdammodo herbīs omnem Rōmānum populum putēs esse saturātum: moritur et ridet.
[*Salvian of Marseilles, *Dē Gubernātiōne Deī* 7.1.6, commenting on the decadence of his day.—**sardonica herba, -ae -ae,** f., prob. *Sardinian crowfoot,* which, when eaten, causes the face to be screwed up, as if in bitter laughter.—**quōdammodo,** adv., *in a certain way, in a measure.*—**saturō** (1), *fill, glut.*] I/M

16.   Proinde sī quisquam dīxerit alicuī nostrum, "Accēpistī Spīritum Sānctum, quārē nōn linguīs omnibus loqueris?" respondēre dēbet, "Loquor sānē omnibus linguīs, quia in eō sum Chrīstī corpore, hoc est in Ecclēsiā, quae loquitur omnibus linguīs. Quid enim aliud tunc Deus significāvit per Sānctī Spīritūs praesentiam, nisi Ecclēsiam suam omnibus linguīs locutūram?"
[*A Certain Sixth-Century African Author, *Sermō* 8.1, in LH 2.791.—**proinde,** adv., *consequently.*—**quisquam, quidquam,** indef. pron., *anyone, anything.*—**sānē,** adv., *indeed.*—**significō** (1), *show, indicate.*—**praesentia, -ae,** f., *presence.*—**locutūram,** supply *esse.*] I/M

17.   Iūs autem cīvīle vel gentium ita dīviditur. Omnēs populī, quī lēgibus et mōribus reguntur, partim suō propriō, partim commūnī omnium hominum iūre ūtuntur. Nam quod quisque populus ipse sibi iūs

cōnstituit, id ipsīus proprium cīvitātis est vocāturque iūs cīvīle, quasi
iūs proprium ipsīus cīvitātis. Quod vērō nātūrālis ratiō inter omnēs
hominēs cōnstituit, id apud omnēs populōs peraequē custōdītur
vocāturque iūs gentium, quasi quō iūre omnēs gentēs ūtuntur.

[*Tribonian, Theophilus, and Dorotheus, *Imperātōris Iūstiniānī
Īnstitūtiōnēs* 1.2.1.—**cīvīlis, -e,** *civil, civic.*—**dīvidō, -ere,**
divide.—**partim,** adv., *partly.*—**cōnstituō, -ere,** *establish.*—**vērō,**
adv., *indeed.*—**peraequē,** adv., *quite equally.*—**custōdiō, -īre,**
guard; observe.—**quō,** for *aliquō.*] M

18. Quae rēs [id est, manūmissiō] ā iūre gentium orīginem sumpsit,
utpote cum iūre nātūrālī omnēs līberī nāscerentur, nec esset nōta
manūmissiō, cum servitūs esset incognita, sed posteāquam iūre
gentium servitūs invāsit, secutum est beneficium manūmissiōnis.

[*Tribonian, Theophilus, and Dorotheus, *Imperātōris Iūstiniānī
Īnstitūtiōnēs* 1.5 *in initiō.*—**manūmissiō, -ōnis,** f., *the freeing
of a slave* by his master.—**orīgō, -inis,** f., *origin.*—**sūmō, -ere,**
sūmpsī, *take up, take.*—**utpote,** adv., *inasmuch as, seeing that.*—
incognitus, -a, -um, *unknown.*—**posteāquam,** conj., *after.*—
invādō, -ere, -vāsī, *get in, enter.*] A

19. Merētur ergō amārī propter sēipsum Deus, et ab īnfidēlī, quī etsī
nesciat Chrīstum, scit tamen sēipsum.

[*St. Bernard of Clairvaux, *Dē Dīligendō Deō* 2.6, with his
argument depending on the fact that humans are made in the
image of God.—**mereor, -ērī,** *deserve, merit.*—**sēipsum,** = *sē
ipsum.*—**īnfidēlis, -e,** *faithless.*—**etsī,** *even if, although.*] M

20. Quāpropter homō, illīs bonīs ūtēns, rēs exteriōrēs quās lēgitimē
possidet nōn tantum tamquam sibi propriās, sed etiam tamquam
commūnēs habēre dēbet, eō sēnsū ut nōn sibi tantum, sed etiam aliīs
prodesse queant.

[*Gaudium et Spēs* no. 69, CDD, p. 793, speaking of our possession
of temporal goods.—**quāpropter,** adv., *on which account,
wherefore.*—**exterior, -ōris,** *outer.*—**lēgitimus, -a, -um,** *lawful,
legal.*—**possideō, -ēre,** *possess.*—**prōsum, prōdesse,** *be useful,
do good, benefit* (+ dat.).—**queō, quīre,** *be able.*] M

CAPVT XXXV

Dative with Adjectives, Special Verbs, and Compounds; **Clauses of Doubting; Clauses of Prevention**

Syntaxis Supplēmentum

Clauses of Doubting. When *dubitō* means "to doubt," instead of "to hesitate," and is not negated, it takes an indirect question introduced by *num* or *an*, whether. The same is true of *dubium est*, it is doubtful. However, when *dubitō* or *dubium est* are negated, they take a clause, developed from the deliberative subjunctive (*Woodcock*, § 178–179), introduced by *quīn*, (but) that, e.g, *nūllī dubium [est] quīn peccētis in Dominum*, no one doubts but that you sin against the Lord (Num. 32:23 V). In EL *quod* is sometimes substituted for *quīn* in this construction, e.g., *nōn dubitō quod Deus precēs et lacrimās meās in conspectū suō admīserit*, I do not doubt but that God has admitted my prayers and tears into his sight (Tob. 7:13 V). See also Sentences 14 and 15 below.

Clauses of Prevention. When they are not negated, certain verbs that signify preventing and hindering take a final clause introduced by *nē* or *quōminus* (= by the which less) and the subjunctive. Among such verbs are *impedīre*, to hinder, prevent, and *prohibēre*, to hinder, forbid. Example: *[Dominus] prohibuit tē nē venīrēs in sanguine.* The Lord hindered you from coming into blood (= shedding blood) (I Sam. 25:26 V). When such verbs are negated, they are followed by a consecutive clause introduced by *quīn* or *quōminus*, e.g., *nec prohibuī cor quīn omnī voluptāte fruerētur*, nor did I hinder my heart from enjoying every pleasure (Eccles. 2:10 V). From the examples given it should be clear that we construct such clauses of prevention in English with a gerund and the preposition *from*. See further Sentences 12 and 20 below.

Verba Memoriā Comprehendenda

quīn (= **quī** instrumental + **nē,** *how not? why not? Woodcock,* § 185), conj., *(but) that* (in a clause of doubting); *from* + gerund (in a clause of prevention)

quōminus, quō minus *(by the which less),* conj., *from* + gerund (in a clause of prevention)

redimō, -ere, -ēmī, -ēmptum, *buy back, redeem*

Sententiae ē Fontibus nōn Antīquīs Haustae

1. Crēdidit Ābraham Deō, et reputātum est illī ad iūstitiam.
   [*Gen. 15:6 V.—**reputō** (1), *calculate; ponder; ascribe*: the subject is the fact of Abraham's belief.] I

2. Parcet pauperī et inopī et animās pauperum salvās faciet.
   [Ps. 71:13 V.—**inops, -opis,** *poor, needy.*] I

3. Quī fēcit lūmināria magna, sōlem ut praeesset diēī, lūnam et stēllās ut praeessent noctī.
   [Ps. 135:7a, 8a, 9a NV, LH 3.948–949.—**Quī,** take as a connecting rel.—**lūmināre, -āris,** n., *that which gives light; a heavenly body.*—**praesum,** see *Wheelock,* 296.] I/M

4. Ūnus ergō introitus est omnibus ad vītam et similis exitus. Propter hoc optāvī et datus est mihi sēnsus, et invocāvī et vēnit in mē spīritus sapientiae; et praepōsuī illam rēgnīs et sēdibus, et dīvitiās nihil esse dūxī in comparātiōne illīus.
   [*Wis. 7:6–8 V.—**introitus, -ūs,** m., *entry.*—**exitus, -ūs,** m., *exit.*—**sēnsus,** here = *understanding,* as frequently in EL.—**invocō** (1), *call (upon).*—**sēdēs, -is,** f., *a throne.*—**comparātiō, -ōnis,** f., *comparison.*] I/M

5. Quī serviunt sapientiae obsequentēs erunt Sānctō, et eōs quī dīligunt illam dīligit Deus.
   [Ecclus. 4:15 V.—**obsequor,** see *Wheelock,* 296. Note the periphrastic fut.] M

6. Quamobrem, rēx, cōnsilium meum placeat tibi, et peccāta tua eleemosynīs redime, et inīquitātēs tuās misericordiīs pauperum. Forsitan ignōscet [Deus] dēlictīs tuīs.
   [*Dan. 4:24 V.—**Quamobrem,** adv., *for which reason, wherefore.*—**eleēmosyna, -ae,** f., *alms.*—**inīquitās, -tātis,** f.,

unfairness.—**pauperum,** an objective genitive. See *Wheelock,* 492.—**forsitan,** adv., *perhaps.*—**dēlictum, -ī,** n., *transgression* (against positive law, according to LS).] M

7.　Et mīrātī sunt omnēs, ita ut conquīrerent inter sē dīcentēs, "Quidnam est hoc? Quaenam doctrīna haec nova, quia in potestāte etiam spīritibus immundīs imperat et oboediunt eī?"
　　[*Mk. 1:27 V.—**conquīrō, -ere,** *search diligently.*—**quisnam, quaenam, quidnam,** *who in the world? what in the world?*— **doctrīna, -ae,** f., *teaching.*—**potestās, -tātis,** f., *power.*— **immundus, -a, -um,** *unclean.*—**oboediō, -īre,** *obey* (+ dat.).] I/M

8.　Āit autem Dominus, "Cui ergō similēs dīcam hominēs generātiōnis huius, et cui similēs sunt? Similēs sunt puerīs sedentibus in forō et loquentibus ad invicem et dīcentibus, 'Cantāvimus vōbīs tībiīs et nōn saltāstis, lāmentāvimus et nōn plōrāstis.'"
　　[*Lk. 7:31–32 V.—**generātiō, -ōnis,** f., *generation.*—**ad invicem,** *to each other.* See Appendix I, § 35.—**cantō** (1), *sing.*—**tībia, -ae,** f., *a reed pipe.*—**saltō** (1), *dance. Saltāstis* is a syncopated form of *saltāvistis.*—**lāmentō** (1), *weep, moan, lament.*—**plōrō** (1), *weep, wail. Plōrāstis* is a syncopated form of *plōrāvistis.*] I

9.　Nōn turbētur cor vestrum. Crēditis in Deum; et in mē crēdite.
　　[*Jn. 14:1 V.—**turbō** (1), *disturb, trouble.*—**crēdere in** + acc., *believe in,* borrowed from biblical Greek. See Appendix I, § 6 N 3.] I

10.　Tē ergō quaesumus, tuīs famulīs subvenī, quōs pretiōsō sanguine redēmistī.
　　[*Tē Deum,* Ad mātūtīnum, Ōrdinārium dīvīnī Officiī, BR 1.(6).—**quaesumus,** = *quaerimus,* here = *beg, beseech.*—**famulus, -ī,** m., *slave, servant.*—**subveniō, -īre,** *come to the help of, relieve* (+ dat.).—**pretiōsus, -a, -um,** *precious.*] I/M

11.　Nūllī igitur nātūrae oboediēns aut subiectus, Deus omnem ergō regit ipse nātūram.
　　[*Salvian of Marseilles, *Dē Gubernātiōne Deī* 1.1.4.—**oboediō, -īre,** *be obedient to, obey* (+ dat.).—**subiciō, -ere, -iēcī, -iectum,** here = *submit to, be subject to.*] I/M

12.　Molītus est [Karolus Magnus] et classem contrā bellum Norðmannicum. . . . Et quia Norðmannī Gallicum lītus atque Germānicum assiduā īnfestātiōne vastābant, per omnēs portūs et ōstia flūminum quā navēs recipī posse vidēbantur, statiōnibus et excubiīs dispositīs, nē quā hostis exīre potuisset, tālī mūnītiōne prohibuit.

[*Einhard, *Vīta Karolī Magnī* 17.4, reporting on the first Viking raids in northern Europe, and, in Sentence 13 below, on the Moorish raids on the Mediterranean littoral.—**Karolus, -ī,** m., *Charles,* i.e., Charlemagne.—**classis, -is,** f., *a fleet.*—**Norðmannicus, -a, -um,** *of* or *pertaining to the Northmen, Scandinavian.* The *eth* (ð) = *th.*—**Norðmannus, -ī,** m., *a Northman,* i.e., a Dane, Swede, or Norwegian.—**Gallicus, -a, -um,** *Gallic, French.*—**Germānicus, -a, -um,** *Germanic, German.*—**assiduus, -a, -um,** *unremitting, incessant.*—**īnfestātiō, -ōnis,** f., *molestation; attack.*—**vastō** (1), *empty; lay waste, devastate.*—**portus, -ūs,** m., *a harbor, port.*—**ōstium, -iī,** n., *a door; entrance.*—**quā,** adv., *where.*—**statiō, -ōnis,** f., here = *a picket.*—**excubiae, -ārum,** f., *watchmen.*—**dispōnō, -ere, -posuī, -positum,** *put in different places, distribute.* —**nē,** note the clause of prevention.—**quā,** adv., for *aliquā, somewhere.*—**exeō, -īre,** here = *avoid, evade.*—**mūnītiō, -ōnis,** f., *a defending, fortifying.*] M/A

13. Fēcit [Karolus Magnus] idem ā parte merīdiānā in lītore prōvinciae Narbōnensis ac Septimaniae; tōtō etiam Italiae lītore usque Rōmam contrā Maurōs nūper pīrāticam exercēre aggressōs, ac per hoc nūllō gravī damnō vel ā Maurīs Italia vel Gallia atque Germānia ā Norðmannīs diēbus suīs affecta est.

[*Einhard, *Vīta Karolī Magnī* 17.4, continued from the previous sentence.—**merīdiānus, -a, -um,** *southern.*—**Narbōnensis, -is,** *pertaining to Narbō,* the modern city of Narbonne, which had been the principal *cīvitās* of the Roman district of *Narbōnensis Prīma,* which stretched along the Mediterranean from the Pyrenees to the Rhone.—**Septimania, -ae,** f., a term for the same region as *Narbōnensis Prīma,* named after the tribe of the Septimani.[21] This land had been settled by the Goths.—**tōtō . . . lītore,** supply *in* (cf. LS s.v. "tōtus," I.A.1).—**Maurus, -ī,** m., *a Moor.*—**pīrātica, -ae,** f., *piracy.*—**exerceō, -ēre,** *practice.*—**aggredior, -gredī, -gressus sum,** *begin, undertake.*—**damnum, -ī,** n., *loss, damage, injury.*—**Gallia, -ae,** f., *Gaul.*—**Germānia, -ae,** f., *Germany.*—**afficiō, -ere, -fēcī, -fectum,** *affect.*] M/A

---

[21] Edward Gibbon, *The History of the Decline and Fall of the Roman Empire,* ed. J. B. Bury, vol. 3 (London: Methuen and Co., 1909), App. 19, p. 532. A helpful map can be found in Edward James, *The Origins of France, From Clovis to the Capetians, 500–1000,* New Studies in Medieval History (London: Macmillan Press, 1982), xx.

14. Sī sīc verbum Deī servāveris, haud dubium quīn ab eō servēris.
   [*St. Bernard of Clairvaux, *Sermō V in Adventū Dominī* 3.— **haud,** adv., *not at all.*—**dubius, -a, -um,** *doubtful.*] M

15. Sermō iste [i.e., Verbum Deī] cum ita vīvus sit, haud dubium quīn et efficāx sit.
   [*Baldwin of Canterbury, *Tractātus* 6, in LH 4.344.—**efficāx, -cācis,** *effective, efficient.*] M

16. Frātrī Antōniō meō frāter Franciscus salūtem. Placet mihi quod sacram theologiam legās frātribus, dummodo inter huius studium ōrātiōnis et devotiōnis spīritum nōn exstinguās, sīcut in rēgula continētur.
   [*St. Francis of Assisi, *Epistola ad S. Antōnium.*—**Antōnius, -ī,** m., St. *Anthony* of Padua.—**Franciscus, -ī,** m., *Francis.*—**salūtem,** on this customary epistolary greeting, see Capvt XI, Sentence 6.— **quod** + subjunctive, where in CL one would have expected either an infinitive clause or an *ut*-clause. Cf. Capvt XXV, Syntaxis.— **theologia, -ae,** f., *theology.*—**inter,** = *in the midst of.*—**ōrātiō, -ōnis,** f., *prayer.*—**dēvōtiō, -ōnis,** f., *consecration.*—**exstinguō, -ere,** *extinguish.*—**rēgula, -ae,** f., *a rule.*] M

17. Adeō mihi certē persuādeō rēs aequābilī ac iūstā ratiōne distribuī aut fēlīciter agī cum rēbus mortālium, nisi sublātā prorsus proprietāte, nōn posse.
   [*St. Thomas More, *Ūtopia* 1, LAM, p. 102, Raphael Hythloday's most provocative opinion.—**adeō,** adv., *so much; to such an extent.*—**persuādeō, -ēre,** *persuade* (+ dat.).—**aequābilis, -e,** *equal; equable.*—**iūstus, -a, -um,** *just, right.*—**distribuō, -ere,** *divide, distribute.*—**prorsus,** adv., *utterly, absolutely.*—**proprietās, -tātis,** f., *property; ownership.*] A

18. Basilīus quoque … dīcit, sī trāditiōnēs nōn scrīptae neglegantur, fore ut Ēvangelium etiam magnum dētrīmentum patiātur.
   [*St. Robert Bellarmine, *Dē Contrōversiīs Fideī: Dē Verbō Deī* 4.4.—**Basilīus, -ī,** m., St. *Basil* the Great, bishop of Caesarea.— **trāditiō, -ōnis,** f., *a tradition.*—**fore ut,** see Capvt XXX Syntaxis.—**dētrīmentum, -ī,** n., *a loss, detriment.*—Note that the conditional in the indirect statement could be either a Future More Vivid or a Future Less Vivid, as these are constructed the same way in indirect statement.] M/A

19. Etiam nunc vidēmus aut maiōrem cāritātem aut certē minus odium
inter dīvīsōs Chrīstiānōs esse quam fuit ante C annōs. Cuius reī
mihi vidētur (sub Deō) prīncipālis causa esse gliscēns superbia et
immānitās īnfidēlium. Hitlerus, īnsciēns et nōlēns, maximē ecclēsiae
prōfuit!

[*C. S. Lewis Domnō Iōannī Calabriae, XX Septembris 1947,
Moynihan, 36.—**odium, -iī,** n., *hatred.*—**dīvīsus, -a, -um,**
separated, divided.—**ante C annōs,** *a hundred years ago.*—
prīncipālis, -e, *chief.*—**gliscō, -ere,** *swell up, blaze up.*—**superbia,
-ae,** f., *pride.*—**immānitās, -tātis,** f., *savageness, inhumanity,
cruelty.*—**īnfidēlis, -e,** *unbelieving, infidel.*—**Hitlerus, -ī,** m.,
Adolf *Hitler.*—**īnsciēns, -entis,** *unknowing.*—**prōsum, -esse,
-fuī,** *be useful, do good, benefit* (+ dat.).] M

20. Plūrimī sānē, quōrum vīta māteriālismō practicō īnficitur, ā clārā
huiusmodī drāmaticī statūs perceptiōne avertuntur, vel saltem
miseriā oppressī, impediuntur quōminus illum cōnsīderent.

[*Gaudium et Spēs 10, CDD, p. 692, speaking of the many divisions
at the heart of modern culture and of modern man.—**sānē,** adv.,
to be sure.—**māteriālismus, -ī,** m., *materialism.*—**practicus,
-a, -um,** *active, practical.*—**īnficiō, -ere,** *dye, stain; poison,
taint.*—**huiusmodī,** *of this kind, such.*—**drāmaticus, -a, -um,**
dramatic.—**status, -ūs,** m., *condition, state.*—**perceptiō, -ōnis,** f.,
comprehension.—**vel,** conj., *or.*—**saltem,** adv., *at least.*—**miseria,
-ae,** f., *wretchedness, unhappy condition.*—**impediō, -īre,** *hinder.*—
cōnsīderō (1), *look at, regard carefully, contemplate.*] A

CAPVT XXXVI

Jussive Noun Clauses; *Fīō*; Infinitive in Indirect Command in EL; Substantive Clauses of Result

Syntaxis Supplēmentum

Infinitive in Indirect Command. CL normally employed the infinitive in indirect commands only with the verbs *iubeō*, command, *vetō*, forbid, and *sinō*, let, allow, permit. EL extended this usage to other verbs, e.g., *rogō*. See Sentence 4 below.

Substantive Clause of Result. Verbs such as *fierī*, *facere*, *efficere*, and *accidere* can govern a result clause. Since the result clause functions with these verbs either as a subject clause or an object clause, depending on whether the main verb is transitive (*facere*, *efficere*) or intransitive (*fierī*, *accidere*), these constructions are called substantive clauses of result.

> *efficere ut*, to bring it about that
>
> *facere ut*, to see to it that, please
>
> *accidit ut*, it happens that
>
> *fit ut*, it happens that
>
> *fierī potest ut*, it is possible that

Note that *efficere* and *facere* sometimes govern *nē* instead of *ut nōn* in this construction. In such cases, the subjunctive suggests the will of the speaker, and the result clause has the sense of a command (*Woodcock*, § 168).

Verba Memoriā Comprehendenda

efficiō, -ere, -fēcī, -fectum, *effect, bring about*
accidō, -ere, -cidī, *fall down on; happen*

SENTENTIAE Ē FONTIBUS NŌN ANTĪQUĪS HAUSTAE

1. Accidit quoque ut vīsum somnium referret frātribus suīs. Quae causa maiōris odiī sēminārium fuit.

   [*Gen. 37:5, Joseph reports his dream to his brothers.—**somnium, -iī,** n., *dream.*—**odium, -iī,** n., *hatred.*—**sēminārium, -iī,** n., *seed bed.*] I/M

2. Et benedīcta tū, quae prohibuistī mē hodiē, nē īrem ad sanguinem et ulcīscerer mē manū meā.

   [*I Sam, 25:33 V, David to Abigail.—**eō, īre,** *go.* The imperfect subjunctive is formed regularly.—**ulcīscor, -ī,** *avenge.*] I/M

3. Et pete ab eō [i.e., Deō] ut viās tuās dīrigat et omnia cōnsilia tua in ipsō permaneant.

   [*Tob. 4:20 V, LH 3.609, from Tobit's advice to his son.—**dīrigō, -ere,** *direct, guide.*—**permaneō,** emphatic form of *maneō.*] I

4. Parentēs eam monuērunt honōrāre socerōs, dīligere marītum, regere familiam, gubernāre domum, et sē ipsam irreprehensibilem exhibēre.

   [Tob. 10:13 V, Raguel and Edna give advice to their daughter Sarah, who is about to be married.—**honōrō** (1), *honor, respect.*—**socerī, -cerōrum,** m., *parents-in-law.*—**marītus, -ī,** m., *a husband.*—**domus, -ūs,** f., *a house.*—**gubernō** (1), *pilot; govern.*—**irreprehensibilis, -e,** *unblamable.*—**exhibeō, -ēre,** *display; make.*] I/M

5. Rēx iussit ignem admovērī et frātrem quī prior fuerat locūtus, adhūc spīrantem, torrērī in sartāgine, in quā, cum diū cruciārētur, cēterī frātrēs ūnā cum mātre invicem sē hortābantur morī fortiter.

   [II Mac. 7:5 V, King Antiochus begins to torture the seven faithful sons of a devout Jewish mother.—**rēx** = Antiochus IV Epiphanes (c. 215–154 BCE).—**admoveō, -ēre,** *apply.*—**fuerat locūtus,** depon. plupf. ind. = *had spoken.*—**adhūc,** adv., *still.*—**spīrō** (1), *breathe.*—**torreō, -ēre,** *roast, bake, burn.*—**sartāgō, -inis,** f., *frying pan.*—**cruciō** (1), *torture, torment.*—**ūnā,** adv., *together.*—**invicem,** adv., *in turn.*] I/M

6. Hodiē per tōtum mundum mellifluī factī sunt caelī.

   [*Respōnsōrium, Lēctiō II, Ad mātūtīnum, In Nātīvitāte Dominī, BR 1.74.—**mellifluus, -a, -um,** *flowing with honey; mellifluous.*] I

7.   Exeuntēs discipulī praedicābant ut paenitentiam agerent.
      [*Antiphona ad "Benedictus," Dominica XV per annum, LH
      3.391.—**exeuntēs,** nom. pl. pres. act. partic. of *exeō, = going out.*—
      praedicō (1), *preach.*—**paenitentiam agerent,** for this idiom see
      Capvt VIII, Sentence 5.] I

8.   Fac ut exemplum tuum puerī imitentur atque sapientiā et grātiā
      semper prōficiant.
      [*Precēs, Fēria III, ad Vesperās, LH 3.601.—**exemplum, -ī,** n.,
      example, model.—**imitor, -ārī,** *imitate.*—**grātia,** here = *grace.*—
      prōficiō, -ere, *make headway, advance; help.*] I

9.   Nunc enim et ipsīus Dominī professiōne et fidē nostrā vērē caro est
      et vērē sanguis est. Et haec accepta atque hausta id efficiunt, ut et nōs
      in Chrīstō et Chrīstus in nōbīs sit.
      [*St. Hilary of Poitiers, *Dē Trīnitāte* 8.14, speaking of the
      eucharistic elements.—**professiō, -ōnis,** f., *declaration.*—**vērē,**
      adv., *truly, really.*—**hauriō, -īre, hausī, haustum,** *draw up* or *out;*
      drink up, absorb; drain, empty; swallow up.] I/M

10.   Vincat fōns sitim tuam, nōn autem sitis fontem vincat, quia, sī sitis
      tua explētur quīn fōns exhauriātur, dēnuō sitiēns iterum ex eō bibere
      poteris; sī vērō, sitī tuā explētā, fōns quoque siccārētur, victōria tua
      in malum tuum verterētur.
      [*St. Ephraem the Syrian, *Commentārium in Diatessarōn* 1.19,
      in LH 3.157, speaking of the Word of God as the fountain of
      life.—**fōns, fontis,** m., *a spring, fountain.*—**sitis, -is,** f., *thirst.*—
      quīn, here introducing a limiting result clause dependent on
      an expression "denying objection, hindrance, prevention, or
      analogous extensions of these" (*Woodcock,* § 187[a]), = *without*
      + gerund.—**exhauriō, -īre,** *draw out; drain dry.*—**dēnuō,** adv.,
      anew.—**sitiō, -īre,** *be thirsty.*—**sitī,** *sitis* occurs only in the sg.,
      and shows the *i*-stem in all cases.—**siccō** (1), *make dry, dry.*] A

11.   Ut discipulōs impedīret, nē eum dē mōmentō adventūs suī
      interrogārent, Chrīstus dīxit, "Dē illā hōrā nēmō scit."
      [*St. Ephraem the Syrian, *Commentārium in Diatessarōn* 18.15, in
      LH 1.146.— **impediō, -īre,** *hinder.*—**mōmentum, -ī,** n., *minute,*
      moment.—**adventus, -ūs,** m., *arrival, advent.*—**interrogō** (1),
      ask.] M

12.   Fierī potest ut ego illum locum minus bene intellegam.
      [*St. Augustine of Hippo, *Dē magistrō* 5.16.] I/M

13. Quod sī quis, eīs forte cōnspectīs cum simul aderō, mē admonuerit,
     dīcēns, "Ecce *sarabārās*," discam rem quam nesciēbam, nōn per verba
     quae dicta sunt, sed per eius aspectum, per quem factum est ut etiam
     nōmen illud quid valēret nōssem ac tenērem.

> [St. Augustine of Hippo, *Dē magistrō* 10.35, Augustine is
> demonstrating that words teach nothing.—**Quod sī,** as often =
> *but if.*—**forte,** *by chance.*—**cōnspiciō, -ere, -spexī, -spectum,**
> *see, observe.*—**simul,** adv., *at the same time.*—**adsum, -esse,** *be
> present.*—**eīs forte cōnspectīs . . . aderō,** = who has by chance
> seen these things (i.e., the *sarabarae*) when I am present at the
> same time.—**admoneō** = *moneō.*—**sarabāra, -ae,** f., a very rare
> word used at Dan. 3:94, which Augustine takes to mean *a head
> covering.*—**aspectus, -ūs,** m., *a seeing.*—**nōmen,** here = *noun.*—
> **nōssem,** = *nōvissem.*] A

14. Coepitque [Augustīnus] epīscopīs fraternā admonitiōne suādēre, ut,
     pāce catholicā sēcum habitā, commūnem ēvangelizandī gentibus prō
     Dominō labōrem susciperent.

> [St. Bede the Venerable, *Historia Ecclēsiastica* 2.2, St. Augustine of
> Canterbury addresses the British bishops.—**Augustīnus, -ī,** m., St.
> *Augustine* of Canterbury.—**epīscopus, -ī,** m., *bishop.*—**frāternus,
> -a, -um,** *brotherly.*—**admonitiō, -ōnis,** f., *advice.*—**suādeō, -ēre,**
> *urge.*—**catholicus, -a, -um,** *universal, catholic.*—**ēvangelīzandī,** a
> gerund in the gen., = *of preaching the Gospel* (+ dat.).] M

15. Ō alme salūtiferque Iēsū, vēre litterārum omnium et ingeniī Deus ac
     largītor, vēre rēx glōriae ac virtūtum domine, tē nunc, flexīs animae
     genibus, supplex ōrō, ut, sī mihi nōn amplius vīs largīrī, haec saltem
     portiō mea sit, ut vir bonus sim, quod, nisi tē valdē amem piēque
     colam, esse nōn possum. Ad hoc enim, nōn ad litterās nātus sum,
     quae, sī sōlae obvēnerint, īnflant dīruuntque, nōn aedificant.

> [*Francesco Petrarca (Petrarch), *Dē Suī Ipsīus et Multōrum Ignōrantiā*
> 2.32–33.—**almus, -a, -um,** *nourishing, kind.*—**salūtifer, -fera,
> -ferum,** *health-bringing.*—**largītor, -ōris,** m., *a liberal giver.*—**flectō,
> -ere, flexī, flexum,** *bend.*—**supplex, -icis,** *humble, suppliant.*—
> **amplius,** adv., *more; longer.*—**largior, -īrī,** *give abundantly, lavish,
> bestow.*—**saltem,** adv., *at least.*—**portiō, -ōnis,** f., *a part.*—**ut . . .
> sim,** an explanatory *ut*-clause. See GL, § 557.—**valdē,** adv., *intensely,
> greatly.*—**colō, -ere,** *cultivate; worship; cherish.*—**obveniō, -īre,
> -vēnī,** *occur, fall to one's lot.*—**īnflō** (1), *puff up, inflate.*—**dīruō, -ere,**
> *pull apart, destroy.*—**aedificō** (1), *build, establish.*] A

16. Tū scīs, Domine, cōram quō omne dēsīderium atque omne suspīrium
     meum est, quod ex litterīs, quandō hīs sōbriē ūsus sum, nihil amplius
     quaesīvī, quam ut bonus fierem, nōn quod id litterās aut (quamvīs id
     ipsum pollicērētur Aristoteles multīque aliī) omnīnō aliquem, nisi tē
     ūnum, facere posse cōnfīderem, sed quod per litterās quō tendēbam
     iter honestius ac certius simulque iūcundius aestimārem,[22] tē duce,
     nōn aliō.
     [*Francesco Petrarca (Petrarch), *Dē Suī Ipsīus et Multōrum
     Ignōrantiā* 2.33.—**cōram,** prep. + abl., *in the presence of.*—
     dēsīderium, -iī, n., *desire, longing.*—**suspīrium, -iī,** n., *a
     sigh.*—**quod,** sets up indirect statement.—**sōbrius, -a, -um,**
     sober; moderate; reasonable, sensible.—**ut . . . fierem,** used here
     instead of the more regular infinitive. See GL, §§ 423.2 N 2, and
     557 N 2.—**quod,** here and below, = *because.*—**id,** this pronoun
     represents the noun clause *ut . . . fierem.*—**litterās . . . aliquem,**
     take as the subjects of *posse.*—**quamvīs,** conj. (+ subjunctive),
     although.—**polliceor, -ērī,** *promise.*—**omnīnō,** adv., *at all.*—
     cōnfīdō, -ere, *be confident.*—**quō,** adv., *(to) where.*—**tendō,**
     -ere, *stretch; go.*—**iter, itineris,** n., *a journey; road.*—**honestus,**
     -a, -um, *respectable; honorable.*—**iūcundus, -a, -um,** *pleasant,*
     agreeable, delightful.—**aestimō** (1), *estimate value; judge.*] A

17. *Caelō et terrae loquī.* Quī frūstrā vōciferāntur, "caelō et terrae loquī"
     dīcuntur.
     [*Desiderius Erasmus, *Adagia* 1.5.75.— **frūstrā,** adv., *in vain.*—
     vōciferor, -ārī, *cry aloud, shout.*] I/M

18. Benedicte Deus, quī effēcistī ut quaecumque scrīpta sunt ad
     nostram doctrīnam scrīberentur, concede nōbīs, ut ita scrīptūram
     attentē audiāmus, legāmus, discāmus, et intellegāmus, sincēreque
     observēmus, ut per patientiam et cōnsōlātiōnem scrīptūrārum
     retineāmus spem vītae aeternae, quam dedistī nōbīs in servātōre
     nostrō Iesū Chrīstō, cuī tēcum et Sānctō Spīrituī sit honor et glōria,
     per omnia saecula saeculōrum. Amēn.
     [*Collecta, Dominica II Adventūs, Liber Precum Pūblicārum in
     Ecclēsiā Anglicānā (1560), one of the few Sunday collects composed,
     not translated, for the new Protestant liturgy of the Church of
     England.—**quīcumque, quaecumque, quodcumque,** *whoever,*

---

22 The text has *extimarem,* which appears to be a form halfway between the CL *aestimarem*
    and the Italian *estimassi.*

whatever.—**doctrīna, -ae,** f., *instruction, learning.*—**concēdō, -ere,** *grant, concede.*—**attentus, -a, -um,** *attentive.*—**sincērus, -a, -um,** *pure; sincere.*—**observō** (1), *watch, attend to, observe.*—**cōnsōlātiō, -ōnis,** f., *consolation, encouragement, comfort.*—**retineō, -ēre,** *hold fast.*—**servātor, -ōris,** m., *a savior.*] A

19.   Secunda obiectiō: ex ōrātiōne nōn intellēctā nūlla ūtilitās sequitur. ... Igitur precēs omnēs tam pūblicae quam prīvātae linguā vulgārī fierī dēbent. Quae obiectiō Calvīnī est, sed facilem habet solūtiōnem. Nam in prīmīs falsum est ex pūblicā ōrātiōne Ecclēsiae nūllum frūctum ā populō percipī, nisi ea ōrātiō ā populō intellegātur. Nam ōrātiō Ecclēsiae nōn fit populō, sed Deō prō populō. Itaque nōn est opus ut populus intellegat, ut eī prōsit, sed satis est sī intellegat Deus. Quemadmodum sī quis apud rēgem Latīnē ōrāret prō aliquō rūsticō, certē rūsticus frūctum inde percipere poterit, etiamsī nōn intellegat ōrātiōnem advocātī suī.

      [*St. Robert Bellarmine, *Dē Contrōversiīs Fideī: Dē Verbō Deī* 2.16, addressing one of John Calvin's arguments against public prayer in Latin.—**obiectiō, -ōnis,** f., *a reproach, objection.*—**ōrātiō, -ōnis,** f., *prayer.*—**ūtilitās, -tātis,** f., *advantage, usefulness.*—**prex, precis,** f., *a prayer.*—**pūblicus, -a, -um,** *public.*—**prīvātus, -a, -um,** *private.*—**vulgāris, -e,** *common, ordinary.*—**Calvīnus, -ī,** m., John *Calvin.*—**solūtiō, -ōnis,** f., *a solution, explanation.*—**in prīmīs,** *in the first place.*—**falsus, -a, -um,** *false.*—**percipiō, -ere,** *gain.*—**est opus,** *there is need that* (+ an *ut*-clause to express what is needed).—**prōsum, -esse,** *be useful to* (+ dat.).—**quemadmodum,** conj., *as for instance.*—**Latīnē,** adv., *in Latin.*—**rūsticus, -ī,** m., *a serf* (see Latham, s.v.); perh. = *peasant* in Bellarmine's day.—**inde,** adv., *thence, from it.*—**poterit,** such modal verbs as *possum* remain in the ind. in the apodosis of an unreal or contrafactual condition. See *Woodcock,* § 200(1).—**etiamsī,** conj., *even if.*—**advocātus, -ī,** m., *an advocate, counsel.*] M

20.   Necesse est multōs ad lēgem nātūrālem revocāre, antequam dē Deō loquāmur. Chrīstus enim prōmittit remissiōnem peccātōrum, sed quid hoc ad eōs quī, cum lēgem nātūrālem ignōrent, nesciunt sē peccāvisse. Quis medicāmentum accipiet, nisi sē morbō tenērī sciat? Relātīvismus mōrālis hostis est quem dēbēmus vincere, antequam Atheismum aggrediāmur. Ferē auserim dīcere, "Prīmō faciāmus iūniōrēs bonōs pāgānōs, et posteā faciāmus Chrīstiānōs."

[*C. S. Lewis Domnō Iōannī Calabriae, xv Septembris 1953, Moynihan, 92.—**necesse est,** *it is necessary* (+ inf.).—**revocō** (1), *call back.*—**ignōrō** (1), *be ignorant of, not to know.*—**medicāmentum, -ī,** n., *a medicine.*—**relātīvismus, -ī,** m., *relativism.*—**mōrālis, -e,** *moral.*—**atheismus, -ī,** m., *atheism.*—**aggredior, -ī,** *approach; attack.*—**ferē,** adv., *almost, nearly.*—**iūnior, -ius,** *younger.*] M

St. Hilary of Poitiers (c.300–c. 368) was a native of Poitiers in Roman Gaul. He converted to Christianity from Neo-Platonism as an adult, and was elected bishop of Poitiers in the early 350s, though a married man. He fought the Arian heresy vigorously, such that the Emperor Constantius II exiled him to Phrygia from 356 to 360. Hilary wrote a number of theological works, the most important of which was the *Dē Trīnitāte*, in which he expressed the subtle thought of the Greek Fathers in Latin for the first time. He was deeply influenced by Origen and St. Athanasius. This illumination is an imaginative depiction of St. Hilary in Codex Bodmer 127, fol. 144r, a manuscript of the twelfth century. Hilary's vestments are in the style of that century. With abbreviations expanded, the title reads, "Incipit vīta sānctī Hilariī epīscopī." The first words are, "Igitur beātus hilarius pictāvōrum urbis epīscopus regiōne ęquītāniā oriundus fuit." Can you find the letter "I" in *Igitur*? Note, too, the confused spelling of the adjective *ęquītāniā*, which should be spelled *aquītāniā*. The e-caudata (*ę*) stands for the diphthong *ae*, and is used here by mistake. (© Wikimedia Commons)

CAPVT XXXVII

Conjugation of *Eō*; Place and Time Constructions; Place Constructions in EL; *Et Factum Est*; Verbs of Remembering and Forgetting

Syntaxis Supplēmentum

Place Constructions. EL sometimes employs prepositions in place constructions in which CL eschews them, e.g., *vēnit iterum in Cana Galilaeae*, he came again to Cana of Galilee (Jn. 4:46). On the other hand, EL sometimes extends the CL usage with the names of cities towns, and small islands to names of countries, e.g., *perrēxit Aethiopiam*, he went to Ethiopia (Jerome, Ep. 53.1). Both examples are found in Blaise, § 75.

Et factum est. The Vulgate sometimes imitates the LXX and Greek NT in advancing an historical narrative with the words *et factum est*, in Greek, καὶ ἐγένετο or ἐγένετο δέ. In this construction, the Greek is imitating the Hebrew idiom *wayəhî wə*.[23] The idiom is also employed in other ecclesiastical compositions. PW § 134 note that generally this idiom is followed by a noun-clause introduced "by *ut* or *quod*" with the subjunctive. The noun-clause is the true subject of the sentence. PW also notice, "Frequently . . . when a *cum* clause intervenes, the connecting conjunction is omitted after *factum est.*" See Sentences 7 and 13 below.

Verbs of Remembering and Forgetting. Verbs that mean "remember" or "forget" often take the genitive of the person or thing forgotten or remembered, but sometimes the accusative, especially of the thing forgotten or remembered.

---

[23] See William F. Arndt and F. Wilbur Gingrich, *A Greek-English Lexicon of the New Testament and Other Early Christian Literature*, 4th ed. rev. and aug. (Chicago, 1957), s.v. γίνομαι I.3.f.

VERBA MEMORIĀ COMPREHENDENDA

licet, to the definitions in *Wheelock,* add *although,* used with a verb in the subjunctive.

meminī, -nisse, defective verb (perf. with pres. force), *remember, recollect* (+ gen. or acc.)

misereō, -ēre, -uī, miser(i)tum or **misereor, -ērī, miser(i)tus sum,** (feel) pity (+ gen. or dat.) See Capvt XXXIX for impersonal use.

SENTENTIAE Ē FONTIBUS NŌN ANTĪQUĪS HAUSTAE

1. Respondērunt frātrēs eius et māter, "Maneat puella saltem decem diēs apud nōs et posteā proficīscētur."
    [Gen. 24:55, Rebecca's family asks a concession from Eliezer.— **saltem,** adv., *at least.*] I/M

2. Quibus explētīs, eādem diē ēgressus est omnis exercitus Dominī dē terrā Aegyptī.
    [*Ex. 12:41.—**Aegyptus, -ī,** f., *Egypt.* For the use of the gen. here, see Appendix I, § 9.] I/M

3. Laetātus sum in hīs quae dicta sunt mihi, "In domum Dominī ībimus." Stāntēs erant pedēs nostrī in atriīs tuīs, Ierūsalem.
    [*Ps. 121:1–2 V.—**laetor, -tārī, -tātus sum,** *rejoice.*—**in domum Dominī,** a CL construction, as the *domus* is regarded here as a house, not a home, as the gen. modifier shows. See GL, § 337.3.— **stāntēs erant,** see Capvt XXIII Syntaxis.—**pēs, pedis,** m., *a foot.*—**ātrium, -iī,** n., *a hall.*] I/M

4. Cum exierit spīritus hominis, revertētur in terram suam; tunc perībunt omnia cōnsilia eius.
    [Ps. 145:4 PIB, Fēria quārta ad Laudēs I, BR 2.480.—**revertor, -ī,** *return.*] I

5. Prope est ut veniat tempus eius, et diēs eius nōn ēlongābuntur. Miserēbitur enim Dominus Iacob et ēliget adhūc Israël et requiescere eōs faciet super humum suam.
    [Is. 14:1 V.—**Prope est ut** + subjunctive, = *the time is near when.*— **ēlongō** (1), *prolong.*—**Iacob,** indecl. Heb. name, m., *Jacob.*— **adhūc,** adv., *still.*] I/M

6.   Et vidit Iōnathās quia tempus eum iuvat, et ēlēgit virōs et mīsit eōs
Rōmam statuere et renovāre cum eīs amīcitiam; et ad Spartiātās et
ad alia loca mīsit epistolās secundum eandem fōrmam; et abiērunt
Rōmam et intrāvērunt cūriam et dīxērunt, "Iōnathās summus
sacerdōs et gēns Iūdaeōrum mīsērunt nōs ut renovārēmus amīcitiam
et societātem secundum prīstinum."

> [*I Mac. 12:1–3 V, Jonathan, son of Mattathias, leader of the
> Maccabean state, positions himself internationally.—**statuō,
> -ere,** *set up; determine.*—**renovō** (1), *renew.*—**Spartiātes, -ae,**
> m., *a Spartan.*—**epistola, -ae,** f., *a letter.*—**secundum,** prep. +
> acc., *according to, in conformity with.*—**abeō, -īre, -iī,** *go away,*
> *depart.*—**cūria, -ae,** f., *the senate chamber.*—**Iūdaeus, -a, -um,**
> *Jewish.*—**societās, -tātis,** f., *fellowship.*—**prīstinum, -ī,** n., *(a)*
> *former condition.*] I

7.   Et factum est, ut discessērunt ab eīs angelī in caelum, pastōrēs
loquēbāntur ad invicem, "Trānseāmus usque Bethlehem et videāmus
hoc verbum quod factum est, quod Dominus ostendit nobis."

> [*Lk. 2:15 V. —**ut,** here introduces a temporal clause, not a noun
> clause.—**pastor, -ōris,** m., *a shepherd.*—**ad invicem,** = *to each*
> *other.* See Appendix I, § 35.—**trānseō, -īre,** *go across.*—**usque,**
> adv., *all the way.*] I/M

8.   Prōtectōr in tē spērantium, Deus, sine quō nihil est validum, nihil
sānctum, multiplicā super nōs misericordiam tuam, ut, tē rēctōre,
tē duce, sīc bonīs trānseuntibus nunc ūtāmur, ut iam possīmus
inhaerēre mansūrīs. Per Dominum.

> [*Ōrātiō 17 dominicālis et cotīdiāna, LH 3.31.—**prōtectōr, -ōris,**
> m., *a protector.*—**validus, -a, -um,** *strong, powerful.*—**multiplicō**
> (1), *increase many times, multiply.*—**rēctōr, -ōris,** m., *a ruler,*
> *governor, director, guide.*—**inhaereō, -ēre,** *cling to, cleave to.*] M

9.   Et tamen post accūsātiōnem fallaciārum et crūdēlitātis meae, [mater
mea,] conversa rursum ad dēprecandum tē prō mē, abiit ad solita, et
ego Rōmam.

> [*St. Augustine of Hippo, *Cōnfessiōnēs* 5.8, Augustine has just left
> his mother on the Carthaginian strand, as Aeneas left Dido.—
> **accūsātiō, -ōnis,** f., *an accusation, indictment.*—**fallācia, -ae,** f.,
> *a deception, trick.*—**crūdēlitās, -tātis,** f., *cruelty.*—**convertor,**
> **-tī, -versus sum,** *turn back.*—**rursum,** adv., *again.*—**ad**
> **dēprecandum tē,** to *pray to you.*—**solita,** supply *loca.*] M/A

10.   Pervēnit autem Theodōrus ad ecclēsiam suam secundō postquam
       consecrātus est annō, sub diē sextō Kalendārum Iūniārum,
       Dominicā; et fēcit in eā annōs vīgintī et ūnum, mēnsēs trēs, diēs
       vīgintī sex.
       [*St. Bede the Venerable, *Historia Ecclēsiastica* 4.2, Theodore, the
       new archbishop of Canterbury, reaches his see from Rome in 669
       CE.—**postquam,** conj., *after.*—**sub,** here = *on.*— **sextus, -a, -um,**
       sixth.—**Kalendae, -ārum,** f. pl., *the Kalends, the first day of the
       month.*—**Iūnius, -a, -um,** *of or pertaining to June, June.*—**sub diē
       sextō Kalendārum Iūniārum** = the classical *ante diem sextum
       Kalendās Iūniās, i.e., May 27th.*—**Dominicā [diē],** = *on the Lord's
       Day, Sunday.*—**vīgintī,** indecl. numeral, *twenty.*—**mēnsis, -is,**
       m., *month.*] M

11.   In quō proeliō [i.e., in ipsō Pȳrēnaeī iugō] Eggihardus rēgiae mēnsae
       praepositus, Anshelmus cōmes palatiī et Hruodlandus Britannicī
       limitis praefectus cum aliīs complūribus interficiuntur.
       [*Einhard, *Vīta Karolī Magnī Imperatōris* 9, speaking of the Battle
       of Roncevaux.—**proelium, -iī,** n., *a battle.*—**Pȳrēnaeum, -ī,** *the
       Pyrenees.*—**iugum, -ī,** n., *a yoke; a* (mountain) *pass.*—**Eggihardus,
       -ī,** m., *Eggihard.*—**rēgiae mēnsae praepositus,** *the royal major-
       domo.*—**Anshelmus, -ī,** m., *Anselm.*—**cōmes palatiī,** *the minister
       of justice.*—**Hruodlandus, -ī,** m., *Roland.*—**Britannicī limitis
       praefectus,** *the count of the Breton march.*—**complūrēs, -plūra,**
       several.] I

12.   Ō Fīlī dīlectissime, quem genuī in visceribus meīs dē vī circueuntis
       rotae sanctae dīvīnitātis, quae mē creāvit et omnia membra mea
       ōrdināvit et in visceribus meīs omne genus mūsicōrum in omnibus
       flōribus tonōrum cōnstituit, nunc mē et tē, ō Fīlī dulcissime, multa
       turba virginum sequitur, quās per adiūtōrium tuum salvāre dignāre.
       [*St. Hildegard of Bingen, *Ō Fīlī dīlectissime,* in *Symphonia,* 260,
       a non-metrical hymn of the Virgin to her Son.—**gignō, -ere,
       genuī,** *bear, bring forth.*—**viscera, -um,** n., *the internal organs;
       the womb.*—**circueō, -īre,** *go around; encircle, encompass.*—
       dīvīnitās, -tātis, f., *the divine nature, divinity.*—**membrum, -ī,**
       n., *a member* of the body.—**ōrdinō** (1), *set in order, arrange.*—
       mūsica, -ōrum, n. pl., *music.*—**flōs, -ōris,** m., *a flower.*—**tonus,
       -ī,** m., *an instrumental tone* or *sound.*—**cōnstituō, -ere, -stituī,**
       place, establish.—**adiūtōrium, -iī,** n., *help, aid.*—**salvō** (1), *save.*—
       dignor, -ārī, *consider worthy; deign.*] I

13. Factum est autem cum pater eius, familiārī causā urgente, aliquantulum ā propriā discessisset, et vir Deī vinctus in domūs ergastulō permanēret, māter eius quae sōla domī cum eō remānserat, factum virī suī nōn probāns, blandīs sermōnibus filium allocūta est.
[*Thomas of Celano, *Vīta prīma S. Franciscī Assisiensis* 13, Francis' father has confined him in the house for his religious enthusiasm.— **familiāris, -e,** *domestic, family.*—**urgeō, -ēre,** *put pressure on.*— **aliquantulum,** adv., *a little while.*—**propriā,** here understand *domō.*—**vinciō, -īre, vinxī, vinctum,** *bind.*—**ergastulum, -ī,** n., *prison.*—**permaneō, -ēre,** *remain, hold out.*—**blandus, -a, -um,** *smooth; pleasant.*—**alloquor, -quī, -locūtus sum,** *speak to; exhort; comfort.*] I/M

14. Nam per sēnās ālas rēctē intellegī possunt sex illūminātiōnum suspensiōnēs, quibus anima quasi quibusdam gradibus vel itineribus dispōnitur, ut trānseat ad pācem per ecstaticōs excessūs sapientiae chrīstiānae.
[*St. Bonaventure, *Itinerārium Mentis in Deum,* Prologus 3, allegorizing the Seraphim.—**sēnī, -ae, -a,** distributive numeral, *six each; six.*—**āla, -ae,** f., *a wing.*—**rēctē,** adv., *correctly.*— **illūminātiō, -ōnis,** f., *a lighting up, enlightening.*—**suspensiō, -ōnis,** f., *an arching* or *vaulting, arched work.*—**quasi,** adv. or conj., *as if, as it were.*—**gradus, -ūs,** m., *a step.*—**dispōnō, -ere,** *set in order, arrange, dispose.*—**trānseō, -īre,** *go across, cross.*— **ecstaticus, -a, -um,** *ecstatic, rapturous.*—**excessus, -ūs,** m., *a departure; a departure from the mental powers, ecstasy.*] M

15. Nempe quibuscumque rēgnī partibus nāscitur lāna tenuior atque ideō pretiōsior, ibi nōbilēs et generōsī atque abbātēs aliquot, sānctī virī, nōn hīs contentī reditibus frūctibusque annuīs quī maiōribus suīs solēbant ex praediīs crescere, nec habentēs satis quod, ōtiōsē ac lautē vīventēs, nihil in pūblicum prōsint, nisi etiam obsint, arvō nihil relinquunt, omnia claudunt pascuīs, dēmōliuntur domōs, dīruunt oppida, templō dumtaxat stabulandīs ovibus relictō, et tamquam parum solī perderent apud vōs ferārum saltūs ac vīvāria, illī bonī virī habitātiōnēs omnēs et quidquid usquam est cūltī vertunt in sōlitūdinem.
[*St. Thomas More, *Ūtopia* 1, LAM, 62, Raphael Hythloday is addressing John Cardinal Morton on the grave economic and social evil of enclosures.—**nempe,** adv., *truly, certainly.*— **quīcumque, quaecumque, quodcumque,** *whoever, whatever.*— **quibuscumque rēgnī [in] partibus.**—**rēgnum, -ī,** n., *a kingdom,*

realm.—**tenuis, -e,** *thin, fine.*—**ideō,** adv., *on that account.*—
pretiōsus, -a, -um, *expensive.*—**nōbilis, -e,** *noble.*—**generōsus,
-a, -um,** *of gentle birth* (describing the gentry).—**abbās, -ātis,**
m., *an abbot.*—**aliquot,** indecl. num., *some, several.*—**contentus,
-a, -um,** *content* (+ abl.).—**reditus, -ūs,** m., *income, revenue.*—
annuus, -a, -um, *annual.*—**praedium, -iī,** n., *a farm, landed
estate.*—**habentēs [id esse] satis quod.*—**ōtiōsus, -a, -um,** *at
leisure, without occupation.*—**lautus, -a, -um,** *washed, bathed;
fine, splendid, elegant.*—**pūblicum, -ī,** n., *the commonwealth.*—
prōsum, prōdesse, *be useful, do good, benefit.*—**obsum, obesse,**
be in the way, be against; hinder, hurt.—**arvum, -ī,** n., *ploughed land,
a field.*—**claudō, -ere,** *close, shut.*—**pascua, -ōrum,** n., *pastures.*—
dēmōlior, -īrī, *throw down, demolish.*—**dīruō, -ere,** *pull to pieces,
demolish.*—**oppidum, -ī,** n., *a town.*—**dumtaxat,** adv., *at most.*—
stabulandīs ovibus, = *for stabling sheep.*—**ovis, -is,** f., *a sheep.*—
solum, -ī, n., *ground, earth, soil.*—**perdō, -ere,** *destroy, ruin, lose.*
—**perderent,** take as if the protasis of a present contrafactual, = *were
destroying.*—**fera, -ae,** f., *a wild beast.*—**saltus, -ūs,** m., *woodland,
forest.*—**vīvārium, -ī,** n., *a game preserve.*—**habitātiō, -ōnis,** f.,
a dwelling.—**usquam,** adv., *anywhere.*—**cultus, -ūs,** m., *tilling,
cultivation.*—**sōlitūdō, -inis,** f., *solitude; a state of desolation.*] A

16.   Ergō ut ūnus helluō, inexplēbilis ac dīra pestis patriae, continuātīs
agrīs, aliquot milia iūgerum ūnō circumdet saeptō, ēiciuntur colōnī;
quīdam suīs etiam aut circumscrīptī fraude aut vī oppressī exuuntur,
aut fatīgātī iniūriīs adiguntur ad venditiōnem.

    [*St. Thomas More, *Ūtopia* 1, LAM, 62, continued from
the previous sentence.—**helluō, -ōnis,** m., *a gormandizer,
squanderer.*—**inexplēbilis, -e,** *insatiable.*—**dīrus, -a, -um,**
fearful, dreadful.—**pestis, -is,** f., *a plague; curse.*—**continuō**
(1), *connect together, make continuous.*—**iūgerum, -ī** (gen. pl.,
iūgerum, i.e., third decl.), n., *a measure of land,* about two-
thirds of an acre.—**circumdō, -dare,** *surround* something in
the acc. with something else in the abl.—**saeptum, -ī,** n., *a
fence, enclosure.*—**colōnus, -ī,** m., *a peasant farmer.*—**suīs,** abl.
of separation with *exuuntur.*—**circumscrībō, -ere, -scrīpsī,
-scrīptum,** here = *ensnared.*—**fraus, fraudis,** f., *deception,
fraud.*—**exuō, -ere,** *strip, deprive.*—**fatīgō** (1), *weary, tire.*—
iniūria, -ae, f., *injustice, wrong.*—**adigō, -ere,** *drive to, force to.*—
venditiō, -ōnis, f., *a selling, sale.*] M/A

17. Itaque quōque pactō ēmīgrant miserī, virī, mulierēs, marītī, uxōrēs, orbī, viduae, parentēs cum parvīs līberīs et numerōsā magis quam dīvite familiā, ut multīs opus habet manibus rēs rūstica, ēmīgrant, inquam, ē nōtīs atque assuetīs laribus, nec inveniunt quō sē recipiant.

[*St. Thomas More, *Ūtopia* 1, LAM, 62, continued from the previous sentence.—**quōque pactō,** *by whichever way it be.*— **ēmīgrō** (1), *move away from a place, migrate.*—**marītus, -ī,** m., *a husband.*—**orbus, -ī,** m., *an orphan.*—**vidua, -ae,** f., *a widow.*— **līberī, -ōrum,** m., (a person's) *children.*—**numerōsus, -a, -um,** *numerous.*—**opus, operis,** n., *a work, task.*—**rūsticus, -a, -um,** *rural.*—**nōtus, -a, -um,** *known, familiar.*—**assuētus, -a, -um,** *customary, usual.*—**lār, laris,** n., *a household divinity* among the Romans; *hearth, home.*—**sē recipere,** *withdraw, retire.*] M/A

18. Ad haec tria [argūmenta] respondet Calvīnus ... Scrīptūrās sacrās discernī ā nōn sacrīs per sē ut lūcem ā tenebrīs, dulce ab amārō. At contrā, nam sī ita esset, cur Lutherus iūdicāret Epistolam Iacōbī strāmineam, et Calvīnus apostolicam?

[*St. Robert Bellarmine, *Dē Contrōversiīs Fideī: Dē Verbō Deī* 4.4, mentioning Calvin's counterarguments to Catholic claims that Scripture does not authenticate itself.—**Calvīnus, -ī,** m., John Calvin.—**discernō, -ere,** *separate; distinguish.*—**amārus, -a, -um,** *bitter.*—**at contrā,** *but on the contrary.*—**Lutherus, -ī,** m., Martin Luther.—**iūdicō** (1), *judge, consider.*—**epistola, -ae,** f., *an epistle, letter.*—**Iacōbus, -ī,** m., *James.*—**strāmineus, -a, -um,** *made of straw.*—**apostolicus, -a, -um,** *apostolic.*] M

19. Ideō addit Calvīnus ... nōn omnibus apparēre hanc differentiam Scrīptūrārum, sed sōlum habentibus Spīritum. Nam etiam lūcem ā tenebrīs nōn discernit caecus. At contrā, nam Calvīnus ... contendit apostolōs et prīmae ecclēsiae fidēlēs habuisse vērum Spīritum, sed illī iūdicābant Librum Sapientiae esse sacrum. ... Tamen librum Calvīnus, quī etiam Spīritum iactat, vult esse profānum.

[*St. Robert Bellarmine, *Dē Contrōversiīs Fideī: Dē Verbō Deī* 4.4, continuing the previous argument.—**ideō,** adv., *on that account, therefore.*—**addō, -ere,** *add.*—**appareō, -ēre,** *be visible, appear.*—**differentia, -ae,** f., *difference.*—**apostolus, -ī,** m., *an apostle.*—**iactō** (1), *boast.*—**profānus, -a, -um,** *lying outside a temple; ordinary, common.*] M

20.   Sed īnstat Calvīnus. Fundāmentum Ecclēsiae sunt Scrīptūrae
      Apostolōrum et Prophētārum . . . Igitur nōn crēdimus Scrīptūrās
      dīvīnās ex Trāditiōne Ecclēsiae, quia tunc fundāmentum Scrīptūrae
      esset Ecclēsia. Respondeō Apostolum nōn dīcere scrīpta Apostolōrum
      et Prophētārum, sed Apostolōs et Prophētās. Istī autem nōn sōlum
      scrīpsērunt, sed etiam ōre trādidērunt, et docuērunt sē scrīpsisse.
      Atque ita ex verbō Apostolōrum nōn scrīptō et per Ecclēsiam nōbīs
      trāditō cognōscimus quod sit verbum Apostolōrum scrīptum.

      [*St. Robert Bellarmine, *Dē Contrōversiīs Fideī: Dē Verbō Deī*
      4.4, continuing the previous argument.—**īnstō** (1), *persist.*—
      fundāmentum, -ī, n., *a foundation.*—**trāditiō, -ōnis,** *tradition.*—
      tunc, adv., *then.*—**Apostolum,** = St. Paul. The text under
      discussion is Eph. 2:20. Both the Vulgate and the Greek NT
      support the saint here.] M

21.   Certē sentiō gravissima perīcula nōbīs incumbere. Haec ēveniunt
      quia maxima pars Eurōpae apostasiam fēcit dē fide Chrīstiānā.
      Hinc status peior quam illum statum quem habuimus ante fidem
      receptam. Nēmō enim ex Chrīstiānismō redit in statum quam habuit
      ante Chrīstiānismum, sed in peiōrem: tantum distat inter pāgānum
      et apostatam quantum innūptam et adulteram. Nam fidēs perficit
      nātūram, sed fidēs amissa corrumpit nātūram. Ergō plērīque hominēs
      nostrī temporis amisērunt nōn modo lūmen supernātūrāle, sed etiam
      lūmen nātūrāle quod pāgānī habuērunt.

      [*C. S. Lewis Domnō Iōannī Calabriae, xv Septembris 1953,
      Moynihan, 90.—**incumbō, -ere,** *burden, oppress, weigh upon*
      (+ dat.).—**ēveniō, -īre,** *turn out, happen.*—**Eurōpa, -ae,** f.,
      Europe.—**apostasia, -ae,** f., *apostasy.*—**hinc,** adv., *hence.*—
      status, -ūs, m., *position, condition, state.*—**Chrīstiānismus, -ī,**
      m., *Christianity.*—**tantum . . . quantum,** *as much . . . as.*—**distat,**
      there is a difference.—**pāgānus, -ī,** m., *a pagan.*—**apostata, -ae,** m.,
      an apostate.—**innūpta, -ae,** f., *an unmarried woman.*—**adultera,**
      -ae, f., *an adulteress.*—**perficiō, -ere,** *perfect.*—**corrumpō, -ere,**
      ruin, corrupt.—**plērusque, -raque, -rumque,** and pl. **plērīque,**
      very many, a large part.—**lūmen, -inis,** n., *light.*—**supernātūrālis,**
      -e, *supernatural.*—**nātūrālis, -e,** *natural.*] I/M

CAPVT XXXVIII

Relative Clauses of Characteristic; Dative of Reference; Supines; **Dative of Purpose and Double Dative; Dative of Possession;** *Opus Est;* **Relative Clause of Result**

Syntaxis Supplēmentum

Dative of Purpose and Double Dative. See *Wheelock*, Appendix, 492; but note that where *Wheelock* sees the double dative as datives of purpose and reference, *Woodcock*, § 68, takes the latter to be "of the person interested," which elsewhere he defines as the dative of advantage or disadvantage (taking § 56 with § 64). A dative of purpose occurs in Capvt XXXIII, Sentence 6. See also Sentences 3, 4, 7, and 9 below.

Dative of Possession. See *Wheelock*, Appendix, 492.

Opus est. *Opus est* can mean, "There is need of." The thing needed is put in the nominative, and sometimes the ablative or genitive, while the person who needs the thing is put in the dative, e.g., *Imāgō enim est īdōlum, et opus est illī adiūtōrium*, An idol is an image, indeed, and it needs help (Wis. 13:16 V). The required action can also be represented by an infinitive (e.g., Sentence 11 below) or by an *ut*-clause (Sentence 20 below).

Relative Clause of Result. Introduced in passing on *Wheelock*, 328–329, the relative clause of result developed from the relative clause of characteristic. According to *Woodcock*, § 156, this construction is used when a relative clause of characteristic, which he himself prefers to call a generic relative clause (§ 155), is predicated with *esse* or "otherwise predicated," e.g., *Nūlla bēstia adeō fera est quae pullōs suōs nōn amet*. No beast is so savage that it does not love its own young. See Sentence 5 below.

VERBA MEMORIĀ COMPREHENDENDA

ambulō (1), *walk*

memor, -oris, *mindful* (+ gen.)

SENTENTIAE Ē FONTIBUS NŌN ANTĪQUĪS HAUSTAE

1. Salvum mē fac propter misericordiam tuam, quoniam nōn est in morte quī memor sit tuī.
    [*Ps. 6:5–6 V.]

2. Nōn est quī faciat bonum, nōn est usque ad ūnum.
    [*Ps. 13:1 V.—**usque ad,** adv. + prep. + acc., *even to, as far as.*] I

3. Eī quī insurgunt in tē sunt mihi taediō.
    [Ps. 138:21, BR 2.569.—**īnsurgō, -ere,** *rise up.*—**taedium, -iī,** n., *weariness.*] I

4. Nōn sīs tū mihi formīdinī. Spēs mea tū in diē afflīctiōnis.
    [*Jer. 17:17 V.—**formīdō, -dinis,** f., *fear, dread.*—**afflīctiō, -ōnis,** f., *pain, torment.*] I

5. Percussī vōs ventō ūrente, et aurūgine et grandine omnia opera manuum vestrārum, et nōn fuit in vōbīs quī reverterētur ad mē, dīcit Dominus.
    [*Hag. 2:18 V, in LH 4.278.—**percutiō, -ere, -cussī,** *strike hard.*—**ventus, -ī,** m., *wind.*—**ūrō, ūrere,** *burn.*—**aurūgō, -inis,** f., *jaundice* in humans; *mildew* in plants.—**grandō, -inis,** f., *hail.*—**revertor, -ī,** *return.*] M

6. Petrus autem dīxit, "Argentum et aurum nōn est mihi. Quod autem habeō, hoc tibi dō. In nōmine Iēsū Chrīstī Nazarēnī surge et ambulā."
    [*Acts 3:6 V, Lēctiō I, Ad mātūtīnum, Dominica Sānctissimī Nōminis Iēsū, BR 1.142.—**argentum, -ī,** n., *silver.*—**aurum, -ī,** n., *gold.*—**Nazarēnus, -a, -um,** *of Nazareth, Nazarene.*] I

7. Neque enim aliquandō fuimus in sermōne adūlātiōnis sīcut scītis, neque in occāsiōne avāritiae, Deus testis est . . . cum possēmus vōbīs onerī esse ut Chrīstī Apostolī.
    [*I Thess. 2:5a, 7a, in LH 3.108.—**aliquandō,** adv., *at any time.*—**in,** here = *found in, using.* See PW, §117.B.1.—**adūlātiō, -ōnis,** f., *cringing, flattery.* This is a qualitative gen., in imitation of the Heb. construct state. The noun in the gen. should be taken as an adj. See

PW, § 20, and Appendix I, § 8.—**avāritia, -ae,** f., *greed.*—**testis, -is,** m./f., *a witness.*—**onus, oneris,** n., *a burden.*—**apostolus, -ī,** m., *an apostle.*] M

8. Profectō prīmum parentem tamquam perditam ovem quaesītum vādit.

   [*An Ancient Holy Saturday Homily from the *Patrologia Graeca*, in LH 2.383, speaking of Christ's Harrowing of Hell.—**profectō,** adv., *truly, indeed.*—**perdō, -ere, -didī, -ditum,** *destroy, ruin, lose.*—**ovis, -is,** f., *a sheep.*—**quaesītum,** acc. supine of *quaerō.*—**vādō, -ere,** *go, hasten, rush.*] M/A

9. Quae [i.e., bona Deī] omnia ubi mente recolō, ut meum affectum prōdam, in horrōrem quendam et terrificum stupōrem incidō, nēquandō ob animī incōnsīderantiam aut propter meam circā rēs vanās occupātiōnem ā Deī dīlectiōne excidēns, Chrīstō sim dēdecorī ac opprobriō.

   [*St. Basil of Caesarea, *Rēgula fusius Tractāta*, Resp. 2.4, Lēctiō Altera, Ad Officium Lēctiōnis, Hebdomada III per annum, Fēria Tertia, LH 3.91.—**recolō, -ere,** *cultivate again; resume; recall.*—**affectus, -ūs,** m., *condition, disposition; feeling.*—**prōdō, -dare,** *give* or *bring forth; produce; reveal.*—**horror, -ōris,** m., *a bristling, shuddering; dread; religious awe.*—**terrificus, -a, -um,** *frightful, terrible.*—**stupor, -ōris,** m., *senselessness; astonishment.*—**incidō, -ere,** *fall in* or *on.*—**nēquandō,** *lest ever.*—**ob,** prep. + acc., *because of.*—**incōnsīderantia, -ae,** f., *want of reflection, thoughtlessness.*—**circā,** prep. + acc., *about, in respect to.*—**vānus, -a, -um,** *empty; vain.*—**occupātiō, -ōnis,** f., *employment, occupation.*—**dīlectiō, -ōnis,** f., *love.*—**excidō, -ere,** *fall out* or *from.*—**dēdecus, -coris,** n., *shame, dishonor, disgrace.*—**opprobrium, -iī,** n., *reproach, scandal, taunt, disgrace.*] A

10. Ad quam [vītam bonam], sī fierī posset, nōn sōlum nōs, vērum etiam cūnctōs hominēs iam pervenīre et eīdem inhaerēre cuperem, sī, ut haec audītū mirabilia, ita essent imitātiōne facilia.

   [*St. Augustine of Hippo, *Dē ōrdine* 10.28, Alypius responds to his friend Augustine's words about the end of human life.—**perveniō, -īre,** (+ *ad*) *reach.*—**inhaereō, -ere,** *cling* or *stick to.*—**ut ... ita,** correlative advs., *as ... so.*—**haec ... mirabilia,** supply *sunt.*—**imitātiō, -ōnis,** f., *imitation*; here an abl. of respect, = *with respect to imitation.* See Capvt XL.] M

11.   Quid opus est quaerere cuius persōnā sententia nostra fulciātur?

      [*St. Augustine of Hippo, *Dē magistrō* 5.15, asserting that his argument has no need of authoritative support.—**persōna,** here = *authority.*—**fulciō, -īre,** *prop up, support.*] M

12.   Nōn dēsint quī etiam significātiōne ista [verba] discernunt, quōrum sententiam modo cōnsīderāre nōn opus est.

      [St. Augustine of Hippo, *Dē magistrō* 6.17, admitting that some scholars may make a certain distinction, but that there is no need to discuss them.—**dēsum, -esse,** *be wanting.*—**significātiō, -ōnis,** f., *meaning.*—**discernō, -ere,** *separate, distinguish.*—**modo,** adv., *now.*—**cōnsīderō** (1), *inspect; consider.*] M

13.   Erat eī [id est, Karolō magnō] ūnica soror nōmine Gisla.

      [*Einhard, *Vīta Karolī magnī* 18.—**ūnicus, -a, -um,** *one and only.*— **Karolus Magnus, -ī -ī,** m., *Charles the Great, Charlemagne.*—**Gisla, -ae,** f., *Gisela.*] I/M

14.   Quid opus est indignārī?

      [*St. Bernard of Clairvaux, *Epistola* 65.2.—**indignor, -ārī,** *resent; be indignant.*] I

15.   Parvulī petiērunt panem: nōn est quī frangat eīs; sperātur id ā benignitāte tuā[, Domine].

      [*St. Bernard of Clairvaux, *Sermō I super Cantica* 2.4.—**parvulus, -a, -um,** *very small, very little.*—**pānis, pānis,** m., *bread.*—**frangō, -ere,** *break, break in pieces.*—**benignitās, -tātis,** f., *kindness.*] M

16.   Ō virtūs Sapientiae, quae circuiēns circuīstī, comprehendendō omnia in ūnā viā quae habet vītam, trēs ālās habēns, quārum ūna in altum volat et altera dē terrā sūdat et tertia undique volat. Laus tibi sit, sīcut tē decet, ō Sapientia.

      [*St. Hildegard of Bingen, *Ō virtūs Sapientiae,* in *Symphonia,* 100, a non-metrical antiphon. Regarding the images, cf. Capvt XXXI, Sentence 13.—**circueō, -īre,** *go around; encircle, encompass.*—**āla, -ae,** f., *a wing.*—**in altum,** = *in heaven.*—**sūdō** (1), *sweat; ooze or exude from.*—**undique,** adv., *from or on all sides, everywhere.*— **decet, -ēre,** impers., *it is fitting, proper.*] I/M

17.   Dēbēmus odiō habēre corpora nostra cum vitiīs et peccātīs, quia Dominus dīcit in ēvangeliō, Omnia mala, vitia et peccāta ā "corde exeunt."

      [*St. Francis of Assisi, *Epistola ad Fidēlēs* (Recensiō Posterior) 37.—**corde exeunt,** Mt. 15:18–19, Mk. 7:23.] I

18. Praetereā nihil est ex omnibus studiīs, quod minus nōbīs auferat temporis; nam et addiscuntur [poētae] in pueritiā, cum aliīs ferē vacāre nōn possumus, et inhaerent memoriae ob rotundam concinnitātem et peregrinantur ūnā nōbīscum et sine librīs ultrō recursant, ut vel aliud agēns hoc etiam agās.

[*Leonardo Bruni, *Dē Studiīs et Litterīs ad Baptistam dē Malatestīs* 23,[24] speaking of the knowledge of the poets. Oh, were it so today!—**praetereā**, adv., *besides.*—**auferō, -ferre,** *bear away, carry off.*—**addiscō, -ere,** *learn.*—**pueritia, -ae,** f., *boyhood, childhood.*—**ferē,** adv., *almost, nearly.*—**vacō** (1), *have time for, have leisure for* (+ dat.).—**inhaereō, -ēre,** *stick in, cling to* (+ dat.).—**ob,** prep. + acc., *on account of, because of.*—**rotundus, -a, -um,** *round; rounded, perfect.*—**concinnitās, -tātis,** f., *elegance of style* produced by harmonious and proportionate arrangement.—**ūnā,** adv., *together.*—**ultrō,** adv., *besides, moreover.*—**recursō** (1), *run back, return.*—**vel,** adv., *even.*] A

19. Est enim nōbilibus animīs quaedam insita generōsa invidia, ut in eōdem studiī genere versantibus postpōnī et quasi hebetiōrēs relinquī ērubescant. Ex quō sequitur ut certātim aemulantēs alter alterum reddant alacriōrēs.

[*Battista Guarino, *Dē Ōrdine Docendī et Studendī* 6.[25]—**nōbilis, -e,** *noble.*—**insitus, -a, -um,** *innate, inborn.*—**generōsus, -a, -um,** *noble; magnanimous.*—**versor, -ārī,** *be engaged in, take part in.*—**postpōnō, -ere,** *put after, consider secondary* (+ dat.).—**quasi,** adv., *as if, as it were.*—**hebes, -etis,** *dull, stupid.*—**ērubescō, -ere,**

---

[24] " ... Battista di Montefeltro (1384–1448) ... was a famous woman scholar of the Renaissance and the wife of Galeazzo Malatesta, the lord of Pesaro." *Humanist Educational Treatises,* ed. and tr. Craig W. Kallendorf, I Tatti Renaissance Library 5 (Cambridge, MA: Harvard University Press, 2002), 328, n. 1.

[25] Apparently, this competitive, aristocratic temper was common in education until recent decades. See Werner Jaeger, *Paideia: The Ideals of Greek Culture,* vol. 1, tr. Gilbert Highet from the second German ed. (New York: Oxford University Press, 1945), 6–7: "Thus the code of the nobility had a twofold influence on Greek education. In the first place, the city-state inherited from it one of the finest elements in its ethical system—the obligation to be brave ... And, secondly, the higher social standards of the polis were derived from aristocratic practice ... It was that chivalrous rivalry which struck out the motto of knighthood throughout the centuries: αἰὲν ἀριστεύειν καὶ ὑπείροχον ἔμμεναι ἄλλων. [Homer, *Iliad* 6.208.] (This motto, which teachers of all ages have quoted to their pupils, modern education 'levellers' have now, for the first time, abandoned.) Into that one sentence the poet has condensed the whole educational outlook of the nobility."

blush, be ashamed (+ inf.).—**certātim,** adv., *eagerly.*—**aemulor, -ārī,** *emulate.*—**alter alterum,** note that *aemulantēs* and *reddant* depend on this phrase, taken as pl.—**reddō, -ere,** *render, cause to be.*—**alacer, -cris, -cre,** *quick, lively.*] M/A

20. Opus est gratiā tuā et magnā gratiā, ut vincātur nātūra ad malum semper prōna ab adulēscentiā suā.
[*Thomas à Kempis, *Dē Imitātiōne Chrīstī* 3.55.2.—**prōnus, -a, -um,** *inclined towards, prone.*] I

21. *Canis in praesaepī.* In eōs dīcitur, quī nec ipsī fruuntur rē quāpiam, neque reliquōs item sinunt ūtī; velutī sī quis ēgregiōs cōdicēs inclūsōs dīligenter adservet, quōs nec ipse umquam ēvolvendī faciat copiam. Quemadmodum "canis in praesaepī" nec ipse vescitur hordeō, et equum vetat vescī.
[*Desiderius Erasmus, *Adagia* 1.10.13.—**canis, -is,** m./f., *a dog, a bitch.*—**praesaepes, -is,** f., *a manger.*—**fruor, -ī,** *enjoy* (+ abl.).—**quispiam, quaepiam, quodpiam,** *anyone, anything, someone, something.*—**reliquus, -ī,** m., *the rest.*—**item,** adv., *likewise.*—**sinō, -ere,** *permit, let, allow.*—**velutī,** adv., *just as.*—**ēgregius, -a, -um,** *extraordinary.*—**cōdex, -dicis,** m., *a book.*—**inclūdō, -ere, -clūsī, -clūsum,** *shut in, enclose.*—**adservō** (1), *guard, watch.*—**ēvolvō, -ere,** *unroll, roll open* (an anachronism).—**copia, -ae,** f., here = *means, opportunity.*—**quemadmodum,** adv., *as, as for instance.*—**vescor, -ī,** *eat, feed upon* (+ abl.).—**hordeum, -ī,** n., *barley.*—**vetō** (1), *forbid, prohibit.*] M/A

22. Labor hūmānus . . . cēterīs elementīs vītae oeconomicae praestat, quippe quae tantum ratiōnem īnstrūmentōrum habeant. Hic enim labor . . . ā persōnā immediātē prōcēdit, quae rēs nātūrae quasi suō sigillō signat eāsque suae voluntātī submittit.
[*Gaudium et Spēs* 67, in CDD, 789.—**elementum, -ī,** n., *an element, first principle.*—**oeconomicus, -a, -um,** *economic.*—**quippe quae,** *as things in fact which.*—**īnstrūmentum, -ī,** n., *a tool; a means to an end.*—**immediātē,** adv., *directly.*—**prōcēdō, -ere,** *go forth, proceed.*—**quasi,** adv., *as if, as it were.*—**sigillum, -ī,** n., *a sign, mark.*—**signō** (1), *sign, mark.*—**submittō, -ere,** *subject, subordinate.*] M

CAPVT XXXIX

Gerund and Gerundive; Impersonal Verbs; Passive of Special Verbs with Dative

Syntaxis Supplēmentum

Impersonal Verbs. The following verbs are commonly used impersonally.

licet, licēre, licuit, it is permitted (introduced by *Wheelock* in Capvt XXXVII)

oportet, oportēre, oportuit, it is necessary, it is fitting, it behooves (introduced in this chapter)

miseret, miserēre, miseruit, it pities, it moves to pity (can also be personal)

piget, pigēre, piguit, it disgusts, it irks

taedet, taedēre, taeduit, it bores, it disgusts, it tires

paenitet, paenitēre, paenituit, it repents (can also be personal in 3rd pers.)

pudet, pudēre, puduit, it shames (can also be personal, usu. 3rd pers.)

necesse est, it is necessary (introduced in this chapter)

interest, -esse, -fuit, it concerns, it is of interest, it is in the interest of

rēfert, -ferre, -tulit, it concerns, it is of interest, it is in the interest of

A table of the basic constructions associated with these verbs follows.

Acc. & Infin.	Dat. & Infin.	Subjunctive Clause (± ut)	Obj. Gen. & Acc.[26]	Gen. & Infin.[27]
oportet		oportet		
necesse est	necesse est	necesse est		
licet	licet	licet		
			miseret piget taedet paenitet pudet	
				interest rēfert

These verbs must be committed to memory.

The Passive of Special Verbs That Take the Dative. In Capvt XXXV certain intransitive verbs that are constructed with the dative were introduced. These verbs are often used in the passive. However, when they are put into the passive, they are necessarily impersonal. The logic is this. When a transitive verb is made passive, the direct object becomes the subject, while the subject is put into an agent contruction, e.g., *crustula amō*, I love cookies, becomes *crustula ā mē amantur*, cookies are loved by me. However, none of the intransitive verbs under consideration takes a direct object, with the result that there can be no specific subject for them in the passive, e.g., *Deus mihi parcit*, God is being sparing to me, God is sparing me, becomes ā *Deō mihi parcitur*, it is being spared to me by God, or in good English, I am being spared by God.

VERBA MEMORIĀ COMPREHENDENDA

mediātor, -tōris, m., *a mediator*

quōmodo, adv., *in what way, how*

---

[26]   Note that the genitive can be replaced by an infinitive, a *quod*-clause, or a neuter pronoun.

[27]   Note that the infinitive can be replaced by an *ut*-clause or a neuter singular demonstrative. Also note that the genitive forms of the personal pronouns are not used in this construction. Instead, the ablative forms of the possessive adjective-pronouns are used. (e.g., Sentences 5 and 18 below)

Sententiae ē Fontibus nōn Antīquīs Haustae

1. Dēdūcis ad īnferōs et redūcis, et nōn est quī effugiat manum tuam.
    [*Tob. 13:2 V, LH 3.590, from Tobit's song.—**dēdūcō, -ere,** *lead down.*—**inferī, -ōrum,** m., *the dead.*—**redūcō, -ere,** *lead back.*—**effugiō, -ere,** *flee from, escape.*] I

2. Mīsistī spīritum tuum et creāta sunt, et nōn est quī resistat vōcī tuae.
    [*Jud. 16:17 V, LH 3.608, from Judith's song.—**resistō, -ere,** *resist, oppose.*] I

3. Cui vae? Cuius patrī vae? Cui rixae? Cui foveae? Cui sine causā vulnera? Cui suffossiō oculōrum? Nōnne hīs quī commorantur in vīnō et student calicibus ēpōtandīs? Nē intueāris vīnum quandō flāvēscet, cum splenduerit in vitrō color eius. Ingreditur blandē, sed in novissimō mordēbit ut coluber.
    [*Prov. 23:29–31.—**rixa, -ae,** f., *a brawl.*—**fovea, -ae,** f., *a pit; pitfall.*—**suffossiō, -ōnis,** f., *an undermining*; perh. here = *blearing.*—**nōnne,** interrog. adv. that introduces a leading question, which expects a positive response, *surely?* See *Wheelock,* 341.—**commoror, -ārī,** *linger.*—**calix, -icis,** m., *a cup.*—**ēpōtō** (1), *toss off, drain.*—**intueor, -ērī,** *look at; contemplate; eye with pleasure.*—**flāvēscō, -ere,** *turn golden.*—**splendēscō, -ere, -duī,** *grow bright.*—**vitrum, -ī,** n., *a glass.*—**color, -ōris,** n., *color.*—**ingredior, -dī,** *go in.*—**blandus, -a, -um,** *flattering; pleasant.*—**in novissimō,** = *in the end.*—**mordeō, -ēre,** *bite.*—**coluber, -brī,** m., *a snake.*] M

4. Et cum trānsīret inde Iēsūs, vīdit hominem sedentem in telōniō, Matthaeum nōmine. Et āit illī, "Sequere mē." Et surgēns secutus est eum.
    [Mt. 9:9 V.—**inde,** adv., *from that place, thence.*—**telōnium, -iī,** n., *a toll-booth.*—**Matthaeus, -ī,** m., *Matthew.*] I

5. Ab iīs autem quī vidēbantur esse aliquid (quālēs aliquandō fuerint, nihil meā interest: Deus persōnam hominis nōn accipit); mihi enim, quī vidēbantur esse aliquid, nihil contulērunt.
    [*Gal. 2:6.—**vidērī aliquid esse,** *seem to be something,* or, as we would say, *somebody.*—**quālis, -e,** *of what sort, of what kind,* here interrogative.—**aliquandō,** adv., *ever.*—**persōnam hominis nōn accipit,** *shows partiality to no man.*] M

6. Ratiō est mentis mōtiō ea quae discuntur distinguendī et cōnectendī
potēns. Quā duce ūtī ad Deum intellegendum vel ipsam quae aut
in nōbīs aut ūsquequāque est animam rārissimum omnīnō genus
hominum potest.

[*St. Augustine of Hippo, *Dē ōrdine* 2.11.30, a definition
of reason.—**mōtiō, -ōnis,** f., *motion.*—**distinguō, -ere,**
distinguish.—**cōnectō, -ere,** *connect.*—**potēns,** here = *capable of*
(+ gen.).—**duce,** take as a pred. complement with *quā.*—**ipsam**
. . . animam, understand *ad intellegendam* with this phrase.—
ūsquequāque, adv., *everywhere,* a suggestion of the Plotinian
hypostasis ψυχή.—**rārus, -a, -um,** *rare.*—**omnīnō,** adv., *wholly,*
altogether.—**rārissimum omnīnō genus hominum,** = *quite the*
rarest class of persons.] A

7. Et quaerēbam viam comparandī rōboris quod esset idōneum ad
fruendum tē, nec inveniēbam, dōnec amplecterer mediātōrem Deī
et hominum, hominem Chrīstum Iēsūm.

[*St. Augustine of Hippo, *Cōnfessiōnēs* 7.18, Augustine draws
nearer to conversion.—**comparō** (1), *acquire.*—**rōbur, -oris,**
n., *an oak; strength.*—**idōneum ad** = *suitable for.*—**fruor,** see
Wheelock, 285.—**amplector, -tī,** *embrace.*] M

8. Cumque ad eum fīnem sermō perdūcerētur, ērigentēs nōs ardentiōre
affectū in id ipsum, perambulāvimus gradātim cūncta corporālia
et ipsum caelum, unde sōl et lūna et stēllae lūcent super terram. Et
adhūc ascendēbāmus, interius cogitandō et loquendō et mīrandō
opera tua, et vēnimus in mentēs nostrās et trānscendimus eās, ut
attingerēmus regiōnem ūbertātis indēficientis, et ibi vīta sapientia
est per quam fīunt omnia ista, et quae fuērunt et quae futūra sunt.

[St. Augustine of Hippo, *Cōnfessiōnēs* 9.10, the vision of St.
Augustine and St. Monica at Ostia.—**perdūcō, -ere,** *bring*
through, conduct.—**ērigō, -ere,** *raise; rouse.*—**ardēns, -entis,**
burning; passionate.—**affectus, -ūs,** m., *affection, love, feeling.*—**id**
ipsum, perh. *the very thing, reality itself.* One translator renders
it "that Self-same".—**perambulō** (1), *walk through, traverse.*—
gradātim, adv., *step by step.*—**corporālis, -e,** *corporeal.*—
lūceō, -ēre, *shine, beam.*—**adhūc,** adv., *still.*—**ascendō, -ere,**
ascend.—**interius,** adv., *more inwardly.*—**trānscendō, -ere, -ndī,**
transcend.—**attingō, -ere,** *touch; arrive at.*—**regiō, -ōnis,** f., *a*
region.—**ūbertās, -tātis,** f., *fertility; plenty.*—**indēficiēns, -entis,**
unfailing.] M

9. Ēvītandō vīvit anima quae appetendō moritur.
[*St. Augustine of Hippo, *Cōnfessiōnēs* 13.21.—**ēvītō** (1), *avoid.*—
appetō, -ere, *strive* or *long for; approach.*] I

10. Et nunc vix contineō lacrimās, ita pudet teporis torporisque
miserabilium temporum.
[*St. Bernard of Clairvaux, *Sermō II super Cantica* 1.1.—**vix,**
adv., *scarcely.*—**lacrima, -ae,** f., *a tear.*—**tepor, -ōris,** m.,
lukewarmness.—**torpor, -ōris,** m., *numbness, sluggishness.*—
miserābilis, -e, *sad, wretched.*] M

11. Et [Pater] vult ut omnēs salvēmur per eum [i.e., Fīlium] et recipiāmus
ipsum pūrō corde et castō corpore nostrō. Sed paucī sunt, quī velint
eum recipere et salvī esse per eum, licet eius "iugum suave" sit et
"onus" ipsius "leve."
[*St. Francis of Assisi, *Epistola ad Fidēlēs* (Recensiō Posterior)
14–15.—**vult,** here takes a final clause, as was common in CL. See
Wheelock, 304.—**salvō** (1), *save.*—**pūrus, -a, -um,** *pure.*—**castus,
-a, -um,** *clean, pure; chaste.*—**velint,** here takes the infin., as was
also done in CL (GL, § 546 R 1).— **iugum, -ī,** n., *a yoke.*—**onus,
oneris,** n., *a burden, load.* Cf. Mt. 11:30.] I/M

12. "Frātrēs meī, volucrēs, multum dēbētis laudāre creātōrem vestrum
et ipsum dīligere semper, quī dedit vōbīs plūmās ad induendum,
pennās ad volandum, et quidquid necesse fuit vōbīs."
[Thomas of Celano, *Vīta prīma S. Franciscī Assisiensis* 21.58, St.
Francis begins a sermon to the birds.—**volucer, -cris, -cre,** *winged;*
as substantive, *a bird.*—**creātor, -ōris,** m., *a creator; the Creator.*—
plūma, -ae, f., *down, downy feathers.*—**induō, -ere,** *cover, clothe,
array.*—**penna, -ae,** f., *a feather;* (usu. pl.) *wings.*—**volō** (1), *fly.*] I

13. Tertium lūmen, quod illūminat ad vēritātēs intelligibilēs
perscrutandās, est lūmen cognitiōnis philosophicae.
[St. Bonaventure, *Dē reductiōne artium ad theologiam* 4.—**lūmen,
-inis,** n., *light.*—**illūminō** (1), *light up, illuminate.*—**intelligibilis,
-e,** *intelligible, intellectual.*—**perscrūtō** (1), *examine thoroughly.*—
cognitiō, -ōnis, f., *knowledge.*—**philosophicus, -a, -um,**
philosophical.] I

14. Quis enim nescit ante omnia tinctum esse oportēre ingenium et quasī
initiātum praeceptōris operā, ut nōn sōlum partēs structūramque
eārum, sed etiam minūtiōra illa ac velut elementa ōrātiōnis agnōscat?
Vērum haec tamquam somniāntēs in pueritiā capimus: posteā vērō

ad maiōra prōvectī, nesciō quōmodo haec ipsa ad ōs revocāmus et quasī rūmināmus, ut tunc dēmum illōrum sūcus saporque vērus exprimātur.

[*Leonardo Bruni, *Dē Studiīs et Litterīs ad Baptistam dē Malatestīs* 4, speaking of the lifelong effects of childhood memory training.— **tingō, -ere, tīnxī, tinctum,** *moisten; dye; imbue.*—**initiō** (1), *initiate.*—**praeceptor, -ōris,** m., *a teacher.*—**opera, -ae,** f., *work, help.*—**partēs,** to be taken with *ōrātiōnis* in the next clause, but not in the narrow technical sense, I think.—**structūra, -ae,** f., *a building, constructing; arrangement of words.*—**minūtus, -a, -um,** *small, little.*—**elementum, -ī,** n., *an element, first principle.*— **agnōscō, -ere,** *recognize.*—**vērum,** adv. acc., *truly.*—**somniō** (1), *dream.*—**pueritia, -ae,** f., *boyhood, childhood.*—**prōvehō, -ere, -vexī, -vectum,** *carry forward.*—**nesciō quōmodo,** = *somehow.*— **revocō** (1), *call back.*—**rūminō** (1), *chew the cud; chew over again.*—**tunc,** adv., *then.*—**dēmum,** adv., *at last.*—**sūcus, -ī,** m., *juice, sap; flavor; vigor.*—**sapor, -ōris,** m., *taste.*—**exprimō, -ere,** *press out, force out.*] A

15.   Antequam tamen ad studendī docendīque praecepta veniāmus, haudquāquam ā prōpositō nostrō aliēnum esse vidēbitur, sī adulēscentēs ipsōs admonuerimus, prīmum ut, quam eīs praeceptor extrīnsecus trādere nōn potest discendī cupiditātem, ipsī per sē sponte illam arripiant.

[*Battista Guarino, *Dē Ōrdine Docendī et Studendī* 3.— **praeceptum, -ī,** n., *a precept.*—**haudquāquam,** adv., *not at all, by no means.*—**prōpositum, -ī,** n., *a design, purpose, plan.*—**aliēnus, -a, -um,** *foreign.*—**admoneō,** = *moneō.*—**prīmum,** adv., *first.*— **quam,** note that the antecedent is *cupiditātem,* which has been incorporated into the rel. clause. See GL, § 616.—**extrīnsecus,** adv., *from outside.*—**sponte,** adv., *willingly, of one's own accord.*— **arripiō, -ere,** *take to oneself, appropriate.*] A

16.   Stōicī negant bonum virum esse posse, nisi quī vacet animī morbīs. Morbōs autem animī cupiditātēs sīve affectūs vocant. Multō magis Chrīstiānōrum est ab hīs esse līberōs, sed omnium maximē prīncipem. Ac rursum plūs quam maximē, prīncipem ac patrem Ecclēsiae, hoc est, caelestis illīus populī caelestem prīncipem.

[*Desiderius Erasmus, *Adagia* 3.3.1.—**Stōicus, -ī,** m., *a Stoic philosopher.*—**vacō** (1), *be free from.*—**sīve,** conj., *or.*—**affectus, -ūs,** m., (among the Stoics) *an ignoble passion.*—**magis,** adv., *more.*—**Chrīstiānōrum,** take as a pred. gen. (Capvt XXV Syntaxis).—**rursum,** adv., *again.*—**caelestis, -e,** *heavenly.*] M

17. Ubi omnia pecūniīs mētīmur, multās artēs necesse est exercērī inānēs ac superfluās, luxūs ac libīdinis ministrōs.

    [*St. Thomas More, *Ūtopia* 2, LAM, 128.—**mētior, -īrī,** *measure.*—**exerceō, -ēre,** *employ, exploit; practice, exercise.*—**inānis, -e,** *empty, vain.*—**superfluus, -a, -um,** *superfluous.*—**luxus, -ūs,** m., *luxury, excess.*—**libīdō, -inis,** f., *violent desire; lust.*—**minister, -trī,** m., *servant; helper.*] M

18. Iam vērō Deī nōtitiam intellegō, quā nōn modo concipimus aliquem esse Deum, sed etiam tenēmus quod dē eō scīre nostrā rēfert, quod ūtile est in eius glōriam, quod dēnique expedit.

    [*John Calvin, *Institūtiō Chrīstianae Religiōnis* 1.2.1 (Amsterdam edition), seeking a ground for the knowledge of God.—**nōtitia, -ae,** f., *knowledge, acquaintance.*—**concipiō, -ere,** *conceive, imagine.*—**expedit,** *it is useful, expedient.*] A

19. Fatendum est hūmānam vītam circā rēs particulārēs saepe errōribus esse obnoxiam, et nātūrae nostrae īnfirmitās agnoscenda est.

    [René Descartes, *Meditātiōnēs dē Prīmā Philosophiae* 6.24.90.—**circā,** prep. + acc., *around; in respect to.*—**particulāris, -e,** *partial, particular.*—**error, -ōris,** m., *a mistake, error.*—**obnoxius, -a, -um,** *liable to, subject to.*—**īnfirmitās, -tātis,** f., *weakness, feebleness.*—**agnōscō, -ere,** *recognize; understand; admit.*] I/M

20. Numquam exinde omīsit Ecclēsia quīn in ūnum convenīret ad paschāle mystērium celebrandum.

    [*Sacrōsānctum Concilium* 6, CDD, 8, in LH 2.538.—**exinde,** adv., *thence; therefore.*—**omittō, -ere, -mīsī,** *let go, omit, cease.*—**conveniō, -īre,** *come together, assemble.*—**paschālis, -e,** *paschal, easter.*—**mystērium, -iī,** n., *a* (sacred) *mystery.*—**celebrō** (1), *celebrate, solemnize.*] I/M

CAPVT XL

-Ne, Num, and Nonne in Direct Questions; Fear Clauses; Genitive and Ablative of Description; Ablative of Cause; Ablative of Specification; Genitive of Material; Compound (Disjunctive) Questions

Syntaxis Supplēmentum

Ablative of Cause. See *Wheelock*, 493. Note that the ablative of cause is used with verbs of emotion. Sometimes the emotion is implicit in the context. See Sentence 7 below.

Ablative of Specification (Respect). See *Wheelock*, 492–493. Sentences 3 and 20 below contain examples.

Genitive of Material. See Wheelock, 491–492. I do not find this classification of the genitive in GL. However, *Wheelock's* example *numerus hostium,* "the number of the enemy," is like the example *vīnī numerus,* "amount of wine," at GL, § 368, which is a type of partitive genitive sometimes called the *genitīvus generis.*

Compound (Disjunctive) Questions. A disjunctive question inquires about alternatives. The questions are conjoined with *or.* Compound questions can be direct or indirect. When indirect, the first question is introduced by *whether.* Thus: *Shall I go or (shall I) not? He asked whether he should go or not.* In compound questions in Latin, whether direct or indirect, the first question generally is introduced by *utrum* or *-ne*. Sometimes too there is no introductory particle. The second question is usually introduced by *an*. In a direct disjunctive question, *or not* is usually *annōn*; in an indirect, generally *necne*.

Verba Memoriā Comprehendenda

ecclēsia, -ae, f., (political) *assembly; church*

numquid, in EL can replace *num* or *-ne?* (see Appendix I, § 71)

Sententiae ē Fontibus nōn Antīquīs Haustae

1. "Terra quam lustrāvimus dēvorat habitātōrēs suōs, populus quem aspēximus prōcērae statūrae est. Ibi vīdimus mōnstra quaedam, fīliōrum Enac dē genere gigantēō, quibus comparātī quasī lōcustae vidēbāmur."

   [*Num. 13:32–33 V, in LH 2.246, from the report on the Promised Land of the Hebrew scouts.—**lustrō** (1), *traverse; observe.*—**dēvorō** (1), *swallow, devour.*—**habitātor, -ōris,** m., *an inhabitant.*—**aspiciō, -ere, -spēxī,** *look at, behold.*—**prōcērus, -a, -um,** *tall, long.*—**statūra, -ae,** f., *height, stature.*—**mōnstrum, -ī,** n., *a monster.*—**Enac,** indecl. Heb. name, m., *Anak.*—**gigantēus, -a, -um,** *pertaining to the giants; gigantic.*—**comparō** (1), *compare.*—**lōcusta, -ae,** f., *a locust.*] M

2. Quae ūtilitās in sanguine meō, dum dēscendō in corruptiōnem? Numquid cōnfitēbitur tibi pulvis aut annuntiābit vēritātem tuam?

   [*Ps. 29:10 V.—**ūtilitās, -tātis,** f., *usefulness, advantage.*—**dēscendō, -ere,** *descend.*—**corruptiō, -ōnis,** f., *corruption.*—**pulvis, -eris,** m., *dust.*—**annuntiō** (1), *announce.*] I

3. Iuxtā est Dominus iīs quī trībulātō sunt corde, et humilēs spīritū salvābit.

   [*Ps. 33:19 V.—**iuxtā,** adv., *close.*—**trībulō** (1), *oppress.*—**salvō** (1), *save.*] I/M

4. Tē per orbem terrārum sāncta cōnfitētur Ecclēsia Patrem immēnsae maiestātis, venerandum tuum vērum et ūnicum Fīlium, Sānctum quoque Parāclitum Spīritum.

   [**Tē Deum,* Ad mātūtīnum, Ōrdinārium dīvīnī Officiī, BR 1.(6).—**orbis, -is,** m., *orb;* **orbis terrārum,** *world.*—**cōnfiteor, -ērī,** *confess.*—**immēnsus, -a, -um,** *immeasurable, endless.*—**maiestās, -tātis,** f., *dignity, majesty.*—**veneror, -ārī,** *worship.*—**ūnicus, -a, -um,** *one and only.*—**Parāclitus, -ī,** m., *Advocate, Paraclete.*] M

5.   Nunc factus est salūs et virtūs et rēgnum Deī nostrī, quia prōiectus est accūsātor frātrum nostrōrum.
     [Canticum (Apoc. 12:10 V), ad Vesperās, Fēria V, Hebdomada IV, LH 3.1003.—**prōiciō, -ere, -iēcī, -iectum,** *throw forward* or *out.*—**accūsātor, -tōris,** m., *an accuser.*] I

6.   Trēs affectūs [scīlicet, īra, avāritia, libīdō], vel, ut ita dīcam, trēs Furiae sunt . . . Hōs affectūs Stōicī amputandōs, Peripatēticī temperandōs putant. Neutrī eōrum rēctē . . . Nōs vērō neque dētrahendōs neque minuendōs esse dīcimus. Nōn enim per sē mala sunt, quae Deus hominī ratiōnābiliter īnsēvit; sed, cum sint utique nātūrā bona, quoniam ad tuendam vītam sunt attribūta, male ūtendō fiunt mala.
     [*Lactantius, *Epitomē Īnstitūtiōnum Dīvīnārum* 61.—**affectus, -ūs,** m., *a mental disposition, affection, mood; a passion.*—**scīlicet,** adv., *namely.*—**avāritia, -ae,** f., *greed, avarice.*—**libīdō, -inis,** f., *inordinate desire, pleasure.*—**Furiae, -ārum, f. pl.,** *the Furies.*—**Stōicus, -ī,** m., *a Stoic philosopher.*—**amputō** (1), *cut off.*—**Peripatēticus, -ī,** m., *a Peripatetic philosopher.*—**temperō** (1), *control, moderate.*—**dētrahō, -ere,** *remove.*—**ratiōnābiliter,** adv., *reasonably, with reason.*—**īnserō, -ere, -sēvī,** *implant.*—**utique,** adv., *at any rate, certainly.*—**tueor, -ērī,** *keep, guard, protect.*—**attribuō, -ere, -uī, -ūtum,** *allot to, assign to.*] M/A

7.   Et cum tacuisset Trygetius egoque mē ipsum nōn caperem gaudiō, quod vidēbam adolescentem carissimī amīcī fīlium etiam meum fierī et tōtō impetū in mediam venīre philosophiam, subitō ille exclāmat, "Ō sī possem dīcere quod volō!"
     [St. Augustine of Hippo, *Dē ōrdine* 1.7.16.—**Trygetius, -ī,** m., *Trygetius,* a pupil of St. Augustine, who had recently returned from military service.—**nōn caperem** = *I could not contain,* a past potential subjunctive.—**adolescēns, -entis,** *adolescent.*—**fīlium,** not Trygetius, but Licentius, the son of Augustine's patron Romanianus.—**impetus, -ūs,** m., *force; ardor.*—**exclāmō** (1), *cry out.*—**Ō sī,** poetic for *utinam.* Licentius was a budding poet.] A

8.   Vereor nē rīdiculus videar.
     [*St. Augustine of Hippo, *Dē magistrō* 8.21.] I

9. Metus est enim nē in odium vel timōrem ratiōnis incidāmus.
   [St. Augustine of Hippo, *Dē magistrō* 10.31.—**incidō, -ere,** *fall (into)*.] I/M

10. Vereor nē quid in tantīs involūcrīs lateat quod aciēs mentis meae lūstrāre nōn possit.
   [St. Augustine of Hippo, *Dē magistrō* 10.31, Adeodatus doubts he can follow the argument.—**involūcrum, -ī,** n., *a wrapping, covering.*—**lateō, -ēre,** *lie hid, lurk.*—**aciēs, -ēī,** f., *a sharp edge* or *point; battle line; keenness, acuteness; power, force.*] M

11. In dōnō tuō requiēscimus, ibi tē fruimur. Requiēs nostra locus noster. Amor illūc attollit nōs et Spīritus tuus bonus exaltat humilitātem nostram dē portīs mortis. In bonā voluntāte tuā pāx nōbīs est. Corpus pondere suō nititur ad locum suum. Pondus nōn ad īma tantum est, sed ad locum suum. Ignis sūrsum tendit, deorsum lapis. Ponderibus suīs aguntur, loca sua petunt. Oleum īnfrā aquam fūsum super aquam attollitur, aqua suprā oleum fūsa infrā oleum dēmergitur. Ponderibus suīs aguntur, loca sua petunt. Minus ōrdināta inquiēta sunt. Ōrdinantur et quiēscunt. Pondus meum amor meus. Eō feror, quōcumque feror. Dōnō tuō accendimur et sūrsum ferimur. Inardēscimus et īmus. Ascendimus ascēnsiōnēs in corde et cantāmus canticum grāduum. Igne tuō, igne tuō bonō inardēscimus et īmus, quōniam sūrsum īmus ad pācem Hierūsalem.
   [*St. Augustine of Hippo, *Cōnfessiōnēs* 13.9, arguing that, as each of the elements—fire, air, earth, water—tends to its own place, so does our soul.—**fruor,** see *Wheelock*, 285.—**requiēs, -ētis,** f., *rest.*—**illūc,** adv., *to that place, thither.*—**attollō, -ere,** *lift* or *raise up.*—**exaltō** (1), *raise, elevate.*—**humilitās, -tātis,** f., *lowness.*—**pondus, -eris,** n., *weight.*—**nitor, -tī,** *lean* or *rest (on); exert oneself.*—**īmus, -a, -um,** *lowest, deepest.*—**sūrsum,** adv., *upwards.*—**tendō, -ere,** *stretch.*—**deorsum,** adv., *downwards.*— **lapis, -pidis,** m., *a stone.*—**oleum, -ī,** n., *olive oil.*—**īnfrā,** prep. + acc., *below, under.*—**fundō, -ere, fūdī, fūsum,** *pour out.*—**super,** prep. + acc., *above, on.*—**dēmergō, -ere,** *plunge (into).*—**ōrdinō** (1), *set in order, order, arrange.*—**inquiētus, -a, -um,** *unquiet, restless.*—**quiēscō, -ere,** *be at rest.*—**quōcumque,** adv., *(to) wheresoever, whithersoever.*—**accendō, -ere,** *enkindle, set on fire.*— **inardēscō, -ere,** *take fire.*—**ascendō, -ere,** *ascend.*—**ascēnsiō,**

-ōnis, f., *an ascent.*—**canticum, -ī,** n., *song.*—**gradus, -ūs,** m., *a step; degree.* The reference is to Psalms 119–133, the "Cantica graduum."] M/A

12.   Temptābat et [Karolus] scrībere tabulāsque et cōdicillōs ad hoc in lectō sub cervīcālibus circumferre solēbat, ut, cum vacuum tempus esset, manum litterīs effigiendīs assuēsceret; sed parum successit lābor praeposterus ac sērō incohātus.

[*Einhard, *Vīta Karolī Magnī Imperātōris* 25.—**Karolus, -ī,** m., *Charles* the Great, Charlemagne.—**temptō** (1), *try.*—**tabula, -ae,** f., *a writing tablet* (made of wood or ivory routed out on one surface, the hollow being filled with wax).—**cōdicillī, -ōrum,** m., *a little book, booklet.*—**lectus, -ī,** m., *a couch, bed.*—**cervīcal, -ālis,** n., *a pillow, bolster.*—**circumferō, -ferre,** *carry around.*—**vacuus, -a, -um,** *empty, free.*—**effigiō, -ere,** = (by back-formation from *effigiēs* or *effigientia*) **effigiō** (1), *form, fashion.*—**assuēscō, -ere,** *grow accustomed; accustom.*—**succēdō, -ere, -cessī,** *turn out well, succeed.*—**praeposterus, -a, -um,** *reversed, unseasonable.*—**sērō,** adv., *late; too late.*—**incohō** (1), *begin, commence.*] M

13.   Īrēna, cum sīs minor aetāte, fītō maior dignitāte.

[*Hrosvitha of Gandersheim, *Dulcitius* 1.5.—**Īrēna, -ae,** f., *Irene.*—**fītō,** fut. imperative of *fierī.*] I/M

14.   "Nōn est bonum," inquit [Deus], "hominī esse sōlum. Faciāmus eī adiūtōrium simile sibi." Nec certē dē similī, vel saltem dē eādem māteriā, hoc adiūtōrium dīvīna virtus fōrmāvit, sed, ad expressius cāritātis et amīcitiae incentīvum, dē ipsīus substantiā masculī fēminam prōcreāvit. Pulchrē autem dē latere prīmī hominis secundus assūmitur, ut nātūra docēret omnēs aequālēs, quasi collaterālēs, nec esset in rēbus hūmānīs superior vel īnferior, quod est amīcitiae proprium.

[*St. Aelred of Rievaulx, *Dē Spirituālī Amīcitiā* 1.57.—**adiūtōrium, -iī,** n., *help, assistance.*—**saltem,** adv., *even* (with a neg.).—**māteria, -ae,** f., *matter, stuff.*—**fōrmō** (1), *form, fashion.*—**expressus, -a, -um,** *clear, plain.*—**incentīvum, -ī,** n., *an incentive.*—**substantia, -ae,** f., *substance.*—**masculus, -ī,** m., *a male.*—**fēmina, -ae,** f., *a female.*—**prōcreō** (1), *beget; produce, make.*—**latus, -eris,** n., *the side.*—**assūmō, -ere,** *take in addition.*—**aequālis, -e,** *equal.*—**collaterālis, -e,** *"by the side of, helping, associated with"* (Latham, s.v.).—**īnferior, -ōris,** *lower.*] I/M

15. Vērē mundō corde sunt quī terrēna despiciunt, caelestia quaerunt et semper adōrāre et vidēre Dominum Deum vīvum et vērum mundō corde et animō nōn dēsistunt.

> [*St. Francis of Assisi, *Admonitiōnēs* 16.—**vērē**, adv., *truly*.— **mundus, -a, -um,** *clean, neat, elegant; morally pure, upright, free from sin*.—**terrēnus, -a, -um,** *earthen; earthly*.—**dēspiciō, -ere,** *regard from above; look down on*.—**caelestis, -e,** *heavenly*.—**adōrō** (1), *entreat; honor, worship*.—**dēsistō, -ere,** *leave off, cease, desist* (+ inf.).] I

16. Habent cēterī animantēs insitum aliquid nātūrā, ut equī currere, avēs volāre, hominibus vērō sciendī cupiditās trādita est, unde et hūmānitātis studia sunt nuncupāta. Quam enim Graecī παιδείαν vocant, nōs ērudītiōnem īnstitūtiōnemque in bonās artēs dīcimus. Eam hūmānitātem quoque veterēs nōminārunt, quia scientiae cūra ex ūniversīs animantibus ūnī hominī data sit.

> [*Battista Guarino, *Dē Ōrdine Docendī et Studendī* 38.—**animāns, -antis,** adj., *living*.—**insitus, -a, -um,** *innate, inborn*.—**avis, avis,** f., *a bird*.—**volō** (1), *fly*.—**hūmānitās, -tātis,** f., *human nature; the education appropriate to human nature*.—**studia hūmānitātis,** = *the disciplines of study appropriate to free men and women*.— **nuncupō** (1), *name*.—**παιδείαν, paideian,** *education, culture*.— **ērudītiō, -ōnis,** f., *instruction; knowledge*.—**īnstitūtiō, -ōnis,** f., *arrangement; custom; education*.—**bonae artēs,** *the liberal arts* (LS, s.v. B.1.a.).—**veterēs,** = *the ancients*.—**nōminō** (1), *name, call*.—**ūniversus, -a, -um,** *all together*.] M

17. *Crocodīlī lacrimae.* Dē iīs [hoc dīcitur], quī sēsē simulant graviter angī incommodō cuiuspiam, cuī perniciem attulerint ipsī, cuiusve magnum aliquod malum mōliantur. Sunt quī scrībant crocodīlum, cōnspectō procul homine, lacrimās ēmittere, atque eundem mox dēvorāre.

> [*Desiderius Erasmus, *Adagia* 2.4.60.—**crocodīlus, -ī,** m., *a crocodile*.—**sēsē,** an emphatic *sē*.—**simulō** (1), *pretend*.— **angō, -ere,** *hurt, distress*.—**incommodum, -ī,** n., *inconvenience; misfortune*.—**quispiam, quaepiam, quodpiam,** *anyone, anything; someone, something*.—**perniciēs, -ēī,** f., *disaster, ruin*.—**attulerint,** here = *cause*. Note the perf. subjunct. in a rel. clause of purpose.— **cōnspiciō, -ere, -spēxī, -spēctum,** *catch sight of, spy*.—**procul,** adv., *afar off, far away*.—**ēmittō, -ere,** *send forth, send out*.— **dēvorō** (1), *swallow, gulp down*.] M/A

18. Gēns facilis ac facēta, sollers, ōtiō gaudēns, corporis labōrum (cum est ūsus) satis patiēns (cēterum aliās haudquāquam sānē appetēns), animī studiīs īnfatīgāta.

[*St. Thomas More, *Ūtopia* 2, LAM, 178, 180, speaking of the nature of the Utopians.—**facētus, -a, -um,** *well-made; polite; merry.*—**sollers, -ertis,** *clever, skillful.*—**patiēns, -entis,** *capable of enduring* (+ gen.).—**cēterum,** adv., *for the rest.*—**aliās,** adv., *otherwise.*—**haudquāquam,** adv., *by no means, not at all.*—**sānē,** adv., *to be sure.*—**appetēns, -entis,** *eager, desirous* (+ gen.).— **īnfatīgātus, -a, -um,** *unwearied.*] M

19. Dum haec dīcit, sublīme in pluteum suprā focum sublāta est; vix tamen sēnsit quōmodo eō pervēnisset. Vitrum sine dubiō dissolvī incipiēbat, velut nebula lucida et fulgida. Alicia statim per vitrum trānsiit, atque in conclāve Intrāspeculāre dēsiluit.

[*Lewis Carroll, *Aliciae per Speculum Trānsitus,* Caput Primum, tr. Clive Harcourt Carruthers.—**sublīme,** adv. from *sublīmis, -e.*— **pluteus, -ī,** m., or **pluteum, -ī,** n., *mantelpiece.*—**suprā,** prep. + acc., *above.*—**focus, -ī,** m., *fireplace.*—**vix,** adv., *hardly, scarcely.*— **eō,** adv., *thither, (to) there.*—**pervenio, -īre, -vēnī,** *arrive at, reach.*—**vitrum, -ī,** n., *glass* (here of a looking glass).—**dubium, -iī,** n., *doubt.*—**dissolvō, -ere,** *loosen, break up; dissolve.*—**velut,** adv., *as, just as.*—**nebula, -ae,** f., *fog, mist, cloud.*—**lūcidus, -a, -um,** *full of light, clear, bright.*—**fulgidus, -a, -um,** *shining, gleaming.*—**Alicia, -ae,** f., *Alice.*—**statim,** adv., *immediately.*— **conclāve, -is,** n., *a room, chamber.*—**intrāspeculāris, -e,** *within the looking glass.*—**dēsiliō, -īre, -siluī,** *jump down.*] I/M

20. Corpore et animā ūnus, homō per ipsam suam corporālem condiciōnem elementa mundī māteriālis in sē colligit, ita ut, per ipsum, fastīgium suum attingant et ad līberam Creātōris laudem vōcem attollant.

[*Gaudium et Spes,* no. 14.—**corporālis, -e,** *corporeal.*—**condiciō, -ōnis,** f., *condition, state.*—**elementum, -ī,** n., *a rudiment; element.*—**māteriālis, -e,** *material.*—**colligō, -ere,** *gather together, collect.*—**fastīgium, -iī,** n., *summit; dignity.*—**attingō, -ere,** *touch; arrive at; appropriate.*—**creātor, -tōris,** m., *a creator; the Creator.*—**attollō, -ere,** *lift up.*] M

Locī Immūtātī

Notā bene! *No word that appears in the complete glossary at the back of Wheelock's Latin, 518–536, will be glossed in these Locī. (Numerals can be found on p. 500 of Wheelock.) Neither will any word in the glossary of this book be annotated. Also, no word will be glossed more than once in the same reading or set of readings. Finally, only those principal parts of a verb necessary to understand the form of the verb in the passage being read will be given in the annotations.*

I. TWO CREATION STORIES

A. *Genesis 1:1–2:3 V*

This is the Priestly (P) account of the creation of the cosmos. The priestly writings are supposed to have been brought together from older traditions during the exile of Israel in Babylon (6th century BCE). This passage, which is read at the Easter Vigil, and the following have been absolutely crucial in the development of Christian theology. Notice the parataxis (Smith, 105).

> [1:1]In prīncipiō creāvit Deus caelum et terram. [2]Terra autem
> erat inānis et vacua, et tenebrae erant super faciem abyssī, et
> Spīritus Deī ferēbātur super aquās. [3]Dīxitque Deus, "Fīat lūx,"
> et facta est lūx. [4]Et vīdit Deus lūcem quod esset bona, et dīvīsit
> 5   lūcem ac tenebrās. [5]Appellāvitque lūcem Diem et tenebrās
> Noctem, factumque est vespere et māne, diēs ūnus.
> [6]Dīxit quoque Deus, "Fīat firmāmentum in mediō aquārum,
> et dīvidat aquās ab aquīs." [7]Et fēcit Deus firmāmentum,
> dīvīsitque quae erant sub firmāmentō ab hīs quae erant
> 10   super firmāmentum, et factum est ita. [8]Vocāvitque Deus
> firmāmentum Caelum, et factum est vespere et māne, diēs
> secundus.

⁹Dīxit vērō Deus, "Congregentur aquae quae sub caelō sunt in locum ūnum, et appāreat ārida," factumque est ita. ¹⁰Et

15 vocāvit Deus āridam Terram congregātiōnēsque aquārum appellāvit Maria, et vīdit Deus quod esset bonum. ¹¹Et āit, "Germinet terra herbam virentem et facientem sēmen, et lignum pōmiferum faciēns frūctum iuxtā genus suum, cuius sēmen in sēmetipsō sit super terram," et factum est ita.

20 ¹²Et prōtulit terra herbam virentem et adferentem sēmen iuxtā genus suum, lignumque faciēns frūctum et habēns ūnumquodque sēmentem secundum speciem suam, et vīdit Deus quod esset bonum. ¹³Factumque est vespere et māne, diēs tertius.

25 ¹⁴Dīxit autem Deus, "Fīant lūmināria in firmāmentō caelī, ut dīvidant diem ac noctem, et sint in signa et tempora et diēs et annōs, ¹⁵ut lūceant in firmāmentō caeli, et illūminent terram," et factum est ita. ¹⁶Fēcitque Deus duo magna lūmināria: lūmināre maius, ut praeesset diēī, et lūmināre minus, ut

30 praeesset noctī, et stēllās; ¹⁷et posuit eās in firmāmentō caelī, ut lūcērent super terram, ¹⁸et praeessent diēī ac noctī, et dīviderent lūcem ac tenebrās. Et vīdit Deus quod esset bonum. ¹⁹Et factum est vespere et māne, diēs quārtus.

²⁰Dīxit etiam Deus, "Prōdūcant aquae rēptile animae

35 vīventis et volātile super terram sub firmāmentō caelī." ²¹Creāvitque Deus cētē grandia et omnem animam vīventem atque mōtābilem, quam prōdūxerant aquae in speciēs suās, et omne volātile secundum genus suum. Et vīdit Deus quod esset bonum, ²²benedīxitque eīs dīcēns, "Crēscite et multiplicāminī

40 et replēte aquās maris, avēsque multiplicentur super terram." ²³Et factum est vespere et māne, diēs quīntus.

²⁴Dīxit quoque Deus, "Prōdūcat terra animam vīventem in genere suō, iūmenta et rēptilia et bēstiās terrae secundum speciēs suās," factumque est ita. ²⁵Et fēcit Deus bēstiās terrae

45 iuxta speciēs suās et iūmenta et omne rēptile terrae in genere suō. Et vīdit Deus quod esset bonum. ²⁶Et āit, "Faciāmus hominem ad imāginem et similitūdinem nostram; et praesit piscibus maris et volātilibus caelī et bēstiīs, ūniversaeque terrae omnīque rēptilī quod movētur in terrā." ²⁷Et creāvit Deus

50 hominem ad imāginem suam; ad imāginem Deī creāvit illum, māsculum et fēminam creāvit eōs. ²⁸Benedīxitque illīs Deus, et

āit, "Crēscite et multiplicāminī et replēte terram et subicite eam
et domināminī piscibus maris et volātilibus caelī et ūniversīs
animantibus quae moventur super terram." [29]Dīxitque Deus,
55   "Ecce, dedī vōbīs omnem herbam adferentem sēmen super
terram, et ūniversa ligna quae habent in sēmetipsīs sēmentem
generis suī, ut sint vōbīs in ēscam, [30]et cūnctīs animantibus
terrae omnīque volucrī caelī et ūniversīs quae moventur in
terrā et in quibus est anima vīvēns, ut habeant ad vēscendum."
60   Et factum est ita. [31]Vīditque Deus cūncta quae fēcit, et erant
valdē bona, et factum est vespere et māne, diēs sextus.
      [2:1]Igitur perfectī sunt caelī et terra et omnis ōrnātus eōrum.
[2]Complēvitque Deus diē septimō opus suum quod fēcerat, et
requiēvit diē septimō ab ūniversō opere quod patrārat.
65   [3]Et benedīxit diēī septimō et sānctificāvit illum, quia in ipsō
cessāverat ab omnī opere suō quod creāvit Deus, ut faceret.

2 **tenebrae, -ārum,** f., *darkness*	**pōmifer, -fera, -ferum,** *fruit-bearing*
faciēs, -ēī, f., *face*	**iuxtā,** prep. + acc., *close to; according to*
abyssus, -ī, f., *a bottomless pit, abyss*	19 **-met,** enclitic pronominal suffix, = *self* (often redundant)
4 **dīvidō, -ere, -vīsī,** *divide*	22 **ūnusquisque, ūnaquaeque, ūnumquodque,** *every*
6 **vespere,** abl. used as an adv., *in the evening, late*	**sēmentis, -is,** f., *a sowing; seed sown*
māne, adv., *in the morning, early*	**speciēs, -ēī,** f., *a seeing; a kind, species*
7 **fīrmāmentum, -ī,** n., *a means of support; the sky fixed above the earth*	25 **lūmināre, -āris,** n., *that which gives light; a heavenly body; a window*
14 **appāreō, -ēre,** *become visible, appear*	27 **lūceō, -ēre,** *be bright, shine (forth)*
āridus, -a, -um, *dry, arid*	**illūminō** (1), *light up, illuminate*
15 **congregātiō, -ōnis,** f., *an assembling together*	34 **prōdūcō,** = *prō* + *dūcō,* i.e., *produce*
17 **germinō** (1), *sprout or put forth*	**rēptilis, -e,** *creeping, reptile*
herba, -ae, f., *a blade, stalk; a green plant*	35 **volātilis, -e,** *winged, flying*
vireō, -ēre, *be green; be vigorous*	
sēmen, -inis, n., *seed*	
18 **lignum, -ī,** n., *wood; a tree*	

36 **cētus, -ī,** n. (the Gr. pl. *cētē* is usu. used), *any large sea animal, a whale, dolphin, seal*

36 **grandis, -e,** *large, great*

37 **mōtābilis, -e,** *that moves, moving*

39 **multiplicō** (1), *increase manifoldly, multiply*

40 **repleō, -ēre,** *fill again* or *up*

43 **iūmentum, -ī,** n., *a beast of burden, draft animal*

47 **similitūdō, -inis,** f., *likeness, resemblance*

48 **ūniversus, -a, -um,** *whole, entire*

49 **movētur,** here and below, take as a Gr. middle voice, = *moves itself*

51 **māsculus, -a, -um,** male; as a subst. = *a male*

fēminam: note that the basic meaning of *fēmina* is *"a female"*

52 **subiciō, -ere,** *throw, place,* or *set under; make subject*

53 **dominor, -ārī,** *rule, be lord* or *master, have dominion* (here + dat.; below + gen., in imitation of Gr. See Appendix I, § 14.)

57 **ēsca, -ae,** f., *food*

animāns, -antis, here n., *an animal*

58 **volucer, -cris, -cre,** *flying, winged*

59 **vēscor, -ī,** *eat, feed on*

61 **valdē,** adv., *very, exceedingly*

62 **ōrnātus, -ūs,** m., *a furnishing, providing, preparing*

63 **compleō, -ēre, -ēvī,** *fill up; complete*

64 **patrō** (1), *to father; accomplish, perform, achieve*

66 **cessō** (1), *stop, leave off*

B. Genesis 2:4–3:24 V

This is the Yahwist's (J) account of creation and the fall. The Yahwist's writings are supposed to have been brought together from much older traditions in the ninth century BCE.

²:⁴ Istae generātiōnēs caelī et terrae, quandō creātae sunt, in diē quō fēcit Dominus Deus caelum et terram ⁵et omne virgultum agrī, antequam orīrētur in terrā, omnemque herbam regiōnis, priusquam germināret. Nōn enim pluerat Dominus

5   Deus super terram, et homō nōn erat, quī operārētur terram; ⁶sed fōns ascendēbat ē terrā īrrigāns ūniversam superficiem terrae. ⁷Fōrmāvit igitur Dominus Deus hominem dē līmō terrae, et īnspīrāvit in faciem eius spīrāculum vītae, et factus est homō in animam vīventem.

10   ⁸Plantāverat autem Dominus Deus paradīsum voluptātis ā prīncipiō, in quō posuit hominem quem fōrmāverat; ⁹prōdūxitque Dominus Deus dē humō omne lignum pulchrum vīsū et ad vēscendum suāve; lignum etiam vītae in mediō paradīsī lignumque scientiae bonī et malī. ¹⁰Et fluvius

15   ēgrediēbātur dē locō voluptātis ad īrrigandum paradīsum, quī inde dīviditur in quattuor capita. ¹¹Nōmen ūnī Phison. Ipse est quī circuit omnem terram Hevilath, ubi nāscitur aurum, ¹²et aurum terrae illīus optimum est, ibique invenītur bdellium et lapis onychinus. ¹³Et nōmen fluviō secundō Gehon. Ipse est quī

20   circuit omnem terram Aethiopiae. ¹⁴Nōmen vērō flūminis tertiī Tigris. Ipse vādit contrā Assyriōs. Fluvius autem quārtus, ipse est Euphrātes.

      ¹⁵Tulit ergō Dominus Deus hominem et posuit eum in paradīsō voluptātis, ut operārētur et custōdīret illum.

25   ¹⁶Praecēpitque eī dīcēns, "Ex omnī lignō paradīsī comede. ¹⁷Dē lignō autem scientiae bonī et malī nē comedās. In quōcumque enim diē comēderis ex eō, morte moriēris."

      ¹⁸Dīxit quoque Dominus Deus, "Nōn est bonum esse hominem sōlum. Faciāmus eī adiūtōrium similem

30   suī." ¹⁹Fōrmātīs igitur, Dominus Deus, dē humō cūnctīs animantibus terrae et ūniversīs volātilibus caelī, addūxit ea ad Adam, ut vidēret quid vocāret ea. Omne enim quod vocāvit Adam animae vīventis, ipsum est nōmen eius. ²⁰Appellāvitque Adam nōminibus suīs cūncta animantia et ūniversa volātilia

35   caelī et omnēs bēstiās terrae. Adae vērō nōn inveniēbātur
       adiūtor similis eius. [21]Immīsit ergō Dominus Deus sopōrem
       in Adam; cumque obdormīsset, tulit ūnam dē costīs eius et
       replēvit carnem prō eā. [22]Et aedificāvit Dominus Deus costam,
       quam tulerat dē Adam, in mulierem, et addūxit eam ad Adam.
40   [23]Dīxitque Adam, "Hoc nunc os ex ossibus meīs et carō dē
       carne meā. Haec vocābitur virāgō, quoniam dē virō sūmpta
       est." [24]Quamobrem relinquet homō patrem suum et mātrem, et
       adhaerēbit uxōrī suae, et erunt duo in carne ūnā. [25]Erant autem
       uterque nūdī, Adam scīlicet et uxor eius, et nōn ērubescēbant.
45   [3:1]Sed et serpēns erat callidior cūnctīs animantibus terrae
       quae fēcerat Dominus Deus. Quī dīxit ad mulierem, "Cūr
       praecēpit vōbīs Deus, ut nōn comederētis dē omnī lignō
       paradīsī?" [2]Cui respondit mulier, "Dē frūctū lignōrum quae
       sunt in paradīsō vēscēmur. [3]Dē frūctū vērō lignī quod est in
50   mediō paradīsī praecēpit nōbīs Deus, nē comederēmus et nē
       tangerēmus illud, nē forte moriāmur." [4]Dīxit autem serpēns ad
       mulierem, "Nēquāquam morte moriēminī. [5]Scit enim Deus
       quod, in quōcumque diē comēderitis ex eō, aperientur oculī
       vestrī et eritis sicut deī, scientēs bonum et malum." [6]Vīdit igitur
55   mulier quod bonum esset lignum ad vēscendum et pulchrum
       oculīs aspectūque dēlēctābile, et tulit dē frūctū illīus et
       comēdit deditque virō suō, quī comēdit. [7]Et apertī sunt oculī
       ambōrum; cumque cognōvissent esse sē nūdōs, cōnsuērunt
       folia ficūs et fēcērunt sibi perizōmata.
60   [8]Et cum audīssent vōcem Dominī Deī deambulantis in
       paradīsō ad auram post merīdiem, abscondit sē Adam et uxor
       eius ā faciē Dominī Deī in mediō lignī paradīsī. [9]Vocāvitque
       Dominus Deus Adam et dīxit eī, "Ubi es?" [10]Quī āit, "Vōcem
       tuam audīvī in paradīsō et timuī, eō quod nūdus essem, et
65   abscondī mē." [11]Cui dīxit, "Quis enim indicāvit tibi quod
       nūdus essēs, nisi quod ex lignō, dē quō tibi praecēperam nē
       comederēs, comēdistī." [12]Dīxitque Adam, "Mulier, quam
       dedistī sociam mihi, dedit mihi dē lignō et comēdī." [13]Et dīxit
       Dominus Deus ad mulierem, "Quārē hoc fēcistī?" Quae
70   respondit, "Serpēns dēcēpit mē et comēdī."
       [14]Et āit Dominus Deus ad serpentem, "Quia fēcistī hoc,
       maledictus es inter omnia animantia et bēstiās terrae. Super
       pectus tuum gradiēris et terram comedēs cūnctīs diēbus vītae

75

80

85

90

tuae. [15]Inimīcitiās pōnam inter tē et mulierem et sēmen tuum
et sēmen illīus. Ipsa conteret caput tuum et tū insidiāberis
calcāneō eius." [16]Mulierī quoque dīxit, "Multiplicābō aerumnās
tuās et conceptūs tuōs. In dolōre pariēs fīliōs, et sub virī
potestāte eris et ipse dominābitur tuī." [17]Ad Adam vērō dīxit,
"Quia audīstī vōcem uxōris tuae et comēdistī dē lignō ex quō
praecēperam tibi nē comederēs, maledicta terra in opere tuō.
In labōribus comedēs eam cūnctīs diēbus vītae tuae. [18]Spīnās et
tribulōs germinābit tibi, et comedēs herbās terrae. [19]In sūdōre
vultūs tuī vēscēris pāne, dōnec revertāris in terram dē quā
sūmptus es, quia pulvis es et in pulverem revertēris." [20]Et
vocāvit Adam nōmen uxōris suae Hēva, eō quod māter esset
cūnctōrum vīventium. [21]Fēcit quoque Dominus Deus Adae et
uxōrī eius tunicās pelliciās et induit eōs. [22]Et āit, "Ecce Adam
factus est quasi ūnus ex nōbīs, sciēns bonum et malum. Nunc
ergō, nē forte mittat manum suam et sūmat etiam dē lignō
vītae et comedat et vīvat in aeternum..." [23]Ēmīsit eum Dominus
Deus dē paradīsō voluptātis, ut operārētur terram dē quā
sūmptus est. [24]Ēiēcitque Adam et collocāvit ante paradīsum
voluptātis cherubim et flammeum gladium atque versātilem ad
custōdiendam viam lignī vītae.

1   **generatiō, -ōnis,** f., *a generating,
generation*

3   **virgultum, -ī,** n., *a thicket, bush,
shrubbery; a slip, cutting*

4   **pluō, -ere, pluī,** *rain* (used both
impersonally and personally)

5   **operor, -ārī,** *work, labor*

6   **ascendō, -ere,** *go up*
    irrigō (1), *water, irrigate*
    superficiēs, -ēī, f., *a surface*

7   **līmus, -ī,** m., *mud, mire*

8   **īnspīrō** (1), *breathe* or *blow upon*
or *into*
    spīrāculum, -ī, n., *an air hole;
breath*

10   **plantō** (1), *plant; make*
    paradīsus, -ī, m., *a park; Paradise*

10–11   **paradīsum voluptātis ā
prīncipiō,** for these words NV
substitutes *in Eden ad orientem*

12   **prōdūcō,** = *prō + dūcō,* i.e.,
produce

14   **fluvius, -iī,** m., *a stream, river*

16   **inde,** adv., *thence, from there*
    Phison, indecl. Heb. name, the
Pison (KJV), an unidentified
river

17   **Hevilath,** indecl. Heb. name,
Havilah (KJV), an unidentified
land

18   **bdellium, -iī,** n., *a fragrant, bitter
gum from the Near East*

19   **lapis onychinus, -idis, -ī,** m.,
onyx stone

Gehon, indecl. Heb. name, the *Gihon* (KJV), the *Nile,* in Jewish and Christian tradition

20   **circueō, -īre,** *go around, surround*

      Aethiopia, -ae, f., *Ethiopia*

21   **Tigris, -gridis,** m., the *Tigris*

      vādō, -ere, *go, hasten, rush*

      Assyrius, -a, -um, *Assyrian*

22   **Euphrātes, -is,** m., the *Euphrates*

24   **custōdiō, -īre,** *guard, watch, keep*

25   **praecipiō, -ere, -cēpī,** *instruct, advise, admonish*

      comedō, -ēsse, -ēdī, *eat* (the whole thing) *up, consume*

26   **quīcumque, quaecumque, quodcumque,** *whoever, whichever*

27   **morte,** = Heb. inf. absolute. See Appendix I, § 26

29   **adiūtōrium, -iī,** n., *help, assistance, support*

29   **adiūtor, -ōris,** m., *a helper*

32   **Adam,** indecl. Heb. name, or **Adam, -ae,** m., *Adam*

36   **immittō, -ere, -mīsī,** *send in, cause to go in*

37   **obdormiō, -īre, -īvī,** *go to sleep, fall asleep*

      costa, -ae, f., *a rib*

38   **repleō, -ēre, -ēvī,** *fill again* or *up*

      aedificō (1), *build; frame*

40   **os, ossis,** n., *a bone*

41   **virāgō, -inis,** f., "*a man-like, vigorous, heroic maiden, a female warrior, a heroine, virago*" (LS)

42   **quamobrem,** adv., *on which account, for which reason*

43   **adhaereō, -ēre,** *stick to, adhere*

44   **uterque, utraque, utrumque,** *each of two, both*

      nūdus, -a, -um, *naked*

      scīlicet, adv., *of course; namely*

      ērubescō, -cere, *grow red, blush*

45   **serpēns, -entis,** m./f., *a creeping thing; a snake*

      callidus, -a, -um, *clever; sly*

51   **forte,** adv., *by chance, accidentally*

52   **nēquāquam,** adv., *not at all, by no means*

53   **aperiō, -īre, -ruī, -rtum,** *open*

56   **dēlēctābilis, -e,** *delightful, pleasant*

58   **ambō, -ae, -ō** (declined like *duo*), *both*

      cōnsuō, -ere, -suī, *sew together*

59   **folium, -iī,** n., *a leaf*

      perizōma, -mata, n., *an apron*

60   **deambulō** (1), *take a walk*

61   **aura, -ae,** f., *air*

      merīdiēs, -ēī, m., *midday, noon*

      abscondō, -ere, -condī, *conceal*

64   **eō quod,** *because*

68   **socia, -ae,** f., *a partner, companion, comrade; wife*

72   **maledictus, -a, -um,** *accursed*

73   **gradior, -ī,** *step, walk*

74   **inimīcitia, -ae,** f., *enmity*

75   **conterō, -rere,** *rub away, grind, pound*

      īnsidior, -ārī, *lie in ambush, lie in wait* (+ dat.)

76   **calcāneum, -ī,** n., *the heel*

      aerumna, -ae, f., *hard labor, toil, hardship*

77 **conceptus, -ūs,** m., *a conceiving, pregnancy*

81 **eam:** NV, *ex eā*

spīna, -ae, f., *a thorn; a thornbush; an anxiety, difficulty*

82 **tribulus, -ī,** m., *a thistle; a land caltrop*

sūdor, -ōris, m., *sweat, perspiration*

84 **pulvis, -eris,** m., *dust, powder*

85 **Hēva, -ae,** f., *Eve*

87 **tunica, -ae,** f., *a tunic; a jacket*

pellicius, -a, -um, *made of skins*

induō, -ere, -duī, *put on; clothe, cover*

90 **ēmittō,** = *ē* + *mittō*. Possibly an example of anacoluthon (Smith, 93);[28] but perh. better, an example of aposiopesis (Smith, 94).

93 **cherub** (pl. **cherubim**), Heb. name, m., *a member of one of the hierarchies of angels*

flammeus, -a, -um, *fiery, flaming*

versātilis, -e, *turning around, revolving*

---

[28] This is the explanation of John Skinner, *A Critical and Exegetical Commentary on Genesis,* 2nd ed., International Critical Commentary (Edinburgh: T. & T. Clark, 1930), 88-89, and of Gerhard von Rad, *Genesis, A Commentary,* tr. John H. Marks, rev. ed., Old Testament Library (Philadelphia, Westminster Press), 1972, 97.

II. Two Passages from the Book of Wisdom

A. Wisdom 2:1–25 V

The Book of Wisdom was written in Greek, probably in the second century BCE. *The passage below, which forms part of a longer reflection on wisdom, justice, and reward, is the speech of the impious as they plot the death of the just man. The depiction of the just man derives from the last Servant Song of Deutero-Isaiah (see No. III below), and has been taken by Christians as a prophecy of Christ.*

2:1Dīxērunt enim apud sē, cogitantēs nōn rēctē: "Exiguum et cum taediō est tempus vītae nostrae, et nōn est refrīgerium in fīne hominis, et nōn est quī agnitus sit reversus ab īnferīs, 2quia ex nihilō nātī sumus et post hoc erimus tamquam nōn

5   fuerimus, quoniam fūmus afflātūs est in nāribus nostrīs et sermō scintillae ad commovendum cor nostrum, 3quia extīncta cinis erit corpus, et spīritus diffundētur tamquam mollis āēr, et trānsiet vīta nostra tamquam vestīgium nūbis, et sīcut nebula dissolvētur quae fugāta est ā radiīs sōlis et ā calōre illīus

10   aggravāta. 4Et nōmen nostrum oblīviōnem accipiet per tempus, et nēmō memoriam habēbit operum nostrōrum. 5Umbrae enim trānsitus est tempus nostrum, et nōn est reversiō fīnis nostrī, quoniam cōnsignāta est et nēmō revertētur.

6"Venīte ergō et fruāmur bonīs quae sunt, et ūtāmur

15   creātūram tamquam in iuventūte celeriter. 7Vīnō pretiōsō et unguentīs nōs impleāmus, et nōn praetereat nōs flōs temporis. 8Corōnēmus nōs rosīs, antequam marcescant. Nūllum prātum sit quod nōn pertrānseat luxuria nostra. 9Ubīque relinquāmus signa laetitiae, quoniam haec est pars nostra et haec est sors.

20   10"Opprimāmus pauperem iūstum et nōn parcāmus viduae, nec veterānī revereāmur cānōs multī temporis. 11Sit autem fortitūdō nostra lēx iniūstitiae. Quod īnfirmum est enim inūtile invenītur. 12Circumveniāmus ergō iūstum, quoniam inūtilis est nōbīs, et contrārius est operibus nostrīs, et improperat

25   nōbīs peccāta lēgis, et diffāmat in nōs peccāta disciplīnae nostrae. 13Prōmittit scientiam Deī sē habēre, et fīlium Deī sē nōminat. 14Factus est nōbīs in trāductiōnem cōgitātiōnum nostrārum. 15Gravis est nōbīs etiam ad videndum, quoniam dissimilis est aliīs vīta illīus, et immūtātae sunt viae eius.

30   16Tamquam nūgācēs aestimātī sumus ab illō, et abstinet sē ā viīs nostrīs tamquam ab immunditiīs, et praefert novissima

iūstōrum, et glōriātur patrem Deum sē habēre. [17]Videāmus
ergō sī sermōnēs illīus vērī sunt, et temptēmus quae ventūra
sunt illī, et sciēmus quae erunt novissima illīus. [18]Sī enim
35   est vērus fīlius Deī, suscipiet illum et līberābit eum dē manū
contrāriōrum. [19]Contumēliā et tormentō interrogēmus eum,
ut sciāmus reverentiam illīus, et probēmus patientiam ipsīus.
[20]Morte turpissimā condemnēmus illum. Erit enim eī respectus
ex sermōnibus illīus."

40   [21]Haec cōgitāvērunt et errāvērunt. Excaecāvit enim
illōs malitia eōrum, [22]et nesciērunt sacrāmenta Deī neque
mercēdem spērāvērunt iūstitiae, nec iūdicāvērunt honōrem
animārum sānctārum, [23]quoniam Deus creāvit hominem
inexterminābilem, et ad imāginem suae similitūdinis fēcit
45   illum. [24]Invidiā autem diabolī mors introīvit in orbem
terrārum. [25]Imitantur autem illum quī sunt ex parte illīus.

1   **exiguus, -a, -um,** *"small, little,*
    petty, short, poor, mean" (LS)

2   **taedium, -ī,** n., *disgust, loathing,*
    weariness, boredom

    refrīgerium, -iī, n., *a cooling;*
    consolation

3   **agnōscō, -ere, -nōvī, -nitum,**
    recognize; acknowledge

5   **fūmus, -ī,** m., *smoke, vapor*

    afflātus, -ūs, m., *a breeze, breath*

    nāris, -is, f., *a nostril*

6   **scintilla, -ae,** f., *a spark; a faint*
    trace

    commoveō, -ēre, *move, rouse,*
    agitate

7   **diffundō, -ere,** *pour in different*
    directions; spread out

    āēr, āeris, m., *the air around us*

8   **trānsiet,** a regular fut. for the
    normal irregular *trānsībit*. See
    LS, s.v.

    vestīgium, -iī, n., *a track, trace*

10 **aggravō** (1), *make heavier*

    oblīviō, -ōnis, f., *forgetfulness,*
    oblivion

12 **reversiō, -ōnis,** f., *a return*
    (either before journey's end
    or at journey's end). The
    construction of this word with
    the gen. is unusual. The LXX
    has ἀναποδισμὸς τῆς τελευτῆς.
    ἀναποδισμός means "a going
    back," in particular the
    "reversal of a planet's motion"
    (LSJ, s.v.). Thus, this phrase
    might be translated, *"the*
    reversal of our end."

13 **cōnsignō** (1), *seal; authenticate;*
    record

14 **fruor,** see *Wheelock's Latin*, 285

15 **creātūram:** note that *ūtī* was
    sometimes used transitively
    in EL, and thus took a dir.
    obj. See Strecker, 66. Cf.
    Blaise, § 74

    iuventus, -ūs, f., *youth*

    pretiōsus, -a, -um, *costly, pricey*

16 **unguentum, -ī,** n., *an ointment,*
perfume

nōn, this would be *nē* in CL. See
Appendix I, § 64 N 1.

flōs, flōris, m., *a flower*

17 **corōnō** (1), *crown with a garland*

marcescō, -ere, *droop, wither,*
decay

prātum, -ī, n., *a meadow*

18 **pertrānseō, -īre,** *go* or *pass*
through or by

ubīque, adv., *everywhere*

19 **laetitia, -ae,** f., *richness, beauty;*
joy, delight

sors, sortis, f., *a lot; share; fate*

20 **vidua, -ae,** f., *a widow*

21 **veterānus, -a, -um,** *old*

revereor, -ērī, *revere, respect, fear*

cānī, -ōrum, m., *gray hair*

22 **fortitūdō, -inis,** f., *stength; courage*
(cf. Plato, *Republic* 338C)

iniūstitia, -ae, f., *injustice, unjust*
proceeding (cf. Plato, *Republic*
338C)

inūtilis, -e, *useless, unprofitable*

23 **circumveniō, -īre,** *surround;*
oppress; cheat

24 **contrārius, -a, -um,** *opposed,*
contrary

improperō (1), *reproach* (someone
in dat. with something in acc.)

25 **diffāmō** (1), *spread an evil report;*
decry; make widely known

peccāta disciplīnae: < LXX
ἁμαρτήματα, *failures to attain;*
fallings away from (Lampe, s.v.
ἁμαρτία I.C and II.A.1.a)

27 **nōminō** (1), *call*

trāductiō, -ōnis, f., *disgrace,*
ridicule

cōgitātiō, -ōnis, f., *thinking; a*
thought

29 **immūtātus, -a, -um,** *unchanged*

30 **nūgāx, -ācis,** *trifling, frivolous*

aestimō (1), *rate, value, judge*

abstineō, -ēre, *hold* or *keep back*

31 **immunditia, -ae,** f., *impurity*

novissima, -ōrum, n., *the end*
(LXX, ἔσχατα)

32 **glōrior** (1), *glory, boast*

33 **temptō** (1), *try, test*

36 **contumēlia, -ae,** f., *outrage*
(physical or verbal)

tormentum, -ī, n., *the rack* or *any*
instrument of torture; anguish,
torment

interrogō (1), *ask, question;*
question judicially

37 **reverentia, -ae,** f., *respect, fear,*
awe

38 **condemnō** (1), *condemn* (+ abl.
of the penalty)

respectus, -ūs, m., *care, regard,*
respect (LXX, ἐπισκοπή). The
regard will be God's, the words
are the just man's own.

40 **excaecō** (1), *blind thoroughly*

41 **malitia, -ae,** f., *wickedness;*
cunning

44 **inexterminābilis, -e,** *that cannot*
be exterminated, immortal

similitūdō, -inis, f., *likeness,*
resemblance

45 **introeō, -īre, -iī,** *go into, enter*

46 **imitor** (1), *imitate; resemble*

ex parte illīus, *on his side,*
belonging to his party (LXX,
τῆς ἐκείνου μερίδος)

B. Wisdom 7:1–8:2 V

This passage contains a portion of "Solomon's" great speech on God's Wisdom. It is especially noteworthy for the author's application of terminology from Middle Platonic and Stoic philosophy to Wisdom in an effort to show that Nous and Logos belong to the Wisdom of the God of the Hebrews.[29]

7:1Sum quidem et ego mortālis homō similis omnibus, et
ex genere terrēnō illīus quī prior factus est, et in ventre mātris
figūrātus sum carō, ²decem mēnsuum tempore coāgulātus in
sanguine, ex sēmine hominis et dēlectāmentō somnī

5   conveniente. ³Et ego nātus accēpī commūnem āerem, et
in similiter factam dēcidī terram, prīmam vōcem similem
omnibus ēmīsī plōrāns. ⁴In involūmentīs nūtrītus sum et
cūrīs magnīs. ⁵Nēmō enim ex rēgibus aliud habuit nātīvitātis
initium. ⁶Ūnus ergō introitus est omnibus ad vītam et similis

10   exitus.
       ⁷Propter hoc optāvī et datus est mihi sēnsus. Et invocāvī
et vēnit in mē spīritus sapientiae. ⁸Et praeposuī illam rēgnīs et
sēdibus, et dīvitiās nihil esse dūxī in comparātiōne illīus. ⁹Nec
comparāvī illī lapidem pretiōsum, quoniam omne aurum

15   in comparātiōne illīus harēna est exigua, et tamquam lutum
aestimābitur argentum in cōnspectū illīus. ¹⁰Super salūtem
et speciem dīlēxī illam, et prōposuī prō lūce habēre illam,
quoniam inextinguibile est lūmen illīus. ¹¹Vēnērunt autem mihi
omnia bona pariter cum illā, et innumerābilis honestās

20   per manūs illīus. ¹²Et laetātus sum in omnibus, quoniam
antecēdēbat ista sapientia, et ignōrābam quoniam hōrum
omnium māter est. ¹³Quam sine fictiōne didicī, et sine invidiā
commūnicō, et honestātem illīus nōn abscondō. ¹⁴Īnfīnītus
enim thēsaurus est hominibus, quō quī ūsī sunt, participēs

25   factī sunt amīcitiae Deī, propter disciplīnae dōna commendātī.
¹⁵Mihi autem dedit Deus dīcere ex sententiā, et praesūmere
digna hōrum quae dantur, quoniam ipse et sapientiae dux
est et sapientium ēmendātor. ¹⁶In manū enim illīus et nōs et
sermōnēs nostrī et omnis sapientia et operum scientiae

30   disciplīna. ¹⁷Ipse enim dedit mihi hōrum quae sunt scientiam

---

[29]   See Addison G. Wright, S.S., "Wisdom," in *The Jerome Biblical Commentary*, vol. 1, ed.
       Raymond E. Brown et al. (Englewood Cliffs, NJ: Prentice-Hall, Inc., 1968), 562, § 26.

vēram, ut sciam dispositiōnem orbis terrārum, et virtūtēs
elementōrum, [18]initium et cōnsummātiōnem et medietātem
temporum, vicissitūdinum permūtātiōnēs et commūtātiōnēs
temporum, [19]annī cursūs et stēllārum dispositiōnēs, [20]nātūrās
35   animālium et īrās bēstiārum, vim ventōrum et cōgitātiōnēs
hominum, differentiās virgultōrum et virtūtēs rādīcum. [21]Et
quaecumque sunt abscōnsa et imprōvīsa didicī. Omnium enim
artifex docuit mē sapientia.

     [22]Est enim in illā spīritus intellegentiae, sānctus, ūnicus,
40   multiplex, subtīlis, disertus, mōbilis, incoinquinātus, certus,
suāvis, amāns bonum, acūtus, quem nihil vetat, benefaciēns,
[23]hūmānus, benignus, stabilis, certus, sēcūrus, omnem habēns
virtūtem, omnia prōspiciēns, et quī capiat omnēs spīritūs,
intellegibilis, mundus, subtīlis. [24]Omnibus enim mōbilibus
45   mōbilior est sapientia. Attingit autem ubīque et capit propter
suam munditiam. [25]Vapor est enim virtūtis Deī, et ēmānātiō
quaedam est clāritātis omnipotentis Deī sincēra, et ideō nihil
inquinātum in eam incurrit. [26]Candor est enim lūcis aeternae,
et speculum sine maculā Deī maiestātis, et imāgō bonitātis
50   illīus. [27]Et cum sit ūna, omnia potest, et in sē permanēns omnia
innovat, et per nātiōnēs in animās sānctās sē trānsfert. Amīcōs
Deī et prophētās cōnstituit. [28]Nēminem enim dīligit Deus, nisi
eum quī cum sapientiā inhabitat. [29]Est enim haec speciōsior
sōle et super omnem stēllārum. Lūcī comparata, invenitur
55   prior. [30]Illī enim succēdit nox, sapientiam autem nōn vincit
malitia. [8:1]Attingit ergō ā fīne usque ad fīnem fortiter, et
dispōnit omnia suāviter. [2]Hanc amāvī et exquīsīvī ā iuventūte
meā, et quaesīvī spōnsam mihi assūmere, et amātor factus sum
fōrmae illīus.

---

2 **terrēnus, -a, -um,** *earthly*
    venter, -is, m., *the stomach; womb*

3 **figūrō** (1), *form, shape*
    coāgulō (1), *cause a fluid to curdle*
      or coagulate

4 **sēmen, -inis,** n., *seed*
    dēlectāmentum, -ī, n., *pleasure,*
      delight

5 **conveniō, -īre,** *meet*

6 **dēcidō, -ere, -cidī,** *fall down*
    (presumably between his
    mother's feet at the moment of
    birth)
    in similiter factam . . . terram,
    < ἐπὶ τὴν ὁμοιοπαθῆ . . .
    γῆν, perh. = *the earth, made*
    similarly (to me).

7 **ēmittō, -ere, -mīsī,** *send forth or*
    out

plōrō (1), *weep, wail*

involūmentum, -ī, n., here = *a swaddling band* or *cloth* (LXX, σπαργάνοις)

8 **nātīvitās, -tātis,** f., *birth*

9 **introitus, -ūs,** m., *an entrance; a beginning*

10 **exitus, -ūs,** m., *a means of going out; an end*

11 **invocō** (1), *call upon for help, invoke*

12 **praepōnō, -ere, -posuī,** *put* or *place before; prefer* (+ dat.)

13 **sēdēs, -is,** f., *a seat; a throne*

14 **comparātiō, -ōnis,** f., *a comparison*

lapis, -idis, m., *a stone*

15 **harēna, -ae,** f., *sand*

lutum, -ī, n., *mud, dirt*

16 **in cōnspectū illīus,** take *illīus* as an objective gen., = *in sight of* or *in comparison with that* (LXX, ἐν συγκρίσει αὐτῆς)

17 **speciēs, -ēī,** f., *a seeing; the outward appearance; beauty*

18 **inextinguibilis, -e,** *that cannot be put out, unextinguishable*

lūmen, -inis, n., *light*

19 **innumerābilis, -e,** *countless, innumerable;* here perh. = *limitless, measureless* (cf. LLMA, s.v. *innumerōsē*)

honestās, -tātis, f., *honorable reputation* or *character;* but here = *profit, advantage* (LLMA, s.v. See also LXX, πλοῦτος; NV, *dīvitiae.*)

20 **laetor, -ārī,** *rejoice, take delight*

21 **antecēdō, -ere,** *go before, precede*

ignōrō (1), *be ignorant of, not know*

22 **fictiō, -ōnis,** f., *a feigning, counterfeiting*

23 **commūnicō** (1), *share; communicate, impart*

abscondō, -ere, *conceal*

24 **thēsaurus, -ī,** m., *a treasure; treasury*

particeps, -cipis, m., *a sharer, partner, comrade*

25 **disciplīna, -ae,** f., *instruction, teaching; training, education; disciplined life*

commendātus, -a, -um, *recommended; esteemed*

26 **ex sententiā:** *according to judgment* or *opinion* (LXX, κατὰ γνώμην)

praesūmō, -ere, here = *infer* (LXX, ἐνθυμηθῆναι)

28 **ēmendātor, -ōris,** m., *a corrector*

31 **dispositiō, -ōnis,** f., *a regular arrangement*

32 **cōnsummātiō, -ōnis,** f., *a summing up; a completion*

medietās, -tātis, f., *the middle, mean*

33 **permūtātiō, -ōnis,** f., *a complete change; an interchange*

commūtātiō, -ōnis, f., *a change, alteration*

36 **differentia, -ae,** f., *difference, distinction*

virgultum, -ī, n., *a bush, shrubbery; slips, cuttings*

rādīx, -īcis, f., *a root*

37 **quīcumque, quaecumque, quodcumque,** *whoever, whichever, whatever*

imprōvīsus, -a, -um, *unforeseen, unexpected*

38 **artifex, -ficis,** *a master craftsman; creator*

39 **intellegentia, -ae,** f., *understanding*

ūnicus, -a, -um, *one, only; alone of its kind*

40 **multiplex, -plicis,** *having many parts; many-sided; versatile*

subtīlis, -e, *slender, fine*

disertus, -a, -um, *clear* (in speaking)

mōbilis, -e, *active, rapid*

incoinquinātus, -a, -um, *undefiled, unpolluted*

41 **acūtus, -a, -um,** *sharp, keen*

benefaciō, -ere, -fēcī, -factum, *do well; do good to* (+ dat.)

42 **benignus, -a, -um,** *kind, friendly*

43 **prōspiciō, -ere,** *see ahead, foresee, provide*

44 **intellegibilis, -e,** *intelligible, intellectual*

mundus, -a, -um, *clean, neat, elegant*

intelligibilis, mundus, subtīlis: NV: *intellegibilēs, mundōs, subtīlēs*

45 **attingō, -ere,** *touch, come in contact with; arrive at, reach*

ubīque, adv., *everywhere*

46 **munditia, -ae,** f., *cleanness, neatness, elegance*

vapor, -ōris, m., *a vapor, steam, exhalation*

ēmānātiō, -ōnis, f., *an emanation*

47 **clāritās, -tātis,** f., *clearness, brightness, splendor*

sincērus, -a, -um, *pure, unmixed*

ideō, adv., *therefore*

48 **inquinātus, -a, -um,** *foul, dirty, polluted*

incurrō, -ere, *attack; meet; extend into*

candor, -ōris, m., *a dazzling whiteness; sincerity*

49 **macula, -ae,** f., *a spot; a moral blemish*

bonitās, -tātis, f., *goodness*

50 **permaneō, -ēre,** *stay, abide; continue, last*

51 **innovō** (1), *renew*

52 **cōnstituō, -ere,** *set up, establish; appoint*

53 **inhabitō** (1), *inhabit*

speciōsus, -a, -um, *beautiful, splendid*

54 **comparō** (1), *compare*

55 **succēdō, -ere,** *follow, succeed*

56 **malitia, -ae,** f., *wickedness; cunning*

57 **dispōnō, -ere,** *distribute; arrange*

exquīrō, -ere, -quīsīvī, *search out, seek out*

iuventus, -ūs, f., *youth*

58 **spōnsa, -ae,** f., *a bride*

assūmō, -ere, *take to oneself*

amātor, -ōris, m., *a lover*

III. Isaiah 52:13–53:12 V

This is the last of the Servant Songs of Deutero-Isaiah. Christians have always taken it as a prophecy of Christ. It is read on Good Friday.

^{52:13}Ecce intelleget servus meus, exaltābitur et ēlevābitur, et sublīmis erit valdē. ¹⁴Sīcut obstupuērunt super tē multī, sīc inglōrius erit inter virōs aspectus eius, et fōrma eius inter filiōs hominum. ¹⁵Iste asperget gentēs multās, super ipsum
5 continēbunt rēgēs ōs suum, quia quibus nōn est nārrātum dē eō vīdērunt, et quī nōn audiērunt contemplātī sunt. ^{53:1}Quis crēdidit audītuī nostrō, et brācchium Dominī cui revēlātum est? ²Et ascendet sīcut virgultum cōram eō, et sīcut rādīx dē terrā sitientī. Nōn est speciēs eī neque decor, et vīdimus
10 eum, et nōn erat aspectus, et dēsīderāvimus eum, ³dēspectum et novissimum virōrum, virum dolōrum, et scientem īnfirmitātem. Et quasi absconditus vultus eius et dēspectus, unde nec reputāvimus eum. ⁴Vērē languōrēs nostrōs ipse tulit, et dolōrēs nostrōs ipse portāvit, et nōs putāvimus eum quasi
15 leprōsum, et percussum ā Deō, et humiliātum. ⁵Ipse autem vulnerātus est propter inīquitātēs nostrās, attrītus est propter scelera nostra. Disciplīna pācis nostrae super eum, et līvōre eius sānātī sumus. ⁶Omnes nōs quasi ovēs errāvimus, ūnusquisque in viam suam dēclīnāvit, et Dominus posuit in eō inīquitātem
20 omnium nostrum. ⁷Oblātus est, quia ipse voluit, et nōn aperuit ōs suum. Sīcut ovis ad occīsiōnem dūcētur, et quasi agnus cōram tondente obmūtescet, et nōn aperiet ōs suum. ⁸Dē angustiā et dē iūdiciō sublātus est. Generātiōnem eius quis ēnārrābit, quia abscīsus est dē terrā vīventium? Propter scelus
25 populī meī percussit eum, ⁹et dabit impiōs prō sepultūrā, et dīvitem prō morte suā, eō quod inīquitātem nōn fēcerit, neque dolus fuerit in ōre eius. ¹⁰Et Dominus voluit conterere eum in īnfirmitāte. Sī posuerit prō peccātō animam suam, vidēbit sēmen longaevum, et voluntās Dominī in manū eius dīrigētur.
30 ¹¹Prō eō quod labōrāvit anima eius, vidēbit et saturābitur. In scientiā suā iūstificābit ipse iūstus servus meus multōs, et inīquitātēs eōrum ipse portābit. ¹²Ideō dispertiam eī plūrimōs, et fortium dīvidet spolia, prō eō quod trādidit in morte animam suam, et cum scelerātīs reputātus est, et ipse peccātum
35 multōrum tulit, et prō trānsgressōribus rogāvit.

1   **exaltō** (1), *raise, elevate, exalt*
     ēlevō (1), *lift up, raise, elevate*

2   **valdē,** adv., *very much*
     obstupescō, -ere, -stupuī,
     become senseless, be astounded

3   **inglōrius, -a, -um,** *without glory,*
     inglorious
     aspectus, -ūs, m., *look,*
     appearance

4   **aspergō, -ere,** *sprinkle upon*

6   **contemplor, -ārī,** *survey, regard,*
     contemplate

7   **audītus, -ūs,** m., *a report*
     bracchium, -iī, n., *an arm*
     revēlō (1), *unveil, uncover*

8   **ascendō, -ere,** *go up, ascend*
     virgultum, -ī, n., *a bush,*
     shrubbery; slips, cuttings
     cōram, prep. + abl., *in the*
     presence of
     rādīx, -īcis, f., *a root*

9   **speciēs, -ēī,** f., *beauty*

10   **dēspectus, -a, -um,** *contemptible,*
     despicable

12   **īnfīrmitās, -tātis,** f., *weakness,*
     feebleness

13   **reputō** (1), *reckon, calculate;*
     ponder, reflect on
     languor, -ōris, m., *weariness;*
     feebleness

14   **portō** (1), *bear, carry*

15   **leprōsus, -a, -um,** *leprous*
     percutiō, -ere, -cussī, -cussum,
     strike, beat
     humiliō (1), *abase, humble*

16   **vulnerō** (1), *wound, injure*
     inīquitās, -tātis, f., *unfairness,*
     injustice

     atterō, -ere, -trīvī, -trītum, *rub*
     away; weaken, ruin

17   **disciplīna, -ae,** f., *instruction;*
     training
     līvor, -ōris, m., *a black and blue*
     spot; envy, spite, malice

18   **ūnusquisque, ūnaquaeque,**
     ūnumquidque, *each one*

19   **dēclīnō** (1), *bend aside, turn away*

20   **aperiō, -īre, -ruī,** *open*

21   **occīsiō, -ōnis,** f., *a killing,*
     slaughter
     agnus, -ī, m., *a lamb*

22   **obmūtescō, -ere,** *become silent,*
     grow speechless

23   **angustia, -ae,** f., *narrowness;*
     difficulty, distress
     sufferō, -ferre, sustulī,
     sublātum, *carry or put under;*
     offer, proffer
     generātiō, -ōnis, f., *a generating,*
     generation

24   **ēnarrō** (1), *narrate, explain*
     abscīdō, -ere, -cīdī, -cīsum, *cut*
     off

25   **impiōs prō sepultūrā:** < τοὺς
     πονηροὺς ἀντὶ τῆς ταφῆς
     αὐτοῦ, perh. = *the wicked to*
     serve as his burial (LSJ, s.v. ἀντί
     A.III.2). Cf. Heb., ʼet-rəšāʻîm
     qibərô, his grave with the
     wicked, and NV, *sepulcrum eius*
     cum impiīs.
     sepultūra, -ae, f., *a burying,*
     burial

26   **dīvitem prō morte suā:** the
     construction in this clause is
     analogous to the construction
     in the previous clause. Cf. NV,
     cum dīvitibus tumulum eius

26 **eō quod,** = *because*

27 **dolus, -ī,** m., *fraud, deceit*

    conterō, -ere, *rub* or *wear away,
destroy*

29 **sēmen, -inis,** n., *seed*

    longaevus, -a, -um, *aged, ancient*

    dīrigō, -ere, *arrange, direct*

30 **saturō** (1), *fill, satisfy*

31 **iūstificō** (1), *do justice to; make
just, justify*

32 **ideō,** adv., *therefore*

    dispertiō, -īre, *separate, divide,
distribute*

33 **dīvidō, -ere,** *divide up*

    spolia, -ōrum, n., *spoils, booty,
plunder*

35 **trānsgressor, -ōris,** m., *an
infringer of the law, transgressor*

IV. St. John 1:1–28 V

This is the prologue of the Gospel according to St. John, along with the first testimony of John the Baptist. The prologue has had an unequaled influence on the development of Christology. It is read on December 31st, within the Octave of Christmas, in the Ordinary form of the Mass. In the Extraordinary Form, it is said as the Last Gospel at every Mass.

[1:1]In prīncipiō erat Verbum, et Verbum erat apud Deum, et Deus erat Verbum. [2]Hoc erat in prīncipiō apud Deum. [3]Omnia per ipsum facta sunt, et sine ipsō factum est nihil quod factum est. [4]In ipsō vīta erat, et vīta erat lūx hominum, [5]et lūx in
5   tenebrīs lūcet, et tenebrae eam nōn comprehendērunt.

     [6]Fuit homō missus ā Deō, cui nōmen erat Iōannes. [7]Hic vēnit in testimōnium, ut testimōnium perhibēret dē lūmine, ut omnēs crēderent per illum. [8]Nōn erat ille lūx, sed ut testimōnium perhibēret dē lūmine. [9]Erat lūx vēra, quae
10   illūminat omnem hominem venientem in mundum. [10]In mundō erat, et mundus per ipsum factus est, et mundus eum nōn cognōvit. [11]In propria vēnit, et suī eum nōn recēpērunt. [12]Quotquot autem recēpērunt eum, dedit eīs potestātem fīliōs Deī fierī, hīs quī crēdunt in nōmine eius, [13]quī nōn ex
15   sanguinibus, neque ex voluntāte carnis, neque ex voluntāte virī, sed ex Deō nātī sunt.

     [14]Et Verbum carō factum est, et habitāvit in nōbīs, et vīdimus glōriam eius, glōriam quasi ūnigenitī ā Patre, plēnum grātiae et vēritātis. [15]Iōannes testimōnium perhibet dē ipsō, et
20   clāmat dīcēns, "Hic erat quem dīxī vōbīs: Quī post mē ventūrus est, ante mē factus est, quia prior mē erat." [16]Et dē plēnitūdine eius nōs omnēs accēpimus, et grātiam prō grātia, [17]quia lēx per Mōÿsen data est, grātia et vēritās per Iēsūm Chrīstum facta est. [18]Deum nēmō vīdit umquam, ūnigenitus Fīlius, quī est in sinū
25   Patris, ipse ēnārrāvit.

     [19]Et hoc est testimōnium Iōannis, quandō mīsērunt Iūdaeī ab Hierosolymīs sacerdōtēs et Lēvītās ad eum, ut interrogārent eum, "Tū quis es?" [20]Et cōnfessus est, et nōn negāvit, et cōnfessus est, "Quia nōn sum ego Chrīstus." [21]Et
30   interrogāvērunt eum, "Quid ergō? Ēlīās es tū?" Et dīcit, "Nōn sum." "Prophēta es tū?" Et respondit, "Nōn." [22]Dīxērunt ergō eī, "Quis es, ut respōnsum dēmus hīs quī mīsērunt nōs? Quid

dīcis dē tē ipsō?" [23]Āit, "Ego vōx clāmantis in dēsertō, 'Dīrigite
viam Dominī!' sīcut dīxit Ēsāiās prophēta." [24]Et quī missī fuerant
35 erant ex Pharisaeīs. [25]Et interrogāvērunt eum, et dīxērunt eī,
"Quid ergō baptīzās, sī tū nōn es Chrīstus, neque Ēliās, neque
prophēta?" [26]Respondit eīs Iōannes dīcēns, "Ego baptīzō in
aquā. Medius autem vestrum stetit quem vōs nōn scītis. [27]Ipse
est quī post mē ventūrus est, quī ante mē factus est, cuius
40 ego nōn sum dignus, ut solvam eius corrigiam calceāmentī."
[28]Haec in Bethaniā facta sunt trāns Iordānen, ubi erat Iōannes
baptīzāns.

3-4 **quod . . . erat:** alternative
punctuation: *Quod factum est
in ipsō vīta erat*

5 **lūceō, -ēre,** *be bright, shine*

6 **missus:** take as adj., not as part
of a periphrasis (< Ἐγένετο
ἄνθρωπος, ἀπεσταλμένος...)
Iōannes, -is, m., *John*

7 **testimōnium, -iī,** n., *witness,
evidence, testimony*
perhibeō, -ēre, *present, produce*
lūmen, -inis, n., *light*

10 **illūminō** (1), *light up, illuminate*

13 **quotquot,** indecl. indef. adj.,
however many

14 **hīs quī crēdunt in nōmine,** <
τοῖς πιστεύουσιν εἰς τὸ ὄνομα,
a peculiarly Johannine usage
with "no real parallel . . . in
LXX or in secular Greek. . . .
With the exception of I John
v 10 *pisteuein eis* is used in the
Johannine writings for belief
in(to) a person. . . . A frequent
synonym is to 'come to' Jesus
. . . Thus, *pisteuein eis* may be
defined in terms of an active
commitment to a person and,
in particular, to Jesus."[30]

18 **ūnigenitus, -a -um,** *only-
begotten, only*

21 **plēnitūdō, -inis,** f., *fullness*

23 **Mōÿses, -is,** m., *Moses*

24 **sinus, -ūs,** m., *the fold of the toga
in front of the upper body,* used
as a pouch; *bosom*

25 **ēnarrō** (1), *narrate, explain*

---

[30] Raymond E. Brown, *The Gospel according to John, I–XII,* 2nd ed., Anchor Bible 29
(Garden City, NY: Doubleday and Company, 1979), 512–513. See also Appendix I, §
42 N 1.

26   **Iūdaeus, -ī,** m., *a Jew.* Apart
     from a few exceptions, "the
     Fourth Gospel uses 'the Jews'
     as almost a technical title
     for the religious authorities,
     particularly those in
     Jerusalem, who are hostile to
     Jesus."[31]

27   **Lēvīta, -ae,** m., *a Levite*

     interrogō (1), *ask, inquire*

29   **Quia nōn sum ego Chrīstus:**
     see Appendix I, § 70 N 2

30   **Ēliās, -ae,** m., *Elijah*

32   **respōnsum, -ī,** n., *an answer*

33   **dēsertum, -ī,** n., *a desert, waste
     place*

dīrigō, -ere, here = *straighten,
     make straight*

34   **Ēsāiās, -ae,** m., *Isaiah*

35   **Pharīsaeus, -ī,** m., *a Pharisee*

38   **medius:** take as a pred. adj.
     modifying the subj. of *stetit,* =
     in the middle

40   **solvō, -ere,** *loosen, untie, unbind*

     corrigia, -ae, f., *a shoelace*

     calceāmentum, -ī, n., *a shoe*

41   **Bethania, -ae,** f., *Bethany*

     Iordānes, -ae, f., *the Jordan River*

42   **baptīzāns:** see Appendix I, § 46

---

[31]   Ibid., LXXI.

V. St. John's Account of the Passion and Resurrection of Christ

These three readings form St. John's account of Christ Jesus' trial before Pilate, his crucifixion and burial, and his resurrection. Sections A and B are read on Good Friday both in the Ordinary and in the Extraordinary Forms of the Mass. Most of section C is read on Easter Sunday or during the Easter Octave.

A. St. John 18:28–19:15 V

[18:28]Addūcunt ergō Iēsūm ā Caiaphā in praetōrium. Erat autem māne, et ipsī nōn introiērunt in praetōrium, ut nōn contāminārentur, sed mandūcārent Pascha. [29]Exīvit ergō Pīlātus ad eōs forās, et dīxit, "Quam accūsātiōnem adfertis
5   adversus hominem hunc?" [30]Respondērunt et dīxērunt eī, "Sī nōn esset hic malefactor, nōn tibi trādidissēmus eum." [31]Dīxit ergō eīs Pīlātus, "Accipite eum vōs, et secundum lēgem vestram iūdicāte eum." Dīxērunt ergō eī Iūdaeī, "Nōbīs nōn licet interficere quemquam," [32]ut sermō Iēsū implērētur, quem dīxit
10   significāns quā esset morte moritūrus.

[33]Introīvit ergō iterum in praetōrium Pīlātus, et vocāvit Iēsūm, et dīxit eī, "Tū es rēx Iūdaeōrum?" [34]Et respondit Iēsūs, "Ā tēmetipsō hoc dīcis, an aliī tibi dīxērunt dē mē?" [35]Respondit Pīlātus, "Numquid ego Iūdaeus sum? Gēns tua
15   et pontificēs trādidērunt tē mihi. Quid fēcistī?" [36] Respondit Iēsūs, "Rēgnum meum nōn est dē mundō hōc. Sī ex hōc mundō esset rēgnum meum, ministrī meī dēcertārent, ut nōn trāderer Iūdaeīs. Nunc autem meum rēgnum nōn est hinc." [37]Dīxit itaque eī Pīlātus, "Ergō rēx es tū?" Respondit Iēsūs, "Tū
20   dīcis quia rēx sum ego. Ego in hoc nātus sum et ad hoc vēnī in mundum, ut testimōnium perhibeam vēritātī. Omnis quī est ex vēritāte audit meam vōcem." [38]Dīcit eī Pīlātus, "Quid est vēritās?"

Et cum hoc dīxisset, iterum exīvit ad Iūdaeōs, et dīcit eīs,
25   "Ego nūllam inveniō in eō causam. [39]Est autem cōnsuētūdō vōbīs, ut ūnum dīmittam vōbīs in Paschā. Vultis ergō dīmittam vōbīs rēgem Iūdaeōrum?" [40]Clāmāvērunt rursum omnēs dīcentēs, "Nōn hunc, sed Barabban." Erat autem Barabbas latrō.

30

19:1Tunc ergō apprehendit Pīlātus Iēsūm, et flagellāvit, 2et
mīlitēs, plectentēs corōnam dē spīnīs, imposuērunt capitī eius,
et veste purpureā circumdedērunt eum, 3et veniēbant ad eum et
dīcēbant, "Avē, rēx Iūdaeōrum," et dabant eī alapās.

    4Exiit iterum Pīlātus forās et dīcit eīs, "Ecce, addūcō vōbīs
eum forās, 5ut cognōscātis quia in eō nūllam causam inveniō."

35

Exīvit ergō Iēsūs portāns corōnam spīneam et purpureum
vestīmentum, et dīcit eīs, "Ecce homō." 6Cum ergō vīdissent
eum, pontificēs et ministrī clāmābant dīcentēs, "Crucifīge,
crucifīge." Dīcit eīs Pīlātus, "Accipite eum vōs et crucifīgite.
Ego enim nōn inveniō in eō causam." 7Respondērunt eī

40

Iūdaeī, "Nōs lēgem habēmus, et secundum lēgem dēbet morī,
quia Fīlium Deī sē fēcit." 8Cum ergō audīsset Pīlātus hunc
sermōnem, magis timuit,9et ingressus est praetōrium iterum et
dīcit ad Iēsūm, "Unde es tū?" Iēsūs autem respōnsum nōn dedit
eī. 10Dīcit ergō eī Pīlātus, "Mihi nōn loqueris? Nescīs quia

45

potestātem habeō crucifīgere tē, et potestātem habeō dīmittere
tē? 11Respondit Iēsūs, "Nōn habērēs potestātem adversum mē
ūllam, nisi tibi esset datum dēsuper. Proptereā quī trādidit
mē tibi maius peccātum habet." 12Exinde quaerēbat Pīlātus
dīmittere eum.

50

    Iūdaeī autem clāmābant dīcentēs, "Sī hunc dīmittis, nōn es
amīcus Caesaris. Omnis quī sē rēgem facit contrādīcit Caesarī."
13Pīlātus ergō cum audīsset hōs sermōnēs, addūxit forās
Iēsūm, et sēdit prō tribūnālī in locum quī dīcitur Lithostrōtus,
Hebraicē autem Gabbatha. 14Erat autem parascēvē Paschae,

55

hōrā quasi sextā. Et dīcit Iūdaeīs, "Ecce rēx vester." 15Illī autem
clāmābant, "Tolle, tolle, crucifīge eum." Dīxit eīs Pīlātus,
"Rēgem vestrum crucifīgam?" Respondērunt pontificēs, "Nōn
habēmus rēgem nisi Caesarem."

---

1   **Caiaphas, -ae,** m., *Caiaphas,* the
high-priest

  praetōrium, -iī, n., usu. *the Roman
governor's official residence
in his province,* but here, *the
governor's residence at Jerusalem,*
which would have included a
courtyard, public and private
rooms, and a barracks.

2   **māne,** indecl. noun, *morning;*
adv., *in the morning, early*

  introeō, -īre, -iī, *go into, enter*

3   **contāminō** (1), *pollute, make
unclean*

  mandūcō (1), *chew; eat*

  pascha, -atis, n., *the Passover
Feast; the Paschal lamb*

4 **Pīlātus, -ī,** m., Pontius *Pilate,*
prefect of Judea 26–36 CE

forās, adv., *outdoors*

accūsātiō, -ōnis, f., *an*
accusation

6 **malefactor, -ōris,** m., *an evildoer,*
malefactor

7 **secundum,** prep. + acc.,
according to

8 **Iūdaeus, -ī,** m., *a Jew.* See note
on this word in Locī IV (on
Jn.1:19).

10 **significō** (1), *indicate, show*

13 **-met,** emphatic enclitic particle,
self (often used, seemingly
redundantly, with *ipse*)

15 **pontifex, -ficis,** m., *a high priest;*
(pl.) *a guild of priests* (at Rome)

17 **minister, -trī,** m., *a servant,*
attendant

21 **testimōnium, -iī,** n., *witness,*
evidence, testimony

perhibeō, -ēre, *present, produce*

25 **cōnsuētūdō, -inis,** f., *a custom,*
usage

27 **rursus,** adv., *again, once more*

28 **Barabbas, -ae,** m., *Barabbas*

latrō, -ōnis, m., *a robber, bandit*

29 **apprehendō, -ere, -dī,** *lay hold*
of, seize

flagellō (1), *whip, scourge*

30 **plectō, -ere,** *plait, braid*

spīna, -ae, f., *a thorn*

impōnō, -ere, -posuī, *put or*
place upon

31 **vestis, -is,** f., *clothing, a garment*

purpureus, -a, -um, *purple-*
colored; dark red, brown, or
violet (like a Roman soldier's
cloak)

circumdō, -dare, -dedī,
surround, put something around
someone or *something*

32 **aveō, -ēre,** *be well;* (imperative)
hail!

alapa, -ae, f., *a slap on the cheek, a*
box on the ear

35 **portō** (1), *carry, bring;* (here =)
wear

spīneus, -a, -um, *of thorns,*
thorny

36 **vestīmentum, -ī,** n., *a garment*

37 **crucifīgō, -ere, -īxī, -īxum,**
crucify

42 **ingredior, -ī, -gressus sum,**
enter, go in

43 **respōnsum, -ī,** n., *an answer*

46 **adversum,** = *adversus*

47 **dēsuper,** adv., *from above*

proptereā, adv., *on that account*

48 **exinde,** adv., (in space) *thence;*
(in time) *after that*

51 **contrādīcō, -ere,** *speak against,*
contradict

53 **tribūnal, -ālis,** n., *a raised*
platform for a magistrate

Lithostrōtus, -ī, m., *the*
Tessalated Pavement

54 **Hebraicē,** adv., *in Hebrew*

parascēvē, -ēs, f., *the day of*
preparation for the Sabbath

55 **quasi,** with numerals, = *about*

B. St. John 19:16–42 V

[16]Tunc ergō trādidit eīs illum, ut crucifigerētur. Suscēpērunt
autem Iēsūm et ēdūxērunt, [17]et bāiulāns sibi crucem, exīvit in
eum quī dīcitur Calvāriae locum, Hebraicē Golgotha, [18]ubi
eum crucifīxērunt, et cum eō aliōs duōs, hinc et hinc, medium

5   autem Iēsūm. [19]Scrīpsit autem et titulum Pīlātus et posuit
super crucem. Erat autem scrīptum, "Iēsūs Nāzarēnus, rēx
Iūdaeōrum." [20]Hunc ergō titulum multī lēgērunt Iūdaeōrum,
quia prope cīvitātem erat locus ubi crucifīxus est Iēsūs, et erat
scrīptum Hebraicē, Graecē et Latīnē. [21]Dīcēbant ergō Pīlātō

10   pontificēs Iūdaeōrum, "Nōlī scrībere ʿrēx Iūdaeōrum,ʾ sed
quia ʿipse dīxit, "Rēx sum Iūdaeōrum." ʾ " [22]Respondit Pīlātus,
"Quod scrīpsī scrīpsī."

     [23]Mīlitēs ergō cum crucifīxissent eum, accēpērunt
vestīmenta eius et fēcērunt quattuor partēs, ūnīcuique mīlitī

15   partem, et tunicam. Erat autem tunica incōnsūtilis, dēsuper
contexta per tōtum. [24]Dīxērunt ergō ad invicem, "Nōn
scindāmus eam, sed sortiāmur dē illā, cuius sit," ut scrīptūra
impleātur dīcēns, "Partītī sunt vestīmenta mea sibi, et in vestem
meam mīsērunt sortem." Et mīlitēs quidem haec fēcērunt.

20   [25]Stābant autem iuxtā crucem Iēsū māter eius et soror mātris
eius, Marīa Cleopae et Marīa Magdalēnē. [26]Cum vīdisset ergō
Iēsūs mātrem et discipulum stantem quem dīligēbat, dīcit
mātrī suae, "Mulier, ecce fīlius tuus." [27]Deinde dīcit discipulō,
"Ecce māter tua." Et ex illā hōrā accēpit eam discipulus in sua.

25   [28]Posteā, sciēns Iēsūs quia iam omnia cōnsummāta sunt,
ut cōnsummārētur scrīptūra, dīcit, "Sitiō." [29]Vās ergō positum
erat, acētō plēnum. Illī autem spongiam plēnam acētō, hyssōpō
circumpōnentēs, obtulērunt ōrī eius. [30]Cum ergō accēpisset
Iēsūs acētum, dīxit, "Cōnsummātum est." Et inclīnātō capite

30   trādidit spīritum.

     [31]Iūdaeī ergō, quoniam parascēvē erat, ut nōn remanērent in
cruce corpora Sabbatō—erat enim magnus diēs ille Sabbatī—
rogavērunt Pīlātum, ut frangerentur eōrum crūra et tollerentur.
[32]Vēnērunt ergō mīlitēs, et prīmī quidem frēgērunt crūra et

35   alterīus quī crucifīxus est cum eō. [33]Ad Iēsūm autem cum
vēnissent, ut vīdērunt eum iam mortuum, nōn frēgērunt eius
crūra, [34]sed ūnus mīlitum lancea latus eius aperuit, et continuō

exīvit sanguis et aqua, ³⁵et quī vīdit testimōnium perhibuit, et
vērum est eius testimōnium, et ille scit quia vēra dīcit, ut et
40   vōs crēdātis. ³⁶Facta sunt enim haec, ut scrīptūra impleātur,
"Os nōn comminuētis ex eō," ³⁷et iterum alia scrīptūra dīcit,
"Vidēbunt in quem trānsfīxērunt."
       ³⁸Post haec autem rogāvit Pīlātum Iōsēph ab Arimathaea, eō
quod esset discipulus Iēsū, occultus autem propter metum
45   Iūdaeōrum, ut tolleret corpus Iēsū, et permīsit Pīlātus. Vēnit
ergō et tulit corpus Iēsū. ³⁹Vēnit autem et Nicodēmus, quī
vēnerat ad Iēsūm nocte prīmum, ferēns mixtūram murrae et
aloēs, quasi lībrās centum. ⁴⁰Accēpērunt ergō corpus Iēsū, et
ligāvērunt eum linteīs cum arōmatibus, sīcut mōs Iūdaeīs est
50   sepelīre. ⁴¹Erat autem in locō ubi crucifīxus est hortus, et in
hortō monumentum novum, in quō nōndum quisquam positus
erat. ⁴²Ibi ergō propter parascēvēn Iūdaeōrum, quia iuxtā erat
monumentum, posuērunt Iēsūm.

2	**bāiulō** (1), *carry a burden*	16–17	**Nōn scindāmus:** note that *nōn*
	crux, crucis, f., *a cross*		is used here with the hortatory
3	**calvāria, -ae,** f., *a human skull*		subjunctive. See Appendix I, §
4	**hinc et hinc,** *on this side and on*		64 N 1
	that	17	**scindō, -ere,** *cut, tear*
	medium: take as a pred. adj., = *in*		**sortior, -īrī,** *cast lots*
	the middle	18	**partior, -īrī, -tītus sum,** *share*
6	**Nazarēnus, -a, -um,** *of Nazareth,*		*out, divide*
	Nazarene	19	**sors, sortis,** f., *a lot.* The
8	**prope,** prep. + acc., *near to*		quotation is of Ps. 21:19 V.
9	**Graecē,** adv., *in Greek*	20	**iuxtā,** adv., *nearby;* prep. + acc.,
	Latīnē, adv., *in Latin*		*close* or *near to*
14	**ūnusquisque, ūnaquaeque,**	21	**Cleopas, -ae,** m., *Cleophas* (<
	ūnumquodque, *every*		Κλωπᾶ)
15	**tunica, -ae,** f., *an undergarment*		**Magdalēnē, -ēs,** f., *of Magdala*
	with sleeves worn by both men	24	**in sua,** take as acc. (< εἰς + acc)
	and women, *a tunic*	25	**consummō** (1), *add together, sum*
	incōnsūtilis, -e, *not sewn*		*up; form a whole, complete*
	together, seamless	26	**vās, vāsis,** n., *a vessel*
16	**contexō, -ere, -texuī, -textum,**	27	**acētum, -ī,** n., *vinegar*
	weave together		**spongia, -ae,** f., *a sponge*
	ad invicem, see Appendix I, § 35		**hyssōpus, -ī,** f., *hyssop*

28 **circumpōnō, -ere,** *put around*

29 **inclīnō** (1), *bend, incline*

32 **sabbatum, -ī,** n., *the* (Jewish)
    Sabbath

33 **frangō, -ere, frēgī,** *break, break
    in pieces, shatter*

    crūs, crūris, n., *the shin,
    shinbone, leg*

37 **lancea, -ae,** f., *a light spear with a
    leather thong in the middle*

    latus, -eris, n., *the side*

    aperiō, -īre, -uī, *uncover; open*

    continuō, adv., *at once*

41 **comminuō, -ere,** *make small,
    break into small pieces.* The
    quotation is perh. of Ps.
    33:21 V.

42 **trānsfīgō, -ere, -fīxī,** *pierce
    through, transfix.* See
    Zechariah 12:10.

43 **Iōsēph,** indecl. Heb. name, m.,
    Joseph

    Arimathea, -ae, f., *Arimathea,
    an unidentified town,* prob. in
    Judea.

43–44 **eō quod,** = *because*

46 **Nicodēmus, -ī,** m., *Nicodemus,* a
    member of the Sanhedrin who
    had come secretly one night to
    speak with Jesus (John 3:1)

47 **mixtūra, -ae,** f., *a mixture*

    murra, -ae, f., *the myrrh-tree;
    myrrh*

48 **aloē, -ēs,** f., *the aloe-plant; aloe*

    libra, -ae, f., *a scales; the Roman
    pound* (= 12 oz.)

49 **arōma, -matis,** n., *a spice*

50 **sepeliō, -īre, -iī, -pultum,** *bury*

51 **monumentum,** here = *tomb*

C. St. John 20:1–25 V

20:1Ūnā autem sabbatī, Marīa Magdalēnē venit māne, cum
adhūc tenebrae essent, ad monumentum, et videt lapidem
sublātum ā monumentō. 2Cucurrit ergō et venit ad Simōnem
Petrum et ad alium discipulum, quem amābat Iēsūs, et dīcit
5 eīs, "Tulērunt Dominum dē monumentō, et nescīmus ubi
posuērunt eum." 3Exiit ergō Petrus et ille alius discipulus, et
vēnērunt ad monumentum. 4Currēbant autem duo simul, et
ille alius discipulus praecucurrit citius Petrō, et vēnit prīmus ad
monumentum. 5Et cum sē inclīnāsset, videt posita līnteāmina.
10 Nōn tamen introīvit. 6Venit ergō Simōn Petrus sequens eum,
et introīvit in monumentum, et videt līnteāmina posita, 7et
sūdārium, quod fuerat super caput eius, nōn cum līnteāminibus
positum, sed sēparātim involūtum in ūnum locum. 8Tunc ergō
introīvit, et ille discipulus quī vēnerat prīmus ad monumentum,
15 et vīdit et crēdidit. 9Nōndum enim sciēbant scrīptūram, quia
oportet eum ā mortuīs resurgere. 10Abiērunt ergō iterum ad
sēmetipsōs discipulī.

   11Marīa autem stābat ad monumentum foris plōrāns. Dum
ergō flēret, inclīnāvit sē et prōspēxit in monumentum, 12et
20 vīdit duōs angelōs in albīs sedentēs, ūnum ad caput et ūnum ad
pedēs, ubi positum fuerat corpus Iēsū. 13Dīcunt eī illī, "Mulier,
quid plōrās?" Dīcit eīs, "Quia tulērunt Dominum meum, et
nesciō ubi posuērunt eum." 14Haec cum dīxisset, conversa est
retrorsum et videt Iēsūm stantem, et nōn sciēbat quia Iēsūs
25 est. 15Dīcit eī Iēsūs, "Mulier, quid plōrās? Quem quaeris?"
Illa, existimāns quia hortulānus esset, dīcit eī, "Domine,
sī tū sustulistī eum, dīcitō mihi ubi posuistī eum, et ego
eum tollam." 16Dīcit eī Iēsūs, "Marīa." Conversa illa dīcit eī,
"Rabbōni," quod dīcitur, "Magister." 17Dīcit eī Iēsūs, "Nōlī mē
30 tangere. Nōndum enim ascendī ad Patrem meum. Vāde autem
ad frātrēs meōs, et dīc eīs, 'Ascendō ad Patrem meum et Patrem
vestrum, et Deum meum et Deum vestrum.'" 18Vēnit Marīa
Magdalēnē annūntiāns discipulīs, "Quia vīdī Dominum et haec
dīxit mihi."

35   19Cum ergō sērō esset diē illō, ūnā sabbatōrum, et forēs
essent clausae, ubi erant discipulī propter metum Iūdaeōrum,
vēnit Iēsūs et stetit in mediō. Et dīcit eīs, "Pāx vōbīs." 20Et hoc

cum dīxisset, ostendit eīs manūs et latus. Gāvīsī sunt ergō
discipulī vīsō Dominō. ²¹Dīxit ergō eīs iterum, "Pāx vōbīs. Sīcut
40   mīsit mē Pater, et ego mittō vōs." ²²Hoc cum dīxisset, īnsufflāvit
et dīcit eīs, "Accipite Spīritum Sānctum. ²³Quōrum remīseritis
peccāta, remittuntur eīs. Quōrum retinueritis, dētenta sunt."

²⁴Thōmās autem, ūnus ex duodecim, quī dīcitur Didymus,
nōn erat cum eīs quandō vēnit Iēsūs. ²⁵Dīxērunt ergō eī aliī
45   discipulī, "Vīdimus Dominum." Ille autem dīxit eīs, "Nisi
vīderō in manibus eius figūram clāvōrum, et mittam digitum
meum in locum clāvōrum, et mittam manum meam in latus
eius, nōn crēdam." ²⁶Et post diēs octō, iterum erant discipulī
eius intus, et Thōmās cum eīs. Venit Iēsūs, iānuīs clausīs, et
50   stetit in mediō et dīxit, "Pāx vōbīs." ²⁷Deinde dīcit Thōmae,
"Īnfer digitum tuum hūc, et vidē manūs meās, et adfer manum
tuam et mitte in latus meum. Et nōlī esse incrēdulus, sed
fidēlis." ²⁸Respondit Thōmās et dīxit eī, "Dominus meus et
Deus meus." ²⁹Dīcit eī Iēsūs, "Quia vīdistī mē, crēdidistī. Beātī
55   quī nōn vīdērunt et crēdidērunt."

³⁰Multa quidem et alia signa fēcit Iēsūs in cōnspectū
discipulōrum suōrum, quae nōn sunt scrīpta in librō hōc.
³¹Haec autem scrīpta sunt, ut crēdātis quia Iēsūs est Chrīstus
Fīlius Deī, et ut crēdentēs vītam habeātis in nōmine eius.

1   **Ūnā ... sabbatī,** on the first *day*
    of the week; < τῇ ... μιᾷ τῶν
    σαββάτων, where the cardinal
    number may be a Semiticism,
    and *sabbaton* can mean *week*.³²

    venit, here, and in what follows,
    I have conformed the tenses of
    this word to the Gr.

2   **lapis, -idis,** m., *a stone*

3   **Simōn, -ōnis,** m., *Simon*

7   **simul,** adv., *at the same time,
    together*

8   **praecurrō, -ere, -cucurrī,** *run
    before, go on ahead*

9   **līnteāmen, -inis,** n., *a linen cloth*

12   **sūdārium, -iī,** n., *a handkerchief,
    towel*

13   **sēparātim,** adv., *apart, separately*
    involūtus, -a, -um, *rolled up*

16   **resurgō, -ere,** *rise up again,
    appear again*

16–17   **ad sēmetipsōs,** an emphatic
    form of the idiom *ad sē, to one's
    home* (LS, s.v. "suī," IV.A)

18   **plōrō** (1), *lament, cry aloud for
    grief*

19   **prōspiciō, -ere, -spēxī,** *look*

20 **alba (vestis),** *a white garment*

23 **convertor, -ī,** = *convertō*

24 **retrorsum,** adv., *backwards, behind*

26 **existimō** (1), *form a judgement, judge*

hortulānus, -ī, m., *a gardener*

27 **dīcitō,** 2nd sg. future (second) imperative of *dīcō* (see Capvt XXVIII Syntaxis)

30 **tangere,** perh. = *take hold of, handle* (LS, s.v., I.B.3.b)

ascendō, -ere, -dī, *go up, ascend*

vādō, -ere, *go, hasten*

33 **annuntiō** (1), *announce, tell*

35 **sērō,** *late*

ūnā sabbatōrum, = *ūnā sabbatī* (see note on 20:1)

foris, -is, f., *a door*

38 **ostendit,** take as perf, following the Gr. aorist

40 **insufflō** (1), *blow* or *breathe into* or *upon*

41 **remittō, -ere, -mīsī,** *send back; let go; relieve; forgive*

42 **retineō, -ēre, -uī,** *hold back* or *fast, not let go*

dētineō, -ēre, -uī, -tentum, *hold away* or *back, detain*

43 **Thōmās, -ae,** m., *Thomas*

didymus, -a, -um, < δίδυμος, η, ον, *double;* (as subst.) *a twin*

46 **figūra, -ae,** f., *form, shape, figure*

clāvus, -ī, m., *a nail*

51 **hūc,** adv., *hither, here*

52 **incrēdulus, -a, -um,** *without faith, incredulous*

56 **cōnspectus, -ūs,** m., *sight, view*

VI. Two Hymns of St. Ambrose of Milan

These readings are hymns composed by St. Ambrose, bishop of Milan. They are among the earliest hymns composed for Christian use, and they are still in use in the Litūrgia Hōrārum *today.*

A. *Hymnus Mātūtīnus, in* March, 8–9 (see Source Texts)

*Mentioned by St. Augustine (*Retractātiōnēs *1.21), this is one of the earliest Latin hymns. The meter of this hymn is quantitative iambic dimeter, i.e., two metra (Smith, 121) of two iambs each (= four iambs). Every foot may be an iamb (⌣ –). A spondee (– –) may be substituted in the first and third foot, a dactyl (– ⌣ ⌣) in the first, and a tribrach (⌣ ⌣ ⌣) in the second. By the rule* brevis in longō *(Smith, 115), a short syllable may be substituted for the final long syllable in each line of verse. Thus, reading column by column:*

The Possibilities for Iambic Dimeter[33]			
First Metron		Second Metron	
First Foot	Second Foot	Third Foot	Fourth Foot
⌣ –	⌣ –	⌣ –	⌣ –
– –	⌣ ⌣ ⌣	– –	⌣ ⌣
– ⌣ ⌣			

Elision is indicated by italics.

> Aeterne rērum conditor,
> Noctem diemque quī regis,
> Et temporum dās tempora,
> Ut allevēs fastīdium;
>
> 5   Praecō diēī iam sonat,
> Noctis profundae pervigil,
> Noctūrna lūx viantibus,
> Ā nocte noctem sēgregāns.

---

[33]   See Thomas Kerchever Arnold, *A Practical Introduction to Latin Verse Composition*, 3rd ed. (London: Francis and John Rivington, 1851), 95.

Hōc excitātus lūcifer
10 Solvit polum cālīgine,
Hōc omnis errōrum chorus
Viam nocendī dēserit.

Hōc nauta vīrēs colligit
Pontīque mītēscunt freta,
15 Hōc ipsa petra ecclēsiae
Canente culpam dīluit.

Surgāmus ergō strēnuē!
Gallus iacentēs excitat,
Et somnolentōs increpat,
20 Gallus negantēs arguit.

Gallō canente spēs redit,
Aegrīs salus refunditur,
Mūcrō latrōnis conditur,
Lāpsīs fidēs revertitur.

25 Iēsū, lābentēs respice,
Et nōs videndō corrige,
Sī respicis, lāpsūs cadunt,
Flētūque culpa solvitur.

Tū lūx refulgē sēnsibus,
30 Mentisque somnum discute,
Tē nostra vox prīmum sonet
Et ōre psallāmus tibi.

---

1 **conditor, -ōris,** m., *a founder; author; the Creator*

3 **temporum dās tempora:** "With ordered times dividing times" (March, 224)

4 **allevō** (1), *lift up; lighten, alleviate*

fastīdium, -iī, n., *disgust; daintiness; aversion*

5 **praecō, -ōnis,** m., *a herald;* here = *a cock,* a symbol of the Resurrection

sonō (1), *sound, resound, make a noise*

6 **profundus, -a, -um,** *deep; high*

pervigil, -ilis, *always watchful* (here with the gen. as an equivalent to the abl. of respect; cf. GL, § 374 N 6)

7   **noctūrnus, -a, -um,** *of the night,*
        by night, nocturnal
        viō (1), *travel, go*

8   **Ā nocte noctem:** i.e., the watches
        of the night (see Connelly, 19).
        sēgregō (1), *separate*

9   **excitō** (1), *arouse; raise up*
        Lūcifer, -ferī, m., *Lucifer, the*
        morning star, i.e., the planet
        Venus

10   **solvō, -ere,** *loosen; free, release;*
        pay as due
        polus, -ī, m., *the end of an axis, a*
        pole; the sky, heavens
        cālīgō, -inis, f., *darkness*

11   **chorus, -ī,** m., *a choral dance; the*
        ordered motions of the heavens;
        a band, troop: with *errōrum,*
        perh. = "the whole dancing
        troop of goings-astray," i.e.,
        the nocturnal activities
        of wicked spirits and evil
        men, as contrasted with the
        harmonious movements of the
        stars

12   **dēserō, -ere,** *abandon, leave*

14   **pontus, -ī,** m., *the sea*
        fretum, -ī, n., *a strait, sound,*
        channel

15   **petra, -ae,** f., *a stone, rock*

16   **dīluō, -ere,** *wash apart, dissolve;*
        resolve, remove

17   **strēnuus, -a, -um,** *nimble, active,*
        prompt, vigorous

18   **gallus, -ī,** m., *a cock*

19   **somnolentus, -a, -um,** *sleepy,*
        dozy, somnolent
        increpō (1), *make a noise; chide,*
        rebuke

20   **arguō, -ere,** *prove; accuse, blame;*
        expose, convict

22   **aeger, -gra, -grum,** *sick, ill*
        refundō, -ere, *pour back, make*
        overflow

23   **mūcrō, -ōnis,** m., *a sharp edge* or
        point, esp. of a sword; *a sword*
        latrō, -ōnis, m., *a robber, bandit*

25   **respiciō, -ere,** *look back; have a*
        regard for, care for

26   **videndō:** cf. Lk. 22:61

28   **flētus, -ūs,** m., *a weeping, wailing:*
        cf. Lk. 22:62

29   **refulgeō, -ēre,** *gleam back, shine*
        brightly

30   **discutiō, -ere,** *strike apart,*
        shatter; disperse, scatter

B. Hymnus Vespertīnus, in March, 9–10 (see Source Texts)

This hymn is also mentioned by St. Augustine (Cōnfessiōnēs 9.12). The meter is the same as above.

Deus, creātor omnium
Polīque rector, vestiēns
Diem decōrō lūmine,
Noctem sopōris grātiā,

5   Artūs solūtōs ut quiēs
Reddat labōris ūsuī,
Mentēsque fessās allevet
Lūctūsque solvat anxiōs;

Grātēs perāctō iam diē
10   Et noctis exortū precēs,
Vōtīs, reōs ut adiūvēs,
Hymnum canentēs solvimus.

Tē cordis īma concinant,
Tē vox canōra concrepet,
15   Tē dīligat castus amor,
Tē mēns adōret sobria;

Ut, cum profunda clauserit
Diem cālīgō noctium,
Fidēs tenebrās nesciat
20   Et nox fidē relūceat.

Dormīre mentem nē sinās,
Dormīre culpa nōverit;
Castōs fidēs refrīgerāns
Somnī vapōrem temperet.

25   Exūta sēnsū lubricō
Tē cordis alta somnient,
Nē hostis invidī dolō
Pavor quiētōs suscitet.

Chrīstum rogēmus et Patrem,
30 Chrīstī Patrisque Spīritum,
Ūnum potēns per omnia
Fovē precantēs Trīnitās.

2 **rector, -ōris,** m., *a ruler, governor, director*

vestiō, -īre, *dress, clothe*

3 **decōrus, -a, -um,** *graceful, beautiful; proper, becoming*

lūmen, -inis, n., *light*

5 **artus, -ūs,** m., *a joint*

7 **fessus, -a, -um,** *weary, tired*

8 **lūctus, -ūs,** m., *sorrow, grief, distress*

anxius, -a, -um, *anxious, troubled*

9 **grātēs, -ēs,** f. pl., *thanks*

peragō, -ere, -ēgī, -āctum, *pass through; complete, finish*

10 **exortus, -ūs,** m., *a rising*

11 **vōtum, -ī,** n., *a vow.* March, 225, identifies this as an abl. of accompaniment, i.e., with *grātēs* and *precēs*.

reus, -ī, m., *a defendant, prisoner, culprit*

12 **hymnus, -ī,** m., *a song of praise, hymn*

13 **īmus, -a, -um,** superl. of *īnferus, -a, -um, lowest, deepest*

concinō, -ere, *sing in a chorus; harmonize; celebrate*

14 **canōrus, -a, -um,** *melodious, harmonious*

concrepō (1), *make a noise*

15 **castus, -a, -um,** *clean, pure*

16 **adōrō** (1), *to speak to,* esp. to a deity; *entreat; worship*

sōbrius, -a, -um, *sober; reasonable*

20 **relūceō, -ēre,** *shine back* or *out, gleam, glitter*

21 **sinō, -ere,** *permit, allow*

23 **refrīgerō** (1), *cool; refresh*

24 **vapor, -ōris,** m., *steam; warmth*

temperō (1), *set limits, keep within bounds*

25 **exuō, -ere, -uī, -ūtum,** *take off; strip, deprive* (+ abl.)

lūbricus, -a, -um, *slippery, smooth; fleeting; deceitful; dangerous*

26 **somniō** (1), *dream*

27 **invidus, -a, -um,** *envious*

dolus, -ī, m., *fraud, deceit*

28 **pavor, -ōris,** m., *a fearful trembling*

quiētus, -a, -um, *resting, sleeping*

suscitō (1), *stir up, make to rise*

31 **ūnum,** March, 225, identifies this as an adv., presumably for *ad ūnum,* all together, or *in ūnum,* together (LS, s.v., I.B.1.a-b)

potēns: take with *Trīnitās* as a vocative (March, 225).

32 **fovē:** an imperative, instead of the expected indirect command

precor (1), *entreat, pray*

Trīnitās, -tātis, f., *the (Holy) Trinity*

VII. VENANTIUS FORTUNATUS, *DĒ PASSIŌNE DOMINĪ*, IN MARCH, 64–65 (SEE SOURCE TEXTS)

The meter of this great hymn, which is still sung at the Adoration of the Cross on Good Friday, is quantitative trochaic tetrameter catalectic (= trochaic septenarius). Thus, there are four metra (Smith, 121) of two trochees each, but the last foot of the fourth metron lacks its last syllable (− ∧). Thus, there are only fifteen syllables. A spondee (− −) may be substituted for a trochee (− ⌣) in the first six feet. Two short syllables may be substituted for any syllable, long or short, except in the last two syllables of the line before the catalexis. Thus, reading column by column,

The Possibilities for Quantitative Trochaic Tetrameter[34]							
First Metron		Second Metron		Third Metron		Fourth Metron	
1st Foot	2nd Foot	3rd Foot	4th Foot	5th Foot	6th Foot	7th Foot	8th Foot
− ⌣	− ⌣	− ⌣	− ⌣	− ⌣	− ⌣	− ⌣	− ∧
⌣ ⌣ ⌣	⌣ ⌣ ⌣	⌣ ⌣ ⌣	⌣ ⌣ ⌣	⌣ ⌣ ⌣	⌣ ⌣ ⌣	⌣ ⌣ ⌣	
− ⌣ ⌣	− ⌣ ⌣	− ⌣ ⌣	− ⌣ ⌣	− ⌣ ⌣	− ⌣ ⌣		
− −	− −	− −	− −	− −	− −		

Recall too the rule brevis in longo *(Smith, 115). Elisions and synaeresis ("consonantal i," Wheelock, xxxviii) are indicated by italics.*

Pange, lingua, glōriōsī proelium certāminis,
Et super crucis tropaeō dīc triumphum nōbilem,
Quāliter redemptor orbis immolātus vicerit.

De parentis protoplastī fraude factor condolēns,
5   Quandō pōmī noxiālis morsū in mortem corruit,
Ipse lignum tunc notāvit, damna lig_nī ut_ solveret.

Hoc opus nostrae salūtis ōrdō dēpoposcerat,
Multīformis prōditōris ars ut artem falleret,
Et medēlam ferret inde hostis unde laeserat.

---

34 See James W. Halporn, Martin Ostwald, and Thomas G. Rosenmeyer, *The Meters of Greek and Latin Poetry* (Indianapolis: Bobbs-Merrill Company, 1963), 77

10   Quandō vēnit ergō sacrī plēnitūdō temporis,
       Missus est ab arce Patris nātus, orbis conditor,
       Atque ventre virgināli carō factus prōdiit.

       Vāgit īnfāns inter arta conditus praesēpia,
       Membra pannīs involūta virgō māter alligat,
15   Et pedēs manūsque crūra stricta cingit fascia.

       Lustra sex quī iam perācta tempus implēns corporis,
       Sē volente nātus ad hoc, passiōnī dēditus
       Agnus in cruce levātur, immolandus stipite.

       Hīc acētum, fel, arundō, spūta, clāvī, lancea;
20   Mīte corpus perforātur, sanguis unda prōfluit,
       Terra, pontus, astra, mundus quō lavantur flūmine.

       Crux fidēlis inter omnēs arbor ūna nōbilis,
       Nūlla tālem silva prōfert, fronde, flōre, germine,
       Dulce lignum dulcī clāvō dulce pondus sustinēs.

25   Flecte rāmōs, arbor alta, tēnsa laxā viscera,
       Et rigor lentescat ille, quem dedit nātīvitās,
       Ut supernī membra rēgis mītī tendās stipite.

       Sōla digna tū fuistī ferre pretium saeculī,
       Atque portum praeparāre nauta mundō naufragō,
30   Quem sacer cruor perunxit fūsus agnī corpore.

---

1   **pangō, -ere,** *fasten, fix; compose,*
     write
   glōriōsus, -a, -um, *famous, glorious*
   certāmen, -inis, n., *a struggle,*
     contest
2   **super:** = *dē,* concerning (LS, s.v.
     "super," II.B.2.b)
   crux, crucis, f., *a cross*
   tropaeum, -ī, n., *a trophy, victory*
     monument, originally a tree
     trunk on the field of battle on
     which were hung arms of the
     conquered; *a victory*

   nōbilis, -e, *renowned; noble*
3   **quāliter,** interrog. adv., *how*
   redemptor, -ōris, m., *a buyer,*
     contractor, tax farmer; the
     Redeemer
   immolō (1), *sacrifice*
4   **prōtoplastus, -a, -um,**
     first-formed
   fraus, fraudis, f., *deceit, fraud;*
     delusion, error; crime, offense
   factor, -ōris, m., *a maker, doer;*
     here = *Christ* (March, 252)

condoleō, -ēre, *suffer greatly;*
sympathize with

5 **noxiālis, -e,** *harmful, noxious*

morsus, -ūs, m., *a bite, biting*

corruō, -ere, -ruī, *fall to the*
ground, sink down

6 **lignum, -ī,** n., *wood; tree*

notō (1), *mark.* Legend has it
that the wood of the Cross
came, by a roundabout way,
from the wood of the tree of
the knowledge of good and evil
(March, 252)

damnum, -ī, n., *loss, damage,*
injury

solvō, -ere, *loosen; free, release;*
pay as due

7 **dēposcō, -ere, -poposcī,**
demand, esp. for punishment

8 **multiformis, -e,** *having many*
shapes, multiform

fallō, -ere, *deceive; lead astray;*
cheat

9 **medēla, -ae,** f., *a healing, a*
remedy

inde, adv., *thence, from there.*
Note the hiatus (Smith,
119–120) at the end of this
word

laedō, -ere, laesī, *strike; injure*

10 **plēnitūdō, -inis,** f., *fullness* (cf.
Gal. 4:4)

11 **nātus, -ī,** m., *a son*

conditor, -ōris, m., *a founder;*
author; the Creator

12 **venter, -tris,** f., *the stomach; the*
womb

virginālis, -e, *of a virgin*

caro factus: cf. Jn. 1:14.

prōdeō, -īre, -iī, *come out, appear*

13 **vagiō, -īre,** *cry, whimper*

īnfāns, -fantis, *unable to speak;*
(as subst.) *a little child*

artus, -a, -um, *narrow, tight*

conditus, here = *positus* (March,
253)

praesēpium, -iī, n., *a manger*

14 **membrum, -ī,** n., *a limb*

pannus, -ī, m., *a cloth, garment; a*
rag; (pl.) *swaddling-clothes*

involvō, -ere, -volvī, -volūtum,
roll in, wrap up

alligō (1), *bind*

15 **crūs, crūris,** n., *the shin, leg* (note
the asyndeton: Smith, 96)

strictus, -a, -um, *tight* (modifies
fascia)

cingō, -ere, *gird, girdle*

fascia, -ae, f., *a band* (take as the
subject)

16 **lustrum, -ī,** n., *a five-year period,*
a lustrum (acc. of extent of
time, March, 253)

peragō, -ere, -ēgī, -āctum, *pass*
through; complete, finish

17 **passiō, -ōnis,** f., *suffering,*
enduring

dēdō, -ere, -didī, -ditum, *give*
up, surrender; dedicate, devote

18 **agnus, -ī,** m., *a lamb*

levō (1), *raise, lift up*

immolandus: take as a simple
fut. pass. participle. See
Appendix I, § 60

stīpes, -itis, m., *a tree trunk, a tree*

19 **acētum -ī,** n., *vinegar*

fel, fellis, n., *the gallbladder; gall,*
bile; bitterness

arundō, -inis, f., *a reed*

spūtum, -ī, n., *spit, spittle*

clāvus, -ī, m., *a nail*

lancea, -ae, f., *a light spear with a leather thong in the middle*

20 **perforō** (1), *pierce through*

prōfluō, -ere, *flow forth or out*

21 **pontus, -ī,** m., *the sea*

quō, take as a connecting rel. following *prōfluit,* and modifying *flūmine*

lavō (1), *wash, bathe*

flūmine: attracted into the rel. clause

23 **frons, frondis,** f., *a leaf*

flōs, flōris, m., *a flower*

germen, -inis, n., *a bud, offshoot*

24 **pondus, -eris,** n., *a weight* used in scales; *a weight, burden*

25 **flectō, -ere,** *bend*

rāmus, -ī, m., *a bough, branch*

laxō (1), *widen, loosen; slacken, relax.* Note the oxymoron *tēnsa laxā* (Smith, 105)

viscera, -um, n. pl., *internal organs; inmost part*

26 **rigor, -ōris,** m., *hardness, rigidity*

lentescō, -ere, *become pliant, soft; weaken, slacken*

nātīvitās, -tātis, f., *birth*

27 **supernus, -a, -um,** *above; celestial*

29 **portus, -ūs,** m., *a harbor, haven*

praeparō (1), *make ready, prepare*

nauta: apparently in apposition to *arbor.* The train of thought seems to be that the wood of the Cross is a ship, and thus a sailor

naufragus, -a, -um, *shipwrecked*

30 **cruor, -ōris,** m., *gore*

perungō, -ere, -unxī, *besmear, anoint*

fundō, -ere, fūsī, fūsum, *pour, pour out*

VIII. Two Readings from St. Augustine of Hippo

A. *Cōnfessiōnēs* 10.24.35–10.27.38, in *Les Confessions, Livres VIII–XIII*, 204–213 (see Source Texts)

In what follows, Augustine concludes his search for God in the world and in his memory, and begins to turn above his mind. This reading is contained in part in the Officium Lēctiōnis, Lēctiō Altera, Hebdomada VIII per Annum, Fēria Quārta, LH 3.215–216.

24.35. Ecce quantum spatiātus sum in memoriā meā quaerēns tē, Domine, et nōn tē invēnī extrā eam. Neque enim aliquid dē tē invēnī, quod non meminissem, ex quō didicī tē. Nam ex quō didicī tē, nōn sum oblītus tuī. Ubi enim invēnī

5   vēritātem, ibi invēnī Deum meum, ipsam Vēritātem, quam ex quō didicī, nōn sum oblītus. Itaque ex quō tē didicī, manēs in memoriā meā, et illīc tē inveniō, cum reminiscor tuī et dēlector in tē. Hae sunt sānctae dēliciae meae, quās dōnāstī mihi misericordiā tuā respiciēns paupertātem meam.

10   **25.**36. Sed ubi manēs in memoriā meā, Domine, ubi illīc manēs? Quāle cubīle fabricāstī tibi? Quāle sānctuarium aedificāstī tibi? Tū dedistī hanc dignātiōnem memoriae meae, ut maneās in eā, sed in quā eius parte maneās, hoc cōnsīderō. Trānscendī enim partēs eius, quās habent et bēstiae, cum

15   tē recordārer, quia nōn ibi tē inveniēbam inter imāginēs rērum corporālium, et vēnī ad partēs eius, ubi commendāvī affectiōnēs animī meī, nec illīc invēnī tē. Et intrāvī ad ipsīus animī meī sēdem, quae illī est in memoriā meā, quoniam suī quoque meminit animus, nec ibi tū erās, quia sīcut nōn es

20   imāgō corporālis nec affectiō vīventis, quālis est, cum laetāmur, contrīstāmur, cupimus, metuimus, meminimus, oblīviscimur et quidquid huius modī est, ita nec ipse animus es, quia Dominus Deus animī tū es, et commūtantur haec omnia, tū autem incommūtābilis manēs super omnia et dignātus es habitāre in

25   memoriā meā, ex quō tē didicī. Et quid quaerō, quō locō eius habitēs, quasi vērō loca ibi sint? Habitās certē in eā, quoniam tuī memini, ex quō tē didicī, et in eā tē inveniō, cum recordor tē.

    26.37. Ubi ergō tē invēnī, ut discerem tē? Neque enim iam erās in memoriā meā, priusquam tē discerem. Ubi ergō tē

30   invēnī, ut discerem tē, nisi in tē suprā mē? Et nusquam locus,
et recēdimus et accēdimus, et nusquam locus. Vēritās, ubīque
praesidēs omnibus cōnsulentibus tē simulque respondēs
omnibus etiam dīversā cōnsulentibus. Liquidē tū respondēs,
sed nōn liquidē omnēs audiunt. Omnēs unde volunt cōnsulunt,
35   sed nōn semper quod volunt audiunt. Optimus minister tuus
est, quī nōn magis intuētur hoc ā tē audīre quod ipse voluerit,
sed potius hoc velle quod ā tē audierit.

      27.38. Sērō tē amāvī, pulchritūdō tam antīqua et tam nova,
sērō tē amāvī! Et ecce intus erās et ego forīs et ibi tē quaerēbam
40   et in ista fōrmōsa, quae fēcistī, dēfōrmis irruēbam. Mēcum
erās, et tēcum nōn eram. Ea mē tenēbant longē ā tē, quae sī
in tē nōn essent, nōn essent. Vocāstī et clāmāstī et rūpistī
surdidātem meam, coruscāstī, splenduistī et fugāstī caecitātem
meam; fragrāstī, et dūxī spīritum et anhēlō tibi, gustāvī, et
45   ēsuriō et sitiō, tetigistī mē, et exarsī in pācem tuam.

---

1 **quantum:** here = how much?

  spatior, -ārī, -ātus sum, *walk,*
take a walk, promenade

3 **ex quō,** sc. *tempore,* = *since* (LS,
s.v. "ex," II.B.)

4 **oblīviscor, -ī, oblītus sum,** *forget*
(+ gen.)

7 **illīc,** adv., *there*

  reminiscor, -ī, *call to mind,*
remember (+ gen.)

8 **dēliciae, -ārum,** f., *allurements,*
charms, delights

  dōnō (1), *give as a present, present*
to

9 **respiciō, -ere,** *look back; have a*
regard for, care for

11 **quālis, -e,** *what sort of?*

  cubīle, -is, n., *a place of rest, a*
bed, a seat

  fabricō (1), *make, construct, forge*

  sānctuārium, -iī, n., *a shrine*

12 **aedificō** (1), *build, erect*

dignātiō, -ōnis, f., *respect,*
esteem; honor, reputation

13 **cōnsīderō** (1), *look at,*
contemplate; consider, weigh

14 **trānscendō, -ere, -scendī,** *climb,*
step, pass over or *across*

15 **recordor, -ārī,** *remember,*
recollect

16 **corporālis, -e,** *corporeal*

  commendō (1), *commit to the*
care of, commit

17 **affectiō, -ōnis,** f., *a state of*
mind, a feeling; here = the four
fundamental passions, desire
and fear, pleasure and pain, as
can be deduced from the next
sentence.

18 **sēdēs, -is,** f., *a seat; throne; abode*

  illī: dat. of possession

20 **quālis, -e,** *such as, as*

  laetor, -ārī, *rejoice, be glad*

21 **contrīstō** (1), *sadden, afflict*

23 **commūtō** (1), *change entirely*

24 **incommūtābilis, -e,**
unchangeable

dignor, -ārī, -ātus sum, *consider worthy; consider worthy of oneself, deign*

habitō (1), *inhabit, dwell*

25 **quō locō,** = *quō in locō*

30 **nusquam,** adv., *nowhere*

31 **ubīque,** adv., *everywhere*

32 **praesideō, -ēre,** *sit before; watch over* (+ dat.); *preside over* (+ dat.)

cōnsulō, -ere, *consult, reflect upon, consider*

simul, adv., *at the same time*

33 **dīversus, -a, -um,** *different, opposed*

liquidē, adv., *clearly, plainly*

35 **minister, -trī,** m., *attendant, servant*

36 **intueor, -ēre,** *pay attention to; here with the infinitive,* = *pay attention to hearing*

38 **sērō,** adv., *late; too late*

40 **fōrmōsus, -a, -um,** *beautifully formed*

dēfōrmis, -e, *deformed, ugly; foul, shameful; formless, shapeless*

irruō, -ere, *rush in*

42 **rumpō, -ere, rūpī,** *break, shatter, burst open*

43 **surditās, -tātis,** f., *deafness*

coruscō (1), *twinkle, gleam*

splendescō, -ere, -duī, *become bright*

caecitās, -tātis, f., *blindness*

44 **fragrō** (1), *emit a sweet smell*

dūxī spīritum, = *I took a breath*

anhēlō (1), *pant for* (+ dat.)

45 **ēsuriō, -īre,** *be hungry; long for*

exardescō, -ere, -arsī, *blaze up; glow; be excited* or *inflamed*

B. Dē Cīvitāte Deī 8.6 and 8.8, in Welldon, 333–338 (see Source Texts)
*In 410 CE, the barbarian Goths sacked the "eternal city," Rome. Pagans blamed
this unprecedented catastrophe on the empire's turning away from the old gods to
the "new" God of the Christians. Augustine wrote the Dē Cīvitāte Deī to prove
this pagan calumny wrong. However, Augustine's argument went far beyond the
actual proof of Books 1–10. In Books 10–22, Augustine developed a Christian
philosophy of history, which showed that the histories of the earthly city—which
we know in the stories of the great empires— and of the heavenly city—known in
the records of Israel and of the Church—display the working out of God's provi-
dential purposes for humankind. The following excerpts on the three branches
of philosophy—natural, logical (omitted in this excerpt), and moral—are introductory to Augustine's argument that Christianity surpasses even the best of the
pagan philosophies—the Platonic—in its conception of the afterlife.*

     6. Vīdērunt ergō istī philosophī, quōs ceterīs nōn immeritō
fāmā atque glōriā praelātōs vidēmus, nūllum corpus esse
Deum, et ideō cūncta corpora trānscendērunt quaerentēs
Deum. Vīdērunt quidquid mūtābile est nōn esse summum
5   Deum, et ideō animam omnem mūtābilēsque omnēs spīritūs
trānscendērunt quaerentēs summum Deum. Deinde vīdērunt
omnem speciem in rē quācumque mūtābilī, quā est quidquid
illud est, quōquō modō et quāliscumque nātūra est, nōn esse
posse nisi ab illō quī vērē est, quia incommūtābiliter est.
10   Ac per hoc sīve ūniversī mundī corpus, figūrās, quālitātēs
ōrdinātumque mōtum et elementa disposita ā caelō usque
ad terram et quaecumque corpora in eīs sunt, sīve omnem
vītam,—vel quae nūtrit et continet, quālis est in arboribus; vel
quae et hoc habet et sentit, quālis est in pecōribus; vel quae
15   et haec habet et intellegit, quālis est in hominibus, vel quae
nūtrītōriō subsidiō nōn indiget, sed tantum continet, sentit,
intellegit, quālis est in angelīs,—nisi ab illō esse nōn posse, quī
simpliciter est, quia nōn aliud illī est esse, aliud vīvere, quasi
possit esse nōn vīvēns; nec aliud illī est vīvere, aliud intellegere,
20   quasi possit vīvere nōn intellegēns; nec aliud illī est intellegere,
aliud beātum esse, quasi possit intellegere nōn beātus, sed quod
est illī vīvere, intellegere, beātum esse, hoc est illī esse.
     Propter hanc incommūtābilitātem et simplicitātem
intellēxērunt eum et omnia ista fēcisse, et ipsum ā nūllō fierī

25 potuisse. Cōnsīderāvērunt enim quidquid est vel corpus
esse vel vītam, meliusque aliquid vītam esse quam corpus,
speciemque corporis esse sēnsibilem, intellegibilem vītae.
Proinde intellegibilem speciem sēnsibilī praetulērunt.
Sēnsibilia dīcimus quae vīsū tactūque corporis sentīrī queunt;
30 intellegibilia, quae cōnspectū mentis intellegī.

Nūlla est enim pulchritūdō corporālis sīve in statū corporis,
sīcut est figūra, sīve in mōtū, sīcut est cantilēna, dē quā nōn
animus iūdicet. Quod profectō nōn posset, nisi melior in illō
esset haec speciēs, sine tumōre mōlis, sine strepitū vōcis, sine
35 spatiō vel locī vel temporis. Sed ibi quoque nisi mūtābilis
esset, nōn alius aliō melius dē speciē sēnsibilī iūdicāret; melius
ingeniōsior quam tardior, melius perītior quam imperītior,
melius exercitātior quam minus exercitātus, et īdem ipse ūnus,
cum prōficit, melius utique posteā quam prius.

40 Quod autem recipit magis et minus, sine dubitātiōne
mūtābile est. Unde ingeniōsī et doctī et in hīs exercitātī
hominēs facile collegērunt nōn esse in eīs rēbus prīmam
speciem, ubi mūtābilis esse convincitur. Cum igitur in eōrum
cōnspectū et corpus et animus magis minusque speciōsa
45 essent, sī autem omnī speciē carēre possent, omnīnō nūlla
essent. Vīdērunt esse aliquid ubi prīma esset incommūtābilis
et ideō nec comparābilis, atque ibi esse rērum prīncipium
rēctissimē crēdidērunt, quod factum nōn esset et ex quō facta
cūncta essent.

50 Ita "quod nōtum est Deī manifestāvit eīs ipse, cum ab eīs
invīsibilia eius, per ea quae facta sunt intellēcta, cōnspecta
sunt; sempiterna quoque virtūs eius et dīvīnitās," ā quō etiam
vīsibilia et temporālia cūncta creāta sunt. Haec dē illā parte
quam physicam, id est nātūrālem, nuncupant, dicta sint. . . .

55 **8.** Reliqua est pars mōrālis, quam Graecō vocābulō dīcunt
ēthicam, ubi quaeritur dē summō bonō, quō referentēs omnia
quae agimus, et quod nōn propter aliud, sed propter sē ipsum
appetentēs, idque adipiscentēs, nihil quō beātī sīmus ulterius
requīrāmus. Ideō quippe et fīnis est dictus, quia propter hunc
60 cētera volumus, ipsum autem nōn nisi propter ipsum. Hoc ergō
beātificum bonum aliī ā corpore, aliī ab animō, aliī ab utrōque
hominī esse dīxērunt.

Vidēbant quippe ipsum hominem cōnstāre ex animō et
corpore, et ideō ab alterutrō istōrum duōrum aut ab utrōque
65   bene sibi esse posse crēdēbant, fīnālī quōdam bonō, quō
beātī essent, quō cūncta quae agēbant referrent atque id quō
referendum esset nōn ultrā quaererēnt. Unde illī, quī dīcuntur
addidisse tertium genus bonōrum, quod appellātur extrinsecus,
sīcutī est honor, glōria, pecūnia et sī quid huius modī, nōn sīc
70   addidērunt, ut fīnāle esset, id est propter sē ipsum appetendum,
sed propter aliud; bonumque esse hoc genus bonīs, malum
autem malīs.

Ita bonum hominis quī vel ab animō vel ā corpore vel ab
utrōque expetīvērunt, nihil aliud quam ab homine expetendum
75   esse putāvērunt, sed quī id appetīvērunt ā corpore, ā parte
hominis dēteriōre; quī vērō ab animō, ā parte meliōre; quī
autem ab utrōque, ā tōtō homine. Sīve ergō ā parte quālibet sīve
ā tōtō, nōn nisi ab homine. Nec istae differentiae, quoniam trēs
sunt, ideō trēs, sed multās dissensiōnēs philosophōrum
80   sectāsque fēcērunt, quia et dē bonō corporis et dē bonō animī
et dē bonō utrīusque dīversī dīversa opīnātī sunt.

Cēdant igitur omnēs illīs philosophīs, quī nōn dīxērunt
beātum esse hominem fruentem corpore vel fruentem animō,
sed fruentem Deō, nōn sīcut corpore vel sē ipsō animus aut
85   sīcut amīcō amīcus, sed sīcut lūce oculus, sī aliquid ab hīs ad
illa similitūdinis adferendum est; quod quāle sit, sī Deus ipse
adiūverit, aliō locō (quantum per nōs fierī poterit) apparēbit.
Nunc satis sit commemorāre Platōnem dētermināsse fīnem
bonī esse secundum virtūtem vīvere, et eī sōlī ēvenīre posse quī
90   nōtitiam Deī habeat et imitātiōnem, nec esse aliam ob causam
beātum. Ideōque nōn dubitat hoc esse philosophārī: amāre
Deum, cuius nātūra sit incorporālis.

Unde utique colligitur tunc fore beātum studiōsum
sapientiae (id enim est philosophus), cum fruī Deō coeperit.
95   Quamvis enim nōn continuō beātus sit, quī eō fruitur quod
amat (multī enim, amandō ea quae amanda nōn sunt, miserī
sunt et miseriōrēs cum fruuntur), nēmō tamen beātus est, quī
eō quod amat nōn fruitur. Nam et ipsī, quī rēs nōn amandās
amant, nōn sē beātōs putant amandō, sed fruendō.

100   Quisquis ergō fruitur eō quod amat vērumque et summum
bonum amat, quis eum beātum nisi miserrimus negat? Ipsum

autem vērum ac summum bonum Platō dīcit Deum, unde vult
esse philosophum amātōrem Deī, ut, quoniam philosophia ad
beātam vītam tendit, fruēns Deō sit beātus quī Deum amāverit.

1   **immeritō,** adv., *undeservedly*

3   **ideō,** adv., *therefore*

4   **mūtābilis, -e,** *changeable, variable*

7   **speciēs, -ēī,** f., here = *species,* or even Gr. ἰδέα, an *"eternally existing archetype of any class of being"* (OLD, s.v. 13)

    quīcumque, quaecumque, quodcumque, *whoever, whichever, whatever*

8   **quōquō modo,** adv., *in what way soever [it exists]*

    quāliscumque, quālecumque, *of whatever kind* or *sort, whatever*

9   **incommūtābilis, -e,** *unchangeable*

    per hoc: supply *vidērunt*

10   **sīve,** conj., *or if;* **sīve . . . sīve,** *whether . . . or*

    ūniversus, -a, -um, *whole, entire*

    figūra, -ae, f., *form, shape, figure*

    quālitās, -tātis, f., *a quality, property*

11   **ōrdinātus, -a, -um,** *in order, orderly*

    mōtus, -ūs, m., *a motion, movement*

    dispōnō, -ere, -posuī, -positum, *distribute; arrange, put in order*

13   **vel . . . vel,** *either . . . or* (it can be repeated several times)

14   **pecus, -oris,** n., *cattle; a herd, flock*

16   **nūtrītōrius, -a, -um,** *nourishing, nutritive*

    subsidium, -iī, n., *help, support*

    indigeō, -ēre, *want, need, require* (+ gen. or abl.)

23   **incommūtābilitās, -tātis,** f., *unchangeableness, immutability*

    simplicitās, -tātis, f., *simpleness, simplicity*

25   **quidquid est:** take as the subject of *esse*

27   **sēnsibilis, -e,** *perceptible to the senses, sensible*

    intellegibilis, -e, *that can be understood, intelligible*

29   **vīsus, -ūs,** m., *seeing, sight*

    tāctus, -ūs, m., *touching, touch*

    queō, quīre, *be able*

31   **corporālis, -e,** *corporeal*

    status, -ūs, m., *position, condition, state*

32   **cantilēna, -ae,** f., *"'a dance'* accompanied, of course, by music, and properly by vocal music" (Welldon, 1.334)

33   **profectō,** adv., *truly, really*

34   **tumor, -ōris,** m., *a swelling; mental excitement; pride*

    mōles, -is, f., *a shapeless mass*

    sine tumōre mōlis, *"'without bulk' or 'size'"* (Welldon, loc. cit.)

    strepitus, -ūs, m., *noise, din*

37   **ingeniōsus, -a, -um,** *naturally clever, talented,* or *able*

imperītus, -a, -um, *unskilled*

38   **exercitātus, -a, -um,** *trained, schooled*

39   **prōficiō, -ere,** *make progress, advance*

40   **dubitātiō, -ōnis,** f., *doubt*

43   **convincō, -ere,** *prove, demonstrate*

44   **speciōsus, -a, -um,** *beautiful, splendid*

46   **prīma:** supply *speciēs*

47   **comparābilis, -e,** *capable of comparison*

50   **manifestō** (1), *make manifest, show clearly*

51   **invīsibilis, -e,** *invisible, unseen*

52   **sempiternus, -a, -um,** *everlasting*

     dīvīnitās, -tātis, f., *divine nature, divinity*

53   **vīsibilis, -e,** *visible, seen*

     temporālis, -e, *temporal*

     parte: supply *philosophiae*

54   **physica, -ae,** f., *physics*, which A. has already defined (8.4) as "[philosophiam] nātūrālem, quae contemplātiōnī dēputata est."

55   **reliquus, -a, -um,** *remaining, left*

     mōrālis, -e, *moral, ethical*, which A. has already defined (8.4) as "[philosophiam] mōrālem, quae maximē in āctiōne versātur."

     vocābulum, -ī, n., *a name; a noun*

56   **ēthica, -ae,** f., *moral philosophy, ethics*

58   **idque,** *and that,* "introducing a qualification or amplification of a previous sb. or phr." (OLD, s.v. "is" B.7)

adipiscor, -ī, *overtake; obtain.* The participle serves as the protasis of an ideal conditional sentence (Future Less Vivid)

quō, introduces a relative clause of purpose under the influence of **ulterius.**

ulterius, adv., *beyond, farther; more*

61   **beātificus, -a, -um,** *that makes happy, beatific*

     uterque, utraque, utrumque, *each of two, both*

64   **alteruter, alterutra, alterutrum,** *one of two*

65   **fīnālis, -e,** *final*

     fīnālī quōdam bonō, in apposition to both *alterutrō* and *utrōque,* and thus dependent on *ab.*

65–66   **quō beātī,** *etc.,* rel. pron. (= abl. of means) with a potential subjunctive (GL, § 627). Take the following subjunctives as potential, too

66   **quō cūncta,** *etc.,* here and in the next clause, adv. with *referre,* = *by reference to which to judge* (OLD, s.v. "referō" 10)

66–67   **atque id quō referendum esset nōn ultrā quaererent,** = *and also they might not seek further a thing by reference to which they ought to judge.* Note that Welldon reads *adque.*

68   **addō, -ere, -didī,** *add*

     extrinsecus, -a, -um, *outer*

69   **sīcutī,** = *sīcut*

71   **bonum,** the dir. obj. of *expetīvērunt*

74 **expetō, -ere, -īvī,** *desire, strive after, head for*

76 **dēterior, -ius,** *lower, inferior, poorer*

77 **quīlibet, quaelibet, quodlibet,** *any you will, any*

78 **differentia, -ae,** f., *difference, distinction*

trēs: i.e., yield only three schools of thought

79 **dissensiō, -ōnis,** f., *a difference in opinion*

80 **secta, -ae,** f., *a way of life; a political* or *philosophical school of thought*

81 **dīversus, -a, -um,** *different, opposed*

83 **fruor,** see *Wheelock,* 285

86 **similitūdō, -inis,** f., *likeness, resemblance*

88 **quod:** take as a connecting relative

dēterminō (1), *set the limits, determine.* Welldon, 336, refers to Gorgias 470D and 508B, as well as to Philebus 11B–C.

90 **imitātiō, -ōnis,** f., *imitation*

ob, prep. + acc., *because of*

91 **philosophor, -ārī,** (1), *philosophize, live the philosophical life, do philosophy*

92 **incorporālis, -e,** *bodiless, incorporeal*

95 **continuō,** adv., *immediately*

100 **quisquis:** the antecedent is the upcoming *eum*

103 **amātor, -ōris,** m., *a friend, a lover*

IX. St. Jerome, *Commentāriōrum in Ēsāiam Liber III*, in Adriaen, 85–87 (see Source Texts)

St. Jerome comments on Isaiah 6:2–4, an excellent example of patristic exegesis.

[VI.]2.3. *Seraphīm stābant super illud, sex ālae ūnī, et sex ālae alterī: duābus vēlābant faciem eius, et duābus vēlābant pedēs eius, et duābus volābant. Et clāmābant alter ad alterum, et dīcēbant: Sānctus, Sānctus, Sānctus Dominus exercituum; plēna est omnis*
5 *terra glōriā eius.* Hoc—quod nōs sequentēs aliōs interpretēs et Hebraicam vēritātem in quā scrīptum est *memmallo,* id est ἐπάνω αὐτοῦ, quod Latīnē dīcitur *super illud,* vertimus—LXX trānstulērunt *in circuitū eius,* ut nōn super templum stāre Seraphīm, sed in circuitū Dominī dēscrībantur. Rursum ubi
10 nōs dīximus quod ūnus dē Seraphīm vēlāret faciem et pedēs *eius,* per quod intellegitur *Deī,* in Hebraeō scrīptum habētur *phanau* et *reglau* quod potest interpretārī et *eius* et *suam,* ut Seraphīm iuxtā Hebraeī sermōnis ambiguitātem et faciem pedēsque Deī, et suam faciem ac pedēs operīre dīcantur.
15 In septuāgēsimō nōnō psalmō legimus *Quī sedēs super Cherubīm manifestāre,* quī in nostrā linguā interpretantur *scientiae multitūdō.* Unde et Dominus in aurīgae modum super Cherubīm apertē sedēre ostenditur. Seraphīm autem, praeter hunc locum, in scrīptūrīs canonicīs alibī lēgisse mē nesciō, quī
20 stāre dīcuntur super templum, vel in circuitū Dominī. Ergō errant quī solent in precibus dīcere: *Quī sedēs super Cherubīm et Seraphīm,* quod scrīptūra nōn docuit.

Seraphīm autem interpretantur ἐμπρησταὶ, quod nōs dīcere possumus *incendentēs* sīve *combūrentēs,* iuxtā illud
25 quod alibī legimus: *Quī facit angelōs suōs spīritūs et ministrōs suōs ignem ūrentem.* Unde et Paulus apostolus in epistulās ad Hebraeōs, quam Latīna cōnsuētūdō nōn recipit, *Nōnne omnēs,* inquit, *ministrī sunt spīritūs, in ministerium missī propter eōs quī hērēditātem acceptūrī sunt salūtis?* Daniēl quoque cum
30 in habitū regnantis Dominum dēscrīpsisset, adiēcit: *Mīlia mīlium ministrābant eī et deciēs mīliēs centēna mīlia assistēbant eī.* In Cherubīm ergō ostenditur Dominus; in Seraphīm ex parte ostenditur, ex parte cēlātur. Faciem enim et pedēs eius operiunt, quia et praeterita ante mundum et futūra post

35   mundum scīre nōn possumus, sed media tantum, quae in sex
      diēbus facta sunt, contemplāmur. Nec mīrum hoc dē Seraphīm
      crēdere, cum et apostolī Salvātōrem crēdentibus aperiant,
      īnfidēlibus abscondant; et vēlum ante arcam fuerit testāmentī.
          Ālās quoque habēre dīcuntur propter vēlōcitātem et in
40   cūncta discursum, sīve quia semper in altiōribus commorantur.
      Neque enim illud quod dē ventīs dīcitur, *Quī ambulat super*
      pennās ventōrum, vērē ventōs iuxtā fābulās poētārum et
      pictōrum licentiam pennās habēre testātur, sed celerem in
      cūncta discursum. Et singulī sēnās ālās, quia dē fabricātiōne
45   tantum mundī et praesentis saeculī nōvimus.
          Quod autem clāmant *alter ad alterum*, vel iuxtā Hebraeōs
      iste ad istum, id est *ūnus ad ūnum*, invicem sē ad laudēs
      Dominī cohortantur et dīcunt, *Sānctus, Sānctus, Sānctus,*
      Dominus exercituum, ut mystērium Trīnitātis in ūnā dīvīnitāte
50   dēmōnstrent, et nēquāquam templum Iūdaeōrum sīcut prius,
      sed omnem terram illīus glōriā plēnam esse testentur, quī
      prō nostrā salūte dignātus est hūmānum corpus assūmere ad
      terrāsque dēscendere. Dēnique et Mōȳsī, cum prō adōrātō
      vitulō Dominum precārētur, ut parceret populō peccātōrī,
55   respondit Dominus, *Propitius erō illīs. Vērumtamen vīvō ego*
      et vīvit nōmen meum, quia implēbitur glōriā meā omnis terra, et
      septuāgēsimus prīmus psalmus canit, *Implēbitur glōriā eius*
      omnis terra. Unde et angelī clāmābant pastōribus, *Glōria in*
      excelsīs Deō, et super terrā pāx hominibus bonae voluntātis.
60   Impiē ergō quīdam duo Seraphīm Fīlium et Spīritum
      Sānctum intellegit, cum, iuxtā ēvangelistam Iōannem et
      Paulum apostolum, Fīlium Deī vīsum in maiestāte regnantis
      et Spīritum Sānctum locutum esse doceāmus. Quīdam
      Latīnōrum duo Seraphīm vetus et novum īnstrūmentum
65   intellegunt, quae tantum dē praesentī saeculō loquuntur. Unde
      et sex ālās habēre dīcuntur, et faciem Deī pedēsque vēlāre, et
      certātim prōferre testimōnium vēritātis, et omne quod clāmant
      Trīnitātis sacrāmenta mōnstrāre; et mīrārī ad invicem, quod
      Dominus Sabaōth, in fōrmā Deī Patris positus, fōrmam servī
70   accēperit et humiliāverit sē usque ad mortem, et mortem
      crucis; et nēquāquam ut prius caelestia eum tantum, sed et
      terrēna cognōscant.

    4. *Et commōta sunt superlīmināria cardinum ā vōce clāmantis;*
et domus implēta est fūmō. Clamantibus Seraphīm et in tōtā

75 terrā Trīnitātis mystērium praedicantibus, quandō passiōnem
Dominī Salvātōris terra ūniversa cognōvit, statim commōtum
est sīve sublātum līmināre templī, et omnēs illīus cardinēs
concidērunt, implētā Salvātōris comminātiōne, dīcentis,
Relinquētur vōbīs domus vestra dēserta. Et quam pulcher ōrdō

80 verbōrum. Postquam terra replēta est glōriā Dominī Sabaōth,
Iūdaeōrum templum implētum est ignōrantiae tenebrīs et
cālīgine et fūmō, quī noxius est oculīs. Vel certē per fūmum
templī mōnstrātur incendium. Prius enim ēvangelium
Salvātōris in tōtō orbe praedicātum est, et post quadrāgintā

85 duōs annōs dominicae passiōnis, capta Hierusalem
templumque succensum est. Iūdaeī putant templum implētum
fūmō thȳmiāma significāre, id est incēnsum, et per hoc
adventum dīvīnae maiestātis.

1 **seraphīm,** indecl. Heb. pl. name, *the Seraphim,* one of the hierarchies of angels	**stāre:** = *as standing*
super illud: the antecedent is *templum*	9 **dēscrībō, -ere,** *transcribe; describe, represent*
āla, -ae, f., *a wing*	**rursum,** adv., *on the other hand*
2 **vēlō** (1), *cover, veil*	11 **Hebraeus, -a, -um,** *Hebrew* (supply *sermōne*)
faciēs, -ēī, f., *face*	**scrīptum habētur:** see Appendix I, § 48 N 1
5 **interpres, -pretis,** m./f., *an expounder, interpreter, translator*	12 *phanau … reglau,* i.e., phānâw … ragəlâw, either *his face … his feet* or *his own face … his own feet*
6 **Hebraicus, -a, -um,** *Hebrew*	**interpretor, -ārī,** (as dep.) *understand in a certain sense, translate;* (in a passive sense) *be understood, translated*
memmallo: i.e., *mimma'al lô,* = ἐπάνω αὐτοῦ, = *super illud*	
7 **vertimus:** i.e., *have translated*	13 **ambiguitās, -tātis,** f., *ambiguity*
Septuāgintā, *the Seventy* (translators of the Septuagint)	14 **operiō, -īre,** *cover*
8 **trānstulērunt:** i.e., *translated*	16 **cherub,** pl., **cherubīm,** *a cherub; the cherubim,* one of the hierarchies of angels
circuitus, -ūs, m., *a circuit, way around; the open space around a building*	**manifestō** (1), *show, reveal*

17 **multitūdō, -inis,** f., *a large number, a multitude.* This etymology of the name *Cherubīm* is also found in Pseudo-Dionysius the Areopagite, *The Celestial Hierarchy* 7.1.

aurīga, -ae, m./f., *a charioteer*

18 **apertē,** adv., *openly*

19 **canonicus, -a, -um,** *according to* rule or *measure; canonical*

alibī, adv., *elsewhere*

23 ἐμπρησταὶ (**emprēstai**), *those who burn*

24 **incendō, -ere,** *set fire, burn*

comburō, -ere, *burn up, completely consume*

iuxtā, prep. + acc., *according to*

25 **minister, -trī,** m., *an attendant, servant*

26 **ūrō, -ere,** *burn*

Paulus, -ī, m., *Paul* (see Hebrews 1:14)

apostolus, -ī, m., *an apostle*

27 **cōnsuētūdō, -inis,** f., *custom, practice* (Hebrews had not yet been admitted into the scriptural canon in the West)

28 **ministerium, -iī,** n., *service, attendance*

29 **hērēditās, -tātis,** f., *inheritance*

Daniēl, -ēlis, m., *Daniel*

30 **habitus, -ūs,** m., *condition, bearing; nature, character*

31 **ministrō** (1), *serve, attend, wait on*

deciēs mīliēs centēna mīlia, 10 x 1,000 x 100,000 = 1,000,000,000 (cf. Dan. 7:10)

assistō, -ere, *stand by*

33 **cēlō** (1), *hide, conceal*

36 **contemplor, -ārī,** *look at attentively, survey, contemplate*

37 **Salvātor, -ōris,** m., *the Savior*

aperiō, -īre, *uncover, expose to view, reveal*

38 **īnfidēlis, -e,** *faithless; unbelieving*

abscondō, -ere, *conceal*

vēlum, -ī, n., *a curtain*

arca, -ae, f., *a box; the Ark*

testāmentum, -ī, n., *a will, testament; here = the Covenant*

39 **vēlōcitās, -tātis,** f., *quickness, rapidity*

40 **discursus, -ūs,** m., *a running up and down* or *to and fro*

sīve, conj., *or if;* **sīve . . . sīve,** *whether . . . or*

commoror, -ārī, *stay, remain*

42 **penna, -ae,** f., *a feather;* (pl.) *a wing* (see Ps. 103:4)

43 **pictor, -ōris,** m., *a painter*

licentia, -ae, f., *freedom, liberty*

testor, -ārī, *prove, demonstrate*

44 **sēnī, -ae, -a,** *six at a time* or *each*

fabricātiō, -ōnis, f., *making, framing*

47 **invicem sē,** = *inter sē* (cf. Appendix I, § 35)

48 **cohortor, -ārī,** *encourage, exhort*

49 **mystērium, -iī,** n., *the secret worship of a deity; a secret thing, mystery; "something transcending mere human intelligence"* (LS, s.v. III.A.1)

trīnitās, -tātis, f., *a triad; the* (Holy) *Trinity*

dīvīnitās, -tātis, f., *divine nature, divinity*

50   **nēquāquam,** adv., *not at all*

52   **dignor, -ārī, -ātus sum,** *consider worthy; consider worthy of oneself, deign*

    assūmō, -ere, *take to oneself*

53   **dēscendō, -ere,** *come down, descend*

    Mōÿses, -is, m., *Moses*

    adōrō (1), *reverence, adore*

54   **vitulus, -ī,** m., *a bull calf;* here = *the (Golden) Calf*

    precor, -ārī, *beg, entreat, pray*

    peccātor, -ōris, m., *a sinner*

55   **propitius, -a, -um,** *favorable, gracious* (see Num. 14:20–21)

    vērumtamen, conj., *nevertheless*

57   **psalmus:** Ps. 71:19

58   **pastor, -ōris,** m., *a shepherd* (see Lk. 2:14)

59   **excelsus, -a, -um,** *lofty, high*

60   **impiē,** adv., *undutifully, disloyally*

61   **ēvangelista, -ae,** m., *an evangelist*

62   **vīsum:** supply *esse*

64   **īnstrūmentum, -ī,** n., *a tool; a document, record* (here = *Testament*)

65   **praesēns, -sentis,** *present*

67   **certātim,** adv., *eagerly*

    testimōnium, -iī, n., *witness, evidence*

68   **mōnstrō** (1), *point out, show*

    mīrārī: supply *dīcuntur*

    ad invicem: see Appendix I, § 35

69   **Sabaōth,** indecl. Heb. pl., *the heavenly hosts* (take as gen.)

70   **humiliō** (1), *humble*

71   **crux, crucis,** f., *a cross* (cf. Phil. 2:7–8)

72   **terrēnus, -a, -um,** *belonging to the earth, terrestrial*

73   **commoveō, -ēre, -mōvī, -mōtum,** *shake*

    superlīmināre, -is, n., *a lintel*

    cardō, -inis, m., *a hinge*

74   **fūmus, -ī,** m., *smoke*

75   **praedicō** (1), *publish, proclaim*

    passiō, -ōnis, f., *a suffering, enduring*

76   **ūniversus, -a, -um,** *whole, entire*

77   **līmināre, -is,** n., *a threshold, lintel* (Latham, s.v. "limen")

78   **concidō, -ere, -cidī,** *fall* or *tumble down to the ground*

    comminātiō, -ōnis, f., *threat*

79   **dēsertus, -a, -um,** *forsaken, abandoned* (Mt. 23:38)

80   **repleō, -ēre, -vī, -plētum,** *fill up again; fill, satisfy*

81   **Iūdaeus, -a, -um,** *Jewish*

    ignōrantia, -ae, f., *ignorance*

82   **cālīgō, -inis,** f., *fog, mist; darkness*

    noxius, -a, -um, *harmful*

83   **incendium, -iī,** n., *a fire*

84–85   **post quadrāgintā duōs annōs dominicae passiōnis,** forty-two years after Christ Jesus' passion (see the examples under the explanatory genitive in Blaise, § 82)

86   **succendō, -ere, -cendī, -censum,** *set on fire from below*

87   **thȳmiāma, -amatis,** n., *incense*

    significō (1), *show, indicate*

    incēnsum, -ī, n., *a lighting; incense*

88   **adventus, -ūs,** m., *an arrival*

X. ST. BEDE THE VENERABLE, *HISTORIA ECCLĒSIASTICA GENTIS ANGLŌRUM* 2.13, IN KING, 1.280–287 (SEE SOURCE TEXTS)

This is the conclusion of the story of the conversion of Edwin (c. 585–633), king of Northumberland, by St. Paulinus of York (d. 644). The narrative begins at the conclusion of a private exhortation to conversion delivered by Paulinus to Edwin. The council or witan *described here took place in Edwin's palace hall at Yeavering. In attendance were his priests and* ealdormen, *or nobles.*[35]

13. Quibus audītīs, rēx suscipere quidem sē fidem, quam docēbat, et velle et dēbēre respondēbat. Vērum adhūc cum amīcīs prīncipibus et cōnsiliāriīs suīs sēsē dē hōc collātūrum esse dīcēbat, ut, sī et illī eadem cum illō sentīre vellent, omnēs
5   pariter in fonte vītae Chrīstō cōnsecrārentur. Et annuente Paulīnō, fēcit ut dīxerat.

Habitō enim cum sapientibus cōnsiliō, scīscitābātur singillātim ab omnibus, quālis sibi doctrīna haec eātenus inaudīta et novus dīvīnitātis quī praedicābātur cultus
10 vidērētur. Cui prīmus pontificum ipsīus Coifi continuō respondit, "Tū vidē, rēx, quāle sit hoc, quod nōbīs modo praedicātur. Ego autem tibi vērissimē quod certum didicī profiteor, quia nihil omnīnō virtūtis habet, nihil ūtilitātis religiō illa quam hūcusque tenuimus. Nūllus enim tuōrum
15 studiōsius quam ego cultūrae deōrum nostrōrum sē subdidit, et nihilōminus multī sunt quī ampliōra ā tē beneficia quam ego et maiōrēs accipiunt dignitātēs magisque prōsperantur in omnibus quae agenda vel acquīrenda dispōnunt. Sī autem dī aliquid valērent, mē potius iuvāre vellent, quī illīs impēnsius
20 servīre cūrāvī. Unde restat ut, sī ea quae nunc nōbīs nova praedicantur meliōra esse et fortiōra, habitā exāminātiōne, perspēxeris, absque ūllō cūnctāmine suscipere illa festīnēmus."

Cuius suāsiōnī verbīsque prūdentibus alius optimātum rēgis tribuēns assēnsum, continuō subdidit, "Tālis," inquiens,
25 "mihi vidētur, rēx, vīta hominum praesēns in terrīs, ad

---

[35] J. Robert Wright, *A Companion to Bede, A Reader's Commentary on* The Ecclesiastical History of the English People (Grand Rapids: William B. Eerdmans Publishing Company, 2008), 53.

comparātiōnem eius quod nōbīs incertum est temporis, quāle
cum, tē residente ad cēnam cum ducibus ac ministrīs tuīs
tempore brūmālī, accensō quidem focō in mediō et calidō
effectō cēnāculō, furentibus autem foris per omnia

30   turbinibus hiemālium pluviārum vel nivium, adveniēnsque
ūnus passerum domum citissimē pervolāverit, quī cum per
ūnum ōstium ingrediēns, mox per aliud exierit. Ipsō quidem
tempore quō intus est, hiemis tempestāte nōn tangitur, sed
tamen, parvissimō spatiō serēnitātis ad mōmentum excursō,

35   mox dē hieme in hiemem regrediēns, tuīs oculīs ēlābitur. Ita
haec vīta hominum ad modicum appāret. Quid autem sequātur,
quidve praecesserit, prorsus ignōrāmus. Unde sī haec nova
doctrīna certius aliquid attulit, meritō esse sequenda vidētur."
Hīs similia et cēterī maiōrēs nātū ac rēgis cōnsiliāriī dīvīnitus

40   admonitī prōsequebantur.

     Adiēcit autem Coifi, quia vellet ipsum Paulīnum dīligentius
audīre dē Deō, quem praedicābat, verbum facientem. Quod
cum iubente rēge faceret, exclāmāvit audītīs eius sermōnibus
dīcēns, "Iam ōlim intellexeram nihil esse quod colēbāmus, quia

45   vidēlicet quantō studiōsius in eō cultū vēritātem quaerēbam,
tantō minus inveniēbam. Nunc autem apertē profiteor, quia in
hāc praedicātiōne vēritās clāret illa quae nōbīs vītae, salūtis, et
beātitūdinis aeternae dōna valet tribuere. Unde suggerō, rēx, ut
templa et altāria quae sine frūctū ūtilitātis sacrāvimus, ōcius

50   anathematī et ignī contrādamus." Quid plūra? Praebuit palam
assēnsum ēvangelīzantī beātō Paulīnō rēx, et, abrenūntiātā
īdōlatrīā, fidem sē Chrīstī suscipere cōnfessus est.

     Cumque ā praefātō pontifice sacrōrum suōrum quaereret,
quis ārās et fāna īdōlōrum, cum saeptīs quibus erant

55   circumdata, prīmus profānāre dēbēret, ille respondit, "Ego.
Quis enim ea quae per stultitiam coluī nunc ad exemplum
omnium aptius quam ipse per sapientiam mihi ā Deō vērō
dōnātam destruam?" Statimque, abiectā superstitiōne vānitātis,
rogāvit sibi rēgem arma dare et equum ēmissārium, quem

60   ascendēns ad īdōla dēstruenda venīret. Nōn enim licuerat
pontificem sacrōrum vel arma ferre vel praeter in equā equitāre.
Accīnctus ergō gladiō accēpit lanceam in manū et, ascendēns
ēmissārium rēgis, pergēbat ad īdōla. Quod aspiciēns vulgus,
aestimābat eum īnsānīre. Nec distulit ille, mox ut appropiābat

65 ad fānum, profānāre illud, iniectā in eō lanceā quam tenēbat;
multumque gāvīsus dē agnitiōne vērī Deī cultūs, iussit sociīs
dēstruere ac succendere fānum cum omnibus saeptīs suīs.
Ostenditur autem locus ille quondam īdōlōrum nōn longē ab
Eborācō ad orientem, ultrā amnem Doruventiōnem, et vocātur
70 hodiē Godmunddingaham, ubi pontifex ipse, īnspīrante Deō
vērō, polluit ac dēstruxit eās quās ipse sacrāverat ārās.

2 **docēbat:** i.e., Paulinus

adhūc, adv., *besides, also; even,
    still*

3 **cōnsiliārius, -iī,** m., *an adviser,
    one of the* ealdormen

5 **cōnsecrō** (1), *consecrate or
    dedicate to the service of a god*

annuō, -ere, *nod assent to, agree*

6 **Paulīnus, -ī,** m., *St. Paulinus*

7 **sciscitor, -ārī,** *inform oneself;
    ask, examine, inquire* (here
    + *ab*)

8 **singillātim,** adv., *one by one*

quālis, -e, *what sort of*

eātenus, adv., *so far*

9 **inaudītus, -a, -um,** *unheard of,
    unusual*

dīvīnitās, -tātis, f., *divine nature,
    divinity*

praedicō (1), *publish, proclaim;
    preach*

cultus, -ūs, m., *worship*

10 **pontifex, -icis,** m., *a pontiff;*
    (pl.) *a guild of priests*

Coifi, indecl. Anglo-Saxon
    name, m., *Coifi*

continuō, adv., *at once*

13 **profiteor, -ērī,** *acknowledge
    publicly, confess*

14 **religiō, -ōnis,** f., *reverence for the
    gods or God, piety, religion*

hūcusque, adv., *hitherto, thus
    far*

15 **subdō, -ere, -didī,** *lay or place
    under; subject* (+ dat.); *bring
    on, furnish*

16 **nihilōminus,** adv., *nevertheless*

amplus, -a, -um, *large, ample;
    great, important; honorable*

17 **prōsperō** (1), *make fortunate or
    happy, prosper*

18 **dispōnō, -ere,** *dispose, determine*

19 **impēnsē,** adv., *at great cost;
    eagerly*

20 **restat,** *it remains* (+ *ut* with the
    subjunctive)

22 **perspiciō, -ere, -spēxī,**
    ascertain

absque, prep. + abl., *without*

cūnctāmen, -inis, n., *a delaying,
    hesitating*

23 **suāsiō, -ōnis,** f., *advice;
    persuasive eloquence*

optimās, -ātis, *aristocratic;* (pl.
    as subtantive) *the aristocrats*

24 **tribuō, -ere,** *allot; give, show;
    yield, concede*

assensus, -ūs, m., *assent,
    agreement*

25 **praesēns, -sentis,** *present*

26 **comparātiō, -ōnis,** f., *a
    comparison*

26   **incertum, -ī,** n., *uncertainty*

       quāle, *as* (correlative with *tālis*)

27   **resideō, -ēre,** *remain sitting, stay*

       minister, -trī, m., *an attendant, servant; a thane* (see King, 282)

28   **brūmālis, -e,** *wintry*

       accendō, -ere, -dī, -cēnsum, *kindle, set on fire*

       focus, -ī, m., *a hearth*

       calidus, -a, -um, *warm, hot*

29   **cēnāculum, -ī,** n., *an eating room;* here presumably, the hall of Edwin's palace, like Hrothgar's "great mead-hall" in *Beowulf.* (See Seamus Heaney's translation, line 69)

       furō, -ere, *rage, rave*

30   **turbō, -inis,** m., *a whirling around*

       hiemālis, -e, *wintry, of winter*

       pluvia, -ae, f., *rain*

       nix, nivis, f., *snow*

31   **pervolō** (1), *fly through* or *around*

       quī, take as a connecting relative in a kind of parataxis (Smith, 105), = *and it* (i.e., the sparrow)

32   **ingredior, -ī,** *go in, enter*

33   **hiems, hiemis,** f., *winter*

34   **spatium, -iī,** n., *space*

       serēnitās, -tātis, f., *fair weather*

       ad momentum, *for a moment*

       excurrō, -ere, -currī, -cursum, *run out, hasten forth*

35   **regredior, -ī,** *go back*

       ēlābor, -ī, *glide away, disappear*

36   **ad modicum,** *for a short time* (Latham, s.v. "ad")

       appareō, -ēre, *become visible, appear*

37   **praecēdō, -ere, -cessī,** *go before, precede*

       prorsus, adv., *utterly*

       ignōrō (1), *not know, be ignorant of*

38   **meritō,** adv., *rightly*

39   **maiōrēs nātū,** *the elders*

       dīvīnitus, adv., *under divine inspiration*

40   **prōsequor, -ī,** *go on* or *proceed with* (in discourse)

42   **verbum facientem:** *talking, discoursing, conversing*

45   **vidēlicet,** adv., *clearly, plainly*

46   **apertē,** *openly, frankly*

47   **praedicātiō, -ōnis,** f., *proclamation, preaching*

       clāreō, -ēre, *be bright; be clear to the mind, be evident*

48   **beātitūdō, -inis,** f., *happiness, blessedness*

       suggerō, -ere, *suggest, advise*

49   **altāria, -ium,** n. pl., *high altars; an altar*

       sacrō (1), *dedicate to a god, consecrate*

       ōcius, adv., *more swiftly*

50   **anathema, -matis,** n., *a curse*

       contrādō, -ere, *deliver entirely*

51   **ēvangelīzō** (1), *preach, proclaim; win to the Gospel by preaching*

       abrenuntiō (1), *renounce*

52   **īdōlatrīa, -ae,** f., *idol worship*

53   **praefātus, -a, -um,** *previously mentioned*

       quaereret: can take the construction *aliquid ab aliquō*

54   **fānum, -ī,** n., *a temple with the land around it*

īdōlum, -ī, n., *an idol*

saeptum, -ī, n., *a wall* or *enclosure*

55 **circumdō, -dare, -dedī, -datum,** *surround*

profānō (1), *profane, desecrate*

56 **stultitia, -ae,** f., *foolishness, folly*

58 **dōnō** (1), *give as a gift, present to*

dēstruō, -ere, *pull down, destroy*

abiciō, -ere, -iēcī, -iectum, *throw down* or *away; get rid of; give up*

superstitiō, -ōnis, f., *unreasonable ideas; superstition*

vānitās, -tātis, f., *emptiness; unreality; boasting*

59 **rogāvit:** understand an omitted *ut.*

equus ēmissārius, *a stallion* (Latham, s.v. "emissio")

60 **ascendō, -ere,** *mount*

61 **equa, -ae,** f., *a mare*

equitō (1), *ride on horseback*

62 **accingō, -ere, -cīnxī, -cīnctum,** *gird*

lancea, -ae, f., *a spear*

63 **pergō, -ere,** *proceed*

64 **aestimō** (1), *estimate, judge, reckon*

īnsāniō, -īre, *be mad, rage*

differō, -ferre, distulī, *scatter; delay, postpone; differ*

mox ut, *as soon as* (Latham, s.v. "mox")

appropiō (1), *approach* (Latham, s.v. "appropiatio")

65 **profānāre:** take with *distulit*

lanceā: just as Woden had defeated his enemies by throwing a spear over them, so Coifi defeats Woden by throwing a spear, presumably into the enclosure over the fence[36]

66 **agnitiō, -ōnis,** f., *recognition; knowledge*

67 **succendō, -ere,** *set on fire from below*

69 **Eborācum, -ī,** n., *York*

oriēns, -entis, m., *the rising sun; the east*

amnis, -is, m., *a stream, river*

Doruventiō, -ōnis, f., *the Derwent*

70 **Godmunddingaham:** commonly thought to be the present Goodmanham, near York. J. M. Wallace-Hadrill doubts the identification, but also cites an interpretation of the name of the place as "enclosure of the godmundings," suggesting "a group of priests."[37]

īnspīrō (1), *breathe upon or into; inspire*

71 **polluō, -ere, -uī,** *defile, pollute*

---

36 Wright, op. cit, 54.

37 See *Bede's Ecclesiastical History of the English People, A Historical Commentary*, Oxford Medieval Texts (Oxford: Clarendon Press, 1988), 72–73.

XI. A Charter of Countess Gunnor, widow of Count Richard I of Normandy and mother of Count Richard II, on behalf of the Monastery of Mont-Saint-Michel (1015 ce), Fauroux, no. 17.[38]

This is an example of an important type of medieval document, the charter. Moreover, Countess Gunnor's gift to an abbey for the sake of her own soul and the souls of her family was a common kind of gift for medieval aristocrats.

In nōmine sānctae et indīviduae Trīnitātis, Patris et Fīliī et Spīritūs Sānctī. Antecessōrum nostrōrum īnstitūtiōnibus sancītum dēcrētumque est quātenus, sī quis suārum facultātum quiddam locō sānctōrum alicuī, vītae supernae accensus
5   amōre, perenniter possidendum trādere voluerit, sollemne exinde idōneārum persōnārum plūrimīs astipulātiōnibus fulcītum, ut id inconvulsum permaneat, testamentum faciat. Quodcirca ego Gunnor esse tam praesentibis quam absentibus, omnibus utique sub Chrīstiānitātis titulō dēgentibus, nōtum
10   volō quod, meōrum immensitātem criminum metuēns, vītaeque caelestis gaudium dēsīderāns, duo alloda, Brittavīllam vidēlicet et Domnum Iōannem, quae mihi meus sānctae recordātiōnis vir Richardus comes cum plūrimīs in dōtalitium dedit, locō beātī Michāēlis frātribusque ibīdem rēgulāriter Deō
15   servientibus, prō animae ipsīus dictī virī praecipuē remediō, deinde prō meae animae et corporis filiōrumque meōrum, Richardī comitis archiepīscopīque Rotbertī et aliōrum salūte, quōrum voluntāte, cōnsēnsū dōnātiōneque id agō, perpetuāliter possidenda trādō et tribuō. Referentibus etenim
20   quam plūrimīs ecclēsiasticīs doctōribus, dinōvī dīvīnum esse praeceptum ut illīc nostrī recondantur thesaurī ubi omnis aberit fūrum formīdō omnisque tineārum dēmōlītiō esseque quoddam peccātōrum purgātōrium eleēmosynam, et quod Deus in largiendō mūnificōs exposcit, quī sē in retribuendō
25   praepārat munificentissimum. Dētur igitur Deō nōn nostrum,

---

38   On the titles of the counts or dukes of Normandy, see the annotations to Capvt XVIII, Sentence 14.

sed suum. Quid enim habēre putāmus quam quod ab eō
accēpimus? Tribuātur frīgidae aquae calix, ut aeterna recipiātur
mercēs. Tantī valēre regnum audīvimus Deī quantum
habēmus. Suffēcit viduae quādrāns, prōfuit et Zachaeō
30   bonōrum dimidium. Quae dēnique ad id quod fīnītur ad id
quod nōn fīnītur comparātiō, prō terrēnīs scīlicet caelestia,
prō peritūrīs merērī perpetua? Hīs igitur et aliīs multimodīs
salūtiferīs incitāta documentīs, praedicta alloda locō praelibātō
cōnferō sub Chrīstī tōtiusque ecclēsiae testimōniō, cum terrīs
35   cultīs et incultīs, cum ecclēsiīs, cum molendīnīs, cum prātīs
et cum omnibus omnīnō appendiciīs, atque cum reditibus et
consuētūdinibus cūnctīs quās in praedictīs vīllīs usque ad diem
istam habuī, eō tenōre, eā lēge ut absque calumniātiōne seu
contrādictiōne omnium succedentium sive parentum
40   sive quōrumque aliōrum praefātus locus et habitāntēs in eō
habeat, teneat, possideat. Quod sī aliquis diabolicae prāvitātis
tēlō iāculātus, huic dōnātiōnī calumniātiōnis alicuius vim
īnferre praesūmpserit, tōtīus excommūnicātiōnis atque
maledictiōnis perennibus perenniter irrētiātur vinculīs.
45   Ut autem huius dōnātiōnis auctōritās vērius crēdātur et
dīligentius per omnia cōnservētur fīrmiusque futūrīs teneātur
temporibus, manibus fīliōrum meōrum, comitis quidem
archiepīscopī, subter firmandam corrōborandamque trādidī. +
Rotbertī archiepīscopī. + Maalgerī. + Rotbertī. + Hugōnis
50   Cōnstanciensis epīscopī. + Hugōnis Baiocacensis epīscopī. +
Hugōnis Sais epīscopī. + Rogērī epīscopī. + Norgotī epīscopī.
+ Heldebertī abbātis. + Willelmī abbātis. + Uspac abbātis. +
Willelmī lāicī. + Robertī comitis. + Godfrēdī. + Willelmī. +
Radulfī. + Turstēnī. + Tescelīnī vicecomitis. + Herluīnī. +
55   Anschetil vicecomitis. + Willelmī fīliī Turstēnī. + Hugōnis
lāicī. + Gerardī. + Osmundī clēricī. + Gaufrēdī. + Arfast. +
Niellī. + Guimundī. + Anschitillī. + Milōnis. + Rainaldī. +
Odōnis. + Rannulfī. [*In a monogram*] Richardus comes.

---

1 **indīviduus, -a, -um,** *indivisible*
    Trīnitās, -tātis, f., *the (Holy)*
    Trinity
2 **antecessor, -ōris,** m., *a*
    forerunner

  īnstitūtiō, -ōnis, f., *arrangement,*
    custom, method
3 **sānciō, -īre, sānxī, sānctum/**
    sancītum, *hallow; ratify, decree*
  dēcernō, -ere, -crēvī, -crētum,
    decide, determine

3   **quātenus,** adv., here = *ut*

4   **accendō, -ere, -cendī, -cēnsum,**
     set on fire

5   **perennis, -e,** *lasting, durable*

     possideō, -ēre, *have, hold.* For
     the use of the gerundive here,
     see Appendix I, § 60.

     sollemne, -is, n., *a solemnity; a
     custom*

6   **exinde,** adv., *thence; accordingly*

     astipulātiō, -ōnis, f., *an
     agreement, confirmation*
     (Latham, s.v.)

7   **fulciō, -īre, fulsī, fultum/
     fulcītum,** *prop up, support*

     inconvulsus, -a, -um,
     undestroyed

     permaneō, -ēre, *remain, abide*

     testamentum, -ī, n., here = *a
     charter* (Latham, s.v.)

8   **Quodcirca:** = *quōcirca, on which
     account* (which one 14th-
     century copy gives)

     Gunnor, -ōris, f., *Gunnor* (c.
     950–c. 1030), countess of
     Normandy, wife of Richard
     I, count of Normandy
     (identifications of persons
     and places are from Fauroux's
     excellent index, pp. 473–560). I
     have derived the quantities of as
     many of these names as possible
     from the verses of William of
     Apulia's *Gesta Robertī Wiscardī.*

     praesēns, -sentis, *present* (in
     time or space)

9   **utique,** adv., *at any rate, certainly*

     Chrīstiānitās, -tātis, f.,
     Christianity (LLMA, s.v.);
     Christendom (Latham, s.v.)

titulus, -ī, m., *title,* (legal)
     right (LLMA, Latham, s.v.);
     headship (Latham, s.v.)

dēgō, -ere, *live*

10   **immensitās, -tātis,** f.,
     immeasurableness

     crīmen, -inis, n., *an accusation,
     charge; the fault, crime with
     which one is charged*

11   **allodis, -is,** n., *an allod, a freehold*
     (LLMA, s.v. "allodis")

     Brittavilla, -ae, f.,
     Bretteville-sur-Odon

12   **vidēlicet,** adv., *namely*

     Domnus Iōannes, -ī, -is, m.,
     Domjean

13   **Richardus, -ī,** m., *Richard*
     I, count of Normandy
     (942–996)

     comes, -itis, m., *a count* (France),
     an earl (England)

     dōtalitium, -iī, n., *a widow's
     dower* (LLMA, s.v.)

14   **Michāēl, -ēlis,** m., *Michael*

     ibīdem, adv., *in the same place*

     rēgulāriter, adv., *according to
     monastic rule* (Latham, s.v.
     "regula")

15   **praecipuē,** adv., *especially*

17   **Richardī comitis,** = *Richard* II,
     count of Normandy (996–
     1026), son of Richard I and of
     Gunnor

     archiepīscopus, -ī, m., *an
     archbishop*

     Rotbertus, -ī, m., *Robert,*
     archbishop of Rouen (989–
     1037) and count of Evreux, son
     of Richard I and of Gunnor

18 **cōnsēnsus, -ūs,** m., *agreement*

dōnātiō, -ōnis, f., *donation; charter of donation; offering*

19 **perpetuāliter,** adv., *permanently*

tribuō, -ere, *distribute, give*

etenim, conj., *for indeed*

20 **ecclēsiasticus, -a, -um,** *of or pertaining to the church*

doctor, -ōris, m., *a teacher, instructor*

dīnōscō, -ere, -nōvī, *know, recognize* (Latham, s.v. "dinotio")

21 **illīc,** adv., *there, at that place*

recondō, -ere, *put away, store*

thēsaurus, -ī, m., *a treasure; a treasury*

22 **fūr, fūris,** m./f., *a thief*

formīdō, -inis, f., *terror, dread*

tinea, -ae, f., *a worm*

dēmōlītiō, -ōnis, f., *a tearing down, demolishing* (see Mt. 6:19–21)

23 **purgātōrium, -iī,** n., *a purification, expiation; Purgatory* (Latham, s.v. "purgamen")

eleēmosyna, -ae, f., *alms* (cf. Tob. 4:11)

24 **largior, -īrī,** *give generously, bestow abundantly*

mūnificus, -a, -um, *generous, liberal*

exposcō, -ere, *require* (Latham, s.v.)

retribuō, -ere, *give again* or *as due*

25 **praeparō** (1), *prepare, make ready*

mūnificēns, -centis, = *mūnificus* (cf. Ps. 17:21)

26 **Quid:** supply *magis* (see Blaise, § 124, and Appendix I, § 39) (cf. I Cor. 4:7)

27 **frīgidus, -a, -um,** *cool, cold*

calix, -icis, m., *a goblet* (Mt. 10:42)

28 **Tantī valēre . . . quantum,** = *to be worth as much . . . as* (see LS, s.v. "tantus" I.A.1 and C.2, and "valeo" II.C.1) (cf. Acts 5:8)

29 **vidua, -ae,** f., *a widow*

quādrāns, -antis, *the fourth part of an as* (Lk. 21:2)

prōsum, prōdesse, -fuī, *be useful, benefit* (+ dat.)

Zachaeus, -ī, m., *Zachaeus* (Lk. 19:8)

30 **fīniō, -īre,** *enclose within limits*

31 **comparātiō, -ōnis,** f., *a comparison*

terrēnus, -a, -um, *of the earth, terrestrial*

scīlicet, adv., *of course; namely*

32 **mereor, -ērī,** *earn, deserve*

perpetuus, -a, -um, *continuous, uninterrupted*

multimodīs, adv., *in many ways, variously*

33 **salūtifer, -fera, -ferum,** *health-bringing*

incitō (1), *urge on*

documentum, -ī, n., *example, proof*

praedictus, -a, -um, *aforesaid*

praelībō (1), *mention beforehand* (Latham, s.v. "prelibamen")

34   **testimonium, -iī,** n., *witness, evidence*

35   **incultus, -a, -um,** *uncultivated*
      molendīnum, -ī, n., *a gristmill*
      prātum, -ī, n., *a meadow*

36   **appendicium, -iī,** n., *an outbuilding* (LLMA, s.v.)
      reditus, -ūs, m., *income, revenue* (sg. or pl.)

37   **cōnsuētūdō, -inis,** f., *a tax, duty* (LLMA, s.v.)
      vīllīs: here = *a village* or *manor*

37–38 **diem istam:** Can you explain why *diēs* is feminine here?

38   **tenor, -ōris,** m., *a condition, stipulation* (Latham, s.v.)
      absque, prep. + abl., *without*
      calumniātiō, -ōnis, f., *"claim, dispute, challenge"* (Latham, s.v. "calumnia")

39   **contrādictiō, -ōnis,** f., *contestation, dispute, litigation* (LLMA, s.v.)
      succēdō, -ere, *come after, follow*
      parentum: here = *kin* (Latham, s.v. "parentes")

40   **praefātus, -a, -um,** *aforesaid*
      habitō (1), *inhabit, dwell.* Note that the reference here is to Mont-Saint-Michel and to the monks who dwelt there.

41   **diabolicus, -a, -um,** *devilish*
      prāvitās, -tātis, f., *perversity, depravity*

42   **tēlum, -ī,** n., *a dart, spear, javelin*
      iaculō (1), *throw, strike, hit*

43   **praesūmō, -ere, -sūmpsī,** *take beforehand; presume; dare*

excommūnicātiō, -ōnis, f., *excommunication*

44   **maledictiō, -ōnis,** f., *the act of cursing, a curse*
      perennis, -e, *lasting, durable*
      inrētiō, -īre, *catch in a net, entangle*

47   **quidem:** a 14th-century copy supplies *atque* here

48   **subter,** adv., *below*
      firmō (1), *make firm, strengthen, secure, establish* (modifying either *auctōritās* or an understood *chartam,* charter)

49   **Maalgerius, -iī,** m., *Malger, Mauger,* count of Corbeil, son of Count Richard I and of Gunnor; supply *signum* (= mark, i.e., the little cross before each name) here and with the other names in the gen. in this list
      Hugō, -ōnis, m., *Hugh, Hugues*

50   **Cōnstanciēnsis, -e,** *of Coutances* (Hugh reigned c. 989–1025)
      epīscopus, -ī, m., *a bishop*
      Baiocacēnsis, -e, *of Bayeux* (Hugh reigned 1015–1049)

51   **Sais, -is** (?), f. (?), *Sées* (?)
      Rogērus, -ī, m., *Roger,* bishop of Lisieux (c. 986–1022)
      Norgotus, -ī, m., *Norgod,* bishop of Avranches (990–1017)

52   **Heldebertus, -ī,** m., *Hildebert,* abbot of Mont-Saint-Michel (Fauroux, p. 508, gives the dates of his reign as 1017–1023, which must be incorrect)

abbās, -ātis, m., *an abbot*

52   **Willelmus, -ī,** m., *William* of
Volpiano, abbot of Fécamp
(1001–1028). German and
French have received the name
Willelmus as *Wilhelm* and
Guillaume.

Uspac, indecl. name, m., *Uspac,*
abbot of Jumièges (1000–1015)

53   **lāicus, -ī,** m., *a layman*

Godfrēdus, -ī, m., *Godfrey,*
Gottfried, Godfroi

54   **Radulfus, -ī,** m., *Ralph, Rudolph,*
Raoul

Turstēnus, -ī, m., prob. *Thorsten*
of Bassebourg

Tescelīnus, -ī, m., *Thescelin*

vicecomes, -itis, m., *a viscount*

Herluīnus, -ī, m., *Herluin*

55   **Anschetil,** (here, at any rate)
indecl. name, m., *Asketill,*
viscount of Bayeux

Willelmī fīliī Turstenī: prob.
= *William* Bertran, *son of*
Thorsten of Bassebourg

56   **Gerardus, -ī,** m., *Gerard,*
Gerhard, Gérard

Osmundus, -ī, m., *Osmund*

clēricus, -ī, m., *a clerk, cleric,*
priest

Gaufrēdus, -ī, m., *Geoffrey,*
Geoffroi

Arfast, indecl. name, m., *Harfast,*
knight, brother of Countess
Gunnor, who, with his son
Osbern, "laid the foundations
of their family's later landed
prosperity" (Bates, op. cit.,
151).

57   **Niellus, -ī,** m., *Nigellus, Nigel,*
Neil (from Celtic *Niall* via
Norse *Njáll* and Norman *Neel*)

Guimundus, -ī, m., *Witmund*

Anschitillus, -ī, m., *Asketill*

Milō, -ōnis, m., *Milo*

Rainaldus, -ī, m., *Reginald,*
Reynaud (Scottish *Ronald*)

58   **Odō, -ōnis,** m., *Otto, Eudes*

Rannulfus, -ī, m., *Randolph*

XII. Geoffrey Malaterra, Dē Rēbus Gestīs Rogēriī Calābriae et Siciliae Comitis et Robertī Guiscardī Ducis Frātris Eius 2.30–31, in Pontieri, 40–41 (see Source Texts)

The Norman knight Tancred of Hauteville (fl. under Count Richard II, 996–1026) had twelve sons and perhaps three daughters. His estate was too small to be divided among all his sons, as was the custom in the days before primogeniture, and eleven of them, as well as one daughter, emigrated in the 1030s and 1040s to Southern Italy and Sicily to participate in seizing them from the Byzantine Greeks, the Lombards, and the Moslems. The greatest of Tancred's sons were the sixth and the twelfth, Robert (d. 1085), called Guiscard or "wily" from his early exploits as a desperado in Calabria, and Roger (d. 1101). Robert rose to become Duke of Apulia, that is, of all of Italy southeast of a line between Termoli and Salerno, while under his aegis Roger conquered Sicily. The following story is part of an account of an incident in that conquest, the siege of Roger with his wife and 300 men in the city of Troina west of Mount Ætna by rebellious Greeks and Moslems during the winter of 1062–1063. One should notice not only Roger's shrewdness and valor, but also the hardihood and practical wisdom of his young Norman wife, Judith of Evreux (d. 1076). Geoffrey Malaterra was a monk at the Benedictine monastery of Sant' Agata in Catania, Sicily, a Norman foundation of 1071.[39]

XXX. Quādam itaque diē certāmine initō, comes equō īnsidēns, ut suīs succurrat, sēsē hostibus medium dedit. Hostēs vērō, eō cognitō, versus eum fortiōrī impetū transientēs, equum eius spīculīs cōnfōdiunt. Ipsum cum equō humī
5   dēiectum manibus corripiunt; quasi taurum ad victimam reluctantem usque ad sibi tūtiōrem locum nītuntur pertrahere pūniendum. Porro comes in tantō discrīmine positus, prīstinārum vīrium nōn immemor, ēnsem quō accinctus erat exercēns in modum falcis virēns prātum resecantis,

---

[39] The best introduction to this period in English is G.A. Loud, *The Age of Robert Guiscard, Southern Italy and the Norman Conquest*, The Medieval World (Harlow, UK: Longman, 2000). A translation can be found in Kenneth Baxter Wolf, tr., *The Deeds of Count Roger of Calabria and Sicily and of His Brother Duke Robert Guiscard by Geoffrey Malaterra* (Ann Arbor: The University of Michigan Press, 2005), 104–106.

10   circumquāque impiger vibrandō dūcēns, plūribus interēmptīs,
      sōlā dextrā et Deī adiūtōriō līberātur, tantā strāge dē inimīcīs
      factā, ut sīcut in condēnsibus saltibus iacērent ā ventō dīrupta
      ligna, sīc circumquāque sibi adiacērent hostium ab ipsō
      perēmpta cadāvera. Hostēs reliquī sēsē in suam mūnītiōnem
15   recipiunt. Ipse, equō āmissō, sellam nē quasī timidus accelerāre
      vidērētur asportāns, versus suōs pedēs regreditur.
           Nostrīs igitur per quattuor mensēs in tam laboriōsō
      discrīmine positīs, hiems asperrima, quae ipsō annō ipsīs in
      partibus fuit occāsiō līberātiōnis, hostibus autem damnātiōnis
20   exstitit. Nam et ā vīcīnitāte Aetnae, quae in eādem prōvinciā
      haud procul exterminat, ibi ita certīs temporibus ab aestuantī
      incendiō sulphureī montis aestās acerrima, itaque certīs
      temporibus minime satis inundātiō tempestātis, procellārum,
      nivis et grandinum asperrima solet fierī. Quamobrem hostēs
25   balneārum aestuātiōnibus aestuārī assuētī, frīgidiōrī aurā
      flante, dum vīnī pōtātiōnibus nātūrālem calōrem intrā
      sē excitāre nītuntur, somnō propter vīnum (ut assolet)
      subsequente, tardiōrēs ad excubiās vigiliārum urbis esse
      coepērunt. Quod cum nostrī cognōvissent, coepērunt et ipsī ex
30   industriā tardiōrēs appārēre, et quamvīs attentissimē vigilārent,
      clāmōribus tamen omissīs—ut illōs dolōsē securiōrēs
      redderent—fingēbant sē quasī nōn vigilēs essent. Quādam ergō
      nocte cum comes, ut semper nūllō labōre dēficiēns, excubiās
      noctis cum suīs armātīs sub algentī brūma, suīs ūtilitātibus
35   accurātissimē intentīs, celebrāret, hostēs somnō gravātōs inter
      suōs mūnītiōnēs, et nēminem eōrum ex tantā multitūdine
      vigilāre dēprehendisset, castra eōrum silenter irrumpit.
      Armātā itaque manū incautōs occupāns, plūribus interfectīs,
      mūnītiōnem accipit. Plūrēs capiuntur. Ex adventīciīs reliquī
40   fugae refugium petunt. Porinus, quī caput prōditiōnis
      exstiterat, cum sibi prīncipāliter assentientibus laqueō
      suspensus, ad exemplum aliōrum vītā prīvātur. Plūrēs dīversīs
      poenīs afficiuntur. Spoliīs itaque triumphālī honōre acceptīs,
      nostrī hāctenus egentēs tantā abundantiā frūmentī, vīnī et oleī
45   et aliārum rērum quae ad ūsum necessāria erant sunt replētī,
      ut meritō ā cōnsimilī argumentō recordārī possent illīus quod
      apud Samarīam, īnspīrātō ā Deō subitō datae abundantiae,
      ad verbum Eliseī dīcentis: "Crās hōrā istā in portā Samarīae

modius similiae ūnō statēre erit," cum in praecēdenti diē nūllō
50   quamvīs magnō pretiō posset invenīrī.

XXXI. Ōrdinātīs itaque rēbus suīs et urbe ad suum libitum
melius fīrmātā, ut suīs equōs quōs āmīserant restituat, versus
Calābriam at Āpūliam acquīsītum vādit, uxōre et mīlitibus suīs
apud Traynam dīmissīs. Quae quamvīs iuvencula, tantā
55   strenuitāte coepit esse sollicita circā castrum tuendum,
ut diātim circuiēns, ubi meliōrandum vidēbat, studēret ut
fierent vigilēs. Reliquōs omnēs quōs sibi dominus suus abiēns
dīmīserat blandē alloquēns, ut sollicitē quae servanda erant
prōvidērent hortābātur, multa in reditū dominī suī
60   reprōmittēns. Sed et trānsāctum periculum, ne segniter agendō
quid simile incurrerent, ad memōriam redūcēbat.

1 **certāmen, -inis,** n., *a military engagement*

comes, -itis, m., *a count,* here Roger of Hauteville

2 **īnsideō, -ēre,** *sit in* or *on* (+ dat.)

sēsē, = *sē*

sēsē dare, *betake oneself*

medius, can modify a person and take a dat., here = *threw himself* (sēsē dedit) *into the midst of* (medium) *the enemy* (hostibus)

3 **versus,** prep. + acc., *to, towards*

impetus, -ūs, m., *an attack*

4 **spīculum, -ī,** n., *a javelin, an arrow*

cōnfodiō, -īre, *dig all around; pierce, transfix*

5 **dēiciō, -ere, -iēcī, -iectum,** *throw down, hurl down*

corripiō, -ere, *seize, take hold of*

taurus, -ī, m. *a bull* or *ox*

victima, -ae, f., *a sacrifice, victim*

6 **reluctor, -ārī,** *struggle against, be reluctant*

nītor, nītī, *strive, endeavor*

pertrahō, -ere, *drag*

7 **porro,** adv., *then, next*

discrīmen, -inis, n., *a critical moment; danger*

8 **immemor, -oris,** *unmindful, forgetful* (+ gen.)

ēnsis, -is, m., *a sword*

accingō, -ere, -inxī, -inctum, *gird on; arm, equip*

9 **exerceō, -ēre,** *work at; employ*

falx, falcis, f., *a sickle*

vireō, -ēre, *be green*

prātum, -ī, n., *a meadow*

resecō (1), *cut off; reap* (cf. Latham, s.v. "resecatio"); here perh. = "mow"

10 **circumquāque, adv.,** *on every side*

impiger -gra, -grum, *unwearied, indefatigable*

vibrō (1), *move quickly back and forth*

dūcēns, here prob. = *swinging*

interimō, -ere, -ēmī, -emptum,
kill, slay

11 **adiūtōrium, -iī,** n., *help, aid*

   strāgēs, -is, f., *an overthrow; a*
   slaughter, carnage

12 **condēnsus, -a, -um,** *very thick*

   saltus, -ūs, m., *woods*

   dīrumpō, -ere, -rūpī, -ruptum,
   break in pieces, break off

13 **lignum, -ī,** n., *wood broken up*
   and suitable for firewood

   adiaceō, -ēre, *lie near, be adjacent*

14 **cadāver, -eris,** n., *a corpse, carcass*

   reliquus, -a, -um, *what is left or*
   remains

   mūnītiō, -ōnis, f., *a fortifying; a*
   fortification

15 **sella, -ae,** f., *a saddle* (Latham,
   s.v.)

   timidus, -a, -um, *fearful, afraid,*
   cowardly

   accelerō (1), *hasten*

16 **asportō** (1), *carry away*

   pedes, -itis, m., *a foot-soldier,*
   infantry-man

   regredior, -dī, *go back, return*

17 **nostrīs,** Malaterra writes as a
   Norman, though this does not
   prove his Norman birth[40]

   per, as in CL, indicates time
   within which (GL, § 336R2)

   labōriōsus, -a, -um, *toilsome,*
   difficult

18 **hiems, -emis,** f., *the winter*

18–19 **ipsīs in partibus,** = *nostrīs in*
   partibus, on our side (see Blaise,
   § 155)

19 **līberātiō, -ōnis,** f., *a getting free,*
   liberation

   damnātiō, -ōnis, f.,
   condemnation; loss, injury
   (Latham, s.v. "damnum")

20 **exsistō, -ere, -stitī,** *emerge,*
   appear; arise, become

   vīcīnitās, -tātis, f., *proximity;*
   region

   Aetna, -ae, f., *Mount Ætna, the*
   famous Sicilian volcano

   prōvincia, -ae, f., *a province*

21 **procul,** adv., *far away*

   exterminō (1), *exile, banish;*
   put aside, remove; delimit,
   demarcate (LLMA, s.v.): here
   prob. = *has its boundaries, i.e.,*
   is situated (the word *sē* would
   clarify the use of *extermināre*
   here)

21–22 **ita . . . itaque,** *in the same way*
   as . . . in like manner

22 **incendium, -iī,** n., *a fire; heat*

   sulphureus, -a, -um, *sulphurous*

   aestuō (1), *rage, toss, boil up; be*
   or feel warm or hot

23 **minimē satis,** *not at all sufficient:*
   best taken as modifying
   inundātiō in litotes (Smith,
   102–103), = *a not at all sufficient*
   inundation, i.e., *an overwhelming*
   inundation, a figure which
   must have been funny to those
   familiar with the climate

   inundātiō, -ōnis, f., *an*
   overflowing, inundation

   procella, -ae, f., *a destructive*
   wind, a tempest

---

[40] Loud, op. cit., 82–84.

24   **nix, nivis,** f., snow

     grandō, -inis, f., *hail, a hail-storm*

     quamobrem, rel. adv., *on which account, wherefore*

25   **balneae, -ārum,** f., *baths* (the old Roman baths still existed: were they fed by thermal springs?)

     aestuātiō, -ōnis, f., *a boiling up*

     aestuārī, perh. here = *to warm themselves up* (middle voice)

     assuēscō, -ere, -suēvī, -suētum, *be accustomed to*

     frīgidus, -a, -um, *cold, chill*

     aura, -ae, f., *a breeze, wind*

26   **flō** (1), *blow*

     pōtātiō, -ōnis, f., *a drinking, drinking-bout*

     calor, -ōris, m., *warmth, heat*

     intrā, prep. + acc., *within*

27   **excitō** (1), *arouse*

     ut assolet, *as is wont to happen*

28   **subsequor, -quī,** *follow immediately*

     excubiae, -ārum, f., *a lying out at night for guard-duty*

     vigilia, -ae, f., *a staying awake to keep watch; a watch*

29–30   **ex industriā,** *on purpose, intentionally*

30   **appāreō, -ēre,** *make one's appearance*

     attentus, -a, -um, *attentive, careful*

31   **clāmor, -ōris,** m., *a loud call;* here = *a watch-cry*

     dolōsus, -a, -um, *cunning, deceitful*

32   **redderent,** here = *render*

     fingō, -ere, *form, make; pretend*

     vigil, -ilis, adj., *wakeful, watchful*

34   **armātus, -a, um,** *furnished with armor and weapons,* which would have included, at least for the richer soldiers, helmet, hauberk, shield, spear, and sword. The Bayeux Tapestry depicts men armed just as these men would have been. (See Image 1, p.3.) A knight equipped with just a sword and a shield was not considered armed by the Normans. See Malaterra, *Dē rēbus gestīs* 2.4

     algēns, -entis, adj., = *frīgidus*

     brūma, -ae, f., *the winter solstice; winter-time; hoar-frost* (Latham, s.v.)

35   **accūrātē,** adv., *carefully, exactly*

     intendō, -ere, -ndī, -ntum, *aim* or *direct at*

     celebrō (1), *frequent, fill; do, make, commit* (LLMA, s.v.)

     hostēs, note the asyndeton (Smith, 96): read *hostēsque*

     gravō (1), *weigh down*

36   **multitūdō, -inis,** f., *a multitude*

37   **dēprehendō, -ere, -ndī,** *find out, detect*

     castrum, -ī, n., *a fort;* **castra, -ōrum,** n., *a military camp*

     silenter, adv., *silently*

     irrumpō, -ere, *burst* or *rush in*

38   **incautus, -a, -um,** *heedless, improvident*

39   **adventīcius, -a, -um,** *extraordinary*

40   **refugium, -iī,** n., *a refuge*

Porinus, -ī, m., apparently, the ringleader of the revolt

prōditiō, -ōnis, f., treason

41 **prīncipāliter,** adv., chiefly

assentior, -īrī, agree with (+ dat.)

laqueus, -ī, m., a noose, snare

42 **dīversus, -a, -um,** different, diverse

43 **afficiō, -ere,** grace with; inflict upon

spolium, -iī, n., an animal's hide; the arms stripped from an enemy's corpse, illustrated in the borders of the Bayeux Tapestry (See Image 1, p.3.); booty, spoil

triumphālis, -e, triumphal

44 **hāctenus,** adv., so far

frūmentum, -ī, n., grain

oleum, -ī, n., olive oil

45 **repleō, -ēre, -ēvī, -plētum,** fill up

46 **meritō,** adv., justly, deservedly

cōnsimilis, -e, entirely similar

argumentum, here = main point of a story

recordor, -ārī, recall, recollect (+ gen.)

illīus, here = of that well-known incident

quod, supply factum est in this rel. clause

47 **Samarīa, -ae,** f., Samaria

īnspīrō (1), blow into; inspire

subitum, -ī, m., a sudden or unexpected occurrence (+ gen.)

48 **ad,** here = according to

Eliseus, -ī, m., Elisha, the prophet (see II Kings 7:1)

49 **modius, -iī,** m., the Roman grain measure, a peck

simila, -ae, f., the best wheat flour

statēr, -tēris, m., a Jewish silver coin

praecēdō, -ere, go before, precede

51 **ōrdinō (1),** set in order, arrange

libitum, -ī, n., or **libitus, -ūs,** m., will, pleasure (Latham, s.v.)

52 **fīrmō (1),** make firm, strengthen

53 **Calābria, -ae,** f., the region of Italy still called Calabria, held in part by Roger by agreement with Robert Guiscard

Āpūlia, -ae, f., the region of Italy now called Puglia, ruled directly by Robert Guiscard

vādō, -ere, go fast, hasten

54 **Trayna, -ae,** f., Troina

dīmittō, here = leave behind

iūvencula, -ae, f., a young girl, though Judith might have been in her early 20s

55 **strēnuitās, -tātis,** f., nimbleness, activity, vigor, the characteristic Norman virtue, in Malaterra's view[41]

circā, prep. + acc., around; with regard to (Latham, s.v.)

tueor, -ērī, defend, protect

56 **diātim,** adv., daily (Latham, s.v.)

circueō, -īre, go around; go the rounds

meliōrō (1), make better, improve

---

41 Loud, op. cit., 5, 84, 167.

58 **blandē**, adv., *softly, carefully, gently*

    alloquor, -quī, *speak to, address*

59 **reditus, -ūs,** m., *a return*

60 **reprōmittō, -ere,** *promise in return*

trānsigō, -ere, -ēgī, -āctum, *pierce; finish, conclude*

segniter, adv. *lazily, slowly*

61 **incurrō, -ere,** *rush upon; happen, occur*

XIII. Two Readings from Hugh of St. Victor

A. *Practica Geōmetriae, III. Dē Cosmimetria 39,* in Baron, 49–51 (see Source Texts)

This passage purports to be an account of how Eratosthenes of Cyrene (c. 285–194 BCE) discovered the circumference of the earth. Hugh attributes two different proofs to Eratosthenes. The first proof, achieved by the measurement of shadows cast by gnomons at different locations, is described inaccurately, a description drawn ultimately from Martianus Capella's report of the same (De Nuptiīs Philologiae et Mercuriī *6.598). W. H. Stahl says, "Eratosthenes' method of measuring the circumference of the globe" was "a simple geometric procedure that no Latin writer, ancient or medieval, understood."[42] The importance of Martianus' account was that it was one of two sources for the medieval world's knowledge of the world's sphericity. The other source was Macrobius. The second proof, which involves the use of an astrolabe, was not attempted by Eratosthenes. Hugh's source for it is unknown.[43]*

Terra igitur, in hōc mundī sēnsibilis globō mediō cōnstitūta
locō, vicem punctī obtinet, quod, in circumferentiā circulī
aequālī undique distantiā ambītum, centrum vocant. Haec
igitur licet, ad illam incomprehēnsibilem sphaerae caelestis
5 quae omnia suō ambitū inclūdit immēnsitātem comparāta,
quōdammodo secundum nātūram punctī indīvīsibilis videātur,
in sē tamen cōnsīderātā nostrīs angustiīs inaestimābilem
magnitūdinem praefert.
Ab hāc igitur tōtīus investīgātiōnis excursus exordium
10 sūmet. Et prīmum ambitus terrae tōtīus quantus sit,
explicandum vidētur, et quemadmodum hūmānus sēnsus ad

---

[42] William Harris Stahl, *The Quadrivium of Martianus Capella: Latin Traditions in the Mathematical Sciences, 50 B.C.–A.D. 1250,* in Stahl, et al., *Martianus Capella and the Seven Liberal Arts,* vol. 1, Records of Western Civilization Series (New York: Columbia University Press, 1971, 1991), 37. Stahl's account (p. 134) of Eratosthenes' proof is concise and helpful. "Cleomedes accurately reports the procedures used by Eratosthenes as follows: assuming Syene to be directly beneath the celestial tropic, Eratosthenes measured the length of the Syene-Alexandria arc and, finding the arc of the gnomon's shadow in a hemispherical bowl placed at Alexandria at noon at the summer solstice to be one-fiftieth of a circle, he multiplied the Syene-Alexandria distance by fifty to get a value for the earth's circumference."

[43] See Frederick A. Homann, S. J., *Practical Geometry [Practica Geometriae], Attributed to Hugh of St. Victor,* Mediaeval Philosophical Texts in Translation 29 (Milwaukee: Marquette University Press, 1991), 81–82.

hunc comprehendendum accesserit, revolvendum.

    Terrae igitur ambitus, ā veteribus in occultā nātūrae
dispositiōne perquīrendā studiōsīs, ducenta quīnquāgintā

15   duo mīlia stadia continēre probātus est. Stadium autem
octāva pars est mīliāris, habēns passūs cxxv. Ducenta igitur
et quīnquāgintā duo mīlia stadia faciunt mīliāria trīgintā et
ūnum mīlia quīngentā. Quae sī per ccclx gradūs dīvidantur,
ēveniunt ūnīcuique stadia septingenta, hoc est octōgintā

20   septem mīliāria et sēmis ūnum, id est dīmidium.

    Huius inventiōnis prīmus auctor Eratosthenēs fertur, quī
in hāc disciplīnā spectābilis et sagācissimus eōrum quae latent
scrūtātor exstitit.

    Hīs itaque, cum terrae ambitum aestimāre dispōneret, tālī

25   arte viam sibi fēcisse dīcitur, et hōc argūmentō satis mīrābilī
ingeniō excōgitātō ūsus memorātur. Nam ā mēnsōribus rēgis
Ptolemaeī adiūtus, quī tōtam Aegyptum tenēbat, ā Syēnē usque
ad Meroen hōroscopicīs vāsibus cum aequālī gnōmonum
dīmēnsiōne dispositīs et per singula vāsa singulōs gnōmonicae

30   supputātiōnis doctissimōs ōrdināns, ūnā diē omnēs umbram
merīdiānam observāre praecēpit. Quā per singulōs gnōmonēs
computātā, comperit quod ultrā septingenta stadia ad ūnīus
longitūdinis gnōmonem umbra nōn respondit.

    Post haec altiōrī ingeniō vēritātem huius reī persequēns,

35   sub stēllāta noctis tempore sūmptō astrolāpsū, quod secundum
ambitum terrae et fīrmāmentī in ccclx gradūs per circuitum
dīviditur, et per utrumque mediclīniī forāmen polō īnspectō,
gradum in quō mediclīnium stetit dīligentī annotātiōne
signāvit, et profectus in rēctā līneā ā merīdiē contrā

40   septemtriōnem, rursus subsequentī nocte polum per utrumque
forāmen mediclīniī contemplātus et tertiō similiter, tandem
ūnō gradū mediclīnium ad superiōra prōmōtum invēnit.

    Tunc dictante ratiōne huius intineris spatium dīligenter
ēmēnsus, invēnit dcc stadia sīve mīliāria lxxxvii et sēmis

45   ūnum, hoc est dīmidium. Post haec datīs ūnīcuique dē ccclx
tōtīus circulī gradibus totidem, inventus est tōtīus terrae
ambitus cclii mīlia stadia sīve xxxi mīlia d mīliāria continēre.
Atque ita probābilī ratiōne conclūdit quod partēs sīve gradus
ccclx, quibus omnis Zōdiacī circulī tractus ac caelestis

50   sphaerae circuitus dīviditur, ad terrās usque perveniant, et pars

quae ibi incompertae et inaestimābilis mēnsurae est in terrā
sub certā mēnsūrā cadat.

1   **sēnsibilis, -e,** *perceived by the senses, sensible*

    globus, -ī, m., *a round ball, globe, sphere*

    cōnstitūtus, -a, -um, *arranged, settled*

1–2 **mediō cōnstitūta locō:** read *mediō in locō cōnstitūta*

2   **(vicis), -is,** f., *place, position*

    punctum, -ī, n., *a point*

    obtineō, -ēre, *hold; maintain*

    circumferentia, -ae, f., *circumference*

    circulus, -ī, m., *a circle*

3   **aequālis, -e,** *equal*

    undique, adv., *from* or *on all sides, everywhere*

    distantia, -ae, f., *distance*

    ambiō, -īre, -iī, -ītum, *go around a thing; surround, encircle, encompass*

    centrum, -ī, n., *the middle point of a circle, the center*

4   **licet,** here = *although*

    incomprehēnsibilis, -e, *incomprehensible*

    sphaera, -ae, f., *a globe, sphere*

5   **ambitus, -ūs,** m., *a revolution, orbit; a circumference, periphery*

    immensitās, -tātis, f., *immeasurableness, immensity*

6   **quōdammodo,** adv., *in a certain way* or *measure*

    indīvīsibilis, -e, *indivisible*

7   **cōnsīderō** (1), *look at* or *regard carefully, contemplate; consider*

    angustiae, -ārum, f., *narrowness*

    inaestimābilis, -e, *that cannot be estimated, incalculable*

8   **magnitūdō, -inis,** f., *greatness*

9   **investīgātiō, -ōnis,** f., *an investigation*

    excursus, -ūs, m., *a running out* or *forth*

    exordium, -iī, n., *a beginning*

12 **revolvō, -ere,** *roll back; go over again*

13 **veterēs,** *the ancients*

    occultus, -a, -um, *hidden, concealed*

14 **dispositiō, -ōnis,** f., *a regular disposition, arrangement*

    perquīrō, -ere, *inquire carefully*

15 **stadium, -iī,** n., *a stade,* a Greek measurement of length, "a distance of 125 paces, or 625 Roman feet, equal to 606 feet 9 inches English; it was an eighth part of a milliarium, or somewhat less than an eighth of an English mile" (LS, s.v.)

16 **probō,** here = *prove, demonstrate*

    mīliāre, -is, n., = *mīliārium,* a Roman *mile*

    passus, -ūs, m., *a pace; the pace,* consisting of five Roman feet

16–18 **Ducenta ... quīngentā:** i.e., 252,000 Greek stadia = 31,500 Roman miles

18   **gradus, -ūs,** m., *an astronomical degree* (Latham, s.v.), i.e., "an arc equal to the 360th part of the circumference of a circle" (OED)

dīvidō, -ere, -vīsī, -vīsum, *separate into parts, divide*

19   **ūnusquisque, ūnaquaeque, ūnumquodque,** *every, everyone*

20   **sēmis, -issis,** m., *the half* of anything, *a half*

21   **inventiō, -ōnis,** f., *a discovery*

Eratosthenēs, -ae, m., *Eratosthenes*

22   **disciplīna, -ae,** f., *a body of knowledge, science*

spectābilis, -e, *notable, remarkable*

sagax, -ācis, *keen, acute*

lateō, -ēre, *lie hid, be concealed*

23   **scrūtātor, -ōris,** m., *an investigator*

exsistō, -ere, -stitī, *stand* or *come forth, appear*

24   **aestimō** (1), *estimate, reckon*

dispōnō, -ere, *settle, determine*

26   **excōgitō** (1), *think out, devise, contrive*

ūsus: supply *esse*

memorō (1), *mention, relate*

mēnsor, -ōris, m., *a measurer; a surveyor*

27   **Ptolemaeus, -ī,** m., *Ptolemy* III Euergetes, reigned 246–221 BCE

Aegyptus, -ī, f., *Egypt*

Syēnē, -ēs, f., *Syene,* a city just below the first cataract of the Nile, now Aswan.

28   **Meroē, -ēs,** f., "a large and celebrated island of the Nile, in Ethiopia," LS, s.v. This is a major mistake in Hugh's account, which was already present in Martianus Capella's report. The other terminus of the arc that Eratosthenes wished to measure was at Alexandria to the north. Eratosthenes chose Syene as the southern terminus because he "observed that at Syene, at noon, at the summer solstice, the sun cast no shadow from an upright gnomon."[44] Another mistake is also implicit here, in that Eratosthenes only took two measurements, one at Syene, the other at Alexandria, not many

hōroscopicus, -a, -um, *indicating the hour*

28   **vās, vāsis,** n., pl. = **vāsa, vāsōrum,** *a vessel, dish; a utensil, implement:* here a *sundial*[45]

gnōmōn, -onis, m., *the upright piece of a sundial, a style, gnomon*

29   **dīmēnsiō, -ōnis,** f., *a measuring; extent, dimensions*

gnōmonicus, -a, -um, *of* or *belonging to a gnomon* or *sundial*

---

44   Thomas L. Heath, *A History of Greek Mathematics, Vol. II, From Aristarchus to Diophantus* (New York: Dover Publications, 1981; orig. pub. 1921), 106.

45   Identified as such by Marshall Clagett, *Greek Science in Antiquity,* rev. ed. (New York: Collier Books, 1963), 117.

30 **supputātiō, -ōnis,** f., *a computation*

ōrdinō (1), *set in order, arrange*

31 **observō** (1), *watch, observe, attend to*

praecipiō, -ere, -cēpī, *instruct*

32 **computō** (1), *reckon together, calculate*

comperiō, -īre, -perī, *find out, discover*

33 **longitūdō, -inis,** f., *length; terrestrial* or *astronomical longitude* (Latham, s.v.)

31–33 **Quā . . . respondit:** i.e., 700 stadia x 360° of longitude = 252,000 stadia, the circumference of the earth

35 **stēllātus, -a, -um,** *starry*

astrolāpsus, -ūs, m., *an astrolabe,* an instrument for taking and predicting the positions of the celestial bodies, and for deriving terrestrial locations and measurements from them

36 **circuitus, -ūs,** m., *circumference, extent*

37 **uterque, utraque, utrumque,** *each of two, both*

mediclīnium, -iī, n., *an alidad,* "the index of an astrolabe, quadrant, or other graduated instrument, carrying the sights or telescope, and showing the degrees cut off on the arc of the intrument. In the astrolabe it revolved at the back, and was called by Chaucer the *Rule*" (OED, s.v. "alidad").

forāmen, -inis, n., *a hole, opening, aperture*

polus, -ī, m., *the end of an axis, a pole; the sky, heavens*

īnspiciō, -ere, -spēxī, -spectum, *view, examine, inspect*

38 **adnotātiō, -ōnis,** f., *an annotation*

39 **signō** (1), *mark*

līnea, -ae, f., *a line*

merīdiēs, -ēī, m., *midday; the south*

40 **septemtriōnēs, -um,** m., *the seven stars* of either the Big Dipper or the Little Dipper; *the north*

rursus, adv., *again*

subsequor, -ī, *follow, follow after*

41 **contemplor, -ārī, -ātus sum,** *survey, regard*

42 **prōmoveō, -ēre, -mōvī, -mōtum,** *advance; increase*

43 **dictō** (1), *say often, repeat; dictate; compose; order, prescribe*

spatium, -iī, n., *space; extent, length*

44 **ēmētior, -īrī, -mēnsus sum,** *measure out*

46 **totidem,** indecl. adj., *just as many* (the subject of *datīs;* the antecedent is *stadia*)

48 **probabilis, -e,** *probable, credible; acceptable, good*

conclūdō, -ere, *bring to a conclusion, argue, infer*

49 **Zōdiacus, -ī,** m., *the Zodiac*

tractus, -ūs, m., *a track, trail*

51 **incompertus, -a, -um,** *of which one has no information, unknown*

mēnsūra, -ae, f., *a measuring; a measure*

B. *Didascalicon dē Studiō Legendī* 3.8–12, in Buttimer, 58–61 (see Source Texts)

Hugh wrote his Didascalicon *as an introduction to the disciplines of knowledge, and to their integration, for the young men who were coming to study at the School of Saint Victor in Paris. This excerpt contains Hugh's very useful observations on reading. Of course, one is aware that, as Ivan Illich says, "The book has now ceased to be the root-metaphor of the age; the screen has taken its place." The scholastic reading that originated with Hugh and which has characterized western culture until the last few decades, may survive, "but outside the educational system which has assumed entirely different functions … [in] something like houses of reading, not unlike the Jewish* shul, *the Islamic* medersa, *or the monastery, where the few who discover their passion for a life centered on reading would find the necessary guidance, silence, and complicity of disciplined companionship needed for the long initiation into one or the other of several "spiritualities" or styles of celebrating the book."*[46]

        8. *Dē ōrdine legendī.* Ōrdō cōnsīderātur alius in disciplīnīs,
ut sī dīxerim grammaticam dialecticā antīquiōrem vel
arithmēticam priōrem mūsicā, alius in librīs, ut sī dīxerō
Catilīnārium Iugurthīnō priōrem, alius in nārrātiōne, quae
5   est in continuā seriē, alius in expositiōne. Ōrdō in disciplīnīs
attenditur secundum nātūram, in librīs secundum persōnam
auctōris vel subiectam māteriam, in nārrātiōne secundum
dispositiōnem. Quae duplex est: nātūrālis, vidēlicet quandō rēs
eō refertur ōrdine quō gesta est, et artificiālis, id est,
10   quandō id quod posteā gestum est prius nārrātur, et quod
prius, postmodum dīcitur. In expositiōne cōnsīderātur ōrdō
secundum inquīsītiōnem. Expositiō tria continet, litteram,
sēnsum, sententiam. Littera est congrua ōrdinātiō dictiōnum,
quod etiam cōnstructiōnem vocāmus. Sēnsus est facilis
15   quaedam et aperta significātiō, quam littera prīmā fronte
praefert. Sententia est profundior intellegentia, quae nisi
expositiōne vel interpretātiōne nōn invenītur. In hīs ōrdō est,
ut prīmum littera, deinde sēnsus, deinde sententia inquīrātur.
Quō factō, perfecta est expositiō.

---

[46]   Ivan Illich, *In the Vineyard of the Text, A Commentary to Hugh's* Didascalicon (Chicago: University of Chicago Press, 1993), 3.

20   *9. Dē modō legendī.* Modus legendī in dīvidendō
cōnstat. Omnis dīvīsiō incipit ā fīnītīs, et ad īnfīnīta usque
prōgreditur. Omne autem fīnītum magis nōtum est et scientiā
comprehēnsibile. Doctrīna autem ab hīs quae magis nōta sunt
incipit, et per eōrum nōtitiam ad scientiam eōrum quae latent
25   pertingit. Praetereā ratiōne invēstīgāmus. Ad quam propriē
pertinet dīvidere, quandō ab ūniversālibus ad particulāria
dēscendimus dīvidendō et singulōrum nātūrās investīgandō.
Omne namque ūniversāle magis est dēterminātum suīs
particulāribus. Quandō ergō discimus, ab hīs incipere dēbēmus
30   quae magis sunt nōta et dētermināta et complectentia, sīcque
paulātim dēscendendō, et per dīvīsiōnem singula distinguendō,
eōrum quae continentur nātūram investīgāre.
        10. Dē meditātiōne. Meditātiō est cōgitātiō frequēns cum
cōnsiliō, quae causam et orīginem, modum et ūtilitātem
35   ūnīuscuiusque reī prūdenter investīgat. Meditātiō prīncipium
sūmit ā lēctiōne. Nūllīs tamen stringitur rēgulīs aut praeceptīs
lēctiōnis. Dēlectātur enim quōdam apertō dēcurrere spatiō,
ubi līberam contemplandae vēritātī aciem adfīgat, et nunc hās,
nunc illās rērum causās perstringere, nunc autem prōfunda
40   quaeque penetrāre, nihil anceps, nihil obscūrum relinquere.
Prīncipium ergō doctrīnae est in lēctiōne, cōnsummātiō in
meditātiōne, quam sī quis familiārius amāre didicerit eīque
saepius vacāre voluerit, iūcundam valdē reddit vītam, et
maximam in trībulātiōne praestat cōnsōlātiōnem. Ea enim
45   maximē est, quae animam ā terrēnōrum āctuum strepitū
sēgregat, et in hāc vītā etiam aeternae quiētis dulcēdinem
quōdammodo praegustāre facit. Cumque iam per ea quae facta
sunt eum quī fēcit omnia quaerere didicerit et intellegere, tunc
animum pariter et scientiā ērudit et laetitiā perfundit,
50   unde fit, ut maximum in meditātiōne sit oblectāmentum. Tria
sunt genera meditātiōnis. Ūnum cōnstat in circumspectiōne
mōrum, aliud in scrūtātiōne mandātōrum, tertium in
investīgātiōne dīvīnōrum operum. Mōrēs sunt in vitiīs et
virtūtibus. Mandātum dīvīnum, aliud praecipiēns, aliud
55   prōmittēns, aliud terrēns. Opus Deī est, et quod creat potentiā,
et quod moderātur sapientiā, et quod cooperātur grātiā. Quae
omnia, quantā sint admīrātiōne digna, tantō magis quisque
nōvit, quantō attentius Deī mīrābilia meditārī cōnsuēvit.

11. *Dē memoriā.* Dē memoriā hoc maximē in praesentī
60 praetermittendum nōn esse existimō, quod sīcut ingenium
dīvidendō investīgat et invenit, ita memoria colligendō
custōdit. Oportet ergō ut quae discendō dīvīsimus,
commendanda memoriae colligāmus. Colligere est ea, dē
quibus prōlixius vel scrīptum vel disputātum est, ad brevem
65 quandam et compendiōsam summam redigere, quae ā
maiōribus epilogus, id est, brevis recapitulātiō suprādictōrum
appellāta est. Habet namque omnis tractātiō aliquod
prīncipium, cui tōta reī vēritās et vīs sententiae innītitur, et ad
ipsum cūncta alia referuntur. Hoc quaerere et cōnsīderāre
70 colligere est. Ūnus fōns est et multī rīvulī. Quid anfractus
flūminum sequēris? Tenē fontem et tōtum habēs. Hoc idcircō
dīcō, quōniam memoria hominis hebes est et brevitāte gaudet,
et, sī in multa dīviditur, fit minor in singulīs. Dēbēmus ergō in
omnī doctrīnā breve aliquid et certum colligere, quod in
75 arculā memoriae recondātur, unde postmodum, cum rēs
exigit, reliqua dērīventur. Hoc etiam saepe replicāre et dē
ventre memoriae ad palātum revocāre necesse est, nē longā
intermissiōne obsoleat. Unde rogō tē, ō lēctor, nē nimium
laetēris, sī multa lēgeris, sed sī multa intellēxeris, nec tantum
80 intellēxeris, sed retinēre potueris. Aliōquī nec legere multum
prōdest, nec intellegere. Quārē superius mē dīxisse recolō eōs
quī doctrīnae operam dant ingeniō et memoriā indigēre.

12. *Dē disciplīnā.* Sapiēns quīdam, cum dē modō et fōrmā
discendī interrogārētur, "Mēns," inquit, "humilis, studium
85 quaerendī, vīta quiēta, scrūtinium tacitum, paupertās, terra
aliēna: haec reserāre solent multīs obscūra legendī." Audīerat,
putō, quod dictum est: "Mōrēs ōrnant scientiam," et ideō
praeceptīs legendī praecepta quoque vīvendī adiungit, ut et
modum vītae suae et studiī suī ratiōnem lēctor agnōscat.
90 Illaudābilis est scientia quam vīta maculat impudīca. Et idcircō
summopere cavendum eī quī quaerit scientiam, ut nōn neglegat
disciplīnam.

1 **disciplīna, -ae,** f., here = *a science, discipline;* below = *an ordered way of life, discipline*

2 **grammatica, -ae,** f., *grammar*

    dialectica, -ae, f., *dialectic, logic*

3 **arithmētica, -ae,** f., *arithmetic*

    mūsica, -ae, f., *music*

4   **Catilīnārius, -a, -um,**
     Catilinarian (i.e., Sallust's
     Bellum Catilinarium)

     Iugurthīnus, -a, -um, *Jugurthine*
     (i.e., Sallust's *Bellum
     Iugurthinum*)

     nārrātiō, -ōnis, f., *a narration,
     narrative*

5   **expositiō, -ōnis,** f., *an exposition,
     explanation*

6   **attendō, -ere,** *direct the attention
     to, attend to, consider*

     subiectus, -a, -um, *subjected,
     subject*

8   **dispositiō, -ōnis,** f., *order and
     arrangement in speech*

     duplex, -plicis, *double, twofold*

     nātūrālis, -e, *of* or *belonging to
     nature*

     vidēlicet, adv., *plainly; namely*

9   **artificiālis, -e,** *of* or *belonging to
     art*

11   **postmodum,** adv., *afterwards*

12   **inquīsītiō, -ōnis,** f., *an
     investigation, examination,
     inquiry*

13   **congruus, -a, -um,** *fit, suitable*

     ōrdinātiō, -ōnis, f., *an
     arrangement*

     dictiō, -ōnis, f., *an utterance, a
     word*

14   **quod etiam,** *etc.*: understand *id*
     as the antecedent

     cōnstructiō, -ōnis, f., *the
     grammatical connection of
     words, construction*

15   **apertus, -a, -um,** *open, clear,
     accessible*

     significātiō, -ōnis, f., *meaning*

     prīmā fronte, = *at first
     appearance*

16   **profundus, -a, -um,** *deep*

     intellegentia, -ae, f., *perception,
     understanding, knowledge*

17   **interpretātiō, -ōnis,** f.,
     explanation

18   **inquīrō, -rere,** *seek* or *search for;
     investigate*

21   **dīvīsiō, -ōnis,** f., *a division; a
     logical* or *rhetorical division*

     fīnītus, -a, -um, *well-rounded,* of
     words (LS, s.v. "finio"); *finite*
     (Latham, s.v. "finis")

     īnfīnītus, -a, -um, *boundless,
     unlimited*

22   **prōgredior, -ī,** *go out; proceed,
     advance*

23   **comprehēnsibilis, -e,** *evident*
     (to the senses); *conceivable,
     intelligible* (to the mind)

24   **nōtitia, -ae,** f., *a knowing,
     knowledge, idea, conception*

25   **pertingō, -ere,** *stretch out, extend*

     praetereā, adv., *besides, further*

26   **ūniversālis, -e,** *general, universal*

     particulāris, -e, *partial,
     particular*

27   **dēscendō, -ere,** *climb* or *come
     down, descend*

28   **dēterminō** (1), *bound, limit,
     determine*

30   **complector, -ī,** *embrace*

31   **paulātim,** adv., *little by little,
     gradually*

33   **meditātiō, -ōnis,** f., *a thinking
     over of anything, meditation;
     a preparation for anything;
     practice in anything*

33 **cōgitātiō, -ōnis,** f., *thinking,* either as the act, i.e., *reflection, meditation,* or as the result, i.e., *a thought, idea*

    frequēns, -entis, *repeated, frequent, constant*

34 **orīgō, -inis,** f., *origin, source, beginning*

36 **lēctiō, -ōnis,** f., *reading*

    stringō, -ere, *bind, tie*

    rēgula, -ae, f., *a ruler; a rule, pattern*

37 **dēcurrō, -ere,** *run* or *hasten down; run in a race; run through, traverse*

    spatium, -iī, n., *space; time, opportunity.* Note that in CL the normal construction with *spatium* would be a gerund in the gen. or *ad* + a gerund, not an infinitive. See LS, s.v. "spatium" II.A.2.a, and Blaise, §§ 327–328.

38 **aciem:** supply *mentis*

    adfīgō, -ere, *fasten to, affix* (+ acc. + dat.). How do you account for the subjunctive? See Capvt XXXIV Syntaxis.

39 **perstringō, -ere,** *touch upon.* I am inclined to take this and the following infinitives as purpose infinitives, but they could possibly be interpreted as substitutes for the supine in dependence on *dēcurrere* (see Blaise, § 330), thus also indicating purpose.

40 **penetrō** (1), *put into; pass into, penetrate*

    anceps, -cipitis, *two-headed; ambiguous*

    obscūrus, -a, -um, *dark, obscure, unintelligible*

41 **cōnsummātiō, -ōnis,** f., *a completion, consummation*

42 **familiāris, -e,** *intimate, friendly*

43 **valdē,** adv., *very much, greatly*

    reddit: take *meditātiō* as the subject

44 **trībulātiō, -ōnis,** f., *distress, trouble*

    cōnsōlātiō, -ōnis, f., *encouragement, comfort, relief.* Hugh is prob. thinking of Boethius' *Cōnsōlātiō Philosophiae* here

45 **terrēnus, -a, -um,** *of the earth, terrestrial*

    āctus, -ūs, m., *impulse, motion; act, performance*

    strepitus, -ūs, m., *any loud, uncomfortable noise*

46 **sēgregō** (1), *separate from the flock, segregate*

    dulcēdō, -inis, f., *sweetness; pleasantness, charm*

47 **praegustō** (1), *taste before.* What construction would CL have used with *facere* instead of the infinitive? See Capvt XXXVI Syntaxis

49 **pariter,** adv., *equally*

    ērudiō, -īre, *instruct, teach*

    laetitia, -ae, f., *fertility; richness, beauty; joy, delight*

    perfundō, -ere, *pour over; fill with a feeling*

50 **oblectāmentum, -ī,** n., *a delight*

51 **circumspectiō, -ōnis,** f., *an examining all around* (Souter, s.v.)

52 **scrūtātiō, -ōnis,** f., *an examining, investigating*

54 **praecipiō, -ere,** *instruct, advise, admonish, teach*

56 **moderor, -ārī,** *regulate; govern*

    cooperor, -ārī, *work together with, combine, unite*

57 **quantā:** take as an indirect question dependent on *novit,* with *Quae omnia* as the subject of *sint.* Note too the connecting relative

    admīrātiō, -ōnis, f., *admiration; wonder*

58 **attentus, -a, -um,** *attentive*

59 **in praesentī:** supply *tempore*

60 **praetermittō, -ere,** *let pass; omit*

    existimō (1), *judge, consider, deem*

62 **custōdiō, -īre,** *guard, watch, keep*

63 **commendō** (1), *entrust to the care* or *keeping of someone* or *something* (+ dat.)

64 **prōlixus, -a, -um,** *wide, broad, long*

65 **compendiōsus, -a, -um,** *abridged, brief but comprehensive*

    redigō, -ere, *bring* or *reduce to a certain condition; lessen*

66 **epilogus, -ī,** m., *the winding up of a speech, peroration*

    recapitulātiō, -ōnis, f., *a restatement of heads, summing up*

    suprādictus, -a, -um, *aforesaid, already mentioned* (Souter, s.v.)

67 **namque,** = an emphatic form of *nam*

    tractātiō, -ōnis, f., here perh. = *a commentary, explanation* (LLMA, s.v.)

68 **innītor, -ī, innixus sum,** *lean upon, rest upon* (+ abl. or dat.)

70 **fōns, fontis,** m., *a spring, fountain*

    rīvulus, -ī, m., *a brook, small stream*

    anfractus, -ūs, m., *a turning, bending, winding*

71 **idcircō,** adv., *therefore*

72 **hebes, -etis,** *blunt*

75 **arcula, -ae,** f., *a little box for valuables* or *perfume,* e.g., *a jewelry box.* Hugh here touches on mnemotechnique. See Illich, op. cit., 35–45.

    recondō, -ere, *put away, store*

76 **dērīvō** (1), *turn into another channel; divert; derive*

    replicō (1), *unroll; review*

77 **venter, -tris,** m., *the belly*

    palātum, -ī, n., *the palate,* thought of as the organ of taste

78 **intermissiō, -ōnis,** f., *an interruption*

    obsoleat here must = **obsolesceat,** > **obsolescō, -ere,** *wear out, fall into disuse, become obsolete,* although LS, s.v. "obsoleo," make the word a by-form of *obsolefaciō,* the transitive form of *obsolescō.* The word appears in no other lexicon that I have been able to consult

79 **laetor, -ārī,** (1), *rejoice*

80 **retineō, -ēre,** *keep, retain*

81 **prōsum, prōdesse,** *be useful, benefit*

81 **recolō, -ere,** here = *recall*

82 **operam dare** + dat. = *work hard at*

indigeō, -ēre, *stand in need of, require* (+ gen. or abl.)

84 **interrogō** (1), *ask, question*

85 **quiētus, -a, -um,** *quiet, peaceful, calm*

scrūtinium, -iī, n., *a search, investigation*

86 **reserō** (1), *unbolt, open; reveal*

87 **ideō,** adv., *therefore*

88 **adiungō, -ere,** *join to*

89 **agnōscō, -ere,** *recognize; understand; acknowledge*

90 **illaudābilis, -e,** *not worthy of praise*

maculō (1), *spot, stain; defile, pollute*

impudīcus, -a, -um, *shameless; unchaste, incontinent*

91 **summopere,** adv., *very much, exceedingly*

cavēre ut + subjunctive = *be sure to* (GL, § 548 N 3)

XIV. St. Bernard of Clairvaux, *Sermōnēs super Cantica Canticōrum, Sermō XI,* in Leclercq-Talbot-Rochais, 1.54–59 (see Source Texts)

The eleventh in St. Bernard's great series on the Song of Songs, this sermon encouraged the monks of Clairvaux to temper godly sorrow with thanksgiving, brought before them the cause of their thanksgiving, viz., redemption, and illustrated the happiness that will fulfil their redemption with a discussion of the redemption of the three spiritual faculties: reason, will, and memory.

I.1. Dīxī in fīne sermōnis, nec mē iterāre piget, quod cupiam omnēs vōs fierī sacrae unctiōnis participēs, illīus vidēlicet in quā Deī beneficia cum laetitiā et grātiārum āctiōne recolit sāncta dēvōtiō. Hoc enim bonum est, tum propter relevandōs

5 vītae praesentis labōrēs, quī utique tolerābiliōrēs nōbīs fīunt exsultantibus in laude Deī, tum quia nihil ita propriē quendam terrīs repraesentat caelestis habitātiōnis statum, sīcut alacritās laudantium Deum, Scrīptūrā dīcente: *Beātī quī habitant in domō tuā, Domine; in saecula saeculōrum laudābunt tē.* Dē hōc

10 praecipuē unguentō putō dīxisse prophētam: *Ecce quam bonum et quam iūcundum habitāre frātrēs in ūnum, sīcut unguentum in capite.* Neque enim priōrī vidētur congruere posse. Illud enim etsī bonum sit, nōn est tamen iūcundum, quia recordātiō peccātōrum amāritūdinem facit, nōn iūcunditātem. Sed nec

15 quī illud faciunt in ūnum habitant, cum quisque peccāta propria lūgeat atque dēplōret. Quī vērō in grātiārum āctiōne versantur, Deum sōlum intuentur et cōgitant, ac per hoc ipsī vērē habitant in ūnum. Bonum est autem quod faciunt, quia servant eī iūstissimē glōriam cuius est, et nihilōminus

20 iūcundum, quia dēlectat.

2. Quamobrem suādeō vōbīs, amīcīs meīs, reflectere interdum pedem ā molestā et anxiā recordātiōne viārum vestrārum, et ēvādere in itinera plāniōra serēniōris memoriae beneficiōrum Deī, ut quī in vōbīs cōnfundimini, ipsīus intuitū

25 respīrētis. Volō vōs experīrī illud quod sānctus prophēta cōnsulit, dīcēns: *Dēlectāre in Dominō, et dabit petītiōnēs cordis tuī.* Et quidem necessārius dolor prō peccātīs, sed sī nōn sit

continuus. Sānē interpolētur laetiōrī recordātiōne dīvīnae
benignitātis, nē forte prae trīstitiā indūrētur cor,

30   et dēspērātiōne plūs pereat. Misceāmus absinthiō mel, ut
salūbris amāritūdō salūtem dare tunc possit, cum immixtō
temperāta dulcōre bibī poterit. Audī dēnique Deum, quōmodo
ipse contrītī cordis temperat amāritūdinem, quōmodo
pusillanimem ā dēspērātiōnis barathrō revocat, quōmodo

35   blandae et fidēlis prōmissiōnis melle maerentem cōnsōlātur,
ērigit diffīdentem. Āit per prophētam: *Ego īnfrēnābō ōs
tuum laude meā, nē intereās*; hoc est: "Nē intuitū facinōrum
tuōrum nimiam incurrās trīstitiam, atque īnstar effrēnis equī
dēspērātus in praeceps ruās et pereās, frēnō tē," inquit,

40   "inhibēbō indulgentiae meae et meīs laudibus ērigam,
respīrābisque in bonīs meīs, quī dē tuīs malīs cōnfunderis,
dum mē sānē benigniōrem quam tē culpabiliōrem inveniēs."
Hōc frēnō sī īnfrēnātus fuisset Cain, nēquāquam dēspērandō
dīxisset: *Maior est inīquitās mea quam ut veniam merear*. Absit,

45   absit! Maior est eius pietās quam quaevīs inīquitās. Ideō iūstus
nōn continuē, sed tantum in prīncipiō sermōnis accūsātor
est suī; porrō autem in Deī laudēs extrēma sermōnis claudere
cōnsuēvit. Vidēte dēnique iūstum hōc ōrdine procedentem:
Cōgitāvī, āit, *viās meās, et convertī pedēs meōs in testimōnia tua*,

50   ut quī vidēlicet contrītiōnem et īnfēlīcitātem in viīs propriīs
perpessus fuerat, in viā testimōniōrum Deī dēlectārētur sīcut
in omnibus dīvitiīs. Et vōs igitur exemplō iūstī, sī dē vōbīs in
humilitāte sentītis, sentīte et dē Dominō in bonitāte. Sīc enim
legitis apud Sapientem: *Sentīte dē Dominō in bonitāte,*

55   *et in simplicitāte cordis quaerite illum*. Hoc autem facile menti
persuādet dīvīnae mūnificentiae frequēns, immō continua
recordātiō. Aliōquī quōmodo implēbitur apostolicum illud:
in omnibus grātiās agentēs, sī ea prō quibus grātiae dēbentur ā
corde recesserint? Nōlō vōs Iūdaïcō notārī opprobriō,

60   dē quibus testātur Scrīptūra quod nōn fuerint memorēs
benefactōrum eius, et mīrābilium eius quae ostendit eīs.

    II.3. Vērum quoniam bona, quae largīrī mortālibus nōn
cessat misericors et miserātor Dominus, recolere et recolligere
omnia omnī hominī impossibile est—*quis* enim *loquētur*

65   *potentiās Dominī, audītās faciet omnēs laudēs eius?*—id saltem,
quod praecipuum est et maximum, opus vidēlicet nostrae

redēmptiōnis, ā memoriā redēmptōrum aliquātenus nōn
recēdat. In quō opere duo potissimum, quae nunc occurrunt,
vestrīs studiīs intimāre cūrābō, et hoc quam paucīs ad
70 compendium poterō, memor illīus sententiae: *Dā occāsiōnem*
sapientī et sapientior erit. Duo ergō illa sunt modus et frūctus.
Et modus quidem Deī exinānītiō est, frūctus vērō nostrī dē
illō replētiō. Hoc meditārī sānctae speī sēminārium est, illud
summī amōris incentīvum. Utrumque prōfectibus
75 nostrīs necessārium, nē aut spēs mercēnāria sit, sī amōre nōn
comitētur, aut amor tepēscat, sī īnfrūctuōsus putētur.

4. Porrō frūctum tālem exspectāmus nostrī amōris, quālem
ipse quem amāmus prōmīsit: *mēnsūram,* inquiēns, *plēnam, et*
cōnfertam, et coagitātam, et supereffluentem dabunt in sinum
80 *vestrum.* Mēnsūra ista, ut audiō, erit sine mēnsūrā.

III. Sed velim scīre cuius reī futūra sit illa mēnsūra, vel
potius illa immēnsitās quae reprōmittitur: *Oculus nōn vīdit,*
Deus, absque tē, quae praeparāstī dīligentibus tē. Dīc nōbīs, tū quī
praeparās, quid praeparās? Crēdimus, cōnfīdimus rēvērā sīcut
85 prōmittis: *Replēbimur in bonīs domūs tuae.* Sed quibus, quaesō,
bonīs, vel quālibus? Forte frūmentō, vīnō et oleō, aurō atque
argentō, lapidibusve pretiōsīs? Sed haec nōvimus et vīdimus, et
vidēmus et fastīdīmus. Id quaerimus quod oculus nōn vīdit, nec
auris audīvit, nec in cor hominis ascendit. Hoc placet, hoc sapit,
90 hoc dēlectat inquīrere, quodcumque est illud. *Erunt,* inquit,
omnēs docibilēs Deī, et ipse erit omnia in omnibus. Ut audiō,
plēnitūdō quam exspectāmus ā Deō, nōn erit nisi dē Deō.

5. Quis vērō comprehendat quam magna multitūdō
dulcēdinis in brevī istō sermōne comprehēnsa sit: *Erit Deus*
95 *omnia in omnibus?* Ut dē corpore taceam, in animā tria intueor,
ratiōnem, voluntātem, memoriam, et haec tria ipsam animam
esse. Quantum cuīque hōrum in praesentī saeculō dēsit dē
integritāte suā et perfectiōne, sentit omnis quī ambulat in
spīritū. Quārē hoc, nisi quia Deus nōndum est omnia in
100 omnibus? Hinc est quod et ratiō saepissimē in iūdiciīs fallitur,
et voluntās quadruplicī perturbātiōne iactātur, et memoria
multiplicī oblīviōne cōnfunditur. Triplicī huic vānitātī nōbilis
creātūra subiecta est nōn volēns, in spē tamen. Nam quī replet
in bonīs dēsīderium animae, ipse ratiōnī futūrus est plēnitūdō
105 lūcis, ipse voluntātī multitūdō pācis, ipse memoriae continuātiō

aeternitātis. Ō vēritās, cāritās, aeternitās! Ō beāta et beātificāns
Trīnitās! Ad tē mea misera trīnitās miserābiliter suspīrat,
quoniam ā tē īnfēlīciter exsulat. Discēdēns ā tē, quantīs sē
intrīcāvit errōribus, dolōribus, timōribus! Heu mē! Quālem
110   prō tē commūtāvimus trīnitātem! *Cor meum conturbātum
est,* et inde dolor; dērelīquit mē virtūs mea, et inde pavor; *et
lūmen oculōrum meōrum nōn est mēcum,* et inde error. Ēn quam
dissimilem Trīnitātem, ō animae meae trīnitās, exsulāns
offendistī.

115   6. Vērumtamen quārē trīstis es, anima mea, et quārē
conturbās mē? Spērā in Deō, quoniam adhūc cōnfitēbor
illī, cum error vidēlicet ē ratiōne, ā voluntāte dolor, atque
ā memoriā timor omnis recesserit, et successerit illa quam
spērāmus mīra serēnitās, plēna suāvitās, aeterna sēcūritās.
120   Prīmum illud faciet vēritās Deus, secundum cāritās Deus,
tertium summa potestās Deus, ut sit Deus omnia in omnibus,
ratiōne recipiente lūcem inexstinguibilem, voluntāte pācem
imperturbābilem cōnsequente, memoriā fontī indēficientī
aeternāliter inhaerente. Vīderitis vōs, rēctēne prīmum illud
125   Fīliō, Spīrituī Sānctō sequens, Patrī ultimum assignētis, sīc
tamen, ut nihil hōrum vel Patrī, vel Fīliō, vel Spīrituī Sānctō
subtrahātis, nē cui forte persōnārum aut plēnitūdinem minuat
distinctiō, aut proprietātem tollat perfectiō. Simul et hoc
advertite, quid simile filiī huius saeculī experiantur dē
130   carnis illecebrīs, dē mundī spectāculīs et dē pompīs Satanae,
cum tamen hoc tōtum sit, unde vīta praesēns ēlūdit miserōs
amātōrēs suōs, dīcente Iōanne: *Quidquid in hōc mundō est,
concupiscentia carnis est, et concupiscentia oculōrum, et ambitiō
saeculī.* Haec dē redēmptiōnis frūctū.

135   7. In modō quoque, quem, sī recolitis, Deī esse
exinānītiōnem dēfinīvimus, tria item praecipuē vōbīs intuenda
commendō. Nōn enim simplex aut modica illa exinānītiō fuit;
sed sēmetipsum exinānīvit usque ad carnem, ad mortem, ad
crucem. Quis dignē penset quantae fuerit humilitātis,
140   mansuētūdinis, dignātiōnis Dominum maiestātis carne induī,
multārī morte, turpārī cruce? Sed dīcit aliquis, "Nōn valuit
opus suum reparāre Creātor absque istā difficultāte?" Valuit,
sed māluit cum iniūriā suī, nē pessimum atque odiōsissimum
vitium ingrātitūdinis occāsiōnem ultrā reperīret in homine.

145 Sānē multum fatīgātiōnis assūmpsit, quō multae dīlēctiōnis
hominem dēbitōrem tenēret, commonēretque grātiārum
āctiōnis difficultās redēmptiōnis, quem minus esse dēvōtum
fēcerat conditiōnis facilitās. Quid enim dīcēbat homō creātus
et ingrātus? "Grātis quidem condītus sum, sed nūllō
150 auctōris gravāmine vel labōre: sīquidem dīxit, et factus sum,
quemadmodum et ūniversa. Quid magnum est, quamlibet
magnā in verbī facilitāte dōnāveris?" Sīc beneficium creātiōnis
attenuāns hūmāna impietās, ingrātitūdinis māteriam inde
sūmēbat, unde amōris causam habēre dēbuerat, idque ad
155 excūsandās excūsātiōnēs in peccātīs. Sed obstructum est ōs
loquentium inīqua. Lūce clārius patet, quantum modo prō tē,
ō homō, dispendium fēcit: dē Dominō servus, dē dīvite pauper,
carō dē Verbō, et dē Deī Fīliō hominis fierī fīlius nōn dēspēxit.
Mementō iam tē, etsī dē nihilō factum, nōn tamen dē nihilō
160 redēmptum. Sex diēbus condidit omnia, et tē inter omnia.
At vērō per tōtōs trīgintā annōs operātus est salūtem tuam
in mediō terrae. Ō quantum labōrāvit sustinēns! Carnis
necessitātēs, hostis temptātiōnēs nōnne sibi crucis aggravāvit
ignōminia, mortis cumulāvit horrōre? Necessariē quidem.
165 Sīc, sīc hominēs et iūmenta salvāstī, Domine, quemadmodum
multiplicāstī misericordiam tuam, Deus.
    8. Haec meditāminī, in hīs versāminī. Tālibus odōrāmentīs
refovēte viscera vestra, quae diū torsit odor molestior
peccātōrum, ut abundētis et hīs unguentīs nōn minus suāvibus
170 quam salūtāribus. Nec tamen adhūc vōs putētis habēre illa
optima, quae in spōnsae ūberibus commendantur. Dē quibus
incipere modo, fīniendī iam sermōnis angustia prohibet. Quae
dicta sunt dē aliīs tenēte memoriā, probāte vītā; et dē hīs iuvāte
mē precibus vestrīs, ut dignē loquī possim quod et dignum sit
175 tantīs spōnsae dēliciīs, et vestrās animās ad amōrem aedificet
spōnsī, Iēsū Chrīstī Dominī nostrī.

1   **sermōnis:** here = *sermon.* The reference is to the previous sermon in the series

2   **unctiō, -ōnis,** f., *an anointing*
     particeps, -ipis, m., *a sharing, participating; a sharer, participant*

vidēlicet, adv., *plainly; namely*

3   **laetitia, -ae,** f., *fertility; richness; joy, delight*
     āctiō, -ōnis, f., *action, doing* (cf. the idiom *grātiās agere*)
     recolō, -ere, *cultivate again; reflect on, recall*

4   **dēvōtiō, -ōnis,** f., *a consecrating, devoting; sorcery; any form of prayer, devotion*

tum . . . tum, *first . . . then, both . . . and*

5   **praesēns, -entis,** *present*

utique, adv., *at any rate, certainly*

tolerābilis, -e, *bearable, endurable*

6   **exsultō** (1), *jump up and down; rejoice greatly, exult*

7   **repraesentō** (1), *make present again, bring back before the eyes* or *mind*

habitātiō, -ōnis, f., *an inhabiting; a habitation*

status, -ūs, m., *a state, condition*

alacritās, -tātis, f., *liveliness ardor, eagerness*

8   **habitō** (1), *inhabit; dwell* (Ps. 83:5)

10 **praecipuē,** adv., *especially, chiefly*

unguentum, -ī, n., *an ointment, perfume*

10–12 **Ecce . . . capite:** Ps. 132:1–2

12 **congruō, -ere,** *correspond with, agree with* (+ dat.)

14 **amāritūdō, -inis,** f., *bitterness of taste; bitterness, sorrow*

16 **lūgeō, -ēre,** *mourn; lament, bewail*

dēplōrō (1), *weep bitterly, lament, deplore*

17 **versō** (1), *turn hither and thither;* (pass. in middle sense) *be engaged* or *employed in*

intueor, -ērī, *look at with attention, contemplate*

19 **nihilōminus,** adv., *nonetheless*

21 **quamobrem,** adv., *wherefore*

suādeō, -ēre, *recommend, advise; convince, persuade* (+ dat.; the construction with the inf. is CL)

reflectō, -ere, *bend* or *turn back*

22 **anxius, -a, -um,** *anxious, uneasy*

23 **ēvādō, -ere,** *go out, climb out, escape*

plānus, -a, -um, *even, level, flat*

serēnus, -a, -um, *bright, serene*

24 **cōnfundō, -ere,** *pour together; throw into disorder; trouble, disturb, confound*

intuitus, -ūs, m., *a look;* (abl. sg.) *with respect to, in consideration of* (LS, s.v.), *in the sight of* (Latham, s.v.), *in the favorable regard of* (LLMA, s.v.)

25 **respirō** (1), *breathe again; recover*

26 **dēlectāre:** take as a passive imperative, = *be delighted (by)* (Ps. 36:4)

petītiō, -ōnis, f., *a request, petition*

28 **continuus, -a, -um,** *unbroken, uninterrupted*

sānē, adv., *indeed*

interpolō (1), *give a new form* or *appearance to a thing*

29 **benignitās, -tātis,** f., *kindness; generosity*

forte, adv., *by chance, accidentally*

prae: here = *on account of* (as often with a neg.)

trīstitia, -ae, f., *sadness, melancholy, dejection*

indūrō (1), *harden*

30 **dēspērātiō, -ōnis,** f., *hopelessness, despair*

absinthium, -iī, n., *wormwood,* a name for certain kinds of bitter, tonic herbs used (nowadays) in aperitifs and (formerly) in medicines

31 **immisceō, -ēre, -uī, -mixtum,** *mix in, intermingle*

32 **temperō** (1), *moderate; mix properly, temper; mix a drink*

dulcor, -ōris, m., *sweetness*

33 **contrītus, -a, -um,** *worn out; trite; contrite*

34 **pusillanimis, -e,** *fainthearted, timid*

barathrum, -ī, n., *a pit, abyss*

35 **blandus, -a, -um,** *flattering, pleasant, agreeable*

prōmissiō, -ōnis, f., *a promise*

maerēns, -entis, *sad, sorrowful*

cōnsōlor, -ārī, *console, comfort, encourage*

36 **ērigō, -ere,** *set upright, lift up; encourage, cheer*

diffīdēns, -entis, *without self-confidence, diffident*

īnfrēnō (1), *rein in; restrain* (Is. 48:9)

37 **intereō, -īre,** *perish, die*

facinus, -oris, n., *a deed; a bad deed, crime*

38 **nimius, -a, -um,** *very great, very much*

incurrō, -ere, *run into; meet*

īnstar, n. (only nom. and acc. sg.), usu. with gen. = *corresponding to, like*

effrēnus, -a, -um, *unbridled, unrestrained*

39 **dēspērō** (1), *be wihout hope, despair*

praeceps, -itis, n., *a steep place, precipice*

frēnō (1), *bridle, curb*

40 **inhibeō, -ēre,** *hold in* or *back, restrain*

indulgentia, -ae, f., *tenderness, gentleness* (take as a dat. of purpose or object for which)

42 **benignus, -a, -um,** *kind; generous*

culpābilis, -e, *blameworthy, culpable*

43 **frēnum, -ī,** n., *bridle, bit*

Cain, indecl. Heb. name m., *Cain*

nēquāquam, adv., *not at all*

dēspērandō: in Late Latin, the abl. gerund can express any circumstance, and consequently often replaces the pres. part. (Blaise, § 343; Appendix I, § 62)

44 **inīquitās, -tātis,** f., *unequalness; unevenness; difficulty; injustice*

mereor, -ērī, *deserve, earn, merit* (Gen. 4:13). Take the *ut-*clause as an explanatory consecutive (result) clause expressing disproportion (GL, §§ 557 N 2, and 298)

45 **pietās, -tātis,** f., *pity, compassion* (LLMA, s.v.)

quīvīs, quaevīs, quodvīs, *any you will, any whatever*

ideō, adv., *therefore*

45–47 **Ideō . . . suī:** cf. Prov. 18:17

46 **continuē,** adv., *without interruption*

47 **porrō,** adv., *further; afterwards*

48 **prōcēdō, -ere,** *go out, proceed, advance*

49　**testimōnium, -iī,** n., *evidence, proof, testimony* (Ps. 118:59)

50　**contrītiō, -ōnis,** f., *a grinding; contrition, grief*

　　īnfēlīcitās, -tātis, f., *unhappiness, misfortune*

51　**perpetior, -ī, -pessus sum,** *endure*

52　**dīvitiae, -ārum,** f., *riches, wealth*

53　**humilitās, -tatis,** f., *a being near to the ground; humility*

　　bonitās, -tātis, f., *goodness, excellence; kindness, benevolence*

55　**simplicitās, -tātis,** f., *simplicity, simpleness; straightforwardness* (Wis. 1:1)

56　**mūnificentia, -ae,** f., *generosity*

　　frequēns, -entis, *repeated, frequent*

57　**apostolicus, -a, -um,** *apostolic*

58　**in . . . agentēs:** I Thess. 5:18

59　**Iūdaïcus, -a, -um,** *Jewish*

　　notō (1), *mark out, distinguish* (+ abl. of means)

60　**testor, -ārī,** *make known, declare* (cf. Ps. 77:11)

61　**benefacta, -ōrum,** n., *good deeds, benefits*

62　**largior, -ī,** *bestow* or *grant abundantly*

63　**cessō** (1), *delay* or *cease work at* (+ inf.)

　　misericors, -cordis, *merciful, compassionate*

　　miserātor, -ōris, m., *one who pities, a commiserator*

　　recolligō, -ere, *gather together again*

65　**potentia, -ae,** f., *power; ability; political power, influence* (used in the pl. by Cicero: this is prob. the meaning here, as it translates LXX δυναστείας, Ps. 105:2)

　　saltem, adv., *at least*

66　**praecipuus, -a, -um,** *special; extraordinary*

67　**redēmptiō, -ōnis,** f., *a buying up; a ransoming, redemption*

　　redimō, -ere, -ēmī, -ēmptum, m., *buy back, redeem*

　　aliquātenus, adv., *in some measure*

68　**potissimum,** adv., *chiefly*

　　occurrō, -ere, *run to meet; come into one's thoughts, occur*

69　**intimō** (1), *put into; publish, make known*

　　quam is sometimes used "in mere intensive expressions" = *exceedingly, very, quite* (LS, s.v. II.B)

　　quam paucīs [verbīs], = *with very few words*

70　**compendium, -iī,** n., *a shortening, abridgement*

　　poterō: supply *facere*

70–71　**Dā . . . erit:** Prov. 9:9

72　**exinānītiō, -ōnis,** f., *an emptying*

73　**replētiō, -ōnis,** f., *a filling again* or *up*

　　sēminārium, -iī, n., *a nursery garden, seed-plot*

74　**incentīvum, -ī,** n., *that which provokes, an incentive*

　　uterque, utraque, utrumque, *each of two, both*

prōfectus, -ūs, m., *advance, progress, increase, growth*

75 **mercēnārius, -a, -um,** *paid, mercenary*

76 **comitor, -ārī,** *accompany, follow*

tepescō, -ere, *grow warm* (not hot); *cool down*

īnfrūctuōsus, -a, -um, *unfruitful; fruitless*

77 **quālis, -e,** correl. with *tālis, such as, as*

78 **mēnsūra, -ae,** f., *a measuring; a measure*

inquiēns, = pres. part. of *inquit* in EL

79 **cōnfertus, -a, -um,** *densely packed* or *compressed*

coagitō, -āre, —, -ātum, *shake together*

supereffluō, -ere, *superabound, overflow* (Luke 6:38)

sinus, -ūs, m., *a curve, fold; the fold of the toga,* which served as a carrying place

82 **immēnsitās, -tātis,** f., *immeasurableness, immensity*

reprōmittō, -ere, *promise in return*

83 **absque,** prep. + abl., *without*

praeparō (1), *make ready, prepare* (Is. 64:4)

84 **rēvērā,** adv., *in truth*

85 **repleō, -ēre,** *fill again, fill up* (Ps. 64:5)

86 **frūmentum, -ī,** n., *grain*

oleum, -ī, n., *olive oil, oil*

87 **lapis, -idis,** m., *a stone*

pretiōsus, -a, -um, *costly, precious*

88 **fastīdiō, -īre,** *loathe; be averse to*

89 **ascendō, -ere, -scendī,** *go up, ascend* (cf. I Cor. 2:9)

sapit, perh. here = *is savory*

90 **inquīrō, -ere,** *seek* or *search for* (take as subject of the three preceding verbs)

quīcumque, quaecumque, quodcumque, *whoever, whatever*

91 **docilis,** *teachable, docile* (Jn. 6:45)

92 **plēnitūdō, -inis,** f., *fullness; abundance*

93 **multitūdō, -inis,** f., *a great number, multitude; a manifold variety, multiplicity* (LLMA, s.v.)

94 **dulcēdō, -inis,** f., *sweetness; charm*

94–95 **Erit . . . omnibus:** I Cor. 15:28

95–97 **Ut . . . esse:** B. here employs the triad discovered by St. Augustine (cf. Capvt XXXIV, Sentence 14).[47]

97 **dēsum, -esse,** *be away* or *absent; fail, be wanting*

97–99 **Quantum . . . spiritū:** cf. Gal. 5:16, 25

98 **integritās, -tātis,** f., *soundness, health; uprightness, integrity*

perfectiō, -ōnis, f., *completion, perfection*

---

47 On whether B.'s use of this triad is more than merely formal, see my "Saint Bernard's Anthropology: Traditional and Systematic," *Cistercian Studies Quarterly* 46 (2011), 415–428 (esp. 421–427).

100 **fallō, -ere,** *deceive*

101 **quadruplēx, -plicis,** *fourfold, quadruple*

   perturbātiō, -ōnis, f., *confusion, disorder; a passion, emotion.* Note that the four passions in Hellenistic philosophy were desire and fear, pleasure and pain, the fulfilment of the first yielding the third, of the second, the fourth.

   iactō (1), *fling* or *throw around*

102 **multiplex, -plicis,** *having many folds, manifold*

   oblīviō, -ōnis, f., *forgetfulness*

   triplex, -plicis, *threefold, triple*

   vānitās, -tātis, f., *emptiness; unreality, untruth; vanity, boasting*

   nōbilis, -e, *well-known; noble*

103 **subiciō, -ere, -iēcī, -iectum,** *throw under; subject*

104 **dēsīderium, -iī,** n., *a desire* or *longing* for an absent or lost person or thing

105 **continuātiō, -ōnis,** f., *a following of one thing after another, an unbroken series*

106 **aeternitās, -tātis,** f., *eternity, immortality*

   beātificō (1), *make happy, bless*

107 **trīnitās, -tātis,** f., *a triad; the (Holy) Trinity*

   miserābilis, -e, *wretched, sad*

   suspīrō (1), *take a deep breath, sigh; long for*

108 **īnfēlīciter,** adv., *unluckily, unfortunately*

   exsulō (1), *be banished, live in exile*

discēdēns: is this usage of the pres. partic. an example of the usage noticed in Appendix I, § 57?

109 **intrīcō** (1), *entangle, confuse*

   Heu mē!: = *Ah, me!* The acc. is used to express the object of "thought, perception, or emotion" in an exclamation (GL, § 343.1).

110 **commūtō** (1), *change; exchange*

111 **inde,** adv., *thence*

   dērelinquō, -ere, -līquī, *leave, abandon, forsake*

   pavor, -ōris, m., *a fearful trembling*

112 **lūmen, -inis,** n., *light*

   ēn, = *ecce*

114 **offendō, -ere, -fendī,** *offend, displease*

115 **vērumtamen,** adv., *but yet, nevertheless*

116–17 **Spērā . . . illī:** cf. Ps. 41:6

118 **succēdō, -ere, -cessī,** *go under; go out from under; go after; succeed*

119 **serēnitās, -tātis,** f., *clearness, serenity*

   suāvitās, -tātis, f., *sweetness, pleasantness*

   sēcūritās, -tātis, f., *freedom from care*

122 **inexstinguibilis, -e,** *inextinguishable*

123 **imperturbābilis, -e,** *that cannot be disturbed, imperturbable*

   cōnsequor, -ī, *get, obtain*

   fōns, fontis, m., *a spring, fountain*

indēficiēns, -entis, *unfailing*

124 **aeternālis, -e,** *enduring forever*

inhaereō, -ēre, *cling* or *cleave to*
(+ dat.)

vīderitis: take as a potential
subjunctive, = *you would see,
know* (GL, § 257.2)

125 **assignō** (1), *allot; ascribe*

127 **subtrahō, -ere,** *draw away
secretly, remove*

128 **distinctiō, -ōnis,** f., *a distinction*

propriētās, -tātis, f., *a property,
peculiarity*

simul, adv., *at the same time*

129 **advertō, -ere,** *turn towards; turn
one's attention to, observe*

130 **illecebra, -ae,** f., *an enticement,
allurement*

pompa, -ae, f., *a solemn
procession; a retinue; a display,
ostentation*

Satanas, -ae, m., *Satan*

131 **ēlūdō, -ere,** *elude; delude*

132 **amātor, -ōris,** m., *a friend; a
lover*

Iōannes, -is, m., *John*

Quidquid . . . saeculi, I Jn. 2:16,
with slight changes

133 **concupiscentia, -ae,** f., *an eager
desire, longing, concupiscence*

134 **Haec . . . frūctū:** a conventional
conclusion of an argument

136 **dēfīniō, -īre, -īvī,** *set limits;
define* (B. is referring to a
previous sermon in the series)

137 **commendō** (1), *commit;
recommend*

modicus, -a, -um, *moderate;
temperate; ordinary*

138 **-met,** an intensive pronominal
enclitic, *self* (with forms of *ipse,*
it is doubly intensive)

139 **crux, crucis,** f., *a cross* (cf. Phil.
2:7f.)

pensō (1), *weigh carefully;
ponder*

quantae: take *quantae,* and the
nouns in the genitive which it
modies, as predicate genitives
(Capvt XXV Syntaxis).
The subject of *fuerit* is each
one of the acc. and infin.
constructions that follows

140 **mansuētūdō, -inis,** f., *mildness,
gentleness, clemency*

dignātiō, -ōnis, f., *respect,
esteem; dignity, honor*

induō, -ere, *clothe, surround; put
on, assume* (+ abl.)

141 **turpō** (1), *befoul, defile; disgrace,
dishonor*

142 **reparō** (1), *restore, renew*

difficultās, -tātis, f., *need,
trouble, difficulty*

143 **odiōsus, -a, -um,** *hateful, odious*

144 **ingrātitūdō, -inis,** f.,
unthankfulness, ingratitude

145 **fatīgātiō, -ōnis,** f., *weariness*

assūmō, -ere, -sūmpsī, *take to
oneself*

quō, = *ut* (usu. with a
comparative, but not always)

145 **dīlēctiō, -ōnis,** f., *love*

146 **dēbitor, -ōris,** m., *a debtor*

commoneō, -ēre, *remind one of*
(+ gen.)

147 **dēvōtus, -a, -um,** *devout, faithful*

148 **conditiō, -ōnis,** f., *a making,
creating*

facilitās, -tātis, f., *easiness, ease*

149 **grātīs,** adv., *for nothing, gratis*

150 **gravāmen, -inis,** n., *trouble*

    sīquidem, conj., *if indeed; since*

151 **ūniversī, -ae, -a,** *all together*

    quamlibet, adv., *how much soever, however much* (take the subjunctive as potential)

152 **creātiō, -ōnis,** f., *a creating, producing*

153 **attenuō** (1), *make thin or weak; weaken, diminish*

    impietās, -tātis, f., *ungodliness, impiety*

155 **excūsō** (1), *excuse; allege or plead as an excuse* (take **excūsātiōnēs** as an internal acc.; cf. Ps. 140:4)

    obstruō, -ere, -xī, -ctum, *stop up, hinder, impede*

155–56 **Sed . . . inīqua:** cf. Ps. 62:12

157 **dispendium, -iī,** n., *expense, cost*

158 **dēspiciō, -ere, -spēxī,** *look down upon; despise, disdain*

159 **mementō:** from *memini;* for the form, see Capvt XXVIII Syntaxis

161 **operor, -ārī, -ātus sum,** *work, be active, operate*

163 **necessitās, -tātis,** f., *necessity, exigency; fate;* (pl.) *necessary things; need, want*

    aggravō (1), *make heavier; make worse; oppress*

164 **ignōminia, -ae,** f., *disgrace, ignominy*

    cumulō (1), *heap up, accumulate, increase*

    horror, -ōris, m., *a bristling; shaking; dread; a horror*

165 **iūmentum, -ī,** n., *a draft-animal*

    salvō (1), *save*

166 **multiplicō** (1), *multiply, increase* (cf. Ps. 35:7–8)

167 **versor, -ārī,** *dwell, live; occupy or busy oneself*

    odōrāmentum, -ī, n., *a perfume, spice*

168 **refoveō, -ēre,** *refresh, revive*

    viscera, -um, n. pl., *the inward parts of the animal body, inwards, viscera*

    torqueō, -ēre, torsī, *twist, bend, wind*

    odor, -ōris, m., *a smell, scent, odor*

169 **abundō** (1), *overflow, abound*

170 **salūtāris, -e,** *healthful, wholesome, salutary*

    adhūc, adv., *until now, as yet*

171 **spōnsa, -ae,** f., *a betrothed woman, a bride*

    ūber, -eris, n., *the organ with which a female mammal nourishes her young, a teat, udder, breast*

172 **fīniō, -īre,** *limit, enclose within limits; restrain, check; finish; terminate*

    angustia, -ae, f., *narrowness* (of space); *shortness* (of time)

175 **dēliciae, -ārum,** f. pl., *delights, pleasures, charms*

    aedificō (1), *build, erect, establish; instruct, edify*

176 **spōnsus, -ī,** m., *a betrothed man, a bridegroom*

XV. THREE READINGS FROM ST. THOMAS AQUINAS

A. Summa Theologiae, Prīma Pars, Quaestiō 66, Articulus 1, in Caramello, 321–323 (see Source Texts)

The following is the first article from the question Dē ōrdine creātiōnis ad distīnctiōnem,[48] *in which Thomas addresses problems regarding the divisions that God made in material creation. In this article, we see him reconciling the Fathers of the Church, as well as other authoritative figures, a fundamental scholastic task. His humility and fairness are remarkable.*

Utrum īnfōrmitās māteriae tempore praecesserit fōrmātiōnem ipsīus

Ad prīmum sīc prōcēditur. Vidētur quod īnfōrmitās māteriae tempore praecesserit fōrmātiōnem ipsīus.

5   **1.** Dicitur enim *Gen.* 1, [2]: *Terra erat inānis et vacua,* sive *invīsibilis et incomposita,* secundum aliam litteram, per quod dēsignātur īnfōrmitās māteriae, ut Augustīnus dīcit. Ergō māteria fuit aliquandō īnfōrmis, antequam fōrmārētur.

    2. Praetereā, nātūra in suā operātiōne Deī operātiōnem
10   imitātur, sīcut causa secunda imitātur causam prīmam. Sed in operātiōne nātūrae īnfōrmitās tempore praecēdit fōrmātiōnem. Ergō et in operātiōne Deī.

    3. Praetereā, māteria potior est accidente, quia māteria est pars substantiae. Sed Deus potest facere quod accidēns sit sine
15   subiectō, ut patet in Sacrāmentō Altāris. Ergō potuit facere quod māteria esset sine fōrmā.

    Sed contrā, imperfectiō effectūs attestātur imperfectiōnī agentis. Sed Deus est agēns perfectissimum, unde dē eō dīcitur, *Deut.* 32, [4]: *Deī perfecta sunt opera.* Ergō opus ab eō creātum
20   numquam fuit īnfōrme.

    Praetereā, creātūrae corporālis fōrmātiō facta fuit per opus distīnctiōnis. Distīnctiōnī autem oppōnitur cōnfūsiō, sīcut et fōrmātiōnī īnfōrmitās. Sī ergō īnfōrmitās praecessit tempore fōrmātiōnem māteriae, sequitur ā prīncipiō fuisse cōnfūsiōnem
25   corporālis creātūrae, quam antīquī vocāvērunt *Chaos.*

---

[48]   Notes on this title: **creātiō, -ōnis,** f., *a creating, producing; ad,* here = in relation to, with regard to, and **distīnctiō, -ōnis,** f., *separation, division, distinction; unlikeness, difference.*

Respondeō dīcendum quod circā hoc sunt dīversae
opīniōnēs Sānctōrum. **Augustīnus** enim **vult quod
īnfōrmitās māteriae corporālis nōn praecesserit tempore
fōrmātiōnem ipsīus, sed sōlum orīgine vel ōrdine nātūrae.**

30 Aliī vērō, ut **Basilīus, Ambrosius, et Chrȳsostomus,
volunt quod īnfōrmitās māteriae tempore praecesserit
fōrmātiōnem.** Et quamvīs hae opīniōnēs videantur esse
contrāriae, tamen parum ab invicem differunt. Aliter enim
accipit īnfōrmitātem māteriae Augustīnus quam aliī.

35 Augustīnus enim accipit īnfōrmitātem māteriae prō carentiā
omnis fōrmae. Et sīc impossibile est dīcere quod īnfōrmitās
māteriae tempore praecesserit vel fōrmātiōnem ipsīus vel
distīnctiōnem. Et dē fōrmātiōne quidem manifestum est. Sī
enim māteria īnfōrmis praecessit dūrātiōne, haec erat iam in

40 āctū. Hoc enim dūrātiō importat. Creātiōnis enim terminus est
ēns āctū. Ipsum autem quod est āctus, est fōrma. Dīcere igitur
māteriam praecēdere sine fōrmā, est dīcere ēns āctū sine āctū,
quod implicat contrādictiōnem. — Nec etiam potest dīcī quod
habuit aliquam fōrmam commūnem, et postmodum

45 supervēnērunt eī fōrmae dīversae, quibus sit distīncta. Quia
hoc esset idem cum opīniōne antīquōrum Nātūrālium, quī
posuērunt māteriam prīmam esse aliquod corpus in āctū,
putā ignem, āerem aut aquam, aut aliquod medium. Ex quō
sequēbātur quod fierī nōn esset, nisi alterārī. Quia, cum illa

50 forma praecēdēns daret esse in āctū in genere substantiae, et
faceret esse hoc aliquid, sequēbātur quod superveniēns fōrma
nōn faceret simpliciter ēns āctū, sed ēns āctū hoc, quod est
proprium fōrmae accidentālis; et sīc sequentēs fōrmae essent
accidentia, secundum quae nōn attenditur generātiō, sed

55 alterātiō. Unde oportet dīcere quod māteria prīma neque fuit
creāta omnīnō sine fōrmā, neque sub fōrmā ūnā commūnī, sed
sub fōrmīs distīnctīs. — Et ita, sī īnfōrmitās māteriae referātur
ad conditiōnem prīmae māteriae, quae secundum sē nōn habet
aliquam fōrmam, īnfōrmitās māteriae nōn praecessit

60 fōrmātiōnem seu distīnctiōnem ipsīus tempore, ut Augustīnus
dīcit, sed orīgine seu nātūrā tantum, eō modō quō potentia est
prior āctū, et pars tōtō.
 Aliī vērō Sānctī accipiunt īnfōrmitātem, nōn secundum
quod exclūdit omnem fōrmam, sed secundum quod exclūdit

65   istam fōrmōsitātem et decōrem quī nunc appāret in corporeā
      creātūrā. Et secundum hoc dīcunt quod īnfōrmitās māteriae
      corporālis dūrātiōne praecessit fōrmātiōnem eiusdem. Et
      sīc secundum hoc, quantum ad aliquid cum eīs Augustīnus
      concordat, et quantum ad aliquid discordat, ut īnfrā patēbit.
70   Et quantum ex litterā *Genesis* 1, [2] accipī potest, triplex
      fōrmōsitās dēerat, propter quod dīcēbātur creātūra corporālis
      īnfōrmis. Dēerat enim ā tōtō corpore diaphanō, quod dīcitur
      caelum, pulchritūdō lūcis, unde dīcitur quod *tenebrae erant*
      super faciem abyssī. Dēerat autem terrae duplex pulchritūdō.
75   Ūna, quam habet ex hōc quod est aquīs discooperta. Et
      quantum ad hoc dīcitur quod *terra erat inānis* sīve *invīsibilis,*
      quia corporālī aspectuī patēre nōn poterat, propter aquās
      undique eam cooperientēs. Alia vērō, quam habet ex hōc quod
      est ōrnāta herbīs et plantīs. Et ideō dīcitur quod erat *vacua,*
80   vel *incomposita,* id est nōn ōrnata, secundum aliam litteram.
      Et sīc, cum praemisisset duās nātūrās creātās, scīlicet caelum
      et terram, īnfōrmitātem caelī expressit per hoc quod dīxit,
      tenebrae erant super faciem abyssī, secundum quod sub caelō
      etiam āēr inclūditur. Īnfōrmitātem vērō terrae, per hoc quod
85   dīxit, *terra erat inānis et vacua.*
           Ad prīmum ergō dīcendum quod *terra* aliter accipitur in
      locō istō ab Augustīnō, et ab aliīs Sānctīs. Augustīnus enim
      vult quod nōmine terrae et aquae significētur in hōc locō ipsa
      māteria prīma. Nōn enim poterat Mōӱses rudī populō prīmam
90   māteriam exprimere, nisi sub similitūdine rērum eīs nōtārum.
      Unde et sub multiplicī similitūdine eam exprimit, nōn vocāns
      eam tantum aquam vel tantum terram, nē videātur secundum
      reī vēritātem māteria prīma esse vel terra vel aqua. Habet
      tamen similitūdinem cum terrā, inquantum subsīdet fōrmīs;
95   et cum aquā, inquantum est apta fōrmārī dīversīs fōrmīs.
      Secundum hoc ergō, dīcitur terra *inānis et vacua,* vel *invīsibilis*
      et incomposita, quia māteria per fōrmam cognōscitur (unde in
      sē cōnsīderātā dīcitur *invīsibilis* vel *inānis*), et eius potentia per
      fōrmam replētur (unde et Platō māteriam dīcit esse *locum*). —
100   Aliī vērō Sānctī per terram intellegunt ipsum elementum. Quae
      quāliter secundum eōs erat īnfōrmis, dictum est.
           Ad secundum dīcendum quod nātūra prōdūcit effectum in
      āctū dē ente in potentiā: et ideō oportet ut in eius operātiōne

potentia tempore praecēdat āctum, et īnfōrmitās fōrmātiōnem.

105 Sed Deus prōdūcit ēns āctū ex nihilō: et ideō statim potest
prōdūcere rem perfectam, secundum magnitūdinem viae
virtūtis.

    Ad tertium dīcendum quod accidēns, cum sit fōrma, est
āctus quīdam. Māteria autem secundum id quod est, est ēns in

110 potentiā. Unde magis repugnat esse in āctū māteriae sine fōrmā
quam accidentī sine subiectō.

    Ad primum vērō quod obicitur in contrārium, dīcendum
est quod sī, secundum aliōs Sānctōs, īnfōrmitās tempore
praecessit fōrmātiōnem māteriae, nōn fuit hoc ex impotentiā

115 Deī, sed ex eius sapientiā, ut ōrdō servārētur in rērum
conditiōne, dum ex imperfectō ad perfectum addūcerentur.

    Ad secundum dīcendum quod quīdam antīquōrum
Nātūrālium posuērunt cōnfūsiōnem exclūdentem omnem
distīnctiōnem, praeter hoc quod Anaxagoras posuit sōlum

120 intellēctum distīnctum et immixtum. Sed ante opus
distīnctiōnis Scrīptūra sacra pōnit [*Gen.* 1:1–2] multiplicem
distīnctiōnem. Prīmō quidem, caelī et terrae (in quō ostenditur
distīnctiō etiam secundum māteriam, ut infrā patēbit), et hoc
cum dīcit, *In prīncipiō Deus creāvit caelum et terram.* —

125 Secundō, distīnctiōnem elementōrum quantum ad fōrmās
suās, per hoc quod nōminat terram et aquam. Āerem autem
et ignem nōn nōminat, quia nōn est ita manifestum rudibus,
quibus Mō̄ysēs loquēbātur, huiusmodī esse corpora, sīcut
manifestum est dē terrā et aquā. Quamvīs Platō āerem

130 intellēxerit significārī per hoc quod dīcitur *spīritus Dominī*
(quia etiam āēr *spīritus* dīcitur), ignem vērō intellēxerit
significārī per caelum (quod igneae nātūrae esse dīxit), ut
Augustīnus refert in VIII librō *Dē cīv. Deī.* Sed Rabbi Mō̄ysēs,
in aliīs cum Platōne concordāns, dīcit ignem significārī per

135 *tenebrās*, quia, ut dīcit, in propriā sphaerā ignis nōn lūcet.
Sed magis vidētur esse conveniēns quod prius dictum est,
quia *spīritus Dominī* in Scrīptūrā, nōn nisi prō Spīritū Sānctō,
cōnsuēvit pōnī. Quī aquīs superferrī dīcitur, nōn corporāliter,
sed sīcut voluntās artificis superfertur māteriae quam vult

140 fōrmāre. — Tertia distīnctiō significātur secundum situm.
Quia terra erat sub aquīs, quibus invīsibilis reddēbātur. Āēr
vērō, quī est subiectum tenebrārum, significātur fuisse super

aquās, per hoc quod dīcitur, *Tenebrae erant super faciem abyssī.*
— Quid autem distīnguendum remanēret, ex sequentibus
145 apparēbit.

1 **īnfōrmitās, -tātis,** f.,
"*formlessness, matter in a
formless state*" (Deferrari, s.v.)

praecēdō, -ere, -cessī, *go
before, precede* (note that the
subjunctive is occasioned by
the indirect question)

2 **fōrmātiō, -ōnis,** f., *a formation,
fashioning; a form, design; a
"granting form"* (Deferrari, s.v.)

3 **Ad prīmum:** supply *articulum,*
from *articulus, -ī,* m., *an article*

prōcēdō, -ere, *go forth, proceed*

5 **Genesis, -is,** f., *Genesis,* the first
book of the Pentateuch

6 **invīsibilis, -e,** *invisible, unseen*

incompositus, -a, -um, "*shapeless,
out of order, wanting in orderly
arrangement*" (Deferrari, s.v.)

aliam litteram: here = *another
translation,* i.e., the LXX as
turned into Latin

7 **dēsignō** (1), *describe, designate,
define*

Augustīnus, -ī, m., St. *Augustine,*
bishop of Hippo, in, for
example, *Cōnfessiōnēs* 12.12.

8 **aliquandō,** adv., *at some time or
other, once*

9 **praetereā,** adv., *besides, moreover*

operātiō, -ōnis, f., *a working,
operation*

13 **potis, pote** (rarely decl. in
positive), *able, capable;
possible;* **potior, -ōris,** *better,
preferable, stronger*

accidēns, -entis, n., "*the
accidental, non-essential quality
of any thing,* τὸ συμβεβηκός
(opp. substantia, the Greek
οὐσία)" (LS, s.v.)

14 **substantia, -ae,** f., "*that of which
a thing consists, the being,
essence, contents, material,
substance*" (LS, s.v.)

quod: = *ut* in a substantive clause
of result (see Capvt XXXVI
Syntaxis; cf. LLMA, s.v. "quod")

15 **subiectum, -ī,** n., *that which
is thrown* or *placed under, a
subject,* esp. *the substance* or *the
matter of a thing*

altar, -āris, n., *an altar*

17 **contrā:** here an adv., = *on the
contrary*

imperfectiō, -ōnis, f.,
imperfection

effectus, -ūs, m., *that which is
produced, an effect*

attestor, -ārī, *give witness to, attest*

18 **agentis:** = "*agent, cause*"
(Deferrari, s.v. "ago")

19 **Deuteronomium, -ī,** n.,
Deuteronomy, the fifth book of
the Pentateuch

21 **corporālis, -e,** *corporeal*

22 **cōnfūsiō, -ōnis,** f., *a mingling;
confusion, disorder*

25 **Chaos,** declension doubtful, n.,
"*the confused formless, primitive
mass out of which the universe
was made, chaos*" (LS, s.v.)

26 **circā,** prep. + acc., *around, about;*
    in respect to

    dīversus, -a, -um, *different,*
    diverse

27 **opīniō, -ōnis,** f., *opinion,*
    conjecture, belief

29 **orīgō, -inis,** f., *earliest beginning,*
    origin

30 **Basilīus, -iī,** m., St. *Basil* the
    Great, bishop of Caesarea

    Ambrosius, -iī, m., St. *Ambrose,*
    bishop of Milan

    Chrȳsostomus, -ī, m., St.
    John *Chrysostom,* bishop of
    Constantinople

33 **contrārius, -a, -um,** *opposite,*
    opposed

    ab invicem: see Appendix I, § 35

    differō, -ferre, *differ, be different*

    aliter, adv., *in another way*

35 **carentia, -ae,** f., *"a lack or want*
    of something, deprivation"
    (Deferrari, s.v.)

36 **impossibilis, -e,** *impossible*

37 **praecesserit:** Why is this verb
    in the subjunctive? See Capvt
    XXV Syntaxis, and Appendix
    I, § 70

38 **manifestus, -a, -um,** *clear, plain,*
    evident

39 **dūrātiō, -ōnis,** f., *"duration,*
    continuance in time . . . time in
    general" (Deferrari, s.v.)

40 **āctus, -ūs,** m., *an action, act*

    importō (1), *carry in; cause;*
    mean (Deferrari, s.v.)

    terminus, -ī, m., *a limit, end*

41 **ēns, entis,** n., *being, a being*
    (Deferrari, s.v.)

43 **implicō** (1), *entangle; involve*

contrādictiō, -ōnis, f., a
    contradiction

44 **postmodum,** adv., *soon;*
    afterwards

45 **superveniō, -īre, -vēnī,** *come*
    upon; arrive

46 **nātūrālis, -e,** *natural* (here
    supply *philosophōrum*)

47 **posuērunt:** here = *maintain,*
    accept as true

48 **putā:** Thomas uses the 2nd sg.
    imperative of *putō* to introduce
    examples, = *namely, for*
    example (Deferrari, s.v.)

    āēr, āeris, m., *air*

    medium: here = *the middle, mean*
    (Deferrari, s.v.)

49 **alterō** (1), *change* (Deferrari,
    s.v.). Cf. Aristotle, *Physics*
    1.4 (187a12), speaking of the
    Ionian Physicists, who posited
    various eternal material
    principles out of which all
    things came to be by change

49 **esse, essendī,** n., *being*
    (Deferrari, s.v.)

53 **proprium, -iī,** n., *"characteristic*
    mark, . . . peculiar quality"
    (Deferrari, s.v.)

    accidentālis, -e, *"accidental,*
    unessential, not belonging to the
    substance" (Deferrari, s.v.)

54 **quae:** take *accidentia* as the
    antecedent, = *according to*
    which

    attendō, -ere, *stretch out towards;*
    direct or *turn towards*

    generātiō, -ōnis, f., *a begetting,*
    generating

55 **alterātiō, -ōnis,** f., *a change*

58 **conditiō, -ōnis,** f., *a making,*
    creating

61 **potentia, -ae,** f., *power; capacity;*
    possibility, potentiality
    (Deferrari, s.v.)

65 **fōrmōsitās, -tātis,** f., *beauty*

    appareō, -ēre, *come into view,*
    appear

    corporeus, -a, -um, *corporeal*

68–69 **quantum ad aliquid ...**
    quantum ad aliquid, *with*
    respect to something ... with
    respect to something, i.e., in
    some respects ... in some respects

69 **concordō** (1), *be of one mind,*
    agree

    discordō (1), *be at variance,*
    disagree

    īnfrā, adv., *below* (i.e., in another
    article)

70 **quantum,** adv., *as far as*

    triplex, -plicis, *threefold, triple*

71 **dēsum, -esse,** *be away* or *absent;*
    be wanting, fail

72 **diaphanus, -a, -um,** *transparent*

74 **faciēs, -ēī,** f., *form, shape; face*

    abyssus, -ī, f., *a bottomless pit,*
    abyss

    duplex, -plicis, *twofold, double*

75 **aquīs:** take as an abl. of
    separation

    discooperiō, -īre, -uī, -pertum,
    uncover, disclose (i.e., the
    beauty that was disclosed by
    the removal of the waters)

76 **quantum ad,** = *so far as concerns*

77 **aspectus, -ūs,** m., *a look, sight;*
    visibility, appearance, look

78 **undique,** adv., *on all sides,*
    everywhere

    cooperiō, -īre, *cover totally,*
    overwhelm

79 **herba, -ae,** f., *grass, green crops*

    planta, -ae, f., *a shoot, slip; a plant*
    (Deferrari, s.v.)

    ideō, adv., *for that reason,*
    therefore

81 **praemisisset:** here = *send forth*
    or *present before* or *in advance*
    (Deferrari, s.v.), i.e., *state first*

    scīlicet, adv., *evidently, certainly*

82 **exprimō, -ere, -pressī,** *press* or
    squeeze out; express, portray

83 **secundum quod,** adv., *according*
    as, in as far as (Deferrari, s.vv.
    "quantus" and "secundum")

86 **prīmum:** supply *obiectum,*
    -ī, n., *a subject; an objection*
    (Deferrari, s.v.; Latham, s.v.
    "objectio")

88 **significō** (1), *show, express,*
    signify

89 **Mōÿses, -is,** m., *Moses* the
    Prophet

    rudis, -e, *rough, raw; rude,*
    ignorant

90 **similitūdō, -inis,** f., *a likeness,*
    resemblance

91 **multiplex, -plicis,** *that has*
    many folds, windings (of hiding
    places); *that has many parts,*
    manifold

94 **inquantum,** adv., *in as far as*
    (Deferrari, s.v. "quantus")

    subsīdō, -ere, *sit* or *settle down;*
    remain; lie in wait for; be
    susceptible to (this last from
    Deferrari, s.v.)

98 **cōnsīderō** (1), *look at closely,*
    consider

99   **repleō, -ēre,** *fill again* or *up;*
     complete

     Platō, -ōnis, m., *Plato* of Athens
     (c. 429–347 BCE)

101 **quāliter,** adv., *how*

102 **prōdūcō, -ere,** *bring out; produce*

106 **magnitūdō, -inis,** f., *greatness*

110 **esse in āctū,** take as the subject

112 **in contrarium:** here T.
     introduces nuanced objections
     to his own two arguments *Sed
     contrā,* with clarifications

114 **impotentia, -ae,** f., *inability*

116 **imperfectus, -a, -um,** *unfinished,
     incomplete*

119 **Anaxagoras, -ae,** m., *Anaxagoras*
     of Clazomenae (c. 500–428
     BCE)

120 **intellēctus, -ūs,** m.,
     understanding; intellect

     immixtus, -a, -um, *unmixed*

126 **nōminō** (1), *call by name, give a
     name to*

128 **huiusmodī,** *of this kind, such*

131 **igneus, -a, -um,** *of fire, fiery*

133 *Dē cīv. Deī:* = *Dē cīvitāte Deī*

     rabbi, indecl. Heb. noun, m.,
     Rabbi

     Mōÿses, -is, *Moses* Maimonides
     (1138–1204)

135 **sphaera, -ae,** f., *a sphere; a
     heavenly sphere*

     lūceō, -ēre, *shine*

136 **conveniēns, -entis,** *appropriate,
     to, fit, suitable*

138 **superferō, -ferre,** *carry over* or
     beyond, place or *put over*

139 **artifex, -icis,** m., *an artist,
     artificer*

     māteriae: why is this in the
     dative?

140 **situs, -ūs,** m., *the situation, local
     position, site*

141 **reddēbatur:** here = *make or
     cause a thing to be* or *appear*
     (Deferrari, s.v.)

B. *Epistola Exhortātōria dē Modō Studendī,* in Verrardo, 451 (see Source Texts)

St. Thomas composed in various genres. Here is a letter that he wrote to a young friar, Brother John, on how to study. It should be compared to Hugh of St. Victor's teaching in Locī XIII.B above. It seems to me that the letter also opens a window on St. Thomas's personality and life.

       Quia quaesistī ā mē, in Chrīstō mihi cārissime Iōannes,
q

āliter tē studēre oporteat in thēsaurō scientiae acquīrendō,
tāle ā mē tibi trāditur cōnsilium:
       1) ut per rīvulōs, nōn statim in mare, ēligās introīre, quia per

5   faciliōra ad difficiliōra oportet dēvenīre.
       2) Haec est ergō monitiō mea et īnstructiō tua.
Tardiloquum tē esse iubeō et tardē ad locūtōrium accēdentem;
       3) cōnscientiae pūritātem amplectere.
       4) Ōrātiōnī vacāre nōn dēsinās;

10   5) cellam frequenter dīligās, sī vīs in cellam vīnāriam
intrōdūcī.
       6) Omnibus tē amābilem exhibē;
       7) nihil quaere penitus dē factīs aliōrum;
       8) nēminī tē multum familiārem ostendās, quia nimia

15   familiāritās parit contemptum, et subtractiōnis ā studiō
māteriam subministrat;
       9) dē verbīs et factīs saeculārium nūllātenus tē intrōmittās;
       10) discursūs super omnia fugiās;
       11) Sānctōrum et bonōrum imitārī vestīgia nōn omittās;

20   12) nōn rēspiciās ā quō audiās, sed quidquid bonī dīcātur,
memoriae recommendā;
       13) ea quae legis et audīs, fac ut intellēgās;
       14) dē dubiīs tē certificā;
       15) et quidquid poteris in armāriolō mentis repōnere,

25   satage, sīcut cupiēns vās implēre;
       16) altiōra tē nē quaesīeris.
       Illa sequens vestīgia, frondēs et frūctūs in vīneā Dominī
Sabaōth ūtilēs, quamdiū vītam habueris, prōferēs et prōdūcēs.
Haec sī sectātus fueris, ad id attingere poteris, quod affectās.

1   **Iōannes, -is,** m., *John*

2   **thēsaurus, -ī,** m., *a treasure; a treasury*

4   **rīvulus, -ī,** m., *a little brook, a tiny stream*

    ēligō, -ere, *choose, elect*

    introeō, -īre, *go in, enter*

5   **dēveniō, -īre,** *come from; arrive at, reach*

6   **īnstructiō, -ōnis,** f., *a constructing; an arranging; instruction*

7   **tardiloquus, -a, -um,** *slow of speech*

    locūtōrium, -iī, n., *the monastic parlor* (Latham, s.v., "locutio")

8   **pūritās, -tātis,** f., *cleanness, purity*

    amplector, -ī, *embrace; cherish*

10 **cella, -ae,** f., *a storeroom, chamber* (here = *the monastic cell*)

    vīnārius, -a, -um, *pertaining to wine, wine*

12 **amābilis, -e,** *worthy of love, amiable*

    exhibeō, -ēre, *show, exhibit*

13 **penitus,** adv., *deeply*

14 **familiāris, -e,** *familiar, intimate, friendly*

    nimius, -a, -um, *excessive, too much*

15 **familiāritās, -tātis,** f., *familiarity, intimacy, friendship*

    contemptus, -ūs, m., *contempt, scorn*

    subtractiō, -ōnis, f., *a drawing back*

16 **subministrō** (1), *give, furnish, supply*

17 **saeculāris, -e,** *pertaining to a saeculum; worldly, profane*

    nūllātenus, adv., *in no way, by no means*

    intrōmittō, -ere, *send in; busy oneself with* (+ *dē,* Deferrari, s.v.)

18 **discursus, -ūs,** m., *a running hither and yon; a conversation, discourse*

19 **vestīgium, -iī,** n., *a footstep; a footprint; a trace, mark*

    nōn: EL can use *nōn* with the optative subjunctive in a prohibition (see example in PW, § 126.1; Appendix I, § 64 N 1)

20 **rēspiciō, -ere,** *look back or behind; have regard; be mindful of, respect*

21 **recommendō** (1), *recommend, entrust to, summarize* (LLMA, s.v.)

23 **certificō** (1), *certify, give guarantees, demonstrate* (LLMA, s.v.)

24 **armāriolum, -ī,** n., *a little chest; a little bookcase; a little cupboard.* The *armārium* or bookcase/book cupboard was used as an image of the memory trained by mnemotechnique in the Middle Ages.[49]

    repōnō, -ere, *put back; store*

25 **satage:** = **satis agō,** *strive, be anxious to do* (Deferrari, s.v. "satis")

---

[49]   See Mary Carruthers, *The Book of Memory: A Study of Memory in Medieval Culture* (Cambridge: Cambridge University Press, 1990), 151–152.

vās, vāsis, n., *a vessel* or
implement of any kind

27 frons, -dis, f., *a leafy branch,*
foliage; a leafy crown

vīnea, -ae, f., *a vineyard*

28 Sabaōth, indecl. Heb. pl., *the*
heavenly hosts

quamdiū, adv., *as long as*

29 sector, -ārī, -ātus sum, *follow*
eagerly or *continually*

attingō, -ere, *touch; reach*

affectō (1), *strive after, exert*
oneself to obtain

C. *Hymnus in Festō Corporis Chrīstī, ad Vesperās,* in March, 168–169 (see Source Texts)

This hymn of St. Thomas' for Corpus Christi is probably his most widely known composition. The hymn is modelled on Fortunatus' Pange, lingua (Locī VII above). Thus, its meter is trochaic tetrameter catalectic. However, while Fortunatus composed in quantitative feet, Aquinas uses accentual measures. He also employs rhyme at the caesura (Smith, 115) and at the ends of lines.

> Pange, lingua, glōriōsī corporis mystērium,
> Sanguinisque pretiōsī, quem in mundī pretium
> Frūctus ventris generōsī rēx effūdit gentium.
>
> Nōbīs datus, nōbīs nātus, ex intāctā virgine,
> 5   Et in mundō conversātus, sparsō verbī sēmine,
> Suī morās incolātūs mīrō clausit ōrdine.
>
> In suprēmae nocte cēnae, recumbēns cum frātribus
> Observātā lēge plēnē cibīs in lēgālibus,
> Cibum turbae duodēnae sē dat suīs manibus.
>
> 10   Verbum carō pānem vērum verbō carnem efficit,
> Fitque sanguis Chrīstī merum; etsī sēnsus dēficit,
> Ad firmandum cor sincērum sōla fidēs sufficit.
>
> Tantum ergō Sacrāmentum venerēmur cernuī,
> Et antīquum documentum novō cēdat rītuī;
> 15   Praestet fidēs supplēmentum sēnsuum dēfectuī.
>
> Genitōrī, Genitōque laus et iūbilātiō,
> Salus, honor, virtūs quoque sit et benedictiō:
> Prōcēdentī ab utrōque compar sit laudātiō.

1   **pangō, -ere,** *fasten, fix; compose, write*

    glōriōsus, -a, -um, *famous, glorious*

    mystērium, -iī, n., a "*divine mystery, that which is so hidden that it cannot be understood, secret rites*" (Deferrari, s.v.)

2   **pretiōsus, -a, -um,** *valuable, precious; costly*

3   **venter, -tris,** m., *belly; womb*

    generōsus, -a, -um, *of noble birth, noble, eminent*

    effundō, -ere, -fūdī, *pour out, shed, spread about*

4 **intāctus, -a, -um,** *untouched,*
uninjured, intact

5 **conversor, -ārī, -ātus sum,**
abide, live, dwell

sēmen, -inis, n., *seed*

6 **suī morās:** supply *temporis,* =
spaces or *periods of his own time*
(see LS, s.v. "mora" II.B)

incolātus, -ūs, m., *a residing,*
dwelling

ōrdine: can = *divine disposition,*
providence in EL, as in the title
of Augustine's *Dē ōrdine*

7 **recumbō, -ere,** *recline at table* (as
in antiquity)

8 **observō** (1), *watch, observe; keep,*
comply with (a law)

cibus, -ī, m., *victuals, food*

lēgālis, -e, *lawful, legal*

9 **duodēnī, -ae, -a,** *twelve each,*
twelve (used here on the model
of an anonymous poet whom
Thomas quotes at ST 3, q.81,
a.1 ad 1, cited by Connelly,
121: perh. = *duodēnārius, -a,*
-um, containing twelve)

10 **carō:** take as in apposition to
Verbum

11 **merum, -ī,** n., *pure, unmixed wine*

12 **fīrmō** (1), *make firm, strengthen,*
support

sincērus, -a, -um, *clean, pure,*
sound

13 **veneror, -ārī,** *worship, adore,*
revere, reverence

cernuus, -a, -um, *with the face*
turned towards the earth,
stooping or *bowing*

14 **documentum, -ī,** n., *a lesson,*
example; here perh. = "*doctrine,*
teaching" (Deferrari, s.v.)

rītus, -ūs, m., "*the form and*
manner of religious observances;
a religious usage or *ceremony, a*
rite" (LS, s.v.)

15 **supplēmentum, -ī,** n., *a filling up,*
supply, supplement

dēfectus, -ūs, m., *a defection,*
revolt; a failing, failure

16 **genitor, -ōris,** m., *a begetter,*
parent, father, creator

gignō, -ere, genuī, genitus,
beget, bring forth, produce;
(pass.) *be born, spring, arise,*
proceed

iūbilātiō, -ōnis, f., *a shouting;*
joy, rejoicing (LLMA, s.v.
"jubilatio")

17 **benedictiō, -ōnis,** f., *a praising,*
lauding; a blessing

18 **prōcēdō, -ere,** *proceed*

uterque, utraque, utrumque,
each of two, both

compar, -paris, *like* or *equal to*
another

laudātiō, -ōnis, f., *a praising,*
praise

XVI. St. Bonaventure, *Itinerārium Mentis in Deum* 2.9–11, in *Tria Opuscula*, 309–312 (see Source Texts)

This reading is an excerpt from St. Bonaventure's argument on the ascent of the mind to God by means of the various mirrors found in creation. Human judgment requires certainty, which can only be found in divine things, of which numbers are one. Therefore, number itself is a primary reflection of God. David P. Goldman has recently pointed to Bonaventure and Augustine's conception of numerī iūdiciālēs, *and to the development of the concept by Nicholas of Cusa, as anticipations of "higher-order number," usually thought to have been the discovery of Newton and Leibniz.*[50]

9. Excellentiōrī autem modō et immediātiōrī dīiūdicātiō
dūcit nōs in aeternam vēritātem certius speculandam. Sī enim
dīiūdicātiō habet fierī per ratiōnem abstrahentem ā locō,
tempore et mūtābilitāte, ac per hoc ā dīmēnsiōne,
5   successiōne et trānsmūtātiōne per ratiōnem immūtābilem
et incircumscrīptibilem et interminībilem, nihil autem est
omnīnō immūtābile, incircumscrīptibile et interminābile, nisi
quod est aeternum. Omne autem quod est aeternum est Deus
vel in Deō. Sī ergō omnia quaecumque certius
10   dīiūdicāmus per huiusmodī ratiōnem dīiūdicāmus, patet
quod ipse est ratiō omnium rērum et rēgula īnfallibilis
et lūx vēritātis, in quā cūncta relūcent infallibiliter,
indēlēbiliter, indubitanter, irrefrāgābiliter, indiiūdicābiliter,
incommūtābiliter, incoartābiliter, interminābiliter,
15   indīvīsibiliter et intellēctuāliter. Et ideō lēgēs illae per
quās iūdicāmus certitūdināliter dē omnibus sēnsibilibus in
nostram cōnsīderātiōnem venientibus, cum sint infallibiles
et indubitābiles intellēctuī apprehendentis, sint indēlēbilēs ā
memoriā recolentis tamquam semper praesentēs, sint
20   irrefrāgābilēs et indiiūdicābilēs intellēctuī iūdicantis, quia, ut
dīcit Augustīnus, "Nūllus dē eīs iūdicat, sed per illās," necesse
est eās esse incommūtābilēs et incorruptibilēs tamquam
necessāriās, incoartābilēs tamquam incircumscrīptās,
interminābilēs tamquam aeternās, ac per hoc indīvīsibilēs

---

[50]   David P. Goldman, "Math and Music," *First Things*, April 2012, 33–39.

25 tamquam intellēctuālēs et incorporeās, nōn factās, sed
increātās, aeternāliter exsistentēs in arte aeternā, ā quā, per
quam et secundum quam fōrmantur fōrmōsa omnia. Et ideō
nec certitūdināliter iūdicārī possunt, nisi per illam quae nōn
tantum fuit fōrma cūncta prōdūcēns, vērum etiam cūncta
30 cōnservāns et distinguēns, tamquam ēns in omnibus fōrmam
tenēns et rēgula dīrigēns, et per quam dīiūdicat mēns nostra
cūncta quae per sēnsūs intrant in ipsam.
  10. Haec autem speculātiō dīlātātur secundum
cōnsīderātiōnem septem differentiārum numerōrum, quibus
35 quasi septem gradibus cōnscenditur in Deum, secundum
quod ostendit Augustīnus in librō *Dē vērā Religiōne* et in
sextō *Mūsicae*, ubi assignat differentiās numerōrum gradātim
cōnscendentium ab hīs sēnsibilibus usque ad Opificem
omnium, ut in omnibus videātur Deus.
40   Dīcit enim numerōs esse in corporibus et maximē in sonīs
et vōcibus, et hōs vocat sonantēs; numerōs ab hīs abstractōs
et in sēnsibus nostrīs receptōs, et hōs vocat occursōrēs;
numerōs ab animā prōcēdentēs in corpus, sīcut patet in
gesticulātiōnibus et saltātiōnibus, et hōs vocat prōgressōrēs;
45 numerōs in dēlectātiōnibus sēnsuum ex conversiōne
intentiōnis super speciem receptam, et hōs vocat sēnsuālēs;
numerōs in memoriam retentōs, et hōs vocat memoriālēs;
numerōs etiam per quōs dē hīs omnibus iūdicāmus, et hōs
vocat iūdiciālēs, quī, ut dictum est, necessāriō sunt suprā
50 mentem tamquam infallibilēs et indiiūdicābilēs. Ab hīs autem
imprimuntur mentibus nostrīs numerī artificiālēs, quōs tamen
inter illōs gradūs nōn enumerat Augustīnus, quia cōnexī sunt
iūdiciālibus; et ab hīs mānant numerī prōgressōrēs, ex quibus
creantur numerōsae fōrmae artificiātōrum, ut ā summīs
55 per media ōrdinātus fīat dēscensus ad īnfima. Ad hōs etiam
gradātim ascendimus ā numerīs sonantibus, mediantibus
occursōribus, sēnsuālibus et memoriālibus.
  Cum igitur omnia sint pulchra et quōdammodo
dēlectābilia, et pulchritūdō et dēlectātiō nōn sint absque
60 proportiōne, et proportiō prīmō sit in numerīs, necesse est
omnia esse numerōsa; ac per hoc "numerus est praecipuum in
animō Conditōris exemplar" et in rēbus praecipuum vestīgium
dūcēns in Sapientiam. Quod, cum sit omnibus ēvidentissimum

et Deō propinquissimum, propinquissimē quasi per septem
65   differentiās dūcit in Deum et facit eum cognōscī in cūnctīs
corporālibus et sēnsibilibus, dum numerōsa apprehendimus,
in numerōsīs proportiōnibus dēlectāmur et per numerōsārum
proportiōnum lēgēs irrefrāgābiliter iūdicāmus.

11. Ex hīs duōbus gradibus prīmīs, quibus manūdūcimur
70   ad speculandum Deum in vestīgiīs quasi ad modum duārum
ālārum descendentium circā pedēs, colligere possumus, quod
omnēs creātūrae istīus sēnsibilis mundī animum contemplantis
et sapientis dūcunt in Deum aeternum, prō eō quod illīus prīmī
prīncipiī potentissimī, sapientissimī et optimī, illīus aeternae
75   orīginis, lūcis et plēnitūdinis, illīus, inquam, artis efficientis,
exemplantis et ōrdinantis sunt umbrae, resonantiae et pictūrae,
sunt vestīgia, simulācra et spectācula nōbīs ad contuendum
Deum proposita et signa dīvīnitus data; quae, inquam, sunt
exemplāria vel potius exemplāta, proposita mentibus
80   adhūc rudibus et sēnsibilibus, ut per sēnsibilia, quae vident,
trānsferantur ad intellegibilia, quae nōn vident, tamquam per
signa ad signāta.

1   **excellēns, -entis,** *high, lofty;*
superior, excellent

immediātus, -a, -um,
unmediated, immediate,
adjacent (cf. Latham, s.v.
"immediatio")

dīiūdicātiō, -ōnis, f., *a judging,*
judgment

2   **speculor, -ārī,** *spy out, watch,*
examine, explore

3   **habet:** see Appendix I, § 55

abstrahō, -ere, *draw away,*
withdraw, abstract

4   **mūtābilitās, -tātis,** f.,
changeableness

dīmēnsiō, -ōnis, f., *a measuring;*
extent, dimensions

5   **successiō, -ōnis,** f., *a following*
after, succeeding, succession

trānsmūtātiō, -ōnis, f., *a*
changing, change

immūtābilis, -e, *unchangeable,*
unalterable

6   **incircumscrīptibilis, -e,**
illimitable (Latham, s.c.
"incircumscriptus")

interminābilis, -e, *endless,*
interminable

9   **quīcumque, quaecumque,**
quodcumque, *whoever,*
whatever

10   **dīiūdicō** (1), *judge by discerning,*
decide, determine

11   **rēgula, -ae,** f., *a rule, ruler; a rule,*
pattern

īnfallibilis, -e, *infallible*
(Latham, s.v., "infallibilitas")

12   **relūceō, -ēre,** *shine back or out*

13 **indēlēbilis, -e,** *indelible, imperishable*

indubitanter, adv., *without doubt, indubitably*

irrefrāgābilis, -e, *unbreakable; definitive* (LLMA, s.v.); *indisputable* (Latham, s.v.)

indiiūdicābilis, -e, *undiscernible, not able to be judged*

14 **incommūtābilis, -e,** *unchangeable, immutable*

incoartābilis, -e, *that cannot be restrained* or *compressed* (LLMA, s.v.)

15 **indīvīsibilis, -e,** *indivisible*

intellēctuālis, -e, *pertaining to the understanding, intellectual*

ideō, adv., *therefore*

16 **certitūdināliter,** adv., *certainly, with certainty* (Latham, s.v. "certitudo")

sēnsibilis, -e, *that can be perceived by the senses, sensible*

17 **cōnsīderātiō, -ōnis,** f., *contemplation, consideration*

18 **indubitābilis, -e,** *that cannot be doubted, indubitable*

intellēctus, -ūs, m., *understanding, comprehension; the faculty of intellect*

apprehendō, -ere, *lay hold of; grasp with the mind, understand, comprehend*

19 **recolō, -ere,** *recall, reflect on*

praesēns, -entis, *at hand, present*

21 **Augustīnus, -ī,** m., St. *Augustine* of Hippo (in *Dē līberō arbitriō* 2.12.34 and *Dē vērā religiōne* 31.58)

22 **incorruptibilis, -e,** *imperishable, incorruptible*

23 **incircumscrīptus, -a, -um,** *unlimited, infinite*

25 **incorporeus, -a, -um,** *incorporeal*

26 **increātus, -a, -um,** *uncreated, not made*

aeternālis, -e, *everlasting*

exsistō, -ere, *step out* or *forth; proceed; exist, be*

27 **fōrmōsus, -a, -um,** *beautifully formed, beautiful*

29 **prōdūcō, -ere,** *lead* or *bring forth; produce*

30 **ēns, entis,** n., *being, a being*

31 **dīrigō, -ere,** *set in a straight line, arrange; direct, guide*

33 **speculātiō, -ōnis,** f., *a spying out, exploration; contemplation, speculation*

dīlātō (1), *spread out, dilate; enlarge, amplify, extend*

34 **differentia, -ae,** f., *a diversity, difference; species*

35 **gradus, -ūs,** m., *a step, pace; a step, degree; a ladder, stair*

cōnscendō, -ere, *mount, ascend*

36 **religiō, -ōnis,** f., *reverence for* or *fear of God; piety, religion* (LS, s.v.) (see *Dē vērā rel.* 40.74–76)

37 **mūsica, -ae,** f., (the art of) *music* (see *Dē mūsicā* 6 passim)

assignō (1), *assign, distribute, allot; attribute, impute*

gradātim, adv., *step by step, little by little, gradually*

38 **opifex, -icis,** m./f., *a maker, fabricator; an artisan, artist*

40 **sonus, -ī,** m., *a noise, sound*

41 **sonō (1),** *make a noise, sound, resound*

42 **occursor, ōris,** m., *a meeter,* (LS, citing Augustine, *Dē mūsicā*); *one who comes to help* (LLMA, citing Pseudo-Isidore); *a sensory nerve* (Latham, s.v. "occursio")

43 **prōcēdō, -ere,** *go out, proceed*

44 **gesticulātiō, -ōnis,** f., *"pantomimic motion, gesticulation"* (LS, s.v.)

     saltātiō, -ōnis, f., *a dancing; a dance*

     prōgressor, -ōris, m., *one that goes out* or *advances* (LS, citing Augustine, *Dē mūsicā*); *a sensory nerve* (Latham, s.v. "progressio")

45 **conversiō, -ōnis,** f., *a turning around, revolving*

46 **intentiō, -ōnis,** f., *a stretching out; a directing of the mind towards; attention*

     speciēs, -ēī, f., *shape, form, figure; sight, appearance; idea, notion*

     sēnsuālis, -e, *endowed with feeling, sensual* (LS, s.v.); *perceptible, affecting the senses* (Latham, s.v., "sensus")

47 **retineō, -ēre, -uī, -tentum,** *hold* or *keep back, not let go; keep, preserve, maintain, retain*

     memoriālis, -e, *pertaining to the memory, memorial*

49 **iūdiciālis, -e,** *pertaining to the courts of justice, judicial* (LS, s.v.; of course, here the courts of justice belong somehow to the mind)

51 **imprimō, -ere,** *press into* or *on, impress, imprint*

     artificiālis, -e, *pertaining to art; requiring* or *produced by art* (Latham, s.v. "artifex")

52 **cōnectō, -ere, -nexuī, -nexum,** *tie* or *bind together, connect*

53 **mānō (1),** *flow*

54 **numerōsus, -a, -um,** *consisting of a great number, numerous; full of rhythm* or *harmony, harmonious, melodious*

     artificiō (1), *design, make, create* (Latham, s.v. "artifex")

55 **ōrdinō (1),** *order, set in order, arrange, dispose, regulate*

     dēscensus, -ūs, m., *a descending way, descent*

     īnfimus, -a, -um, *lowest, last*

56 **ascendō, -ere,** *mount up, ascend, climb*

     mediō (1), *be in the middle, be between; mediate* (Latham, s.v. "medium")

58 **quōdammodo,** adv., *in a certain way*

59 **dēlectābilis, -e,** *delightful, agreeable*

60 **prōportiō, -ōnis,** f., *proportion, symmetry, likeness*

61 **praecipuus, -a, -um,** *particular, peculiar; special, chief, principal*

62 **conditor, -ōris,** m., *a builder, maker, framer.* The citation is from Boethius, *Dē īnstitūtiōne arithmētica* 1.2.

     vestīgium, -iī, n., *a footstep; a footprint; a trace, mark*

63 **ēvidēns, -entis,** *apparent, visible, evident, manifest, clear*

64 **propinquus, -a, -um,** *near,*
   neighboring

69 **manūdūcō, -ere,** *lead, guide*
   (Latham, s.v. "manuductio")

70 **ad modum** + gen., = *in the*
   manner of, like

71 **dēscendō, -ere,** *fall* or *sink down,*
   descend

   circā, prep. + acc., *around, on the*
   sides of (see Is 6:2, and Jerome's
   commentary above in Locī IX)

72 **contemplor, -ārī,** *look at, behold,*
   consider, contemplate

73 **prō eō quod,** = *because*

75 **orīgō, -inis,** f., *earliest beginning,*
   source, origin

   plēnitūdō, -inis, f., *fullness,*
   plenitude; completeness

76 **exemplō** (1), "*adduce as an*
   example, model, pattern
   or *original to be copied* or
   imitated" (Deferrari, s.v.)

   resonantia, -ae, f., *an echo*

   pictūra, -ae, f., (the art of)
   painting; a painting, picture

77 **simulācrum, -ī,** n., *a likeness,*
   image, form, semblance

   contueor, -ērī, *look* or *gaze at,*
   behold, survey, consider with
   close attention

78 **dīvīnitus,** adv., *from heaven, by*
   divine providence

80 **adhūc,** adv., *hitherto, until now*

   rudis, -e, *rough, uncultivated*

81 **intelligibilis, -e,** *that can*
   be understood, intelligible,
   intellectual

82 **signō** (1), *set a mark upon, seal;*
   point out, designate, signify,
   indicate

APPENDIX I

Some Developments in Latin Grammar Found in Ecclesiastical and Medieval Latin

The following primers and grammars have been consulted in the preparation of this short (and very basic) manual: Blaise, Collins, GL, PW, MRi, Nunn, and Strecker.

Unless otherwise noted, the scriptural translations which follow have been taken from *The Holy Bible Translated from the Latin Vulgate ... The Old Testament first Published by the English College at Douay, A.D. 1609, and The New Testament first Published by the English College at Rheims, A.D. 1582* (Baltimore: John Murphy Company Publishers, 1914).

A. Etymology

Pronunciation

Contemporary Pronunciation of Ecclesiastical Latin (adapted from Collins, § 1)

1. Vowels:

    ā   as in *farm*
    ă   as in *careen*
    ē   as in *fey*, but a pure sound, not a diphthong
    ĕ   as in *pet*
    ī   as in *police*
    ĭ   as in *pip*
    ō   as in *spoke*, but a pure sound, as in the Annapolis Valley, Nova Scotia, not a diphthong
    ŏ   as in *song*

ū   as in *tuber,* as in American English

ŭ   as in *bully*

y   as in *mitt*

Note 1. In chant, all vowels tend to be pronounced as if long, although the stresses of CL are maintained.

2.   Diphthongs:

ae   like ē

au   like *ou* in *house* in ordinary American

oe   like ē

ui   as in classical Latin

3.   Consonants:
Just note the following differences from Classical Latin:

c   before *e, i, ae,* or *oe,* like *ch* in *cheese*

g   before *e, i,* or *y,* like *j* in *juice*

gn   like *ny* in *banyan*

h   sounded in speech, but not in chant, except between two vowels, as in *mihi = miki*

sc   before *e* or *i,* like *sh*

ti   followed by a vowel, like *tsĭ,* unless preceded by *s, t,* or *x*

v   as in English

Orthography

4.   The spelling of this book has been standardized. The interested student may consult MRi, pp. 79–80.

Inflection

5.   The inflection of Ecclesiastical/Medieval Latin remained largely the same as that of Classical Latin. However, it would be helpful for the student to look at MRi, pp. 83–84.

B. LEXICON

6.   The lexicon of Latin was greatly expanded in late antiquity and the Middle Ages by borrowings from other languages, by new definitions for old words, and by coinages. There is no single Medieval Latin dictionary that one can consult. LS is usually the best place to start,

when trying to figure out a word's meaning. See MRi, pp. 103–105, for a bibliography of lexical resources. Note that PW contains many neologisms and new usages *passim*, as do Blaise, Nunn, and Strecker. However, the following must be noticed here.

Note 1. *Valeō* often does service for *possum*.

Note 2. *Licet* frequently means "although," thus being used as a conjunction in construction with the subjunctive. This usage was known in CL.

Note 3. On *crēdere in* + acc. or abl., a uniquely Christian construction originating with St. John, indicating "an active commitment to a person and, in particular, to Jesus," see Locī IV, note on Jn. 1:12 ("quī crēdunt in nōmine").

Note 4. The second person plural personal pronoun (*vōs*) can be used in polite speech when addressing a single person. See Capvt XXVIII, Sentence 12.

C. SYNTAX

Cases

Genitive:

7. The genitive of description (or quality) sometimes occurs without an adjective in violation of the classical rule, e.g., *in odōrem suāvitātis*, "for an odour of sweetness" (Eph. 5:2), as opposed to *vir magnae auctōritātis*, "a man of great authority" (Caesar, *Bell. Gall.* 5.35.6).

   Note 1. Cf. the predicate genitive of possession, Capvt XXV Syntaxis.

   Note 2. Blaise, § 84.5, notices a genitive of appurtenance or belonging, which shows the relationship of one person to another, e.g., *Marīa Cleophae*, Mary the wife of Cleophas (Jn. 19:25). It occurs but rarely in CL (GL, § 362 N 1, the "family genitive"), though it is common in Greek.

8. The Hebrew construct state, in which "the former, not the latter, of two nouns is inflected ('man-of blood' not 'man of-blood')" (PW, § 20), is imitated by a descriptive or qualitative genitive (see § 7), e.g., *in brachiō fortitūdinis suae*, "by the arm of his strength" (Is. 62:8). This construction is also used "to heighten the meaning of the first word and raise it to a superlative" (PW, loc. cit.), e.g., *in saecula saeculōrum*, for ever.

9. The genitive is sometimes used for the second term in a place construction, e.g., *urbs Rōmae* instead of *urbs Rōma*, as in CL. Blaise, § 91, calls this the topographic genitive. It is also called the chorographic genitive.

10. The genitive is often employed with a partitive adjective, e.g., *in extrēmā īnsulae* instead of *in extrēmā īnsulā*.

11. The genitive of origin (Blaise, § 83) is also used, e.g., *per iūstitiam fideī*, "through the justice of faith" (Rom. 4:13). This might be seen as an extension of the subjective genitive (cf. *Woodcock*, § 72[2]), but, as a direct translation of the Greek διὰ δικαιοσύνης πίστεως, it certainly represents the Greek genitive of source.[51]

12. In imitation of Greek, the subjective genitive is used with adjectives and participles, e.g., *docibilēs Deī*, "taught of God" (Jn. 6:45). Cf. Capvt XX Syntaxis.

13. In imitation of Greek, the objective genitive is used with nouns that have the sense of an intransitive verb, e.g., *potestātem omnis carnis*, "power over all flesh" (Jn. 17:2). Cf. Capvt XX Syntaxis.

14. In imitation of Greek, verbs meaning "to rule" can govern the genitive, e.g., *dominantur eōrum*, "[they] lord it over them" (Lk. 22:25).

Accusative:

15. The accusative of motion towards with the names of cities, towns, and small islands, and with *domus*, is sometimes constructed with *ad* or *in*.

16. The Greek accusative of respect is sometimes found, e.g., *ablūtī corpus aquā mundā*, "our bodies washed with clean water," but literally = "washed respecting the body" (Hebrews 10:22). This is sometimes called the Greek accusative.

17. Accusative objects sometimes occur with passive verbs, as if the verbs were really middle in sense, e.g., *amictī stolās albās*, "clothed with white robes" (Apoc. 7:9). This and the previous usage are also found in the classical poets.

18. Accusative objects are often retained with gerunds, e.g., *omnis quī vīderit mulierem ad concupiscendum eam iam moechātus est eam in corde suō*, "whosoever shall look on a woman to lust after her, hath already committed adultery with her in his heart" (Mt. 5:28) for *ad concupiscendam eam*.

---

51   Herbert Weir Smyth, *Greek Grammar*, rev. Gordon M. Messing (Harvard, MA: Harvard University Press, 1956, 1984; orig. pub. 1920), § 1410.

19. The accusative often replaces the dative after *crēdere* and *benedīcere*.

Ablative:

20. Rules governing the ablative absolute are not always observed, i.e., the noun in the absolute construction is sometimes the same as the subject or object of the main clause, e.g., *et ascendente eō in nāviculum, secūtī sunt eum discipulī eius,* "And when he had entered into the boat, his disciples followed him" (Mt. 8:23), for *ascendentem in nāviculum secūtī sunt discipulī eius.*

21. The ablative of means/instrument can occur with *ab* or *in* in imitation of the Hebrew construction with *bə*, e.g., *ego baptīzō in aquā,* "I baptise with water" (Jn. 1:26), for simple *aquā.* See Capvt XIV Syntaxis.

22. The ablative of separation with the names of cities, towns, and small islands is sometimes constructed with *ab* or *ex.*

23. The ablative of time is sometimes constructed with *in.* See Capvt XV Syntaxis.

24. The ablative of time is extended to express duration. See Capvt XV Syntaxis.

25. The Hebrew cognate accusative is represented by the cognate ablative, e.g., *scrūtantēs scrūtiniō* = searching (with) a search, i.e., diligently (Ps. 63:7).

26. The Hebrew infinitive absolute, which was "prefixed . . . to the finite verb to emphasize the certainty of an action or fact" (PW, § 26), is sometimes represented by a modal ablative, e.g, *morte moriēris,* "you shall die the death," but KJV: "thou shalt surely die" (Ex. 21:7).

Locative:

27. The indeclinable names of cities such as *Ierusalem* are constructed with *in.*

Pronouns

28. *Iste* almost = *is,* and sometimes any other demonstrative, e.g., *Vōs ascendite ad diem festum hunc: ego nōn ascendō ad diem festum istum,* "Go you up to this festival day, but I go not up to this festival day" (Jn. 7:8). See Capvt IX Syntaxis.

29. The reflexive adjectives and adjective-pronouns are frequently misused, e.g., *dispersit superbōs mente cordis suī*, "he hath scattered the proud in the conceit of their heart" (Lk. 1:51), and *ōrābat Dominum . . . ut dīrigeret viam eius*, "she prayed to the Lord . . . that he would direct her way" (Jud. 12:8). Thus, *proprius* is often made to do service for *suus*. Cf. Capvt XIII Syntaxis.

30. In imitation of Hebrew, a redundant demonstrative is sometimes added to a relative pronoun, e.g., *sermōnum quōrum nōn audiantur vocēs eōrum*, "where their voices are not heard" (Ps. 18:4). See Nunn, § 68, and PW, § 24.

31. In some writers, *ille* and *ipse* approach the meaning of a definite article, while *quīdam* approaches the meaning of the indefinite. Cf. Capvt IX Syntaxis.

32. The possessive pronoun/adjective can have the sense of the objective genitive, e.g., *in meam commemorātiōnem*, "for a commemoration of me" (Lk. 22:19).

33. *Ut quid* is employed as a translation of ἵνα τί and εἰς τί (= for what? why?).

34. The indefinite pronoun *quis, quae* or *qua, quid* is sometimes used instead of *aliquis, aliquid* as a translation of τις, τι, e.g., *Īnfirmātur quis in vōbīs?*, "Is any man sick among you?" (James 5:14).

35. Instead of *alius alium, alter alterum*, or *inter sē*, EL often uses *invicem*, treated as an indeclinable pronoun, or *alterutrum*, e.g., *nōlī murmurāre in invicem*, "Murmur not among yourselves" (Jn. 6:43).

36. *Huiusmodī* and *eiusmodī* are often used as if they were pronouns, e.g., *Prō huiusmodī glōriābor*, "For such an one I will glory" (II Cor. 12:5).

Adjectives

37. On partitive adjectives, see § 10.

38. Neuter adjectives can be used as abstract substantives, e.g., *salutāre*, "salvation" (Lk. 2:30).

39. As regards comparison, in imitation of Greek the positive form of the adjective can be used for the comparative with *quam*, e.g., *bonum tibi est . . . quam*, "it is better for thee . . . than" (Mt. 18:9).

40. The comparative is sometimes used for the superlative, e.g., *maior est cāritās*, "the greatest of these is charity" (I Cor. 13:13).

41. The superlative is sometimes expressed by *ante/super/inter* + the positive form of adjective in imitation of Hebrew, e.g., *benedicta inter mulierēs,* "blessed among women," but better, "most blessed of women"[52] (Judg. 5:24; cf. Lk 4:2).

Prepositions

42. The number and uses of prepositions are expanded and extended considerably. See the appropriate sections of the grammars cited above.

> Note 1. Do note, however, that *in* + abl. is sometimes used "wrongly for εἰς" + acc. (PW, § 117.B(7)).

> Note 2. Note too that *dē* takes on a partitive role that anticipates the use of *de* and *di* in French and Italian, e.g., *effundam dē Spīritū meō,* "I will pour out of my Spirit" (Acts 2:17). See PW, § 117 *de* (3).

Verbs

Future Tense:

43. The future indicative can be deliberative, e.g., *Quid faciēmus?*, "What shall we do?" (Acts 2:37).

44. It can be jussive, e.g., *vocābis nōmen eius Iēsūm,* "thou shalt call his name Jesus" (Mt. 1.21).

45. It can be prohibitive, e.g., *nōn eritis ut hypocritae,* "you shall not be as the hypocrites" (Mt. 6:5).

Periphrastic Tenses:

46. In imitation of Greek, *sum, erō,* and *eram* with the present participle can form periphrastic or analytic present, future, and imperfect tenses, e.g., *est... dēscendēns, = dēscendit,* "is... descending," but KJV, "descendeth" (James 3:15), *stellae... erunt dēcidentēs, = dēcident,* "the stars... shall be falling down" (Mk. 13:25), and *erat expectāns, = expectābat,* "was... looking for" (Mk. 15:43). These are progressive in meaning. Cf. Capvt XXIII Syntaxis.

---

[52] See J. Weingreen, *A Practical Grammar for Classical Hebrew,* 2nd ed. (Oxford: Clarendon Press, 1959), § 62.

47. It is common to find *fuī* with the perfect passive participle for the perfect passive tense, e.g., *dictum fuit* for *dictum est*. *Fueram* with the perfect passive participle often forms the pluperfect passive tense, e.g., *dictum fuerat* for *dictum erat*. *Fuerō* with the perfect passive participle can form the future perfect passive tense, e.g., *dictum fuerit* for *dictum erit*.

> Note 1. In CL such forms were used to emphasize the completion of the act, or when the speaker was thinking of the participle as an adjective (GL, § 250). No such nuances seem to exist regularly in EL, according to the grammars.

> Note 2. Sometimes *sum* + perfect passive participle could simply be the sum of its parts, e.g., *amata est* = "she is loved," rather than "she was loved." (Example from MRi, p. 85.) This usage exists also in CL.

48. The present tense of *habēre* in combination with the accusative perfect passive participle can serve for the perfect active tense, e.g., *cuius etiam capillōs tū, Domine, numerātōs habēs*, = *numerāvistī*, "even whose hairs you, Lord, have numbered" (Augustine, *Conf.* 44.14). This yielded the *passé composé* in French (Blaise, § 219). The imperfect tense of *habēre* with a neuter singular accusative perfect passive participle can also be substituted for the ordinary pluperfect active tense, e.g., *tantum autem audītum habēbant*, = *audīverant*, "but they had heard only" (Gal. 1:23). This construction became the pluperfect tense in French and Italian (Nunn, § 93).

> Note 1. However, CL did employ the perfect passive participle in the accusative with *habēre* to stress "*the maintenance of the result.*" See GL, § 238.

Iteration:

49. Hebrew expresses repeated action "by prefixing the verb 'to add'" (PW, § 28). This sometimes appears in Latin, e.g., *addidit . . . mittere*, "again he sent" (Lk. 20:11, 12). Other verbs, such as *adiciō* and *adpōnō*, can also be used in this sense.

Infinitive:

50. The infinitive can be used in substitution for a purpose clause, e.g., *nōn enim mīsit mē Chrīstus baptīzāre, sed ēvangelīzāre*, "for Christ sent me not to baptize, but to preach the gospel" (I Cor. 1:17), for *ut baptīzārem, sed ēvangelīzārem*. See Capvt XXVIII Syntaxis.

Note 1. As regards expressions of purpose, the infinitive is often substituted for the supine with verbs of motion, e.g., *exiit in montem ōrāre* (= *ōrātum*), "he went out into the mountain to pray" (Lk. 6:12). See Blaise, § 330.

51. The infinitive, with an accusative subject, can be used in substitution for an indirect command, e.g, *rogāvit eum ā terrā redūcere pusillum*, "he desired him to draw back a little from the land" (Lk. 5:3), for *ut ā terrā redūceret*. See Capvt XXXVI Syntaxis.

52. The infinitive can be used in substitution for a clause of prevention, e.g., *impediēbar . . . venīre ad vōs*, "I was hindered . . . from coming to you" (Rom. 15:22), for *quōminus venīrem ad vōs*.

53. The infinitive can be used in substitution for a clause of fearing, e.g., *timuit illūc īre*, "he was afraid to go thither" (Mt. 2:22), for *nē illūc īret*.

54. The infinitive can be used in substitution for a result clause, e.g., *quis vōs fascināvit nōn oboedīre vēritātī?*, "who hath bewitched you that you should not obey the truth?" (Gal. 3:1), for *ut nōn oboediātis*.

55. In imitation of Greek, *habēre* with the infinitive can mean "to be able to . . ." This classical usage was extended to express obligation, e.g., *habēbat inquīrī ut occīderētur*, "he had to be sought so as to be killed" (Irenaeus 4.20.12). Finally, this usage came to convey a sense of future necessity, e.g., *Habēs, homō, imprīmīs aetātem venerāre aquārum*, "In the first place, o man, you will have to revere the age of the waters" (Tert., *De bapt.* 3). This usage gave rise to the future tense in French and Italian (See Blaise, § 221 for examples).

56. The infinitive can be used as the object of a preposition, e.g., *prō velle*, "in accordance with one's wish." (Example from MRi, p. 85.)

Participle:

57. The present participle is sometimes used for the Greek aorist active participle, e.g., *clāmāns . . . ēmīsit spīritum*, κράξας . . . ἀφῆκε τὸ πνεῦμα, "crying . . . [he] yielded up the ghost" (Mt. 27:50).

58. The Hebrew infinitive absolute (see § 26) can be represented by the present participle of the main verb, e.g., *benedīcēns benedīcam*, "blessing I shall bless" (Hebrews 6:14).

59. Participles are often used as substantives, e.g., *crēdentēs*, "believers."

60. The future passive participle (gerundive) is sometimes used as a simple future passive participle, i.e., it is employed without any nuance of obligation or necessity, e.g., *Quid est quod factum est? Ipsum quod faciendum est,* "What is it that hath been done? the same that shall be done" (Eccles. 1:9, cited in PW, § 130(1)(a)).

Gerund:

61. The Hebrew infinitive absolute (see § 26) can be represented by the ablative of the gerund, e.g., *praecipiendō praecēpimus,* "commanding we commanded," but KJV: "did not we straitly command" (Acts 5:28).

62. The gerund in the ablative of attendant circumstances sometimes replaces the present participle, e.g., *ambulandō loquebāmur* for *ambulantēs loquebāmur.* (The example is from MRi, p. 85.)

63. Gerundival attraction does not always happen where you would expect it. See § 18 above.

Complex Sentences
Prohibitions (see also § 45):

64. The present subjunctive can be used in particular prohibitions, e.g., *Nōn mirēris quia dīxī tibi,* "Wonder not, that I said to thee" (Jn. 3:7). See Capvt XXXII Syntaxis.

   Note 1. Notice that *nōn* is used in the example above, as frequently in EL, for *nē* with the optative subjunctive. See Nunn, § 99, and PW, §126(1). Cf. GL, §§ 260 and 263.2.

65. A prohibition can be formed with *vidē(te)* followed by a negative and the present or perfect subjunctive, e.g., *vidē neminī dīxeris,* "see thou tell no man" (Mt. 8:4). Cf. GL § 548N3.

66. In imitation of Hebrew, an emphatic prohibition can be formed with *omnis* and a verb in the present subjunctive with *nōn,* e.g., *Omnis sermō malus ex ōre vestrō nōn praecēdat,* "Let no evil speech proceed from your mouth" (Eph. 4:29).

Dependent Clauses:

67. The indicative is sometimes retained in indirect questions for vividness, e.g., *intellige quid loquitur,* "Understand what it says" (Jerome, *Pelag.* 3.8, cited in Blaise, § 270), for *quid loquātur.* See Capvt XXX Syntaxis.

68. The indicative and the subjunctive are used in temporal clauses with *dum, dōnec, antequam,* and *priusquam* without apparent difference in meaning. This is also true of causal clauses introduce by *quod, quia, quoniam,* and *eō quod.* See Capvt VIII Syntaxis and Capvt XXX Syntaxis.

69. The subjunctive is used in temporal *cum*-clauses sometimes. On the other hand, the indicative is sometimes used in causal and concessive *cum*-clauses. *Quod* + indicative can = result. The subjunctive is also used in this construction.

70. In imitation of Greek, *quod, quia,* and *quoniam,* (and less often *quātenus, quāliter,* and *quōmodo*) with a finite verb in the indicative or subjunctive can be used for indirect statement rather than the accusative and infinitive construction, e.g., *scīmus quia nihil est idōlum in mundō, et quod nūllus Deus nisi ūnus,* "we know that an idol is nothing in the world, and that there is no God but one" (I Cor. 8:4), for *nihil esse idōlum in mundō et nūllum Deum [esse] nisi ūnum.* See Capvt XXV Syntaxis.

Note 1. Nunn, § 135, sees no difference between the indicative and subjunctive in such constructions, while PW, § 134(ii)(a)(1), says "the Indicative Mood lays stress on the fact, the Subjunctive denotes a thought or mental concept." Blaise, §§ 261–263, notices that the subjunctive is used with *quod* more often than with the other conjunctions. Nunn, § 113, notices two uses in early Latin of a *quod*-clause in apposition to verbs of saying or feeling. He gives this example: *Equidem sciō iam [id] fīlius quod amet meus istanc meretrīcem,* "Of course, I know [it] already, that my son loves that damned whore" (Plautus, *Asinaria* 52). In each case cited by Nunn, the verb in the *quod*-clause is in the subjunctive. This usage may have survived in "street" Latin, and found its employment extended much later in what we call Vulgar Latin and EL under the influence of Greek idiom. The subjunctive would be logical in dependence on verbs of saying and feeling, as it expresses an idea, not a fact.

Note 2. Direct quotations are sometimes introduced by *quia* or *quoniam,* in imitation of the Greek. See PW, § 134.a.ii.α.1. See Capvt XXV Syntaxis.

Direct Questions:

71. Both *an?* and *numquid non?* can replace *nōnne?. Numquid?* can replace *num?.* However, *numquid?* can also replace the enclitic particle *-ne?.*

Varia:

72. Hebrew causative constructions (*hiphil* and *hophal*) are generally represented by *facere* and *dare* with the infinitive, e.g., *nec dabis sānctum tuum vidēre corruptiōnem*, "nor wilt thou give thy holy one to see corruption" (Ps. 15:10).

73. The Greek ἐγένετο, which itself represents Hebrew *wayǝhî*, "it came to pass," is represented by *factum est* followed by either an *ut*-clause or an accusative and infinitive or a verb in the indicative with no conjunction, e.g., *factum est . . . ut intrāret in synagōgum*, "it came to pass . . . that he entered into the synagogue" (Lk. 6:6). See Capvt XXXVII Syntaxis.

APPENDIX II
Brief Biographies of Authors Cited in the *Sententiae* and *Locī*

Aelred, St., (1109–1167), abbot of Rievaulx (northern England), Anglo-Saxon, Cistercian, author of spiritual and hagiographical works, adapted Cicero's *Dē amicītiā.*

Ambrose, St. (c. 339–397), Roman statesman, bishop of Milan (Italy), opponent of Arianism, helped adapt Plotinian Neoplatonism to Christianity, author of theological works, introduced hymnody to the western liturgy, adapted Cicero's *Dē officiīs*, one of the four Latin Doctors.

Anselm, St. (c. 1033–1109), native of Lombardy (northern Italy), prior and abbot of Bec (Normandy), archbishop of Canterbury (England), Platonist, author of works of theology and works on the arts, discovered the famous "ontological argument."

Arnold (d. after 1156), abbot of Bonneval near Chartres (France), co-biographer of St. Bernard of Clairvaux, author of sermons and biblical commentaries.

Augustine, St. (354–430), bishop of Hippo (North Africa), rhetorician, brilliant stylist, completed the assimilation of Plotinian Neoplatonism to Christianity, author of many works of theology, and some on the arts, his *Cōnfessiōnēs*, *Dē Trīnitāte*, and *Dē cīvitāte Deī* are foundational for western Christianity and culture, one of the four Latin Doctors.

Baldwin (d. 1190), archbishop of Canterbury (England), Cistercian, author of theological works, died in the Holy Land on the Third Crusade.

Basil the Great, St. (c. 330–379), bishop of Caesarea (Cappadocia, Asia Minor), monk, one of the three Cappadocian Fathers, deeply influenced by Origen, great controversialist against the Arians and others.

Bede the Venerable, St. (c. 673–735), Anglo-Saxon, monk of Jarrow (northern England), historian, biblical commentator, computist.

Bellarmine, St. Robert (1542–1621), native of Tuscany (Italy), Jesuit, cardinal, archbishop of Capua (Italy), scholar, controversialist against the Protestants, instrumental in the revision of the Vulgate.

Benedict XVI, Pope (Josef Ratzinger), (1927–), native of Bavaria (Germany), distinguished Roman Catholic theologian in the Platonic tradition, ecclesiastical statesman.

Bernard, St. (1090–1153), abbot of Clairvaux (Burgundy, France), caused the twelfth-century explosion in Cistercian vocations, prolific letter writer, preacher, and theologian, brilliant stylist, known as the "last of the Fathers."

Boethius (c. 480–c. 524), Roman consul, prolific translator of Greek philosophical texts, theologian, called the "last of the Romans and first of the scholastics."

Bonaventure, St. (c. 1217–1274), Italian, Franciscan, Minister General of the Friars Minor, conservative Platonist theologian and mystic, prolific theological author.

Bruni, Leonardo (1370–1444), Florentine, humanist, a disciple of a disciple of Petrarch's, one of the first Renaissance students of Greek, translator, historian.

Calvin, John (1509–1564), French, one of the magisterial Reformers, his *Īnstitūtiō Chrīstiānae Religiōnis* is the greatest and most systematic work of reformed theology.

Carroll, Lewis, the pseudonym of C. L. Dodgson (1832–1898), Anglican clergyman, Oxford don, mathematician, author.

Cyprian of Carthage, St. (d. 258), North African bishop, theologian, martyr.

Descartes, René (1596–1650), French, Jesuit-educated, mathematician, scientist, metaphysician (deeply influenced by Augustine).

Einhard (c. 770–840), servant and friend of Charlemagne, historian, wrote in the style of Sallust.

Ephraem the Syrian (c. 306–373), native of Nisibis, settled later at Edessa, deacon, biblical exegete, composed hymns that were influential in Syrian and Greek liturgy.

Erasmus, Desiderius (1466/9–1536), Dutch, humanist, brilliant linguist, prodigious scholar, critical of abuses in the Church, but remained a Catholic, friend of St. Thomas More.

Eriugena, John Scotus (c. 810–c. 877), Irish, scholar and theologian at the court of Charles the Bald, attempted the reconciliation of Plotinian Neoplatonism (Augustine) with Procline Neoplatonism (Pseudo-Dionysius, Maximus the Confessor).

Ficino, Marsilio (1433–1499), Florentine, humanist, Neoplatonist philosopher, translator of Plato, Catholic priest.

Francis of Assisi, St. (1181/2–1226), native of Umbria (Italy), friar, deacon, founder of the Friars Minor, made living the Catholic faith viable for the people of the towns of Italy, which were rapidly industrializing as capitalism was being invented, received the Stigmata.

Gaudentius, St. (4th–5th century), bishop of Brescia (Italy), friend of St. Ambrose, ecclesiastical statesman, author of sermons.

Geoffrey Malaterra (d. in or after 1098), "from the regions over the Alps," Benedictine monk, brought to Sicily prob. in 1091 to assist in Count Roger's efforts to re-establish Latin Christianity, solicited by Count Roger to write the history of his achievements.

Gregory of Nazianzus, St. (329/30–389/90), monk, bishop of Constantinople, one of the Cappadocian Fathers, deeply influenced by Origen, author of theological orations.

Gregory the Great, Pope St. (c. 540–604), monk, author, ecclesiastical statesman, fostered liturgical chant, one of the four Latin Doctors.

Guarino, Battista (1434–?), Italian, humanist, teacher.

Hilary, St. (c. 315–367/8), bishop of Poitiers (France), exiled for outspoken defense of orthodoxy against Arianism, author of a great work on the Trinity, as well as of commentaries and hymns.

Hildegard of Bingen, St. (1098–1179), from the Rhineland (Germany), Benedictine, abbess of Rupertsberg, visionary mystic from childhood, illuminator, poetess, composer, hagiographer, letter writer, scientific writer, influenced by Pseudo-Dionysius and Eriugena.

Hrosvitha (10th century), native of Saxony (Germany), canoness of Gandersheim, poetess, modeled her plays on Terence.

Hugh (d. 1142), canon of St. Victor (Paris), possibly a Saxon, teacher, scholar, author of works on the arts, Scripture, and theology.

Ignatius, St. (c. 35–c. 107), bishop of Antioch (Syria), letter writer, martyr.

Isaac, Blessed (c. 1100–c. 1178), abbot of Stella (near Poitiers, France), then of the Île de Ré (off La Rochelle), Cistercian, Platonist, homilist and spiritual writer.

Isidore, St. (c. 560–636), bishop of Seville (Spain), author most notably of the *Etymologiae*, an encyclopedia fundamental to the scholarship of the Middle Ages.

Jerome, St. (c. 345–420), Italian, Ciceronian, monk, controversialist, wrote letters and commentaries, revised the Latin translation of the Bible, a revision now known as the Vulgate, one of the four Latin Doctors.

John of Salisbury (c. 1115–1180), English, humanist, servant and friend of St. Thomas Becket, author of works on the arts, politics, and history, bishop of Chartres (France).

Lactantius (c. 250–c. 325), rhetorician, author of several theological works in a Ciceronian style.

Leo Marsicanus (11th century), monk of Monte Casino (Italy), cardinal bishop of Ostia (Italy), chronicler.

Leo the Great, Pope St. (d. 461), ecclesiastical statesman, raised the status of the Holy See, author of letters and sermons.

Lewis, C. S. (1893–1963), native of Northern Ireland, scholar of medieval literature, popular Anglican theological writer and novelist.

Marius Victorinus Afer (4th century), rhetorician, Neoplatonist philosopher both before and after conversion, translator, author of works that anticipate Augustine to some extent.

More, St. Sir Thomas (1478–1535), English, humanist, lawyer, statesman, author, Catholic martyr.

Niceta, St. (d. c. 414), bishop of Remesiana (Serbia), theologian, there is a slight possibility that he composed the *Te Deum*.

Nicholas of Cusa (Cues) (1401–1464), German, cardinal, bishop of Brixen (Germany), ecclesiastical statesman, humanist, historian, Neoplatonist spiritual writer.

Peter Chrysologus, St. (c. 400–450), bishop of Ravenna (Italy), author of sermons.

Peter Lombard (c. 1100–1160), from Lombardy (Italy), teacher at the Cathedral of Paris, bishop of Paris, author of commentaries and a systematic theology, the *Sententiae*, which became the standard theological textbook of the Middle Ages, called "the Master of the Sentences."

Peter the Venerable (1092 or 1094–1156), abbot of Cluny (Burgundy, France), friend of St. Bernard, author of letters and controversial works.

Petrarca (Petrarch), Francesco (1304–1374), Tuscan, humanist and poet, often called "the Father of Humanism" and "the Father of the Renaissance."

Posthius, Johannes (1537–1597), Dutch, physician, poet.

Salvian of Marseilles (c. 400–c.480), Catholic priest, ecclesiastical author.

Suger (c. 1081–1151), abbot of St. Denis (Paris), adviser to Kings Lewis VI and Lewis VII, Platonist theorist of Gothic architecture.

Thomas à Kempis (prob. Thomas Hemerken) (c. 1380–1471), Dutch, mystic, influenced by the Brethren of the Common Life, a Canon Regular.

Thomas Aquinas, St. (c. 1225–1274), Neapolitan, Dominican, scholastic theologian, poet; a more radical theologian than Bonaventure, he attempted a reconciliation of traditional Plotinian Neoplatonism (Augustine and his western heirs) both with Procline theology (the *Liber de Causis*, Pseudo-Dionysius) and with Aristotle.

Thomas of Celano (c. 1190–1260), joined St. Francis' friars c. 1214, earliest of the biographers of St. Francis.

Thomas of Eccleston (13th century), Franciscan, scholar at Oxford (England), historian.

Tribonian, Theophilus, and Dorotheus (6th century), Roman legists, largely responsible for the great legal codifications under Emperor Justinian.

William of Poitiers (c. 1020–after 1087), native of Normandy (France), knight, priest, chaplain to William the Conqueror, biographer.

William Calculus (12th century), native of Normandy (France), monk of Jumièges (Normandy), historian.

William (1075/80–1148), abbot of St. Thierry (near Rheims, France), close friend and co-biographer of St. Bernard of Clairvaux, became a Cistercian in 1135, author of theological and spiritual works.

Wipo (d. after 1046), native of Swabia (Germany), priest, chaplain to the Emperors Conrad II and Henry III, poet, biographer.

A List of the *Verba Memoriā Comprehendenda*

Ābraham, indecl. Heb. name, or **Ābraham, -hae,** m., *Abraham.* 1

accidō, -ere, -cidī, *fall down on; happen.* 36

aeternus, -a, -um, *eternal.* 16

aliquī, aliquae/aliqua, aliquod, indef. pronominal adj., *some.* 29

ambulō (1), *walk.* 38

amīcitia, to the definitions in *Wheelock* add *a compact, treaty.* 10

angelus, -ī, m., *a messenger; angel.* 11

anima, -ae, f. (dat. and abl. pl. sometimes **animābus**), *breath; vital principle; life; soul; mind.* 2

antequam, conj., *before.* 32

benedīcō, -ere, -dīxī, -dictum, *speak well of* (+ dat.); *bless* (+ dat. or acc.). 19

baptīzō (1), *baptize.* 32

cantō (1), *make melody* (with instrument or voice); *sound* (of an instrument); *play* (of an instrument); *sing* (of a voice); *sing* (a song); *use enchantments.* 18

cāritās, -tātis, f., *costliness, high price; affection, love; charity.* 9

carō, carnis, f., *flesh.* 15

cēterī, -ae, -a, or **caeterī, -ae, -a,** *the others, the rest.* 27

Chrīstiānus, -a, -um, *Christian.* 30

chrīstus, -ī, m., *the anointed;* **Chrīstus, -ī,** m., *the Anointed, the Messiah, (the) Christ,* a Greek borrowing. 4

cibus, -ī, m., *food.* 13

clāmō (1), *shout.* 10

cor, cordis, n., *heart; mind.* 9

cornū, cornūs, n., to the meaning in *Wheelock* add *power, might* (by analogy with the horn of a bull), coming both from CL and as a Hebraism (LS, s.v. II). 20

cūnctī, -ae, -a, *all together, all* (the sg. number is found less frequently than the pl.). 12

Dāvīd, indecl. Heb. name, or **Dāvīd, -vīdis,** m., *David,* second king of Israel. 1

dīvīnus, -a, -um, *divine.* 9

dominus, -ī, m., *a master, owner, lord; the Lord.* 3

dōnec, conj., *while, as long as, at the same time that, until* + indicative; *until* + subjunctive. 8

ecce, interj., *behold.* 3

ecclēsia, -ae, f., *a (political) assembly; church.* 40

efficiō, -ere, -fēcī, -fectum, *effect, bring about.* 36

ēligō, -ere, -lēgī, -lēctum, *choose.* 26

enim, postpositive conj., *truly; for.* 2

ergō, adv., *therefore.* 5

ēvangelium, -iī, n., *good news; the Gospel.* 34

faciēs, -ēī, f., *a face; appearance.* 34

faciō, see *salvus, -a, -um*

fōns, fontis, m., *a spring; fountain.* 21

gaudium, -iī, n., *joy, delight.* 14

habitō (1), *dwell.* 34

Ierūsalem or **Hierūsalem,** indecl. Heb. name, or **Hierosolyma, -ae,** f., or **Hierosolyma, -ōrum,** n., *Jerusalem.* 7

Iēsūs, -ū, -ū, -ūm, -ū, -ū, m. irreg., *Joshua; Jesus* (Collins' quantities are followed). 7

impius, -a, -um, *undutiful; impious.* 20

inimīcus, -ī, m., *a (personal) enemy.* 6

interest, -esse, -fuit, *it concerns, it is of interest, it is in the interest of.* 39

Israël or **Israhel,** indecl. Heb. name, or **Israël/Israhel, -ēlis,** m., *Israel.* 5

iūstitia, -ae, f., *justice; righteousness.* 23

iūstus, -a, -um, *just, righteous.* 17

licet, to the definitions in *Wheelock* add *although*, used with a verb in the subjunctive. 37

Marīa, -ae, f., *Mary.* 11

mediātor, -tōris, m., *a mediator.* 39

meminī, -nisse, defective verb (perf. with pres. force), *remember, recollect* (+ gen. or acc.). 37

memor, -oris, *mindful* (+ gen.). 38

misereō -ēre, -uī, miser(i)tum or **misereor, -ērī, miser(i)tus sum,** *(feel) pity* (+ gen. or dat.). 37

miseret, miserēre, miseruit, *it pities, it moves to pity.* 39

misericordia, -ae, f., *mercy, pity.* 28

mulier, -eris, f., *a woman; wife.* 9

nātūrālis, -e, *natural.* 18

necessitās, -tātis, f., *necessity; poverty.* 25

numquid, in EcL = can replace *num?* or *-ne?* (see Appendix I, § 71). 40

paenitentia, -ae, or **poenitentia, -ae,** f., *a change of mind; repentance; penance.* For the idiom *paenitentiam agere,* see Capvt VIII, Sentence 5. 30

paenitet, paenitēre, paenituit, *it repents.* 39

peccātum, -ī, n., *an error; sin.* 4

persōna, -ae, f., *an actor's mask; the character played by an actor; the function performed, or part maintained, by any person in the world, a personage; a grammatical person; one of the subsistent relations of the Holy Trinity.* 33

Petrus, -ī, m., *Peter.* 12

piget, pigēre, piguit, *it disgusts, it irks.* 39

pius, -a, -um, *dutiful; pious.* 20

potentia, -ae, f., *power.* 21

prex, precis, f., *a prayer.* 15

priusquam, conj., *before.* 32

prophēta, -ae, m., *a prophet.* 32

proprius, -a, -um, *one's own, special, particular, proper, characteristic* (opposed both to *commūnis* and to *aliēnus*); often used in EL as a substitute for the reflexive possessive (Appendix I, § 29). 17

psallō, -ere, psallī, *play upon a stringed instrument; sing the Psalms of David* (EL). 14

psalmus, -ī, m., *a psalm.* 15

pudet, pudēre, puduit, *it shames.* 39

quamvīs, *although* (+ subjunctive). 31

quia, conj., *because; that.* 25

quīn (= **quī** instrumental + **nē,** *how not? why not? Woodcock,* § 185), conj., *(but) that* (in a clause of doubting); *from* + gerund (in a clause of prevention). 35

quōminus, quō minus (*by the which less*), conj., *from* + gerund (in a clause of prevention). 35

quōmodo, adv., *in what way, how.* 39

ratiōnālis, -e, *rational, reasonable.* 24

redimō, -ere, -ēmī, -ēmptum, *buy back, redeem.* 35

rēfert, rēferre, rētulit, *it concerns, it is of interest, it is in the interest of.* 39

rēgnum, -ī, n., *royal rule; a kingdom.* 27

sacer, -cra, -crum, *sacred, holy.* 11

sacrāmentum, -ī, n., *a sum deposited in a suit by the two parties involved; a civil suit; an army recruit's initial promise of service; the military oath of allegiance; a solemn obligation;* (in EL) *a secret; a mystery; a sacrament.* 24

saeculum, -ī, n., *a race, breed; an ordinary lifetime, a generation; a maximum lifetime, a century; an indefinitely long time, an age.* 28

salvus, -a, -um, to the definitions in *Wheelock* add *saved* (from sin by Christ). To the meanings of **faciō** in *Wheelock* add this Biblical idiom, **salvum, -am, -um facere,** = *save* (someone or something, also in the acc.). 6, 13

sanguis, -inis, m., *blood; a blood relationship.* 19

sānctus, -a, -um, *sacred, holy;*
m./f. substantive, *a saint.* 3

scrīptūra, -ae, f., *a writing;* (Holy)
Scripture. 7

sēcrētus, -a, -um, *secret, hidden.*
25

sermō, -ōnis, m., *talk,*
conversation, discourse; a sermon.
21

sīcut, adv. and conj., *as, just as.* 22

stultus, -a, -um, *foolish, simple,*
silly. 16

super, prep. (+ abl.), *over, above,*
concerning, about, besides,
beyond; (+ acc.) *over, above, upon,*
beyond, besides. 2

superbia, -ae, f., *pride, arrogance.*
33

taedet, taedēre, taeduit, *it bores,*
it disgusts, it tires. 39

tenebrae, -ārum, f. pl., *darkness.*
22

trādō, -ere, -didī, -ditum, *hand*
over; hand down, transmit. 26

tunc, adv., *then, at that time.* 31

utinam, adv., *if only, how I wish*
that, would that (archaic), used
sometimes to introduce the
optative subjunctive. 29

valeō, in EL *valeō* often = *possum.*
8

voluntās, -tātis, f., *will, wish,*
inclination. 13

vōx, vōcis, f., *a voice; word.* 23

A List of Source Texts Not Included in the Abbreviations

This is not a complete list of authors and works cited in the Sententiae *and* Locī. *Such a list will be found in the indices. Other texts used in this volume can be found in the Abbreviations.*

Adriaen, Marc, ed., *Sancti Hieronymi Presbyteri Opera* 1.2, Turnhout: Brepols, 1963

Aelred of Rievaulx, St., *De Spirituali Amicitia*, in J.-P. Migne, ed., *Patrologiae Cursus Completus, Series Secunda, Patrologiae Tomus CXCV*, Paris: apud J.-P. Migne Editorem, 1855, coll. 659–702

Ambrose of Milan, St., *De Officiis Ministrorum Libri Tres*, in J.-P. Migne, ed., *Patrologiae Cursus Completus, Series Latina Prior, Patrologiae Latinae Tomus XVI*, Paris: apud Garnier Fratres, Editores et J.-P. Migne Successores, 1880, coll. 25–194

Idem, *Dē virginibus*, in J.-P. Migne, ed., *Patrologiae Cursus Completus, Series Latina Prior, Patrologiae Latinae Tomus XVI*, Paris: apud Garnier Fratres, Editores et J.-P. Migne Successores, 1880, coll. 198–244

Idem, see March for hymns

Anselm of Canturbury, St., *De Humanis Moribus*, in R. W. Southern and F. S. Schmitt, ed., *Memorials of St. Anselm*, Auctores Britannici Medii Aevi 1, Oxford: Published for the British Academy by Oxford University Press, 1969

Idem, *Proslogion*, in M. J. Charlesworth, ed., *St. Anselm's* Proslogion *with A Reply on Behalf of the Fool by Gaunilo and The Author's Reply to Gaunilo*, Notre Dame, IN: University of Notre Dame Press, 1979 (orig. pub. 1965)

Arnold of Bonneval, *Liber de Cardinalibus Christi Operibus,* in my dissertation *The* Liber de Cardinalibus Christi Domini nostri Operibus *of the Lord Arnold, Abbot of Bonneval, Introduction and Critical Text with Notes* (Dalhousie University, Halifax, Nova Scotia, Canada, 1991)

Augustine of Hippo, St., *Confessiones,* see *Les Confessions*

Idem, *De Civitate Dei,* see Welldon

Idem, *De Immortalitate Animae,* in *Soliloquies and Immortality of the Soul,* ed. G. Watson, Aris and Phillips Classical Texts, Eastbourne: Aris and Phillips, 2008 (orig. pub. 1990)

Idem, *De Magistro,* in *Oeuvres de Saint Augustin 6, Première Série: Opuscules, Dialogues Philosophiques III, De Magistro - De Libero Arbitrio,* 3rd ed., ed. Goulven Madec, Institut d'Etudes Augustiniennes, Turnhout: Brepols, 1999

Idem, *De Ordine,* in *Oeuvres de Saint Augustin 4/2, Dialogues Philosophiques, De Ordine - L'Ordre,* ed. Jean Doignon, Bibliothèque Augustinienne, Paris: Institut d'Etudes Augustiniennes, 1986

Idem, *De Trinitate,* see *La Trinité*

Idem, *Sermones ad Populum, Classis IV. De Diversis,* in J.-P. Migne, ed., *Patrologiae Latinae,* vol. 39, Turnhout: Brepols, 1991 (orig. pub. 1841)

Idem, *Soliloquia,* in *Soliloquies and Immortality of the Soul,* ed. G. Watson, Aris and Phillips Classical Texts, Eastbourne: Aris and Phillips, 2008 (orig. pub. 1990)

Baron, Abbé Roger, ed., *Hugonis de Sancto Victore Opera Propaedeutica, Practica Geometriae, De Grammatica, Epitome Dindimi in Philosophiam,* Publications in Mediaeval Studies 20, Notre Dame, IN: University of Notre Dame Press, 1966

Bede the Venerable, St., *Historia Ecclesiastica Gentis Anglorum,* see King

Bellarmine, St. Robert, *Controversiae de Verbo Dei Quattuor Libris Explicatae,* in *Ven. Cardinalis Roberti Bellarmini Politiani S.J. Opera Omnia,* ed. Justinus Fèvre, vol. 1, Paris: Apud Ludovicum Vivès, Editorem, 1870

Benedict XVI, Pope, *Litterae Encyclicae Deus Caritas Est,* http://www.vatican.va/holy_father/benedict_xvi/encyclicals/documents/hf_ben-xvi_enc_2, retrieved 6/26/2007

Bernard of Clairvaux, St., *De Diligendo Deo,* in Leclercq, vol. 3

Idem, *Epistola* 65, in Leclercq, vol. 7

Idem, *Sermo 5 in Adventu Domini*, in Leclercq, vol. 4

Idem, *Sermones super Cantica*, in Leclercq, vols. 1–2

Boethius, *The Theological Tractates* [incl. De Trinitate, De Fide Catholica, and Contra Eutychen], *The Consolation of Philosophy*, new ed., ed. H. F. Stewart, E. K. Rand, and S. J. Tester, Loeb Classical Library, Cambridge, MA: Harvard University Press, 1973

Bonaventure, St., see *Tria Opuscula*

Bruni, Leonardo, *De Studiis et Litteris Liber*, in Kallendorf, 92–125

Buttimer, Brother Charles Henry, ed., *Hugonis de Sancto Victore Didscalicon de Studio Legendi, A Critical Text*, Studies in Medieval and Renaissance Latin 10, Washington, DC: Catholic University of America Press, 1939

Calvin, John, *Institutio Christianae Religionis*, ed. A. Tholuck, Pars Prior, Berlin: apud Gustavum Eichler, 1834 (1549 ed.)

Caramello, Pietro, ed., *Sancti Thomae Aquinatis Summa Theologiae, Prima Pars*, Turin: Marietti, 1950

Carroll, Lewis, *Aliciae Per Speculum Transitus*, tr. Clive Harcourt Carruthers, London: Macmillan and Company, 1966

Cyprian of Carthage, St., *De Ecclesiae Catholicae Unitate*, in Maurice Bévenot, ed. *Cyprian, De Lapsis and De Ecclesiae Catholicae Unitate*, Oxford Early Christian Texts, Oxford: Clarendon Press, 1971

Descartes, René, *Meditationes de Prima Philosophia / Meditations on First Philosophy, A Bilingual Edition*, ed. George Heffernan, Notre Dame, IN: University of Notre Dame Press, 1990

Einhard, *Vita Karoli Magni Imperatoris*, in *Eginhard, Vie de Charlemagne*, ed. Louis Halphen, Les Classiques de l'Histoire de France au Moyen Âge, Paris: Société d'Édition «Les Belles Lettres», 1938

Erasmus, Desiderius, *Adagia*, in *Opera Omnia*, vol. 2, Leiden: Petrus Vander Aa, 1703

Eriugena, John Scotus, *De Divisione Naturae Libri Quinque*, in J.-P. Migne, ed., *Patrologiae Cursus Completus, Series Secunda, Patrologiae Tomus CXXII*, Paris: apud J.-P. Migne Editorem, 1853, coll. 439–1022

Esser, Kajetan, St., ed., *Die Opuscula des Hl. Franziskus von Assisi*, new critical ed., Grottaferrata (Rome): Collegii S. Bonaventurae ad Claras Aquas, 1976

Ficino, Marsilio, *Theologia Platonica de Immortalitate Animorum*, in *Platonic Theology*, vol. 1, Books 1–4, and vol. 2, Books 5–8, ed. James Hankins and William Bowen, I Tatti Renaissance Library 2 and 4, Cambridge, MA: Harvard University Press, 2001

Francis of Assisi, St., *Admonitiones*, in Esser, 106–117

Idem, *Epistola ad Clericos*, in Esser, 163–165

Idem, *Epistola ad Fideles* (recensio prior), in Esser, 178–180

Idem, *Epistola ad Fideles* (recensio posterior), in Esser, 207–213

Idem, *Epistola ad S. Antonium*, in Esser, 153

Idem, *Exhortatio ad Laudem Dei*, in Esser, 282–283

Geoffrey Malaterra, see Pontieri

Guarino, Battista, *De Ordine Docendi et Studendi*, in Kallendorf, 260–309

Hilary of Poitiers, St., *De Trinitate Libri XII*, Innsbruck: Libraria Academica Wagneriana, 1887

Hildegard of Bingen, St., *Physica seu Subtilitatum Diversarum Naturarum Creaturarum Libri Novem*, in J.-P. Migne, ed., *Patrologiae Cursus Completus, Series Latina Prior, Patrologiae Latinae Tomus CXCVII*, Paris: apud Garnier Fratres, Editores et J.-P. Migne Successores, 1882, coll. 1117–1352

Hrosvitha of Gandersheim, *Dulcitius* and *Paphnutius*, in *Hrosvithae Opera*, ed. H. Homeyer, Munich: Verlag Ferdinand Schöningh, 1970

Hugh of St. Victor, *De Grammatica*, see Baron

Idem, *De Sacramentis Fidei Christianae*, in J.-P. Migne, ed., *Patrologiae Cursus Completus, Series Latina Prior, Patrologiae Latinae Tomus CLXXVI*, Paris: apud Garnier Fratres, Editores et J.-P. Migne Successores, 1880, coll. 173–618

Idem, *Didascalicon*, see Buttimer

Idem, *Practica Geometriae*, see Baron

Isidore of Seville, *Isidori Hispalensis Episcopi Etymologiarum sive Originum Libri XX*, ed. W. M. Lindsay, 2 vols., Oxford Classical Texts, Oxford: Clarendon Press, 1957

Jerome, *Commentariorum in Esaiam Libri I–XI*, see Adriaen

John of Salisbury, *Metalogicon*, ed. J. B. Hall and K. S. B. Keats-Rohan, Corpus Christianorum, Continuatio Mediaevalis 98, Turnhout: Brepols, 1991

Kallendorf, Craig W., ed., *Humanist Educational Treatises*, I Tatti Renaissance Library 5, Cambridge, MA: Harvard Universaity Press, 2002

King, J. E., ed. and tr., *Bede, Historical Works*, vol. 1, Loeb Classical Library, Harvard: Harvard University Press, 1930

Lactantius, *Firmiani Lactantii Epitome Institutionum Divinarum / Lactantius' Epitome of the Divine Institutes*, ed. E. H. Blakeney, London: SPCK, 1950

La Trinité, Livres VIII–XV, Oeuvres de Saint Augustin 16, Bibliothèque Augustinienne, Paris: Études Augustiniennes, 1991

Leclercq, J., C. H. Talbot, and H. M. Rochais, ed., *Sancti Bernardi Opera*, Rome: Editiones Cistercienses, 8 vols., 1957–1977

Leo Marsicanus, *Chronica Monasterii Casinensis*, in J.-P. Migne, ed., *Patrologiae Cursus Completus, Series Latina, Patrologiae Latinae Tomus CLXXIII*, Paris: apud J.-P. Migne Editorem, 1895, coll. 183–812

Les Confessions, Livres VIII–XIII, Oeuvres de Saint Augustin 14, Bibliothèque Augustinienne, Paris: Descleé de Brouwer, 1962

Liber Precum Publicarum in Ecclesia Anglicana, in *Liturgical Services: Liturgies and Occasional Forms of Prayer Set forth in the Reign of Queen Elizabeth*, ed. William Keatinge Clay, Parker Society, Cambridge: Cambridge University Press, 1847

March, F. A., *Latin Hymns with English Notes. For Use in Schools and Colleges*, Douglass Series of Christian Greek and Latin Writers for Use in Schools and Colleges 1, New York: Harper and Brothers Publishers, 1879

Marius Victorinus Afer, *De Physicis Liber*, in J.-P. Migne, ed., *Patrologiae Cursus Completus, Series Prima*, Paris: excudebat Vrayet, 1844, coll. 1295–1310

Nicholas of Cusa, *Sermones*, in *Writings on Church and Reform*, various editors, I Tatti Renaissance Library 33, Cambridge, MA: Harvard University Press, 2008

Peter Lombard, *Sententiarum Libri Quattuor*, in J.-P. Migne, ed., *Patrologiae Cursus Completus, Series Secunda*, Paris: apud Editorem, 1846, coll. 11–452

Peter the Venerable, *Epistola* 21, in Giles Constable, ed., *The Letters of Peter the Venerable*, vol. 1, Cambridge, MA: Harvard University Press, 1967

Petrarca (Petrarch), Francesco, *De sui Ipsius et Multorum Ignorantia / Della mia Ignoranza e di quella di molti Altri*, ed. Enrico Fenzi, Milan: Mursia, 1999

Pontieri, Ernesto, ed., *De Rebus Gestis Rogerii Calabriae et Siciliae Comitis et Roberti Guiscardi Ducis Fratris Eius Auctore Gaufredo Malaterra*, Rerum Italicarum Scriptores, nuova edizione, Tomo V, Parte I, Bologna: Nicola Zanichelli, 1925–1928

Posthius, Iohannes, *Tabacum*, in I. D. McFarlane, *Renaissance Latin Poetry*, Literature in Context, Manchester: Manchester University Press, 1980

Salvian of Marseilles, *De Gubernatione Dei*, in *Opera Omnia*, ed. Franciscus Pauly, Corpus Scriptorum Ecclesiasticorum 8, Vienna: apud C. Geroldi Filium Bibliopolam Academiae, 1883

Suger of St. Denis, *Vita Ludovici Grossi Regis*, in *Vie de Louis VI le Gros*, ed. Henri Waquet, 2nd ed., Les Classiques de l'Histoire de France au Moyen Âge 11, Paris: Société d'Édition «Les Belles Lettres», 1964 (orig. pub. 1929)

Thomas à Kempis, *De Imitatione Christi Libri IV*, Leipzig: Sumptibus et Typis Car. Tauchnitii, 1840

Thomas Aquinas, St., *Compendium Theologiae ad Fratrem Reginaldum*, in Verrardo, 13–138

Idem, Corpus Christi hymn, see March

Idem, *In Librum Beati Dionysii de Divinis Nominibus Expositio*, ed. Ceslai Pera, Turin: Marietti, 1950

Idem, *Epistola Exhortātōria dē Modō Studendī*, see Verrardo, 451

Idem, *Summa Theologiae*, see Caramello

Thomas of Celano, *Legenda Sanctae Clarae Virginis*, ed. Francesco Pennacchi, Società Internazionale di Studi Francescani in Assisi, Assisi: Tipografia Metastasio, 1910

Idem, *Vita Prima S. Francisci Assisiensis et Eiusdem Legenda ad Usum Chori*, ed. Patres Collegii S. Bonaventurae, Quaracchi: Ex Typographia Collegii S. Bonaventurae, 1926

Thomas of Eccleston, *De Adventu Fratrum Minorum in Angliam*, in *Monumenta Franciscana*, ed. J. S. Brewer, London: Longman, Brown, Green, Longmans, and Roberts, 1858

Tria Opuscula Seraphici Doctoris S. Bonaventurae: Breviloquium, Itinerarium Mentis in Deum, et De Reductione Artium ad Theologiam, 5th ed., ed. Patres Collegii S. Bonaventurae, Quaracchi: Typographia Collegii S. Bonaventurae, 1938

Tribonian, Theophilus, and Dorotheus, *Institutionum sive Elementorum Libri Quattuor,* in *Imperatoris Iustiniani Institutionum Libri Quattuor,* ed. J. B. Moyle, Oxford: Clarendon Press, 1903

Venantius Fortunatus, see March

Verrardo, Raymondo A., O. P., ed, *S. Thomae Aquinatis Opuscula Theologica, Volumen I, De Re Dogmatica et Mōrālī,* Turin: Marietti, 1954

Welldon, J. E. C., ed. *S. Aurelii Augustini Episcopi Hipponensis De Civitate Dei contra Paganos Libri XXII,* vol. 1, London: Society for Promoting Christian Knowledge, 1924

William Calculus, *Historiae Northmannorum Libri Octo,* in J.-P. Migne, ed., *Patrologiae Cursus Completus, Series Latina Prior, Patrologiae Tomus CXLIX,* Paris: apud Garnier Fratres, Editores et J.-P. Migne Successores, 1882, coll. 779–914

William of Poitiers, *Gesta Guillelmi Ducis Normannorum et Regis Anglorum,* in *Guillaume de Poitiers, Histoire de Guillaume Le Conquérant,* ed. Raymonde Foreville, Les Classique de l'Histoire de France au Moyen Âge 23, Paris: Société d'Édition «Les Belles Lettres», 1952

Wipo, *Gesta Chuonradi Imperatoris,* in *Die Werke Wipos,* 3rd ed., ed. Harry Bresslau, Scriptores Rerum Germanicarum in Usum Scholarum, Hanover and Leipzig, 1956

INDICES

Index I: Passages from the Old and New Testaments

Proverbs (Prov.)

Ecclesiastes (Eccles.)

Song of Solomon (Song)

Wisdom (Wis.)

Ecclesiasticus (Ecclus.)

Isaiah (Is.)

Index II: Passages from Liturgical and Magisterial Documents

Index III: Passages from Ecclesiastical and Other Non-Classical Authors

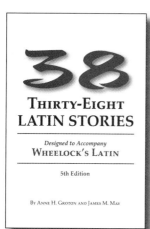

38 Latin Stories

Anne H. Groton and James M. May

Student Text: vi + 104 pp. (5th edition, 1995) 6" x 9"
Paperback, ISBN 978-0-86516-289-1

Originally designed as a supplement to the Latin course by F. M. Wheelock, this book is well suited for use in any introductory or review course. All the stories in the book are based on actual Latin literature, with the stories simplified at first and made gradually more complex as the work progresses. Students will learn how classical Latin was really written as they become familiar with the works of the great Latin authors.

> "I would enthusiastically recommend *Thirty-eight Latin Stories* to all those who teach elementary Latin via Wheelock and wish to provide their students from the start with continuous passages of interesting and idiomatically sound Latin Prose."
> – Richard A. LaFleur,
> *Classical Outlook*

Find Them

Latina Verba Mixta
for WHEELOCK'S LATIN

Sally Proctor

vi +54 pp. (2013) 5" x 7¾" Paperback
ISBN 978-0-86516-793-3

Students can challenge their command of common vocabulary and cultural references with puzzles keyed to each of the forty chapters of *Wheelock's Latin*. A full answer key is provided. Latin students at any level and using any textbook will enjoy these puzzles.

BOLCHAZY-CARDUCCI PUBLISHERS, INC.
WWW.BOLCHAZY.COM

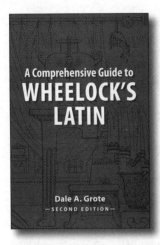

A Comprehensive Guide to *Wheelock's Latin*
2nd Edition

Dale A. Grote

Updated to Coordinate with *Wheelock*, 7th Edition
xix + 307 pp. (2011) 6" x 9" Paperback
ISBN 978-0-86516-773-5

This guide expands and explains more fully important grammatical concepts introduced in the Wheelock text. The guide can also be used to review beginning Latin.

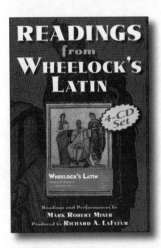

Readings from *Wheelock's Latin*

Mark Robert Miner
(readings and performances)
and Richard A. LaFleur (producer)

280 minutes on 4 CDs (2006)
Audio CDs with 8-page booklet
ISBN 978-0-86516-638-7

This 4-CD audio package has recitation in restored classical pronunciation of all vocabulary and paradigms in *Wheelock's Latin*, as well as dramatic readings of *Sententiae Antiquae* and narrative passages, and lively performance of selections from the *Loci Antiqui* and select *Loci Immutati*. Also available as an MP3 digital download.

BOLCHAZY-CARDUCCI PUBLISHERS, INC.
WWW.BOLCHAZY.COM

Wheelock's Latin GrammarQuick!

Richard A. LaFleur and Brad Tillery

6 (2 sided cards) (2007) 8½" x 11" Laminated Cardstock, ISBN 978-0-86516-666-0

A quick and complete overview of Latin grammar—both forms and usage—on six durable double-sided laminated cards, three-hole punched for easy insertion into notebooks.

Cumulative Chapter Vocabulary Lists for *Wheelock's Latin*
2nd Edition

Richard A. LaFleur and Brad Tillery

Updated to Coordinate with *Wheelock*, 7th Edition
iv + 292 pp. (2011) 6" x 8½" Paperback, ISBN 978-0-86516-770-4

These 40 cumulative vocabulary lists for all chapters of *Wheelock's Latin* each contain all the words for each chapter as well as for all chapters preceding that one.

Vocabulary Cards and Grammatical Forms Summary for *Wheelock's Latin*
2nd Edition

Richard A. LaFleur and Brad Tillery

Updated to Coordinate with *Wheelock*, 7th Edition
(2011) 8½" x 11" Paperback, Perforated Sheets (cards = 1⅞" x 3⁵⁄₁₆")
ISBN 978-0-86516-771-1

Repetitio est mater memoriae: these vocabulary cards allow students an easy way to memorize Latin vocabulary words as they appear in each chapter of *Wheelock's Latin*. Also available as a digital download for iPods.

BOLCHAZY-CARDUCCI PUBLISHERS, INC.
WWW.BOLCHAZY.COM

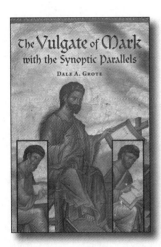

The Vulgate of Mark
with the Synoptic Parallels
Dale A. Grote

xxii + 442 pp., 1 map (2016) 6" x 9" Paperback
ISBN 978-0-86516-835-0

The Vulgate of Mark with the Synoptic Parallels empowers intermediate Latin students to read an engaging narrative in accessible prose. Parallel passages from Matthew and Luke, along with historical and grammatical notes, introduce students to a historical-textual approach to reading and interpreting these texts.

The readings from Matthew and Luke allow students to see how real authors expressed similar ideas in different ways, inviting students to think critically about the texts.

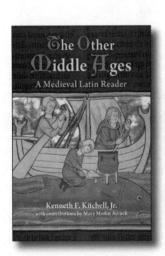

The Other Middle Ages
A Medieval Latin Reader
Kenneth F. Kitchell, Jr.

Student Text: xxxvii + 357 pp., 26 illustrations (2016)
6" x 9" Paperback, ISBN 978-0-86516-837-4
Teacher's Guide: xi + 180 pp. (2016)
6" x 9" Paperback, ISBN 978-0-86516-839-8

The Other Middle Ages introduces selections that cover all aspects and all walks of life, from bawdy songs to somber religious rituals and impudent parodies of the same, from short anecdotes and fables to excerpts from the bestiary tradition. Intermediate Latin students can expect to finish one or more of these enjoyable readings in one sitting, developing their reading skills and giving them a sense of accomplishment.

While some selections have been edited for clarity and length, most are unadapted. Notes and vocabulary guide students accustomed to classical Latin through reading medieval texts drawn from a wide range of centuries, geographical locations, and genres.

BOLCHAZY-CARDUCCI PUBLISHERS, INC.
WWW.BOLCHAZY.COM